A View of Juelich Around 1750
From an engraving by Leopold
in *Die Stadt Jülich* (Essen: 1952).

von Brumbach

from the library
of
HAROLD B. BRUMBAUGH

European
Origins
of the
Brethren

1708 – 1958

250ᵗʰ *Anniversary*

CHURCH of the BRETHREN

Schwarzenau

Photo by Graydon Snyder

European Origins
of the
Brethren

A Source Book on the Beginnings of the
Church of the Brethren in the Early Eighteenth Century
A Two-Hundred-Fiftieth Anniversary Volume

COMPILED

AND TRANSLATED BY

DONALD F. DURNBAUGH

THE BRETHREN PRESS
ELGIN, ILLINOIS

Book Design by Paul Dailey

Printed in the United States of America

Table of Contents

Foreword

"This volume is now given to the public with the prayerful desire that it may quicken our love for the church and, under the blessing of God, be the means of doing some good for the Master." In these words Martin Grove Brumbaugh, a minister in the Church of the Brethren and later the governor of Pennsylvania, presented to the church in 1899 the first major attempt at a comprehensive history of the Brethren. This statement appropriately expresses the purposes of the committee on the two-hundred-fiftieth anniversary of the Church of the Brethren as we give to the church in this anniversary year of 1958 this volume entitled *European Origins of the Brethren*.

The Brethren have always recognized that the roots of the church were in Europe even though our life on that continent was of short duration. Our fathers were labeled heretics early in their history because they rejected the dogma, the teaching, and the practices of the established order. As such, they were objects of bitter persecution by the provincial governments and the state churches of Germany. Forced to leave that country almost en masse, they left nearly everything behind—including practically all records of their beginning.

Brethren scholars and historians have assumed that the archives of Europe, especially those of Germany, would undoubtedly throw important light on the beginnings of the church; but no such investigation had ever been undertaken. This conviction deepened among Brethren as visitations back to the scenes of our origin increased before and following World War II. M. R. Zigler, director of Brethren Service in Europe and Church of the Brethren representative to the World Council of Churches, through his service and acquaintanceship in Europe greatly sharpened that conviction and repeatedly urged research into the European origins of the Brethren.

Convinced that records in Germany, and perhaps in other European countries, would yield fruitful results for Brethren history, the Two-hundred-fiftieth Anniversary Committee determined to arrange to carry on such investigation as an anniversary project. It seems providential that the services of Donald F. Durnbaugh and his wife, Hedda, became available for such an enterprise. They have labored patiently, ardently, and long in this difficult task. Their labors have yielded fruitage far beyond our dreams, to which this volume bears eloquent testimony. The historical library of the church has also been enriched by the purchase of many volumes relating to our history and scores of documents have been microfilmed and are now in the Elgin archives and available to the scholars and historians of the church.

Donald F. Durnbaugh is a native of Detroit, Michigan. He graduated, Bachelor of Arts degree with distinction, from Manchester College in 1949. He received his Master of Arts degree from the University of Michigan in 1953 and after five years in Brethren Service in Europe is currently a candidate for the Doctor of Philosophy degree at the University of Pennsylvania. Mrs. Durnbaugh, before their marriage in 1952, was Hedda Raschka of Vienna, Austria. She studied at the Kautetzky school of languages in Vienna and was a student also at the University of Vienna. She later taught English in the schools of Vienna as a certified teacher. Her linguistic talent, her familiarity with the German language, and her ability to read and transcribe German script have been an indispensable factor in this project.

The Two-hundred-fiftieth Anniversary Committee of the Church of the Brethren presents to the Brotherhood this anniversary volume as a source book on the early European beginnings of the Brethren in the prayerful hope that it may quicken our love for the church and advance among us the cause of our Lord and Master, Jesus Christ.

The Anniversary Committee:

Paul H. Bowman, Chairman, Timberville, Virginia
Nevin H. Zuck, Secretary, Elizabethtown, Pennsylvania
Norman J. Baugher, Elgin, Illinois
DeWitt L. Miller, Hagerstown, Maryland
Donald E. Rowe, Elgin, Illinois
B. F. Waltz, Philadelphia, Pennsylvania
William G. Willoughby, Bridgewater, Virginia

Preface

History is to the group what memory is to the individual. No sensible person ignores his past experiences when an important decision must be made. He may decide to act differently than he did in the past because of changed circumstances, but his judgment is tempered by past successes and failures. Similarly, for a group to act intelligently it must be informed of its heritage. It must understand how it came to be what it is, in fact, today.

Religious denominations have almost always been keenly interested in their fathers of the faith. Tradition has played a much stronger role in some communions than in others, but, even in the latter, doctrines and practices have been more dependent upon the past than often recognized. More than once in church history it has been a renaissance in interest in and knowledge of its history by a particular fraternity which has sparked in that fraternity a vital period of awakening and growth.

Inspiration is perhaps the most common reason for looking to the past. Although conditions have changed, the basic verities and values of human life are the same throughout history. There are even surprising correlations, as if a cycle had come full turn. Present-day difficulties assume proper proportion when the overwhelming problems of the "founding fathers" are realized. What Methodist has not been encouraged by the heroic efforts of a Wesley? What Presbyterian by a Calvin? What Lutheran by the indomitable Reformer of Wittenberg?

Although the early Brethren were small in numbers and made little impact in their native Europe, the quarter-century or more of Brethren beginnings contains much which should inspire their descendants. A fearlessness, a selflessness, and a devotion were evidenced among the early members which no degree of oppression and hardship could shatter. The heart-warming prison narrative of the Solingen Brethren, for example, glows with simple faith and steadfastness despite extreme trials. The zeal of the handful of craftsmen and farmers was noted by all. Yet, which of the contemporary observers could possibly have foreseen that the fellowship of eight religious refugees in Schwarzenau in 1708 would develop into a church in America which would minister to other refugees in Schwarzenau (and all over the world) two hundred forty years later?

Human weaknesses were not lacking among the first Brethren. By their own admission, their early years in Wittgenstein were marred by contention over church practices. The unfortunate quarrel in Krefeld estranged scores of interested persons. The very beginning in America was endangered by the schism of Beissel and his followers. Nevertheless, it is just as important to learn from the negative aspects of history as from the inspiring.

The bicentennial observance of the Church of the Brethren in 1908 saw a revival of writing on Brethren history, after a full century of comparative neglect. It is hoped that the present volume, prepared for the two-hundred-fiftieth anniversary, will encourage interest in the early Brethren. Ideally, this source material, along with other collected but unpublished documents, should stimulate the preparation of numerous studies—theological, sociological, and other—which will sharpen awareness of what Brethren were, what they are, and what they should be.

This was a labor of love. The writer wishes that each reader may find as rich a benefit in the understanding of and increased appreciation for the early Brethren in the reading as did he in the writing.

EXPLANATIONS

This book contains the fruits of recent research conducted in Europe beginning in 1954, but especially in the period from September 1955 to August 1956, in somewhat more than one hundred public and private archives, libraries, and collections in six countries. The aim was to locate and secure, usually by means of microfilming, all documentary evidence still available on the origin of the Church of the Brethren. While an effort was made at thoroughness, it is probable that more material could be found, especially in archives within the German Democratic Republic (former Soviet Zone of occupation). It may be that this publication will stimulate the location of presently unknown contemporary sources.

Although this research is the first study of its kind on Brethren origins to be made by an American writer, earlier investigations have been made by German scholars. The writer is especially indebted to the thorough scholarship of Dr. Heinz Renkewitz and the late Lic. Friedrich Nieper. The former in the course of his exhaustive research on the radical Pietist leader, Hochmann von Hochenau, discovered the basic documentary sources for early Brethren history. Pastor Nieper contributed a most valuable study of the Brethren in the Lower Rhine area of Germany in his expanded doctoral dissertation on German migration from Krefeld to America. The present study used these two investigations as the beginning point. As is the case with both of the above works, it draws heavily from the three-volume *Geschichte des christlichen Lebens,* by Max Goebel, which (although over one hundred years old) is still the standard source for German nonchurch religious activity of the seventeenth and eighteenth centuries.

Before further acknowledgments are made, some comments on the content of the following source material are necessary. The overriding aim in this compilation has been to let the documents speak for themselves as far as possible. An attempt has been made to organize them in such a way that they tell the story of the Brethren beginnings. The scarcity of material in certain sections has made an integrated narrative impossible. As will be seen, editorial comment has been kept to a minimum, and, in sections I to VI, has been printed in smaller type, so that more space could be given to the documents themselves (about one fourth of those collected). The source of each document printed is given in notes at the end of the volume, where is also to be found brief bibliographical information.

The materials are largely taken from the records of various governmental bodies and established churches. Brethren activity was understandably considered heretical, and even criminal, by the authorities. The reader should not be disturbed by the critical tone of these documents. They provide facts otherwise unavailable, as original materials from the Brethren themselves are scanty. The early Brethren felt little need of documenting their activities. Their private correspondence has been almost entirely lost. Information on them, with some exceptions, is fragmentary. The present collection is an attempt to bring together the most interesting of the available sources.

Translation can never hope to capture the flavor of the original, and the writer is keenly aware that success in the present translation is only partial. An effort has been made to make the translations as close to the originals as possible, while still being readable. Particularly a problem was the translating of the stilted and pompous eighteenth-century official style found in many of the documents. Certain key words proved difficult to translate precisely. There seems to be no exact English equivalent of the German *Gemeinde* and *Gemeinschaft* when used in their religious sense. They signify more than *congregation* and less than *church*, bear more religious connotation than *fellowship*, and are not exactly equivalent to *community* or *brotherhood*. *Church fellowship* has generally been used, but with reservations. Similarly, the very names given to the early Brethren create questions. In the sources they are generally called *Täufer* (Baptists), but also *Neutäufer* (New Baptists), *Schwarzenau Täufer* (Schwarzenau Baptists), *Tunck Täufer* (Dippers), and *Dompelaars* (the Dutch equivalent of *Täufer*). At the risk of confusion with the English Baptists, *Täufer* has been consistently translated as *Baptists* but refers only to the early Brethren. (The actual Baptist development in Germany did not begin until the early nineteenth century.) In cases of doubtful meaning, the original German phrase has generally been given in brackets in addition to the suggested translation.

The translations are those of the writer, although in a very few cases other English translations exist. One exception to the statement is the use of the English translation of the *Chronicon Ephratense (Ephrata Chronicle)* made by Dr. J. Max Hark; excerpts from his translation have been revised. A second exception is that Ralph W. Schlosser of Elizabethtown, Pennsylvania, and Ora W. Garber of Elgin, Illinois, have provided the translations of early Brethren hymns included in the section entitled "Publication." The few documents not originally in German have been identified in the notes as being Dutch or French.

Punctuation has been modernized, and the intolerably long sentences so cherished in that day have been broken into several shorter ones. All editorial comments within or additions to the documents have been placed within brackets. Material within parentheses was contained in the original. Omissions have been invariably indicated by the use of three dots. This device has been especially used to deflate the swollen salutations and complimentary closes. It should be noted that the use of *etc.* is never an editorial addition, but instead appears on the drafts and even original letters to indicate the customary flowery phrases.

Forenames of persons have been Anglicized. The widely varying spellings of family names have been unified, except in a few instances where the variant has been given in brackets. It was felt that most readers would appreciate this simplification. The spelling of place names has followed modern European usage with a few exceptions for the sake of clarity. Dates are given without correction from Old Style to New Style.

The photographic illustrations without specific identification were taken by the writer. The two maps were prepared by my wife.

No attempt has been made to provide the modern dollar equivalents of the currencies mentioned in the documents. The extreme fluctuation in the value of coins from one area to another and the great differences in prices and values between that time and the present make any figure little better than a guess. For some idea of the relationships between coins, the following may be helpful, but it must be stressed that these do not hold true in every case: the standard and largest unit was the *Reichstaler* (from which is obtained *dollar*). It was equivalent to one and one-half *Gulden (Guilder)* or *florin;* six *Kopfstück* (although this term was used for any coin bearing the head of a ruler, and therefore varies greatly in value); eighteen *Batzen;* forty-five *Albus;* ninety *Kreutzer;* or three hundred sixty *Pfennig.* The *stiver, pistol, ducat,* and *dubloon* were foreign coins or monetary values also used in the Holy Roman Empire.

ACKNOWLEDGMENTS

My first and deepest obligation is to my wife, Hedda. The nature of her contribution might well have been recognized by the placing of her name on the title page. Her facility in reading German script enabled her to do much of the archival research. She transcribed all of the documents, corrected the translations, did the translations of Dutch materials, and typed the entire manuscript. Without her full assistance in every stage of research and translation, this volume would never have been possible.

The Two-hundred-fiftieth Anniversary Committee of the Church of the Brethren, the chairman of which is Dr. Paul H. Bowman, enabled this research to be done through grants for travel in Europe and the translating in America. Their generosity and their faith in the writer greatly lightened the burden of producing this book. Norman J. Baugher, in his capacity as general secretary of the General Brotherhood Board of the Church of the Brethren and Brotherhood staff member of the Anniversary Committee, did much to facilitate the project. The representative of the Church of the Brethren in Europe, M. R. Zigler, has long been interested in a research project on early Brethren history. W. Harold Row, executive secretary of the Brethren Service Commission, helped to make this undertaking possible by releasing the author from his duties as director of the Austrian program of the Brethren Service Commission. Also participating in initial planning was Dwight Horner, now of Washington, D. C. Professor William G. Willoughby of Bridgewater College and Ora W. Garber, editor of book publications, General Brotherhood Board— Church of the Brethren, were especially helpful as members of the subcommittee on publication.

One of the most delightful aspects of this research has been the invariable courtesy and kindness extended to us by many persons in Europe. Dr. Heinz Renkewitz, Arnoldshain/Taunus, may be mentioned first because of his helpful counsel and assistance in many ways. Some of the others to whom we are deeply indebted for information, permission to use privately owned materials, or other assistance, are: Herr Hermann Aupperle, Schwäbisch-Gmünd; Pastor em. Gustav Bauer, Bad Rothenfelde; Herr Fritz Behmenburg, Duisburg-Meidrich; Professor Ernst Benz, Marburg; Dr. S. J. Bouma, Groningen; Dr. Hermann Brunn, Schriesheim; Dr. J. F. Gerhard Goeters, Bonn; Dr. Karl Hartnack, Laasphe; Dr. Franklin H. Littell, Bad Godesberg; Pastor Erich Müller, Schwarzenau; Studienrat Erich Neweling, Berleburg; Rektor Wilhelm Niepoth, Krefeld; Pastor Karl Pabst, Wülfrath; Dr. Walther Risler, Krefeld; Dr. W. Rocholl, Trier; Pastor L. Schnell, Elsoff; Mr. A. Tjoelker, Surhuisterveen; and Ds. A. Zwartendijk, Surhuisterveen.

The helpfulness of the custodians of archives and libraries made our work much easier. We wish to recognize especially the following, among many: Archivrat Walter Schmidt, Archiv der Evangelischen Kirche im Rheinland, Düsseldorf; Dipl. theol. J. Storz, Archiv der Franckeschen Stiftungen, Halle/Saale; Mrs. Y. de Swart-Pot,

Doopsgezinde Bibliotheek, Amsterdam; Oberinspektor Henk and his staff, Fürstlich Sayn-Wittgenstein-Hohensteinisches Archiv at Laasphe; Dr. D. Reimers, Dr. Karl Dielmann, and Oberinspektor August Scheid, Fürstlich Ysenburg-und Büdingisches Archiv, Büdingen; Dr. Ernst Crous, Mennonitische Forschungsstelle, Göttingen; Dr. Carl Müller, Städtisches Archiv, Krefeld; and Dr. Theo Clasen, Universitätsbibliothek, Bonn.

All quotations from the Old and the New Testament are from the Revised Standard Version, copyright 1952 and 1946 by the Division of Christian Education of the National Council of the Churches of Christ in the United States of America. The quotations from the Apocrypha are from the translation by Edgar Goodspeed, copyright 1939 by the University of Chicago.

—Donald F. Durnbaugh
Philadelphia, Pennsylvania
October 1957

Introduction

To understand the origins of the Brethren movement, it is necessary to have some conception of the conditions prevailing in their homeland. This was Germany, taken in its broader sense to include the territory of modern Germany and the German-speaking areas of France and Switzerland. The early eighteenth century in Europe was a time of change and turmoil. The two leading royal houses, those of France and Austria, were struggling for the supremacy on the Continent. The modern state system of political powers was in the making. Long periods of bitter warfare kept the suppressed populace in unrest. The discoveries of Newton and others had revolutionized the thought of the educated few. Religious ferment was in the air. All of these changes were felt within the smaller German states, although the latter played relatively minor roles on the European stage. Let us consider conditions in the Germanies at the turn of the century.

POLITICAL CONDITIONS

The Germanic area of Central Europe in the year 1700 was a patchwork of some three hundred sovereign principalities and territories. There were fifty-one free cities, and over eighty independent districts a dozen square miles or less in area. This did not include the holdings of fifteen hundred imperial knights whose average territory was one eighth of a square mile. All of these territories were loosely organized in the Holy Roman Empire—which, in the epigram attributed to Voltaire, was neither holy, Roman, nor an empire. It was the sad remnant of the once-proud vision of a united Europe under one temporal ruler, knit together by the one true Roman Catholic Church. This concept, which had dominated European political thought for centuries, had been shaken by the Reformation and shattered by the arrangements of the Treaties of Westphalia of 1648. The form lingered on, but the shell that was left was but a "constituted anarchy."[1]

The emperor, by tradition a member of the Hapsburg dynasty,

was elected by the nine electors of the empire—Bohemia, Bavaria, Saxony, Brandenburg, Rhenish Palatinate, Hannover, and the three ecclesiastical provinces of the bishop-princes of Mainz, Trier, and Köln (Cologne). Although crowned with pomp and circumstance in Frankfurt/Main, the emperor had seen his power dwindle by this time to the right of creating nobility and granting certain pensions. His lack of authority did not imply a small bureaucratic apparatus; estimates on the number of imperial attendants and officials in Vienna vary from twenty-five thousand to forty thousand. For the education and care of the fifteen boys of nobility who attended the emperor, there were five professors, two dancing instructors, a fencing master, eight servants, four cooks, one steward, and a schoolmaster. The highest nobility of the realm served the emperor at dinner while kneeling.[2]

The chief institutions of the empire were the Diet or Parliament which met in Regensburg, and the Imperial Supreme Court located in Wetzlar, north of Frankfurt. The Diet was composed of three houses or "benches"—the nine electors, the lesser princes (gathered into four groups or "colleges"), and the free cities. The imperial knights had no representation. Originally called by the emperor at various places on special occasions, since 1663 it had been in perpetual session at Regensburg with the rulers represented by deputies. Much of the time was spent in interminable wrangling over matters of prestige and protocol. For example, it had long been the exclusive right of the electors or their representatives to have their chairs on the carpet in the conference hall. The lesser princes objected to this, and after long and bitter negotiations, the following compromise was made: the chairs of their representatives might be placed with the front legs on the fringe of the carpet.[3]

The Imperial Court was notoriously slow-moving, despite the great number of officials and clerks. It was not seldom that the litigants in a case died long before the decision was forthcoming. One case took one hundred eighty-eight years to complete. Moreover, once the decision was made, there was little power available to enforce it, if the defendant was an important prince.

The actual power was centered in the hands of the rulers of the separate territories. Brandenburg-Prussia had become the leading state in northern Germany in the late seventeenth century under the vigorous ruler, Frederick William. The "Great Elector" had centralized the administration, expanded territorial holdings, and attracted thousands of industrious Protestant refugees from France with his famous grant of toleration, the Edict of Potsdam of 1685. The emperor, though weak in his imperial capacity, still exercised the most power in Germany by virtue of his great hereditary possessions centering around Austria. As the leading representative of the House of Hapsburg, he was the chief antagonist of the French ruler, Louis XIV.

The theory of the divine right of kings had become firmly established. The rulers felt themselves responsible to no one except God, and in practice they were not prepared to stand for much nonsense from even Him. A publicist wrote to Prince Ernest Louis of Hesse: "If God were not God, who would have more right to be God than Your Princely Serenity?"[4] The earlier checks and balances imposed by the feudal system—the rights of the peasantry and townspeople, and, above all, the immense power of the church—had vanished. Land and subjects were considered the personal property of the sovereign to be used or abused as his whim indicated.

Thus, Germany presented the spectacle of hundreds of petty sovereigns, supreme within their own borders, deadly suspicious of one another, and virtually powerless in any crisis. Each ruler attempted to imitate Louis XIV, the king of France, and his court at Versailles. The "Sun-King" had become the symbol of all that was desirable. Each sovereign, no matter how small his possessions, had to have a pompous court, an opera company, and especially a gorgeously costumed army for parades.

The most invidious feature of the aping of the French was the lowering of moral standards. With some few exceptions, the German nobility hit a low of debauchery and depravity. August the Strong of Saxony is reputed to have had three hundred fifty-four children by a series of mistresses. Far from daring to criticize the excesses of their masters, the subjects and most of the clergy cried, "The king can do no wrong," and applauded each successive act of degradation. That an occasional voice was raised against this folly is shown by the statement of the Stuttgart prelate, Osiander. When the dissolute ruler of Württemberg, Eberhard Louis, ordered him to include the name of the current mistress in the pastoral prayer as well as that of the duke, the minister answered that special mention was not necessary; she was already included in the Lord's Prayer, when he prayed, "Deliver us from evil."[5]

War Events

It is not surprising that in this state of mutual suspicion, extravagance, and moral decay, the German borders were encroached upon by greedy neighbors. Renewed Turkish aggression from the East penetrated as far as the Enns River in Upper Austria and besieged Vienna in 1683. Louis XIV had earlier utilized German weakness to extend the French borders over the Rhine, annexing Strassburg and many other areas under the legal fictions of the "Courts of Reunion." Then, when the Hapsburgs were in a life-and-death struggle in their homeland of Austria, he treacherously attacked the Spanish Netherlands and later the Palatinate. The second campaign is infamous for the unparalleled reign of destruction which scarred the fertile valleys of the Neckar and the Rhine. Heidelberg was twice burned and

A Contemporary Broadside Depicting the Horrors of the Thirty Years' War
Engraving by Jakob van der Heyden, from the facsimile in W. Hadorn, *Geschichte des Pietismus in den Schweizerischen Reformierten Kirchen* (Konstanz and Emmishofen: 1901).

Mannheim literally leveled. Many of the surrounding Palatine villages were reduced to smoking ruins and crops were wantonly destroyed. Indescribable outrages were committed upon the civilian populace. The aim was to make the area unfit for human habitation.

The Treaty of Ryswick of 1697 brought this phase of the war to a close. Although the French were forced to relinquish their claims upon the Palatinate, they cleverly introduced a clause which provided that the Catholics should retain all of the church property which they had recovered during the French occupation. The "Ryswick clause" was to cause endless strife, as will be seen later.

Elsewhere, the conflict broadened to become the first real world war. Known in Europe as the War of the Spanish Succession, it was called Queen Anne's War in America, where there was bitter fighting between the French and the English forces. The drawn-out war in Europe was primarily one of maneuvering and sieges; it was concluded by the Treaties of Utrecht and Rastatt in 1713. A northern war involving Russia, Sweden, Poland, Denmark, and some German states dragged on until 1721. The era was one of continual conflict.[6]

FRANCE

Louis XIV is said to have summed up his view of government by saying, "I am the state." This absolutist figure epitomized the age. The elaborate ritual at Versailles, which centered upon the person of the monarch, was designed to impress the world with his splendor. The king led the life of an actor whose every waking moment was observed by many, and was carefully prescribed and regulated. Beginning with the *lever,* the ceremony of rising, which was attended by scores of the highest nobility, and concluding with a similar ceremony at night, the day was filled with ritual and pageant. It took four people to hand the king a glass of water. During the splendid meals, the soup had to be tasted by so many official tasters that it was invariably cold by the time it reached the royal mouth from one of the hundreds of Versailles kitchens. Louis XIV gathered around him all of the formerly independent and proud nobility of France, who hung on his every word and for whom absence from Versailles was unbearable. It was only at the court that the largess of the state was distributed.

However, from 1685 when the king's advisers induced him to revoke the Edict of Nantes, which had granted toleration to the French Protestants, the glory and power of France declined. Thousands of skilled Huguenots left the country despite severe penalties against leaving, rather than accept the Roman Catholic faith. Their tales of French intolerance did much to arouse the neighbors of France against her, and the refugees contributed valuable talents to the places of asylum. The costly and vainglorious wars of Louis XIV ruined the financial structure of the country, already heavily burdened under the immense cost of the spendthrift court. (The clergy and the nobility were freed from taxes.) When the king died in 1715, France had lost much of its former status, and his dying words to his great-grandson and heir were supposedly a warning against the folly of making war.

ECONOMIC CONDITIONS

The continual wars also drained the economies of the Germanies. The peasants, whose fields were repeatedly overrun and destroyed, lost interest in replanting. Those not directly affected by enemy action were smothered under taxes of every conceivable kind created to finance the expensive armies. Under the vicious method of "tax-farming," local collectors were given the right of extracting taxes from peasant and townsman, withholding a commission for their efforts. One was taxed for being born and for dying, and during the time in between. As any display of prosperity would bring on heavier assessments, properties were allowed to deteriorate. Excise taxes and state monopolies on many necessities such as salt especially hurt the poorer class. In the face of ever greater expenses, monarchs created offices and titles of nobility to be sold to the highest bidder.

Commerce was hampered by the many borders, where taxes were imposed on merchandise passing through each territory. The money system was a nightmare. Many sovereigns possessed the right of coinage, and there was no set relationship between the great number of different coins and currencies. Foreign money was also used. The earlier important trade monopolies had been lost to the coastal countries.

The feudal obligations of the peasants were continually increased, until some had to work five days a week for their lord and on the sixth day earn their livelihood and the means to pay taxes. There is a record of peasants being forced to continue their work in their master's fields even though they saw their homes burning in the nearby village. The nobility commonly thought more highly of their hunting dogs than of their subjects.

The passion of the lords for hunting was in itself a great economic problem. In order to preserve the wild game, the peasants were forbidden to kill any of the animals even though they destroyed the seed planted and ruined harvests. Packs of wild boars were particularly destructive. When the hunt was on, the peasants' fields were thoughtlessly trampled by the riders.

The most-hated practice was the commonly occurring sale of subjects as troops to foreign nations. German sovereigns found this an easy way to raise money to help pay off their crushing debts. As the subjects were considered as chattel, or *Leibeigene,* there was no legal barrier to this traffic in lives. Americans are familiar with the role of the Hessians (citizens of the state of Hesse) in the British forces during the Revolutionary War.

SOCIAL AND CULTURAL CONDITIONS

Depopulation and loss of civil rights were the chief factors in the social structure. Many areas had still not replaced their losses of the Thirty Years' War, when death, disease, and migration drastically reduced the populace. Many of the once-independent townspeople and peasants had lost their rights during the recent upheavals and found themselves the puppets of the absolutist rulers. The cities were usually dominated by a few families, who monopolized all offices through interlocking arrangements.

Culturally, Germany was at a low ebb. The fashion was to imitate France. Women's dress styles were French, the upper class spoke French exclusively and corresponded in French, and many French phrases found their way into even the everyday language of the poorer classes. Having an outward French polish did not, however, remove a vulgar and mean core. Society took its cue from the outwardly glittering but inwardly corrupt court life, and strove for unlimited pleasure and sensual delights. One historian compared the age with the person of Louis XIV—outwardly resplendent with gold and purple raiment and

topped with an imposing wig, the king repelled because of the evil
stench of his unwashed body upon closer approach.[7]

The demands of cleanliness were met by an occasional rinsing of
the hands with water and application of perfume to the face. Bathing
was little practiced, and even considered unhealthy. The wig may be
taken as a symbol of the age. Powdered and perfumed, it was the
ultimate in artificiality and concealed filth beneath its impressive
exterior. Ladies' wigs grew to be of such towering dimensions that
cartoons of the day showed servants looking through telescopes to
see the top of the hairpiece. As its arrangement took so long, the wig
was often left on for long periods of time, and lice were therefore
common.

The swollen titles considered necessary for salutations present
another clue to the spirit of the time. The simple *sir* had been expanded
to page-length lists of exaggerated expressions of esteem for the one
being spoken or written to, and of humility on the part of the speaker
or writer. Examples of this will be found in the documents given later.

Baroque is an art term which has been expanded to include all
aspects of the period. The word itself is of uncertain origin, but
bears the connotation of the grotesque or the perverse. There seems to
be no precise definition of *Baroque,* but it can be described by listing
some of its characteristics: it is dynamic, stresses curved and inter-
twining lines instead of straight lines, utilizes illusion, is highly
emotional, organizes space well, and strives for a unity of all elements.
It can be seen in its fullest form in the palaces and their surroundings
of the period, and in the grand opera which developed at that time.

It was primarily introduced by the Roman Catholic Church during
the Counter Reformation. In this stage it is best demonstrated by
the cathedrals and monasteries of southern Germany, Austria, and
Italy. The Protestant Anglo-Saxon visitor may be estranged at the
sight of these palatial edifices to the honor of God and the power of
the church, but he is usually overwhelmed by the sheer richness,
profusion, color, and general effect of these buildings. One writer has
called Baroque the Catholic answer at that time to the growing
rationalism introduced by the Enlightenment. This "refined narcosis"
was designed to silence the religious doubts of the Rationalists by
massive emotional power.[8]

The monarchs of the day were not slow in seizing upon the new style for building structures aimed at self-glorification rather than the honor of God. The sprawling palace of Versailles was finished at this time, and is Baroque in over-all design and landscaping, although the architecture itself might better be called Renaissance. In Austria and Germany, more unified examples of Baroque can be seen in the palaces of Belvedere in Vienna, the Nymphenburg of Munich, Sans-Souci near Berlin, and Wilhelmshöhe in Kassel. Immense sums were poured into the building and outfitting of these magnificent palaces and their expansive gardens. One room in the palace of Schönbrunn in Vienna is said to have cost one million *Guilders* because of its especially ornate furnishings. They are today the showplaces of Europe.

On the educational scene, the universities were staffed with professors who were pedantic and hair-splitting scholastics. The students were notoriously riotous and vulgar; the swords which were part of student dress were often put to use in dueling or street fighting. In one university they were forbidden to wear swords, so they took delight in carrying them along in wheelbarrows.

"The masses reveled in obscenities,"[9] and superstition was rife. The tremendous sufferings of the war years called for scapegoats, and these were found predominantly in the persons of women who were accused of witchcraft. Under the torture of the rack and other instruments of pain commonly used in the questioning of persons suspected of crimes in that day, the unhappy creatures were glad to "confess" fantastic tales of pacts with the devil and hexes on neighbors' livestock in order to escape further agony. They were forced to incriminate others, who in turn cast suspicion on still others; so the chain grew. Thousands of individuals are said to have been executed as witches between the years 1575-1700 in this area.[10] The last "witch" to be burned in Germany died in 1775 in Kempten. Both the Catholic and the Protestant clergy were active in prosecuting persons for witchcraft, and developed a highly organized system of accusations and punishments. Belief in alchemy—the making of gold from base substances—was accepted by many throughout the eighteenth century.

RELIGIOUS CONDITIONS

The three established churches in the Holy Roman Empire were the Roman Catholic, the Lutheran, and the Reformed. After the bloody religious battles of the sixteenth century and the first half of the seventeenth, the final compromise, established in the Peace of Augsburg of 1555 and confirmed and expanded in the Treaties of Westphalia of 1648, was summed up by the phrase *cuius regio, eius religio* (the ruler determines the religion). This gave each sovereign the choice of one of the three churches as the official faith in the area over which he ruled. Subjects must belong to the state church but had the right (in theory) to migrate to another territory where their faith was recognized. Dissenters such as the Anabaptists were specifically excluded from this arrangement, and were to be expelled or even executed. Under this arrangement, southern Germany and Austria, as well as certain ecclesiastical territories in Germany, were Catholic; the Lutherans controlled all of northern, middle, and eastern Germany; the Reformed were found in a narrow strip extending from the Netherlands along the Rhine to Switzerland. Although actual hostilities had ceased, the hatred among the confessions continued. Lutheran hated Reformed and vice versa every bit as much as the Protestants hated their Catholic neighbors.

The inherent danger in the Reformers' dependence upon the territorial rulers had been completely revealed by this time. The churches in the Protestant territories, and to some extent in the Catholic, were *Caesaro-papist*—that is, they were controlled by the temporal powers. All ministers were state officials, and the church hierarchy was dominated by the sovereign. Although the extent of interference varied greatly from area to area, the ruler was supreme in matters of faith. "The Reformation had broken Rome's monopoly on religion, only to replace it with a series of smaller state monopolies."[11] The high positions in the churches tended to be filled with political appointments, and many incumbents did not pretend to live up to the teachings of the church. In practice, there was little difference between the Lutheran and the Catholic churches, with somewhat greater efforts made by the Reformed to maintain strict church discipline in some areas.

The main interest of the Protestant clergy was guarding the "true doctrine" and the "symbolic books." These were the catechisms and creeds established by the theologians of the sixteenth century. One German Protestant writer said that the Lutheran church was maintaining the dogmatic crust of Luther's faith, but had lost all of his dynamic

Christianity.[12] A Lutheran church historian wrote: "In spite of all their subtlety, they [the Lutheran clergy] really thought of God as a great Lutheran pastor who hit out in defense of his honor."[13] The dispute-loving Protestant theologians fell back into the narrow scholasticism against which the Reformers had revolted. The minutest details were subjects of vitriolic debates. In 1733, the *eighth* edition of a work by the prominent Lutheran theologian, John George Walch, was printed; its title: *Thoughts on the Faith of Children in Their Mothers' Wombs and the Basis for the Salvation of Those Children of Christian Parents Who Died Before Being Baptized [Gedancken vom Glauben der Kinder im Mutterleibe und dem Grunde der Seeligkeit der verstorbenen ungetaufften Christenkinder].*[14]

Congregations were offered violent attacks against other faiths and learnéd exercises of academic eloquence on fine points of theology in sermons. The most insignificant Biblical details were used for these displays of erudition. One contemporary writer pokes fun at the fashion of preaching in the "remotive" style. This consisted of a demonstration, on any given issue, why certain factors could *not* have played a role. For example, he described one pastor who discussed what kind of cheese David took to his brothers in the camp (1 Samuel 17:18). The preacher went through all of the varieties of cheeses— Swiss, Edam, Emmentaler, etc.—showing in each case in detail why these could not have been used by David. Although this may be more satire than fact, it indicates the style of preaching common in that day. All too often, this mixture of hyperorthodoxy, dogmatic doctrine, and scholastic quibbling left the average churchgoer cold.

It must be mentioned that church attendance was not optional, at least in most areas. Especially in the rural communities, absence from church services was immediately noticed, and the guilty called to account before the church consistory. If the case was deemed serious, it was turned over to the authorities for disciplinary action. In sections of Switzerland, officials were sent to visit each household on Sunday morning to make sure that all those not really needed at home were attending church. A fixed system of church fees, often paid in kind in rural areas, provided the support of the clergy. A later contemporary, the professor and author Henry Jung-Stilling, told of a Pastor Stolbein, who often said, when members of his parish went

to other churches: "Each sow should remain at her own trough."[15]
This inelegant but telling remark reveals the attitude of some of the
clergy in that era.

Particularly offensive to many were the worldly lives of a great
number of the clergy. The Reformed consistory in Heidelberg felt
it necessary to issue a general reprimand in 1707 to its pastors concerning the "irresponsible evils in doctrine and life." Reformed pastors
were reported as being publicly drunk at feasts after such ceremonies
as baptisms and marriages.[16] The behavior of the Catholic clergy is
said to have been generally worse than that of the Protestants.[17] The
official Catholic and Lutheran position that the validity of the sacraments was independent of the conduct of the priest or pastor was not
acceptable to many. Jesuit casuistry—the explaining away of virtually
all sins by finding quotations in the writings of the church fathers
which would minimize them—although earlier damaged by the attack
by Pascal, was still flowering.

THE PALATINATE

The sorry state of affairs catalogued above seemed to have been
concentrated even more heavily in the Palatinate. One of the most
heavily devastated areas in the Thirty Years' War, it had hardly been
built up again under the wise rule of the Elector Charles Louis (who
permitted Mennonites and other outlawed dissenters to settle in his
land because of their skill and industry), when the destructive French
forces again desolated the area. The excuse for the invasion was a
weak claim upon the area after the death, in 1685, of Charles's successor,
who had left no heirs. Sovereignty passed to the Palatine-Neuburg
line, who were Roman Catholic and much influenced by Jesuits.
Unable to protect—and perhaps uninterested in protecting—his newly
acquired land against the French forces, the Elector John William
(who ruled from 1690 to 1716) behaved as if his aim was to reconvert
the populace to Catholicism.

The Electoral Palatinate had become Lutheran in 1556, and then
Reformed in 1560. From 1576 to 1583 a new elector reintroduced
Lutheranism, only to have this faith replaced by the Reformed until
1620. During the Thirty Years' War, the Spanish and Bavarian Catholics were twice dominant, but the Treaties of Westphalia placed a

Reformed elector on the throne. After each change, the new party attempted to repress completely the other faiths. In other words, within the space of one hundred fifty years the official religion had been changed eight times!

The clause in the Treaty of Ryswick, mentioned previously, provided that all of the churches and church properties in the hands of the Catholics in 1697 should remain theirs even though they had come into possession of them during the French occupation. Hundreds of Reformed churches were thus recovered by the Catholics, who sent monks to take possession of them as the number of Catholics was small. In 1698 the so-called *Simultaneum,* which ostensibly provided for the toleration of all three established churches, was introduced. In practice, the Protestants complained that it gave the Roman party a foothold in many more Protestant churches. As part of its provisions, many villages with only one church building were directed to hold services for all three confessions at alternate times in their church. In the bitter atmosphere of that time, this arrangement meant continual bickering and quarreling. The archives are full of bitter complaints from pastors who were indignant at having to wait overtime for the services of the others to be concluded. (In some areas of the Palatinate, this arrangement continues to this day.)

Particularly galling to the Protestants was the elector's order that they must observe Catholic holidays, kneel when the Catholic processions passed through the streets, and contribute material for these processions. The main struggle, however, revolved around the control of the extensive church property and land holdings, which provided considerable income. The Protestants took their complaints to the foreign Protestant states such as Brandenburg-Prussia, the Estates General of the Netherlands, and England. The latter put pressure on the elector, which resulted in the so-called Interim Agreement of 1705, which settled some of the outstanding issues. Its main proviso was that the Reformed should retain five sevenths of the church property with the Catholics obtaining two sevenths. The Lutherans were not included. The Reformed complained that actually the Catholic officials saw to it that the Catholic two sevenths was more like one half. The religious strife in the Palatinate in this era is certainly one of the saddest chapters in church history.

PIETISM

Given the above conditions, a reaction was inevitable. Many devout laymen and clergymen deplored the unfortunate decline in religious affairs and strove for a more satisfying faith. These reformers were called Pietists. This Pietistic movement can best be defined as a continuation of the sixteenth-century reformation of doctrine through a reformation of life. The Pietist was a person who studied God's Word and sought to order his life by it. As with the names of many religious movements, such as *Quaker* or *Methodist,* the term *Pietist* was a name of reproach coined by its enemies.

Philip Jacob Spener
From the painting by J. G. Wagner engraved by B. Kilian in W. Hadorn, *Geschichte des Pietismus in den Schweizerischen Reformierten Kirchen* (Konstanz and Emmishofen: 1901).

There are certain elements of the earlier Catholic reform movement called Quietism in the origins of Pietism, but it primarily came to Germany through Reformed influences from the Netherlands and Puritan ideas from England. It first took root in the Reformed Church, especially in northern Germany and the lower Rhine area close to the Netherlands. Theodore Untereyk (1635-1693) and Frederick Lampe (1683-1729) are representative figures. They were both clergymen and had parishes in various places, but for both of them Bremen was the scene of their most important endeavors. They especially stressed Bible study and the teaching of the catechism and opposed such features of church life as fees for confession, which they found un-Christian. Lampe was especially important as a professor of theology and a widely read writer.[18]

It was within the Lutheran Church, however, that the most famous Pietist leaders emerged. Although not the first to raise his voice on behalf of reform, the man generally considered to be the father of Lutheran Pietism was Philip Jacob Spener (1635-1705). Of Alsatian birth, he became the head pastor in Frankfurt/Main. In 1670 he introduced the *collegia pietatis*—regular conventicles of earnest Christians from his congregation who met to discuss the sermons and study the Bible (today they would be called cell groups). In 1675 he published a foreword to a new edition of one of the works of John Arndt (1555-1621), who may be called a forerunner of Pietism. In this writing, *Pious Desires (Pia desideria)*, he called for a reform of church life, which met with instant approval throughout Germany, showing that Spener had voiced a need felt by many. After castigating the laxness of the clergy and the shortcomings of the church, he proposed a six-point plan for improvement: (1) more intensive Bible study, (2) more lay activity, (3) Christianity to be practiced in daily life, (4) no coercion in religious matters, (5) a reform of theological training, and (6) more edifying preaching instead of rhetoric and dogma. The measures sound rather tame today, but they were considered radical by many in the seventeenth century.[19]

A more forceful leader than the diffident Spener was August Herman Francke (1663-1727). He organized a Bible study group among fellow graduate students at Leipzig, for which he was expelled from the university. It was during this time that he experienced a profound conversion. He was driven from a pastorate in Erfurt, but was called to Halle. Besides being a pastor there, he became a professor in the newly founded (1694) university. His immense drive and organizing talent led to an amazing adventure of faith in establishing a great foundation at Halle. Beginning with taking some orphaned children into his home, he developed a complex of an orphanage, hospital, schools, seminary, and mission and Bible societies. Halle became the center of world-wide Pietist activity in the early eighteenth century.[20]

August Herman Francke

An engraving by B. Vogel in W. Hadorn, *Geschichte des Pietismus in den Schweizerischen Reformierten Kirchen* (Konstanz and Emmishofen: 1901).

RADICAL PIETISM

Although Pietism as such was a reform movement *within* the organized Protestant church, some "awakened" souls were led to break completely with the established churches. They felt that true reform demanded separation from a structure which showed all-too-many signs of human frailty. They were usually intensified in this belief by the repression of church authorities who had little tolerance for such ideas. These radical Pietists came to be known as separatists.

The most influential figure in this group was Gottfried Arnold (1666-1714). After earning his way through the University of Wittenberg by tutoring, he found employment in positions recommended by Spener as tutor and chaplain with noble families. His first major work, *The First Love, That Is the True Portrayal of the First Christians (Die erste Liebe . . . Das ist Wahre Abbildung der Ersten Christen),* published in 1696, met with instant success; it was republished five times before 1732, and was translated into several foreign languages. This learnéd description of the way of life of the early Christians earned him a professorship at the University of Giessen in 1697.

To the astonishment of his friends and the entire religious and academic world, he resigned his position of prestige one year later. In a printed defense of his unprecedented action, he explained that academic life fostered pride and that true Christianity could not be practiced in that secular atmosphere. He devoted himself in the next few years to the writing of his monumental *Impartial History of the Church and the Heretics (Unpartheyische Kirchen-und Ketzer-Historie)* (1699-1700). This scholarly work traced the course of ecclesiastical history up through the Christian era to the eighteenth century. Arnold attempted to show that often those groups and individuals repressed as heretical had actually been the true Christians and their oppressors false leaders. Although his history is biased in favor of the heretical groups, and contains some factual errors, it has been considered the first modern church history in its use of the documents of various groups as sources rather than accepting at face value the condemnations of the official church. It was the source book for many of the sectarian movements of the eighteenth century. It greatly influenced such figures as Goethe; and so recent an authority as Ernst

Troeltsch has praised it highly. Arnold's writings greatly influenced the early Brethren, who found there the description of the early church after which they wished to pattern themselves.[21]

A friend of Arnold, and the one person who most influenced the Brethren, was Ernest Christopher Hochmann von Hochenau (1670-1721). Born of a noble family in northern Germany, he followed family tradition and studied law at several universities. In Halle he experienced a conversion or awakening which changed his whole life, causing him to abandon a promising career which his older brother, a high imperial official in Vienna, had arranged for him. Instead of honor and security, he chose to become an itinerant preacher of the gospel, roaming Germany (and Switzerland and the Netherlands). Welcomed in both the castle of the nobility and the hut of the humblest peasant, he developed a following of sincere seekers throughout the country. A powerful speaker, he always spoke simply and testified of his ardent love for Jesus. He was imprisoned many times and was mistreated so often that he said that "he was so used to enduring a 'backful of blows' for Jesus' sake, that it did not bother him any more."[22]

Hochmann found a retreat from his strenuous travels in Wittgenstein, where he was welcomed both at Berleburg and at Schwarzenau/Eder. In the latter village, he built a simple hut, which he called the Castle of Peace *(Friedensburg)*, where he lived very ascetically. The creed which he wrote in the prison of the castle of Detmold in 1702, as a condition of his release, was cherished by the Brethren and is as close to a written confession of faith as they came. They had it reprinted in Pennsylvania in 1743. All of the contemporary and later writers considered Hochmann to be the most winsome personality of the Pietist movement.[23]

It was Hochmann who "awakened" most of those people who became the early Brethren. Although they were later to break with him over the question of church organization, they originally looked to him as their spiritual guide. The first main story in the early history of the Brethren is the process of separation from the state or established churches. As these earnest seekers endeavored to translate Christianity into their daily lives they found that the church and the state were determined to suppress any change in the existing situation.

I. Separation

It pleased the good God in His mercy at the very beginning of this present century and age to support His saving grace, which appears to all men, through some voices calling for repentance and awakening. In this way He awakened many people from the death and sleep of sin. They then sought to find righteousness in Christ. However, they immediately saw to their sorrow great decay almost everywhere. Therefore they felt impelled to give many sincere testimonies of truth about this. Here and there private meetings (in which the newly-awakened souls sought their edification) were established alongside of the usual church organizations. However, because of the spiritual envy of the clergy, the hearts of the authorities were embittered, and persecution began to take place here and there. This happened in Switzerland, the state of Württemberg, in the Electoral Palatinate, in the state of Hesse, and many other places.

—Alexander Mack, Jr.[1]

Records have been preserved of separatist activity involving members of the Reformed and Lutheran churches, who were to become the first Brethren, in three areas—the Heidelberg-Mannheim territory of the Electoral Palatinate, the vicinity of Strassburg in France, and the district of Basel in Switzerland. The reports of government and church officials, and especially minutes of hearings which they held, disclose the pattern of events through which men and women, generally considered to be devout and faithful church members, came to take the drastic step of defying the authorities for the sake of newly won religious beliefs.

Dissatisfaction with the lack of piety in the lives of their pastors and their fellow parishioners appears as the basic reason for attempts at holding private meetings for mutual edification. With a harshness hardly imaginable today, church and civil agencies suppressed these harmless gatherings. Expulsion was the usual lot for those found guilty of "Pietism." Seldom did the Pietists resolve to break with their churches until that was the only way left them to stay true to their convictions.

PIETISM IN THE PALATINATE

The great majority of the early Brethren were natives of the Electoral Palatinate—an irregularly shaped section of Germany south and west of Frankfurt/Main along the Rhine River valley. The particularly disturbed religious and political situations there have been previously described. With the established churches engaged in bitter in-fighting, it is not surprising that some of the populace would be receptive to new religious ideas promising more genuine spirituality. The repeated invasions and continuing threats of war disrupted the conservative forces of tradition and custom. Wandering prophets proclaimed the impending end of the world. The times were insecure and unsettled, the burdens of the sovereign crushing, the future dark.

The records of the Palatine government (now kept at Karlsruhe) show that separatist activities began in the Palatinate at the very beginning of the century.[2] In 1702 Mathew Baumann openly attacked the established church in his home Lambsheim near Frankenthal.[3] He early migrated to Pennsylvania, where he became the leader of the "New Born," who believed that they had become perfect and therefore could not sin. In 1705, four Lambsheim citizens—John Traut, Jacob Bossert, Jacob Berg, and Adam Pfarr—refused to swear oaths of allegiance because they said that oath-taking was forbidden in the Bible. They were accused of Pietism and were to be imprisoned until they were willing to profess themselves again to one of the established churches.[4] These men later appeared in the Marienborn area east of Frankfurt, where Bossert and Traut became Brethren.

It was, however, with the appearance of Ernest Christopher Hochmann von Hochenau in the Palatinate in 1706 that a real movement began which caused the church and the government authorities much concern. Hochmann came first to Schriesheim, five miles north of Heidelberg on the Bergstrasse, at the invitation of Alexander Mack.[5] A miller by trade, Mack (1679-1735) was to become the organizer and leader of the Church of the Brethren. He had become acquainted with Hochmann during visits to meetings in the Marienborn area.

THE PIETISTS IN SCHRIESHEIM AND MANNHEIM

Activity in Schriesheim

A report from the Reformed church council at Heidelberg to the Palatine government gave warning of the evangelistic activity of Hochmann, Mack, and the others.

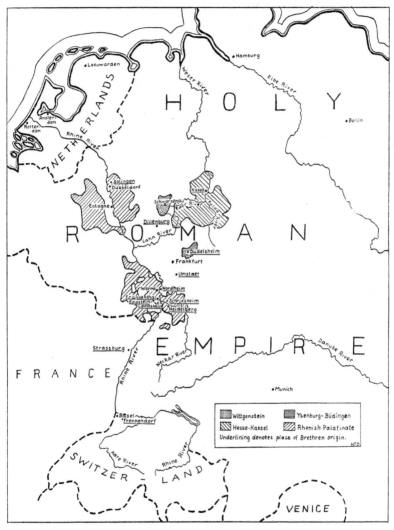

Map by Hedda Durnbaugh

Where the Brethren Originated

For some time the so-called Pietists have been getting the upper hand here in the city as well as in various places in the country, especially in Schriesheim. They meet from time to time in their homes and hold conventicles. They also preach in the streets, sing, and distribute books in order to attract the inhabitants when the latter return from the fields to their homes. Through this, the congregation might become upset or led astray by their errors. Many souls might be caused to doubt through this hypocrisy. Therefore the most praiseworthy Electoral Palatine government is hereby respectfully requested to check this evil before it spreads further, and to condemn it strongly, through the high authority based on the Electoral Palatine regulation, title 28, page 227.

Heidelberg, August 7, 1706

Consistorial councilor,
Mr. Creutz.[6]

Pietists Dispersed

This report was forwarded to a Heidelberg official for investigation. His letter to the Elector Palatine affirmed the success which the Pietists were having with the inhabitants of Schriesheim and vicinity. Although he dispersed them, the group fled before the summoned soldiers arrived to arrest them.

Princely Elector, Gracious Lord, etc.

That which the Reformed church council respectfully reported to Your Princely Highness on the seventh of this month, and which Your Highness graciously communicated to us on the twenty-first of this month, is not without some truth. Namely, some days ago several so-called Pietists came together in a mill a quarter of an hour distant from Schriesheim, among whom were two leaders—one from Nürnberg [Hochmann], and the other a native of Switzerland [Erb]. This pernicious sect has spread there to such an extent that about fifty men and women, who had come there from the above-mentioned Schriesheim, as well as Heidelberg and Ladenburg, have already succumbed to this Pietism.

They would have certainly gained a majority and captured many hundred souls in a short time, if we had not gone in person to the scene at Schriesheim to disrupt and drive away this heretical pack.

After we had spoken to them sharply, and had examined them, the county clerk wanted to withdraw from their synagogue in the mill in the above-mentioned Schriesheim. He intended having a company from the Haxthausen regiment, quartered in Weinheim, come to secure these dangerous persons by arresting them until instructions could be obtained. However, they decamped in the same moment with bag and baggage and fled here.

We could not determine exactly what these people teach or preach, except that they cited some texts from Dr. Martin Luther's Bible which speak of spirit, brethren and sisters in Christ, and similar things. This they interpret according to their own caprice and supposed benefit, and delude the poor rabble with it. From all of their gestures and actions we can perceive nothing else but pure hypocrisy and willful idleness. Incidentally, as far as we are now informed, no Catholic person has gone over to this Pietism, but rather it occurs most among the Reformed. Therefore the first mentioned Reformed church council has indeed grounds to be the main opponents of this new sect. We remain herewith with most humble respect,

Your Princely Highness'
most humble, loyal and obedient
servant

Heidelberg,   Superior bailiwick [*Oberamt*], Heidelberg,
August 25, 1706.   Schumm.[7]

Pietists Arrested

Most of the dispersed Pietists went to the nearby city of Heidelberg, where, however, they were driven away. The next mention of them in the records was at the home of a Mennonite, John Bechtoldt, in the village of Zuzenhausen southeast of Heidelberg. After being forced by the authorities to leave his home, they went to Mannheim, where they were finally arrested. The group included the leaders, Hochmann and Christian Erb, and eight others. The councilors of the Elector Palatine issued an order sentencing the Pietists to hard public labor.

Heidelberg, September 13, 1706, Sunday.

The Mannheim city council has informed us with a report of the ninth of this month that the so-called Pietist sect has begun to spread there also. Some time earlier there was a rumor that such sectarians were in Mannheim, and were holding their secret conventicles. The said city council therefore investigated, and finally learned some days ago that several were staying in the home of a shoemaker and were about to hold a sermon. This pack was immediately seized and taken to prison. They were interrogated and a report was made of their statements, which is enclosed in the city council's report as well as the forwarded minutes and enclosures pertaining to it.

His Electoral Highness is to be informed about the present case by means of the sending of the above-mentioned report along with its enclosures. His Highness should be further notified that steps have not been lacking, as reports received indicate, to eradicate this sect here in the city and in Schriesheim, as well as in the Dielsperg bailiwick, where the sect has established itself. It is not to be doubted that the fanatics, who have infiltrated from time to time, have set foot in almost all of the territory. This is a very dangerous sect, which indeed simulates outward sanctimony without neglecting to try to get others under their will. They attempt to evade the power of the authorities, in that they expressly profess that they cannot be forced to obey in matters against the Word of God, which they interpret according to their perverse minds and fanatical spirit in disobedience. They also vagabond around the country after abandoning their livelihood, properties, and trades, and give themselves over to idleness from which evil results must necessarily come.

Therefore we have found it fitting to sentence those imprisoned at Mannheim, as well as all others who are caught professing this sect, or who may join it in the future, to public work on the fortifications or other labor on a bread-and-water diet. They will be kept at it until they have learned better and again professed one of the three churches tolerated in the empire. This decree is to be distributed in the whole county to the end that we may be rid of and done with them.

> [Palatine councilors]
> (Read and approved in
> consistory on September 18.)[8]

Pietists Questioned

One of the enclosures mentioned in the above order was a record of the interrogation of the imprisoned group soon after their arrest. Their replies not only give personal information but reveal their dissatisfaction with the Reformed Church and the worldly lives of the Reformed clergy as well. The record of the questioning of the last two prisoners, Clemens Heruse and Louis Reno [Renaud], both of whom were residents of Mannheim, is here omitted. An additional entry in the minute book shows that Alexander Mack came to visit his friends and barely escaped imprisonment himself.

Mannheim city council minutes, September 7, 1706.
Examination of the imprisoned Pietists . . .

After having arrested and imprisoned some Pietists yesterday evening upon received order, they were examined under today's date, as follows:

General interrogation of the first two.
Question 1. What are their names?
    a. Hochmann.
    b. Christian Erb.
2. How old are they?
    a. Will be thirty-seven years old.
    b. Thirty years old.
3. Where were they born?
    a. In Lauterburg in Lower Saxony.
    b. In Switzerland at Stefansburg, six hours from Bern.
4. What are their professions?
    a. A Christian; previously he served the devil, but now he seeks to serve Christ.
    4a. Has he [Hochmann] studied at a university?
        a. He was taught by God. He attended classes at the universities of Giessen, Leipzig, Erfurt, and Jena, but these were only outward studies. Now he has received the true doctrine from Jesus Christ.
    b. He has not learned a trade.
5. Are they married? If so, do they have children, and where do the same live?
    a. No, he has no outward wife, but is married to Christ.
    b. No, he is still single.
    5a. Why then does he [Erb] write a letter to his "dear housekeeper" [*Hausfrau*]?
    b. They had resided there.

A View of Schriesheim

5b. How long had he already traveled with Hochmann?
    b. About two years.

Detailed interrogation.

Question 1. How long have they been gone from home?
    a. It has been many years. He has traveled occasionally in Switzerland and other places, and can determine no fixed time.
    b. It will be three years at the next trade fair.
2. For what purpose have they come into this land?
    a. To honor God and Christ and to call the people to repentance.
    b. They were called here, specifically, by the so-called Sanden [Alexander Mack] of Schriesheim, who was once with them at Marienborn, six hours from Frankfurt.
3. To what church do they belong?
    a. The Christian church; his Savior knows of only one church.
    b. He does not profess any church, but only Christ. He was previously Reformed, but abandoned this church because he did not find there the right life, in which one could be saved.
4. Whether they do not know that in the Holy Roman Empire only three churches are tolerated?
    a. He knows the imperial regulations very well outwardly, but Jesus Christ curses such regulations.
    b. They are not making a new religion but rather seek to unite themselves with God.
5. Why do they then dare to preach and spread new heretical teachings and sectarianism?
    a. He does not preach any new doctrines but only the ancient teachings which Jesus Christ taught.
    b. They are not heretical teachings.
6. Whether they have not found any congregations among the three churches in the Palatinate where they have time enough daily to sing and pray?
    a. There are enough outward temples, but Christ is himself the true temple.
    b. Yes, they are here for that reason. He does not find, however, any people in them who have the love of God.

7. Why do they then hold such forbidden private and secret conventicles and sermons?

   a. He is not permitted to preach in public churches; so it makes no difference to him where he preaches.

   b. They do not hold secret conventicles, but rather wherever they come and the people visit them, they cannot possibly turn them away.

8. Whether they were not recently disrupted and dispersed in Schriesheim and in Heidelberg?

   a. The magistrate had come to them and warned them that they should go away; they would not be tolerated there. He went there again afterwards, however. (He then gave them an example—an allegory—that whoever attacked him attacked God since he was a son of God.)

   b. Yes.

9. Why did they then further dare to wander about the country, like those fanatics, and mislead the poor, simple subjects to accept their superstition, and rouse them against their government?

   a. When the government orders something that is against the will of God, they need not respect and obey it. Otherwise they do nothing against the authorities.

   b. They are not vagabonds, but rather travelers. If they are called for, they cannot decline it.

10. How can they dare to be so arrogant and wicked as to manufacture false passes, and order therein the authorities to respect them? Under what authority did they undertake such wickedness?

   a. This pass was given only to show who they were.

   b. He knows of no false passes; they are only admonitions to turn to God.

11. Whether they do not know that the heresies, the practiced falseness, and incitement of the subjects are forbidden under the heaviest penalties, and whether he must not admit that he has committed the same?

   a. He knows it well, but he has not done anything like that.

   b. Everything that is against God and His commandments is forbidden, but they do not seek to do such things. (They alleged this and that text to show that they respected the authorities in that which the latter were empowered to command.)

The third.

His name is John Jost Hahn; comes from the Dillenburg area; was expelled from that part of the country because he tried to conform to Christ's teachings and to seek salvation. He had been of Reformed faith, however, is seeking now to follow Christ and do what Jesus commands. He has traveled around with Hochmann; before that, he earned his living as a farmer. He now seeks his living in Christ. The grace of God is in him, which he concluded from the fact that his sins—the sins of anger, strife, jealousy, etc.—had subsided within him.

The fourth.

John Jacob Haller of Heidelberg; is about twenty-five years old. He has no trade, except that he seeks to be a Christian. Previously he was of the Reformed faith, but because there are so many godless persons in the congregation at Heidelberg, who are also admitted to communion, he rejected that congregation.

The fifth.

Martin Lucas of Heidelberg, a buttonmaker. The reasons for accompanying the first two [Hochmann and Erb] here were that he had not seen or heard anything bad about them. He follows after Christ because of them, and strives to be a Christian.

The sixth.

Peter Hilpert, born at Waltzheim, but recently a resident of Ebstadt; was formerly of the Reformed faith; however, now seeks to become a Christian, as he could not learn anything in the Reformed Church. The pastors themselves do not practice what they preach. He has no other teacher than Jesus Christ. He will not enter a church, but would rather suffer death and shame for Christ's sake.

The seventh.

Jost Henry Frantz, from the Dillenburg country. He has no other trade than that he is going out of the darkness, and seeks to serve God only. Previously, he earned a living as a farmer, and seeks now to study through the Spirit of God. He had been Reformed, but because he had become acquainted with the preacher Hochmann, he had to leave the county with him, etc.

The eighth.

John Henry Dietz, a journeyman joiner, confesses that the shoemaker [Clemens Heruse] called for him and wanted to persuade him to join them. He has, however, nothing to do with them.

. . .

The same day. Afternoon.

A sackmaker from Heidelberg has come here again, who violently demanded to see his brethren. As he refused to be persuaded otherwise, he was put in the innermost tower because of such wickedness.

Similarly, on Wednesday, September 8, there arrived here a miller from Schriesheim [Alexander Mack] and a single fellow from Heidelberg, who demanded to see their brethren. As there are not enough prisons to detain such people, they were expelled from the city.[9]

Edict of the Elector Palatine

The Elector Palatine considered the Pietist movement so dangerous that he at once issued a severe edict to all of the governmental offices and the three main cities ordering that all Pietists found gathering in homes must be seized and placed at hard labor without trial or hearing. He was determined to prevent the spread of Pietism in his land. The edict became the basis for the future punishment of those accused of Pietism, and resulted in the flight or eventual expulsion of many of his subjects.

John William by God's grace Count of the Rhenish Palatinate, Lord High Treasurer and Elector of the Holy Roman Empire, Duke of Bavaria, Jülich, Cleve, and Berg, etc.

First our gracious greetings, most learnéd, honorable, dear, and faithful [councilors]. We have learned to our great displeasure from several reports to what extent the new, self-proclaimed so-called Pietist sect is trying to make inroads in various villages in our electorate of the Rhenish Palatinate. This is happening although we have had the necessary action taken through our officials to scatter them through expulsion and in other ways in those places wherever any have joined this damnable heresy and been caught holding secret meetings.

It is not untimely to fear that this evil might infiltrate into the other cities and the county through religious fanatics wandering around in the territory, and may spread further. This is to be prevented in time with all sternness and emphasis. It is extremely urgent that this sect—which has an outward hypocritically good appearance, and is therefore much more misleading, but is in itself exceedingly dangerous—should be smothered in its first evil brood.

Therefore it is to this end our gracious will and strict command herewith once and for all that you should have all those people in the city, who profess this error and hold secret conventicles in homes or elsewhere, carefully watched, especially the leaders. Those who commit this evil and who do not respond either to kindly or severe warnings to abandon these wicked intentions and maintain this especially stubbornly are to be arrested at once without special authorization. They are to be put in prison, and as many of them as there are must be locked to wheelbarrows and kept on public work on the fortifications or at other common labor. They are to be separated from one another in various places, and put on a bread-and-water diet. You are to publish this present gracious decree of ours in the entire city so that everyone can conduct himself accordingly and know how to avoid trouble. This is done through our serious decision, and we remain favorably inclined toward you.
Heidelberg, September 14, 1706.[10]

Punishment a Failure

A Palatine official at Mannheim reported to the elector one week later that the punishment of the group had not succeeded very well. The Mannheim populace had flocked to hear Hochmann, who preached instead of working. The Catholic official tried to use the Pietists to discredit the local Reformed congregation, illustrating the bitter Catholic-Protestant controversy in that area.

Illustrious Elector, etc., Gracious Lord, etc.

I have had published at the local city council the gracious decree which Your Electoral Highness has recently issued against the Pietists in arrest here. On the basis of this, they were sentenced to public labor on the Neckar River in the hope that others of their ilk would be intimidated. However, it is impossible to describe what a great sympathy all of the Reformed subjects have shown for them. They have defended the Pietists' teachings, and said that nothing could be found deserving punishment in such pious Christians as far as they could see or hear. They have unashamedly proclaimed and made this their own cause. In addition, they immediately began going in processions to the prisoners outside of the city, not out of curiosity but to spend all day listening to them. The prisoners preached continually instead of doing the assigned labor. They have also sent them plenty to eat and drink despite the published prohibition.

The civil guard appointed to watch them was powerless to prevent this, and was no longer sure of his own safety because of the open threats against him. I was finally forced to request a military guard and ordered him to go there. The latter gave the leader, the so-called Hochmann, a few harmless blows, because the latter would neither stop his continual preaching nor accommodate himself to working.

This caused such compassion, tumult, and exaggeration from the Reformed party as if these "innocent" people were being treated barbarously, so that an open rebellion was to be feared. This was even though I had released the two local citizens among the prisoners upon their declaration that they would again profess the Reformed faith. The Reformed party demonstrated such an unusual hatred for me because of this that one can obviously see that most of the Reformed have fallen prey to this Pietistic error and conspire with them.

Last night the German Reformed pastor and the elders of that congregation went to the Pietists in the prison. According to the information I have received, they comforted them and told them that they had already written to Heidelberg on their behalf. They had expressed in the petition how cruelly the Pietists had been treated, and had related that some of the latter had already fallen ill because of the beatings and other harsh treatment. Therefore they are to have patience and should not be of little faith. The prisoners are encouraged by this to manifest stubbornness.

As their complaint or intercession which they might have made or which might yet be presented is founded on an insincere basis, I wanted to describe obediently this disgraceful state of affairs to Your Electoral Highness. It is my humble opinion that a still harsher edict should be drawn up against this Pietistic sect and their defenders. This should be made known publicly, and then the local Reformed congregation should be required to state whether they profess the Reformed faith or Pietism. If they favor the latter, then they could no longer enjoy the privileges granted by the peace treaties in favor of the Protestants or Reformed. Besides this, they have left unbuilt the favorable church site restored to them half a year ago, and have not shown the slightest intention of building. Rather, as far as can be seen, they prefer to associate with the private conventicles. I humbly commend myself herewith to the most gracious electoral favor.

Your Electoral Highness'

Mannheim,   humble, loyal, and obedient servant
September 21, 1706.   Lippe.[11]

Pietists Released

An appeal for release from their harsh imprisonment was received by the Palatine government from Hochmann, Erb, and a certain Baumann, probably the sackmaker from Heidelberg who was imprisoned later. The councilors ordered the Mannheim city council to release the three, who were not Palatine subjects, but kept the others in prison. The latter were not freed until November, after having been made to promise that they would abandon their Pietist beliefs.

Our honorable sirs, etc.

You will have by now obediently received our recent gracious decree concerning the three persons—Hochmann, Erb, and Baumann—imprisoned because of their Pietism. As these prisoners have obediently appealed again for merciful amelioration by the enclosed submissive petition, we have thereupon graciously resolved to dismiss the same at this time. They are to be expelled with the stern warning that they must never set foot in Mannheim or any other place in the territory of our Electoral Palatinate or spread their false teaching in the future, under penalty of much more severe treatment. Therefore you are to take the necessary action, and report now and later what has happened. We remain, etc.

Heidelberg, September 28, 1706.   [Palatine councilors][12]

RENEWED ACTIVITY IN SCHRIESHEIM

Pietists Arrested in Schriesheim

One of the results of the sharp repressive measures taken by the Elector Palatine was Alexander Mack's leaving Schriesheim. During

October 1706, Mack sold considerable property and left his home. He had earlier (March 5, 1706) sold to his brother, John Jacob, his half of the mill *(Talmühle)* bequeathed by their father, John Philip Mack, to the two brothers on October 24, 1702. At that time Mack had reserved the use of the kitchen and the large room, and it was undoubtedly there that the Pietists' meetings had been held.

Mack's father (1636-1706) was an influential and respected man. He was an elder of the Reformed church, a long-time member of the town council, and had served as mayor in 1690 and 1696. Mack married Anna Margaret Kling, daughter of another important townsman, on January 18, 1701. Two sons, John Valentine (November 13, 1701) and John (April 19, 1703), were born to them in Schriesheim.

Mack and his family eventually settled at Schwarzenau in the county of Wittgenstein, but it is not known whether they went there directly. In 1707, Mack sold the rest of his property while away from Schriesheim— on January 23, February 5, and October 1.[13] It may be that Mack traveled at this time with Hochmann, as one writer states.[14]

Despite governmental repression, the Pietists continued to hold their meetings in the area. John Valentine Kling (1651-1714), Mack's father-

Birth [Baptismal] Entries, Reformed Church Book, Schriesheim
Upper: Alexander Mack, Sr., July 27, [1679]. *Lower:* Anna Margaret Kling, December 5, [1680].

Marriage Entry, Reformed Church Book, Schriesheim
"Alexander Mack, legitimate son of Mr. John Philip Mack, the councilor, and Anna Margaret, legitimate daughter of Mr. John Valentine Kling, also councilor. [Proclamations:] 1st Sunday in Advent, 2nd Sunday in Advent, 3rd Sunday in Advent. [Witnesses:] Signature by Superior Bailiwick. [Marriage:] here, Jan. 18 [1701]."

Birth [Baptismal] Entries, Reformed Church Book, Schriesheim
Upper: John Valentine Mack, November 13, 1701. *Lower:* John, April
19, 1703. These were two of the three sons of Alexander and Anna
Margaret Mack.

in-law, became suspect when he refused to sign a petition denouncing
Mack. A meeting in his home was broken up by the authorities on May
1, 1708, and the participants were arrested. The same Heidelberg official
who had earlier dispersed the Pietists at Schriesheim reported to the
Elector Palatine the imprisonment of Kling and three others, one of whom
was Martin Lucas, who had been with Hochmann in Mannheim.

Your Electoral Highness, Gracious Lord, etc.

Your Electoral Highness is humbly referred to his decree issued
on September 14, 1706, concerning the spreading of the so-called
Pietistic sect. At that time it was ordered that the Pietists be kept
under close observation and seized upon committing the offense
without waiting for further instruction. As many as were involved
were to be locked without fail to the wheelbarrows and kept at public
labor on the fortifications or other lowly work on a bread-and-water
diet. Moreover, this said gracious decree was to be duly publicized
immediately after receiving it and to be made known to everyone.

In addition, this gracious decree was sent by the court clerk to
John Valentine Kling, a citizen of Schriesheim, who was formerly an
elder of the Reformed church and also a member of the town council.
He was ejected from these positions because of this Pietism in the
hope that he would then withdraw from this vulgar sect at some future
date and rejoin one of the three churches tolerated in the empire. He
was shown this decree, warned, and reminded that he must obey the
same. He must withdraw from the sect and cease to receive and give
shelter to such people, failing in which the above decree would have
to be executed upon him to the letter.

This well-intended warning has had no effect on Kling to date,
and he has not professed himself to any church. He has actually been
expelled from the Reformed church, as Annex A shows. Therefore

the court clerk proceeded to make an arrest in accordance with the gracious decree last Sunday, the first of this month, as the Pietists were holding a conventicle. They had gone together to Leutershausen, and were spending the evening together. In order finally to disrupt the conventicle, the court clerk arrested the three from Heidelberg— namely, Martin Lucas, buttonmaker, who has professed the sect for three years already, Stephen Stutzenegger, linen weaver, who [has professed the sect] for two years, and Esbert Bender, a wool spinner, who has professed the sect for only a half year [and John Valentine Kling].

We have therefore humbly reported this herewith, and would like to request further instruction. As a matter of fact, we are of the unauthoritative and humble opinion that they should be given a money fine of one hundred *Reichstaler* because they stubbornly and maliciously refuse to obey the gracious order which has been issued. As the Catholics must build a new church at Schriesheim, and this is a very extraordinary project, we suggest that they be forced to pay the fine in cash to the Catholic church building project. In addition, they should be sharply enjoined that they must submit authentic proof to which church they belong within a previously appointed time, failing in which they should be proceeded against according to the letter of the decree. We, of course, leave this to the gracious disposition of Your Electoral Highness. I remain,

your Electoral Highness'
most humble, loyal and obedient
servant
Schumm.[15]

Heidelberg,
May 4, 1708.

The Klings Excommunicated

The annex mentioned in Schumm's letter is a certificate from the presbytery of the Reformed church in Schriesheim that Kling and his wife had been excommunicated. The John Philip Mack whose signature is included among the elders is not Alexander Mack's father, but rather another Schriesheim resident having the same name.

Annex A.

Mr. John Valentine Kling, along with his wife, as well as John Jacob Hoffsteiter, has stayed away from holy communion, after the

A Street Scene in Schriesheim
The home of John Valentine Kling is at the right, that of the county
clerk at left center.

former became attached to the so-called Pietists. The first two have not, or only seldom, appeared to hear God's Word for over a year's time, and have separated themselves from our church. The latter, however, has for some time been making his appearance again to hear God's Word. The first two will, therefore, no longer be recognized or considered as members of our church, inasmuch as they were admonished often enough by us at the regular visits to their home, unless they again begin to present themselves among us with earnest repentance. This is hereby attested upon request.

Louis Philip Agricola, Sr., pastor
John Stephen Höltzel, elder
John Philip Mack, elder
John Böckel, elder
John Peter Krebs, almoner
John Philip Artlepp, elder
John Valentine Hoffman, elder[16]

Schriesheim,
December 8, 1707.

Schriesheim Pietists Fined

The Palatine councilors responded to Schumm's letter by approving the fine, but directed that it be sent to the government rather than be used for a Catholic church in Schriesheim, as had been suggested.

This is in reply to the last report made to us on the fourth of this month by the superior bailiwick of Heidelberg concerning the former Pietists who gathered again and were thereupon arrested. The above, for their part, are again instructed that they should fine such Pietists one hundred *Reichstaler* and send this to the government. They should at the same time threaten the Pietists that the latter must betake themselves to one of the three churches tolerated in the Roman Empire within four weeks, consequently desist from this sect, and bring authentic proof that this is the case. If they do not comply with this, they shall be proceeded against much more severely, and will no longer be tolerated in this territory.

Heidelberg, May 10, 1708.   [Palatine councilors][17]

Reformed Consistory Intervenes

The imprisoned Pietists appealed to the Reformed church authorities in Heidelberg, stressing their loyalty to the Reformed faith, and asked for a hearing. Upon receipt of the appeal, the Reformed consistory interceded on their behalf with the Palatine government.

Extract from the Reformed consistory minutes, dated May 25, 1708. [Present:] Rev. Heyles, Rev. Dr. Mieg, Rev. Creutz, Rev. Dr. [illegible], Rev. Dr. Kirchmeier, Rev. Pastoir.

. . .

Resolution: These people, as far as is known, are not to be considered as belonging to the so-called Pietists, who are swarming around and setting themselves against all spiritual and civil regulations. The latter could never be aided by the consistory. Further, in the petition they still profess the Reformed faith, and one cannot reject anyone who offers to give an accounting of his faith. Therefore such request should be granted as far as it concerns the consistory. As they are still imprisoned, however, and cannot present themselves, this petition should be sent to the praiseworthy government and the same should be respectfully requested that they might be so good as to order the officials to set these people at liberty immediately. It has not been proved that they belong to a sect which is forbidden in this territory, but rather they still profess themselves to the Reformed church. Even on the day of their arrest they attended a public worship service conducted by a Reformed preacher.

> Vice president and council
> by authority of the
> Elector Palatine.[18]

Schriesheim Pietists Appeal to Consistory

[Enclosure]
[To the Reformed Consistory]
Sirs, etc. Most Noble . . . Dread Sirs, etc.

We, who have been imprisoned and arrested in Schriesheim for praising God, humbly report to the most worthy council that three weeks ago we were in the Reformed church at Gross-Sachsen, and then went home to Schriesheim. We sang a psalm, and during this we were arrested and have been imprisoned to this date without a hearing or being found guilty of anything. We have been sentenced to pay a fine of one hundred *Reichstaler*. All four of us were born and raised in the Reformed faith, and have up to the present not separated ourselves from the true members of the said church. We have rather striven with them to penetrate deeper into the fellowship of the saints. Moreover, we know that we have not acted contrary to the Holy Scriptures or the Reformed Church or any Christian regulation by singing, for which we were seized.

We therefore humbly appeal to the praiseworthy council, to whom belongs in our opinion the examination of this matter, to question us on our faith. We are ready to give an accounting of our faith, reporting in greater detail than could be done by others. We will gladly submit ourselves to this high, authoritative trial in order that the gracious council will then, we hope, have a more favorable opinion of us. We remain with trust in the most gracious and speedy granting of our request. To the most worthy council, your honorable lords' humble servants,

John Valentine Kling,
Esbert Bender from Herborn,
Stephen Stutzenegger from Altstätten in Switzerland,
Heidelberg,
May 24, 1708.

Martin Lucas, citizen of Heidelberg.[19]

Schriesheim Pietists Released

The Palatine councilors ordered the release of the four, and arranged for a hearing, in a letter to Councilor Becker.

To Councilor Becker:

John Valentine Kling, Esbert Bender from Herborn, Stephen Stutzenegger from Altstätten, Switzerland, and Martin Lucas, citizen of Heidelberg, have made themselves so suspect of Pietism that they were imprisoned by the superior bailiwick of Heidelberg on that account. Now, however, upon the intercession of the Reformed consistory, they have been released although the pronounced punishment is kept in abeyance. The said persons are to give an accounting for the reason mentioned above as need requires before the above-mentioned consistory, each one being heard separately. The consistory is to make a decision about them.

Councilor Becker is hereby commissioned to summon the above-mentioned and to examine them with the aid of the local dean, Dr.

Bockreisz, calling in also the older Professor Father Zinck as well as two persons who are to be appointed by the Reformed consistory using their own means. They are to see whether and which of the churches tolerated in the Roman Empire the said persons profess. The findings are to be sent immediately to the electoral government along with the minutes kept and the report of the commission which is to be attached and attested as well as their decision.

[Palatine councilors][20]

Martin Lucas to Christian Liebe

Before their release, the prisoners attempted to send letters to their families and friends from their place of imprisonment in the tower of the Heidelberg gate on the south side of Schriesheim. However, the fellow prisoner being released to whom they entrusted their messages turned these over to the local official, who forwarded them to the Palatine government. These letters were later to be used against them during the hearings.

May the love of Jesus increase in us all. Amen.
Written from the prison tower in the bailiwick of Schriesheim.
My Dear Brother Christian Liebe.

The great Jehovah has considered me and my dear brethren worthy enough to be led into this imprisonment on April 29. We are to be kept here until our Patron orders that this bond be broken. I rejoice along with my dear brethren about the light of grace of the dearest Holy Spirit of God. The great God has performed a great miracle which happened to me today, the fourteenth day as we were in prayer in the morning [?]. May the Shepherd of our souls be praised and glorified for ever and ever. Amen.

I send greetings to my dear wife and to my dear sister Liz. I send you warm greetings as well as all of our dear brethren in Eppstein and in Frankenthal, and to all dear sisters who love Jesus. My dear wife, I ask you once again to greet your dear mother for her sake. I also send greetings to the dear brother Trumpfft, along with his dear wife and his son. I commend you to the protection of the Most High.

Done at Schriesheim,   [Martin] Lucas, your dear
May 27, 1708.   brother to the death.[21]

Stephen Stutzenegger to Christian Liebe

May 27, 1708.

May the King of Salem be your salvation, and God's grace and faithfulness grow in each of you. Amen.

Dear Brother Christian Liebe.

I cannot let this good opportunity pass without visiting you [by writing] several lines and telling you something of our situation. I am lying imprisoned in Babel for as long as the Lord wills. We leave the rest in the hands of God, the intercessor and breaker of all bonds. He is just as much with us here in the tower as if we were in church. We hope to learn from the strangled Lamb how to follow and how to walk in the footsteps of Him who himself endured cross and affliction, and to learn to be faithful in all trials. The Lord goes before us, and will lead and guide us to all eternal truth. Amen.

The dear brother from Mannheim, Nägele, has visited us, and stayed with us one night, as well as the two dear brethren, Dibere [Düpel ?] and Müller. Therefore may the Lord be praised and blessed for His great love and faithfulness which He shows to His children. Concerning myself and my fellow prisoners, we are still, thank God, faithful to our calling. The dear Brother Hochmann has written a dear letter to us and has sent his most friendly greetings to all of us. He also wrote that he was likewise faithful in his calling. He said that the best policy was to remain composed in the Lord through all trials.

We send our warmest greetings to all of the brethren and sisters, and to all those who want to travel to the holy mountain of Zion. We four brethren—that is [Esbert] Bender, the brother-in-law of Deilber [?], [Martin] Lucas, John Valentine Kling, and Stephen Stutzenegger— send our warmest greetings to you, Christian Liebe, and to all those in Eppstein and Frankenthal. Wherewith I remain, I and my fellow prisoners, your faithful and humble brother. I close, greet, and kiss you once again, I, Stephen Stutzenegger, from the prison in the tower at Schriesheim.

The dear brother Nicholas has also visited us in our tower. He sends his greetings to you and all good friends. Amen.[22]

Letters Confiscated

When the three so-called Pietists in prison learned that the shoe-maker Winckler was to be released, they wrote the enclosed letter[s], and gave it to the latter to deliver to Christian Liebe in Eppstein. When he, however, notified me about it, I took the letter from him, and I am hereby forwarding it to the praiseworthy superior bailiwick. From this can be seen, among other things, the communication among the Pietists, and that they by no means intend to desist therefrom. Schriesheim, June 6, 1708.   John Himberger, court clerk.[23]

THE PIETISTS' HEARINGS

Kling, Lucas, Stutzenegger, and Bender were questioned by a board composed of a Palatine councilor and Reformed and Catholic clergy. Kling explained the reason for his falling out with the Reformed pastor of Schriesheim. They were made to divulge the names of like-minded friends, many of whom lived around Frankenthal on the other side of the Rhine River.

Four Pietists Questioned by Officials

Minutes, June 8, 1708.
Present:

Hon. Councilor Becker   Hon. Consistory Councilor
                                     Dr. Mieg

Hon. Dean Dr. Bockreisz   Hon. Consistory Councilor
                                     Dr. Kirchmeier

Hon. Prof. Father Zinck, Society of Jesus

In response to the governmental decree issued on the twenty-sixth of last month to Elector Palatine Councilor Becker, the following persons accused of Pietism were examined about this and the character and principles of their conventicles and newly begun sect. The record was taken as follows:

[*John Valentine Kling*]
Question 1. Into what church was he born?
        Into the Reformed Church.
    2. To what church did his parents belong?
        Also the Reformed Church.

3. Whether he had attended the Reformed church previously?
   He was even shortly before his imprisonment in the Reformed church at Gross-Sachsen.
4. Whether he is still faithfully Reformed?
   Yes.

Detailed interrogation.

Question 1. On what does he base his faith?
   On the merits of Christ.
2. From what did he learn his faith?
   From the Word of God.
3. Whether he accepts the Heidelberg Catechism?
   Yes; it is taken from God's Word.
4. Whether he has any scruples about attending the Reformed church?
   No.
5. Why then did he prefer to go to church in Gross-Sachsen rather than in Schriesheim?
   Because the pastor at Leutershausen evidences greater love for him.
6. Whether he would hesitate to attend holy communion with the Reformed, be it at Schriesheim or at Leutershausen?
   If he had an inclination thereto in his soul, he would have no scruples against it.
7. What grounds does he have against the pastor in Schriesheim to listen to the pastor in Leutershausen, and not to him?
   He was [formerly] an elder and had spoken zealously against the vices, but the pastor cut him short gruffly and defamed him. However, he reconciled himself with the pastor and attended holy communion. Later, the pastor had all church elders called together and sought to obtain all sorts of testimonies against his son-in-law, Alexander Mack, even from women, maidservants, and others. He demanded from him that he should sign a drafted testimony against Mack along with the others, but because he refused to do this, the pastor burst out against him and called him a scoundrel. Upon this the town council of Schriesheim, of which he had been a member up to that day, asked him to resign and did not want to admit him to their sessions any more. This then caused him

not to listen to the pastor's sermons any longer and to avoid the church at Schriesheim, which he has done until now.

8. What, then, were they doing when they were arrested?

They had come from church in Gross-Sachsen and went with the pastor to his home in Leutershausen. They stayed there for a while and toward evening went to Schriesheim together. They went to his, Kling's, house and had supper together. After the meal they prayed and sang; just as they had begun another hymn, the court clerk came with four soldiers and a sergeant-major, asked them what they were doing here together, and told them they were to be arrested, which they immediately carried out.

9. Whether he thought his comrades were of his faith?

He only knows that they are Reformed just as he is. During their meetings they spoke only about the lives of the Christians, and exhorted one another to live the good life and shun evil ways.

Martin Lucas.

Question 1. Where was he born?

In Bayonne, France.

2. Of what faith were his parents?

Catholic parents.

3. How old is he?

Fifty-seven years old.

4. What is his faith?

Reformed.

5. How long has he belonged to the Reformed church?

Thirty-two years.

6. Where did he join the same?

At Bern in Switzerland.

7. Where does he live?

Has been a citizen and buttonmaker in Heidelberg for twenty-seven years.

Detailed interrogation.

Question 1. On what does he base his faith?

On the teachings of Christ, namely the Holy Scriptures of the Old and New Testaments.

2. What is his opinion of the Heidelberg Catechism?

    He has read it and wishes that he could live up to it in all points.

3. Which are the ones that seem hard for him to keep?

    In article one, that he should belong to Christ with body and soul, and article seventy-six, that he should truly be united with Christ.

4. Whether he attended the Reformed Church?

    He went to church at Leutershausen several times.

5. Why did he not go to church here instead of at Leutershausen?

    He prefers the pastor at Leutershausen and is edified by him.

6. Whether he has any scruples against attending the local church?

    If he feels inspired to do so, he has no scruples at all against it.

7. What sort of an inspiration is that?

    It is an inner impulse which means to him a calling.

8. Whether he has not occasionally had such an inspiration to attend church here?

    He has not had such for some time.

9. Whether he would also hesitate to take holy communion?

    If he is ready for it, he would not hesitate.

10. Whether he has any scruples against taking holy communion here in Heidelberg?

    He has no other scruples than that he sees that there is no improvement on the part of many.

11. Whether he considers those outside the city, where he attends, to be good?

    He understands that because the congregation out there is not so large, the pastor can pay more attention about whom he admits to holy communion to see if they are worthy of it.

12. Whether one cannot worthily take holy communion if there are others present that are not worthy of it?

    As long as they are not repentant he cannot receive it with them.

13. Whether he did not consider to be good the things which the local honorable clergy teach?

    Basically, he thinks, everything is good.

14. Whether, then, he criticizes the way and manner of the outward worship service?

No, because he is still going to church, and he has no other way to sing and to pray than as do the local Reformed.

15. Whether he would have any scruples against obeying if he were ordered to attend church here?

He has freedom of conscience and may seek to worship anywhere.

16. Whether they have regular meetings?

No, but whenever they come together as the occasion arises they exhort one another from the Scriptures and sing psalms.

17. Whether they arrange this by writing?

No, but as mentioned before, only by occasion, when one comes to the other.

18. Who are those that come together now and then?

They are Esbert Bender, a settler here, Stephen Stutzenegger, journeyman linen weaver [who lives] on the castle hill, also the two Diehl brothers, both citizens and tailors here.

19. Whether there are any in Frankenthal who belong to the brotherhood?

Yes, there used to be some, but he has been told that they left.

20. Who were those and what are their names?

Schatz, a baker; also two brothers, who were sackmakers, and their father, whose names are not familiar; also Schatz' brother-in-law, and several others, whose names he does not know.

21. Whether there are any in Eppstein that belong to his brotherhood?

There is one named Trumpff[t]; another is Christian Liebe—as far as he was told, the latter has supposedly left—and another, whose name is Wüst, if he remembers rightly. He was further told of one, whose name is Mathew [Matheisz] but is commonly called Theisz. They also told of the hangman of Frankenthal, but he has heard that he has turned away again.

22. Who then were the sisters who have sent their greetings?

The sackmakers' unmarried sister and the wife of Schatz.

23. Why did these from Frankenthal and Eppstein mentioned above leave?

He has heard that they had been imprisoned because of their private devotions; afterwards they left.

24. Why do they call one another "brother" and "sister"?

Because it says in the Bible that the Christians should call one another by this, as did the apostles.

25. Whether he considers all other Reformed his brethren and sisters?
Only those who live according to the commandments of Christ.

Stephen Stutzenegger.

Question 1. Where was he born?
Four hours from St. Gallen in the Upper Rhine valley in Switzerland.

2. Of what faith were his parents?
He was born of Reformed parents.

3. How old is he?
Thirty-one years old.

4. Where does he live actually?
On the hill with the linen weaver, where he is a journeyman.

5. What is his matrimonial state?
Still unmarried.

6. What is his faith?
Reformed.

7. How long has he been here?
For ten years here and at Neuburg monastery.

Detailed interrogation.

. . .

19. Who are the persons who had been in the fellowship with them to the present, and whom he called brethren?
One is named Christian Liebe from Eppstein; one named Peter from Frankenthal or Eppstein; one named Clemens [Heruse], a shoemaker with wife and five children in Mannheim, but as far as he knew, was to have moved across the Rhine River, because the mayor there would not tolerate the common people. Also two bakers from beyond the Rhine, whose names he does not know; also two local tailors, who are brothers; and the four being questioned; as well as John Adam Haller, former clerk of the Imperial Chamber, who had recently held school for children here illegally and therefore was examined by the city council; Abraham, a shepherd, it seems to him, from Frankenthal or Eppstein; also one named

Mathew from Eppstein, a vintner, as far as he knows; also the wigmaker [John Martin] Reinhard, here at Heidelberg; also one named Nägele, to his knowledge a former dealer in flour residing in Mannheim; also one named Müller, and another named Düpel [Dibere?], who, however, only visited him and his brethren in prison in passing through.

20. Where the letter has gotten to, which he alleged in his letter to have received from Hochmann, and who has the same now?

The letter was taken to their brethren from one place to another, and he does not know where it is now.

21. What does he understand by the term *office* which is set off therein?

He considers his imprisonment the office, which is laid upon him now; in several places imprisonments are thus called.

22. What does he understand by the word *Babel* in his letter?

He calls everything that is godless Babel, and he has called this place of his imprisonment Babel because Hochmann had called it thus in his letter.

Esbert Bender.

Question 1. Where is his home?

At Herborn in the Dillenburg area.

2. Of what faith were his parents?

Both were Reformed.

3. How old is he?

About forty years of age.

4. Of what trade?

He prepares wool for the stocking weavers here in Heidelberg.

5. How long has he been here?

Over two years here in Heidelberg; before that, however, he lived in Frankfurt.

6. Of what faith is he really?

Reformed faith.

. . .

12. Why did he recently go to Leutershausen?

In order to have edification for his salvation from the sermon.

13. What was he doing when he was arrested together with his comrades?

The same as the above.

14. How did he become acquainted with these people?

> Because he wanted to avoid wicked company and turn to a good one, and because he had never heard or seen anything evil about them.

15. Whether he has also separated himself from the Reformed worship here?

> Never; he does not have in mind to do so either.

16. Whether he would attend the Holy Ghost church if the honorable clergy ordered him to avoid such meetings?

> He hopes that it will not be forbidden to him to praise God either in one place or another, because God said, "Where two or three are gathered in my name, there am I in the midst of them" [Matthew 18:20].

17. Whether there are not more who gather together with him in the same instances?

> There are the two local tailors, the Diehls; the wife of the buttonmaker, Martin Lucas; as for the Eppstein or Frankenthal group, he knows none of them.

18. Where did they meet the last time?

> In the house of the buttonmaker, Martin Lucas.

19. What do they do when they gather in such groups?

> They fall to their knees, pray, and then sing from the Halle hymnal [John A. Freylinghausen, *Geistreiches Gesangbuch* . . .].

20. How long has he been acquainted with these people and how often has he met with them?

> He has not been acquainted with them long and has joined them because of their good lives.

Resolution:

In order to put an end to these sects or conventicles, the Catholic as well as the Reformed theologians will present their deliberations upon the minutes in writing, so that they may be turned in to the praiseworthy government.[24]

FURTHER HEARINGS

Imprisonment did not stifle the striving of the Palatine Pietists for a purified church. Almost exactly one year after their previous arrest, some of the same members of the group were seized at the home of Martin Lucas in Heidelberg. The outcome of this experience was to be more severe, however.

Heidelberg Pietists Questioned

Heidelberg records.
Tuesday, April 30, 1709.
Present: Councilor and Police Commissioner Becker, Syndic and Mayor Arnold, [recorded by] John George Schell, city clerk.

The following was proposed by Councilor and Police Commissioner Becker: A most gracious and strict Electoral Palatine decree has been repeatedly issued and communicated, respectively, for due observance by virtue of which the stated degree of punishment concerning Pietism (which has infiltrated these Electoral Palatine territories) was to take effect. This movement, which is becoming the fashion, is very much to the disadvantage of public life. Especially as it is contrary to the religious peace treaty, it is to be completely eradicated.

Notwithstanding, such a pack was again apprehended last Sunday in the home of the citizen and buttonmaker of this city, Martin Lucas. In order to comply humbly with Your Excellency, the Elector Palatine's, intention, the lord councilor was induced to have them arrested immediately and interrogated to see how far they had become addicted to this punishable movement. Therefore they were examined one by one and a record was made of their statements and testimonies. Consequently, he wishes to solicit the decision of Your Excellency, Our Most Gracious Lord, the Elector Palatine, or at least that of the honorable council. For this reason the examination was carried out according to the following:

[John Henry Rosenbach, a Lutheran separatist, was examined in the first session.]

[*Nicholas Diehl.*]

Continuation of protocol of May 2, 1709.

Present were: Councilor and Police Commissioner Becker; Syndic and Mayor Arnold, [written by] John George Schell, city clerk, Mr. John Peter Kling, councilor.

The examination of the imprisoned persons accused of suspected Pietism was continued.

General interrogation.
Question 1. What is the defendant's name?
　　　Nicholas Diehl.
　2. How old is he?
　　　Not sure whether he is thirty-six or thirty-seven years old.
　3. Who was his father?
　　　George Bernard Diehl, local citizen and tailor.
　4. Whether he is married? If so, how many children does he have?
　　　He is married and has four children. The oldest is thirteen
　　years old, but does not have any faith yet.
　　　4a.　Why does this child not have any faith yet, although it
　　　　　is already thirteen years old?
　　　　　　Because it does not yet understand the Bible.
　　　4b.　Can such a child be saved, who is incapable of under-
　　　　　standing any doctrine?
　　　　　　Yes, certainly, such a child can be saved.
　　　4c.　Through what means, does he think, can such a child
　　　　　be saved?
　　　　　　If such children have parents who are striving after
　　　　　the teachings of God; but even if the parents are
　　　　　godless, such a child can still be saved through the
　　　　　grace of God.
　　　4d.　If a man had a child that is not baptized which grows to
　　　　　be ten, twelve, or older, can it yet be saved?
　　　　　　Yes, certainly, if it otherwise does not lead a sinful
　　　　　life.
　　　4e.　Whether a minor, who was not baptized, is free from
　　　　　original sin?
　　　　　　Yes, all are freed through the suffering and death of
　　　　　Christ Jesus; infant baptism is not necessary, because
　　　　　Christ the Lord has called the children to Him,
　　　　　Mark 10 and Luke 18, and said, "Let the children
　　　　　come to me . . . for to such belongs the kingdom of
　　　　　God" [Mark 10:14].
　5. What is his trade?
　　　Has been master tailor here for ten to eleven years.
　6. What is his faith?
　　　He professes nothing else but being a Christian and knows

nothing of the three churches tolerated in the empire.

7. Does he have property here?

Yes, a house.

Detailed interrogation.

Question 1. Does he know how many churches are tolerated in the Holy Roman Empire?

According to outward things, Catholics, Lutherans, and Reformed are tolerated.

2. Of what faith was he previously, and why has he not remained in it?

Reformed; he has not remained in it because he has found that most of them did not live according to the teachings of Jesus. Paul says in the fifth chapter of First Corinthians, "Drive out the wicked person from among you" [verse 13], and also in Second Corinthians, "Come out from them," and "Do not be mismated with unbelievers" [6:17 and 14]. Because most of the Reformed are wicked he and his comrades went out from them.

3. Does he take holy communion and does he attend church?

No.

4. Why does he not take holy communion and attend church?

Because he loathes the doctrine and way of living of the Reformed, and does not want to share in the others' sins; God punishes the entire congregation if there is one sinner among them, as is taught by the Heidelberg Catechism. He refers to the example of Joshua, chapters six and seven.

5. Whether he believes that he could be saved in one or the other of the churches tolerated in the Holy Roman Empire?

No, he does not believe that, because most of their members lead wicked lives, and God punishes the others with them for their sins.

5a. Whether those, who lead pious lives, could not be saved among the Catholics, Reformed, and Lutherans?

Yes, many of them, because one achieves salvation here on earth, the other there in eternity, for Christ died for us all.

6. What kind of books does he have, from which he takes the bases
    for his doctrine?
>   The Bible, because such is the Word of God.
>   6a. How does he know that the Bible is the Word of God?
>   Because he has tested it inwardly in his soul as well
>   as outwardly.

[*John Diehl and Martin Lucas.*]

(The second defendant [Nicholas Diehl] was asked whether the rest
of his comrades professed all that to which he had now testified, and
do not recognize any further or different doctrine. He answered, yes,
that they, having previously been Reformed, agree with him in all
points. Therefore, in order to avoid prolixity, they shall be included
in the further interrogation. They have also professed and testified as
follows, after answering the general questions.)

7. How long has it been since the defendants have been to church?
>   Second defendant: It must have been two or three years last
>   Easter.
>   Third defendant: John George Diehl, born here, married, two
>   children (one is a daughter), remarried, about forty-six
>   years old, tailor by trade, owns a house. Answers, he has
>   not been to any church for four or five years.
>   Fourth defendant: Martin Lucas, born in Bayonne in France,
>   of Catholic parents, later turned Reformed in Bern, Swit-
>   zerland, at present local buttonmaker and citizen, fifty-eight
>   years old, married, two children, also one house here. An-
>   swers, he has not been to the Reformed church for about
>   four years.

8. Why does he not go to church, but only to those common meetings
    and private homes?
>   Second defendant: The Apostle Paul says in First Corinthians
>   2: "A man and a woman can raise a holy hand anywhere."
>   Third defendant: Because there is no command in the Bible
>   to attend church, as God says that the heaven is His throne
>   and the earth His footstool. He wants to erect His temple
>   in man and not in a house made by man's hands.
>   Fourth defendant: He agrees in all points with the third.

9. What do they do during those meetings in the homes?

Second, third, and fourth defendants unanimously: When they
come together they sing two or three hymns, as God moves
them; then they open the Bible and whatever they find
they read and explain it according to the understanding
given to them by God, for the edification of their brethren.
After they have read, they fall to their knees, raise their
hands to God and pray for the authorities, that God might
move them to punish the evil and protect the good; then
they praise God that He has created them for this purpose.

9a. Is not God praised also in the church into which they
were born?

All three defendants answered in the negative, because the churches did not have the grace of God
and have barred themselves from it.

9b. Whether they then believe that they have the grace of
God now?

Yes, they believe that.

9c. What gives them proof for this belief?

Because they keep away from sin and the light has
begun to shine in them, just as with all people who
accept this. The door of grace is open, for them, as
God says, "Come to me, all who labor and are heavy-
laden, and I will give you rest" [Matthew 11:28].

9d. Whether a sinner does not live in the grace of God in
this way also?

Yes, if he repents, and does not sin any more, for
the Lord does not hear sinners.

9e. What, then, do they believe to be the grace of God?
The remission of sins.

9f. Whether God does not also forgive the sins in the Catholic, Reformed, or Lutheran churches?

Yes, if they repent, for God is no respecter of persons.

9g. Whether a Jew, Turk, or heathen will be saved, even if
he remains in his religion and repents therein?

Yes, if they but recognize Christ and repent.

9h. Whether a Jew, Turk, or heathen will be saved even if
he is not baptized?

Yes, if he but obeys God's commandments.

9i. Whether a man can be saved without even being baptized?

>Yes, without the natural water, certainly; if he is only baptized by the fire of the Holy Spirit, he can indeed be saved, and all people can attain this. John the Baptist had, indeed, baptized in water (Matthew 3) but aimed at repentance.

9j. Whether they believe that they have more grace in their Pietism than they had before in their Reformed faith?

>Yes, because they have separated themselves from sins and are increasing in grace daily by avoiding sin.

9k. What had been the motivation for the defendants to become Pietists?

>Because they had lived in sin before.

9l. What is a Pietist according to the defendants' opinion?

>A devout Christian, who leads a pious life in Christ and God.

9m. Whether the Catholics, Reformed, and Lutherans are not also leading pious lives?

>Very few of them lead pious lives because they do not follow Christ's teachings.

9n. Whether they themselves do what Christ teaches?

>They are striving to do so in whatever they are still failing in.

9o. Whether they are still lacking in some of the good works that are proper for a Christian?

>Yes, in many.

9p. What is it, in which they are lacking?

>They often sin unintentionally and do not obey Christ's commandment, who has said, "Sell all that you have . . . and follow me" [Luke 18:22].

9q. Whether they know anyone among the Catholics, Reformed, or Lutherans who is striving after the same things and obeys Christ?

>They do not know anyone from among the Catholics who would want to join their fellowship and yield himself to perfection, but there are some among

the Reformed and the Lutherans who wished to follow their doctrine.

9r. Who are the ones among the Reformed and the Lutherans that have joined their fellowship or wished to do so?

They know none among the Lutherans except [John] Henry Rosenbach, local journeyman spurmaker; from among the Reformed, however, there are besides the three of them, his (the defendant Lucas') wife Anna Margaret; Esbert Bender, who is staying with him; Stephen Stutzenegger, a journeyman linen weaver living on the castle hill; a student named [John] Adam Haller; Christine Schmid, daughter of the late needlemaker, John Schmid; also a widow who is staying with a cabinetmaker on Mittelbad Lane, and who earns her living by linen-printing and has three children; Mr. Pastoir's wife, who lives at the apothecary's home, but has never come to their meetings; Mr. John Philip Ehrwald's eldest daughter Rosina. Other than these they know of no one in the city, and outside the city only John Valentine Kling at Schriesheim. They do wish, however, that all people would accept their doctrine; they would regret it, if one soul were lost.

10. How often do they meet?

They do not have appointed days, but come together on Sundays, holidays, or workdays, as God moves them. They enjoy free exercise of religion in Marienborn, four hours distant from Hanau, and in the county of Wittgenstein. Often forty, fifty, or sixty of them meet at one time. So, for instance, the shoemaker Eichhorn from here moved there already two years ago, also many from Frankenthal, Eppstein, and other places in the Palatinate; also some from Mannheim, and the above-named places in the Electoral Palatinate migrated to the island [*sic*] of Pennsylvania six weeks ago, expecting to find there free exercise of religion as in Holland and England.

11. Whether they preach during their meetings?

No, they explain the Bible to one another, according to their grace from God.

11a. Who explains it to them when they differ in their
       opinions?
            When they differ, they pray to God until He grants
            them His grace, through which they remain in love
            and thus can agree.
11b. Whether they do not think that a learnéd clergyman
       could solve such doubts better than they could among
       themselves, since they are only craftsmen who have no
       time to devote to this as do the clergymen?
            No, the clergymen cannot explain it better to them
            than they do themselves, because the first teachers
            were also common people like fishermen and rug
            weavers (1 Corinthians).
11c. Whether the defendants are of the opinion that God gives
       the present craftsmen today the same grace as He did to
       His apostles?
            Yes, the door of grace is open for all people, and
            God is still the same God, which He was from
            eternity, who can give them grace as He did to the
            twelve apostles.
11d. Whether the defendants know any craftsmen who have
       the grace of explaining the Scriptures as did the apostles?
            Yes, the son-in-law of Kling at Schriesheim, Alex-
            ander Mack, who is now at Schwarzenau in Wittgen-
            stein, and many in the Marienborn area, even a
            nobleman, by name of Ernest Hochmann from
            Nürnberg.
11e. Whether they themselves have received their doctrine
       from such people?
            They have indeed heard their doctrine often, but do
            not yet have the grace from God to retain it.
12. Whether then they are obliged to keep other points of doctrine
      besides their meetings?
            Yes, for they love foremost God and their neighbor as them-
            selves, even their enemies, and are obliged to feed them, and
            give them to eat and to drink.
13. Whether they have community of goods among themselves?

Yes, they are obliged to share with one another as long as they have anything.

14. Whether the defendants do not know that meetings and doctrines which are not of the three churches are prohibited by His Excellency, the Elector Palatine, our most gracious lord?

Yes, the most gracious lordship has the power to order and prohibit, but if they are not tolerated, then they are content to suffer according to their crime.

14a. But if the most gracious lordship confiscated all their belongings because they have not obeyed his orders, would he not be right?

They will thank God if they have to suffer something for Christ's sake, even if it be death, because they cannot bind themselves to any authority in matters of conscience.

15. Whether the defendants have been punished for such doctrine here or elsewhere?

The buttonmaker, Lucas, for his part, knows only that he was imprisoned here twice, and at Schriesheim and Mannheim once each, because of this, and that he performed hard labor at Mannheim without complaint. The two Diehls, however, had been imprisoned here once for four days.

15a. Why did they not desist, then, from such meetings and new doctrine as they had been punished?

Because primarily they owe obedience to God in matters of conscience, and to the worldly authorities in matters of police regulations. This is no new doctrine either, but rather Christ's, for which they are ready to sacrifice everything they have, their bodies and their lives, for they are only dust and ashes.

Written by
John George Schell,
notary public and city clerk.[25]

Government Orders Compliance

The government responded to the submitted report of the hearing by ordering that the prisoners must join one of the three recognized churches under severe penalties for noncompliance. The next document in the file is a reminder from Becker that the sentence had not been carried out, even though the prisoners had not accommodated themselves to affiliating with one of the three churches. The edict was then issued ordering that the Pietists be sent to Brabant, a duchy in the Netherlands, now located half in northern Belgium, half in southern Netherlands.

Martin Lucas' wife was also expelled, his house sold, and his children placed under the protection of guardians. It was this kind of harsh suppression which resulted in the exodus of the Palatine Pietists to other sections of Germany.

To Councilor Becker.

In response to the minutes taken last April 30 by Electoral Palatine Councilor Becker about the Pietists held in arrest here, the latter is herewith instructed to remind them emphatically that they must profess themselves immediately to one of the three churches tolerated in the Holy Roman Empire. They must promise to produce each month authentic certificates of this from their pastors. If they will not submit to this, they are to be turned over to the local militia. The carrying out of this order is to be reported.

Heidelberg, May 13, 1709.   [Palatine councilors][26]

Government Reminded by Becker

Most Praiseworthy Councilors:

In carrying out the commission placed upon me by the most praiseworthy councilors to draw up a protocol on the Pietists apprehended here and to report it, I would like to remind the former that these sentenced Pietists are to be expelled with the Freudenberg regiment to Brabant as punishment. The house of the buttonmaker [Martin Lucas], who is among the group, is to be sold for a good profit (because his wife also follows the Pietist doctrine) and the proceeds thus realized are to be employed for the children through appointed guardians. The wife is to be expelled. The edict concerning this case which was decided upon more than five weeks ago has neither come to me nor to the city council to date. I therefore wanted to call attention to this in order to expedite matters. . . .

Heidelberg, July 1, 1709.   J. R. Becker.[27]

Government Issues Final Order

To Councilor Becker.

In response to the reminder of the first of this month from Councilor and Police Commissioner Becker, the edict already decided upon is hereby enclosed. This concerns the said buttonmaker, who was sent away with the Freudenberg regiment along with others of his kind. This also concerns the sale of his house, and the appointing of some guardians for the children left behind, and the arrangements for the care of the same. . . .

Heidelberg, July 3, 1709.   [Palatine councilors][28]

Guardians Needed for the Lucas Children

To the Heidelberg City Council.

It is necessary that the children of the buttonmaker, who has been expelled and assigned to the Freudenberg regiment because of his Pietism, should be given guardians by the authorities. Therefore, the city council is to charge two suitable citizens with this, and to appoint the same in conformity with the prescribed governmental regulations. The council is to consider along with the guardians, whether, under the present circumstances, it would be more useful and profitable for the children to dispose of the house by means of a public auction for as much as possible or whether it should be retained. The city council is to undertake the further steps necessary.

Heidelberg, July 6, 1709.   [Palatine councilors][29]

Guardians Appointed for the Lucas Children

Heidelberg city council minutes, July 11, 1709.

¶3. Upon receiving the most gracious order from our most praiseworthy council, Valentine Müller, master tailor, and John George Unger, butcher, were accepted and sworn in as guardians for the two children of Martin Lucas, buttonmaker.[30]

PIETISM IN STRASSBURG

Strassburg had been one of the most tolerant cities during the Reformation century, and it is not surprising that with the spread of

A View of Strassburg in the Seventeenth Century

An engraving by Mathew Merian from Bernhard Erdmannsdörffer, *Deutsche Geschichte vom Westfälischen Frieden bis zum Regierungsantritt Friedrichs des Grossen. 1648-1740* (Berlin: 1888).

Pietism the city on the Rhine became a center of this reform movement. Philip Jacob Spener, the first and outstanding Lutheran Pietist leader, was born in the Alsace, not far from Strassburg. The movement in the border city, which had been in French hands since 1681, was centered around visitors from Germany such as John Henry Kraft, ministerial students such as John Frederick Klein and John Frederick Haug (who achieved fame later as the editor of the Berleburg Bible), and local inhabitants of whom Michael Eckerlin was the most outstanding.

Eckerlin (1643-c. 1720), a tailor and capmaker, and according to a later source a member of the city council, was the pivot around which the Pietists revolved. Many meetings were held in his home on Fladder Lane, in the shadow of the great cathedral. Much of the voluminous correspondence of the Pietists went through his hands. After being expelled from Strassburg in 1705 he went to Schwarzenau/Eder, where he became a member of the young Brethren movement.

After his death, his widow and four sons—Israel, Samuel, Emanuel, and Gabriel—emigrated in 1725 to Pennsylvania, where the sons later became leaders in the Ephrata community. All of the brothers except Emanuel left the Cloister because of differences with Conrad Beissel and pioneered in an area then in the western part of the colony of Virginia, first in what is now West Virginia and then in what is now western Pennsylvania. Israel and Gabriel were seized by the French and their Indian allies, taken to Montreal, and delivered to a Jesuit monastery as prisoners. They were taken to France, where, according to tradition, they became monks, and died not far from their original home.[31]

Pastor Kraft Denounced

One of the earliest documents on Pietism in Strassburg is a report about John Henry Kraft. The local Protestant clergy submitted a denunciation of the unwanted visitor from Germany. The first part of the statement tells of Kraft's association with Eckerlin.

A True Report about Pastor Kraft, a suspicious person—because of his fanatical doctrine and life.

He is a shoemaker by trade, which, however, he has abandoned, and resided for many years in the area of Giessen in Hesse as a schoolmaster. He appeared at Strassburg some time previously—about a year ago. Warnings soon came from the authorities to beware of him as a man who threatened both the state and the church, whereupon the ministry upon carefully looking into the matter found out the following very dangerous facts:

The church wardens of the New Church have recently told him [Kraft] not to hold school for young children in his house, and, further, neither to induce anyone to visit his home or to hold conventicles. In defiance of this, however, he has already held secret conventicles daily for four weeks in the home of Eckerlin, a local citizen and capmaker. He often stays there in the daytime, and from time to time at night, although he has rented several rooms in the noble Kippenheimer house on Brand Street.

There are no grounds to doubt the truth of the report about such conventicles because (1) there are eyewitnesses available, who for good reasons (partly private and partly official) had been told to pay strict attention. They testify with the greatest veracity that they observed eight persons, men and women, go into the above-mentioned house of Eckerlin at about seven o'clock last Friday; at about ten o'clock they came out again after conducting their worship; (2) Jacob Henry Steinmetz, a local citizen and blacksmith, told me personally that he did not deny that they gathered there, and that he well knew that their names were all taken down. He did not worry about it, if his name was only found in the Book of Life, because they were innocent of committing harlotry or wicked deeds at that place.

However, we, the teachers and believers in the pure, unchanged Augsburg Confession, consider such conventicles in our city to be seditious and pernicious for the church as well as for the state. . . [c. 1701].[32]

Andrew Gross to Michael Eckerlin

The letter from Andrew Gross is noteworthy for its reference to Dr. John William Petersen (1649-1727), who was one of the most influential figures in radical Pietism. With his wife, an important author in her own right, Dr. Petersen especially stressed the doctrine of universal restoration and the belief in an early end of the world. Both of these teachings influenced early Brethren. Andrew Gross was a native of Strassburg who moved to Esslingen and then to Frankfurt. There he was known as an "arch-separatist," and, through his trade as a book dealer, did much to spread radical Pietist views within Germany. He was a close friend and business agent of Christopher Sauer I.[33]

Immanuel! Dearly Beloved Brother:

The enclosed is sent with warm greetings from dear Brother Klein. At the same time I wanted to learn how things stand with you. You no doubt have many temptations and trials, but I am assured of the certain guidance and working of the eternal Spirit above you. May He firmly keep you and our brethren in the world until the end. Amen.

Here Satan has raged for some time, especially because of the worldly priests, and we do not yet know what the enemies of the cross of Christ will undertake. They wanted to expel me from the city without formality (which was all the same to me). Some have just recently voted in the city council that I should be gone by New Year's, but nothing further has come of it to date. I am perhaps not yet worthy of it.

Our Rector Ditzinger is becoming even more powerful in deeds and words, in humility, love, and wisdom—and must suffer very much. The Lord, however, leads him through to victory. Hallelujah! We often hold meetings now at his home, and the number has increased rather greatly, through much opposition, threats, and blasphemies. The Lord has still spared us from the violence with which wicked citizens, who wanted to use the soldiers, have threatened us.

In general, I do not know of anything else to write, except that the work of the Lord is very intensely pursued in our whole county and everywhere, especially now in the Limburg area. This has caused the worldly people much unrest and special commissions. May the Lord himself rise in the midst of His enemies and comfort Israel against all of her enemies, and so arrange that one can teach without fear.

Mrs. Fellenberger recently wrote from the home of Dr. Petersen: "If you write to Strassburg, send my greetings to Mr. Eckerlin, and to his dear wife also. I can still not forget her, etc." Herewith, I greet you, dear brother, and our dear Ann, from all of us.

How is our dear Brother Kraft? What are the other friends and brethren among the students doing? I, as well as our brethren here, commend you to the Holy Spirit and His guidance. May He strengthen you and all the elect saints both in your and our homes. Let us daily remain in good posture and readiness, for He who is to come is coming. Let us arise while it is still day and work before the image is erected.

Oh, Lord, keep our lamps burning, and prevent any of us from receiving the mark of the beast.

                         I remain, your loyal fellow brother
Esslingen, January 10, 1704   Andrew Gross.[34]

Pastors Röderer and Ruopp Questioned

The authorities became seriously disturbed by the continuing Pietist
movement and determined to stamp it out. Spies were planted among
the Pietists and their correspondence was seized. Among those brought
before the church consistory for questioning were two pastors of nearby
villages. Portions of their testimony are here given.

Examination of Pastor [John George] Röderer of Barr.
  I. Whether he still admits, as he confessed to the president, that
     as long as Eckerlin is not brought to order there is no hope
     for lasting peace from the Philadelphian fanaticism?

     He testifies that when the president talked with him re-
     garding Eckerlin, he had agreed with him that if said
     Eckerlin is not brought to order, nothing could be done
     with the rest.

. . .

  IV. Why did he recommend [the writings of Gottfried] Arnold
      to Mr. Schmidt at Barr?

      He asserts that he did not recommend the writings of
      Arnold but that, when Mr. Schmidt saw them at his home,
      and asked to read them, he gave them to him at his request
      to take home. It was not the *History of the Heretics,* but
      another book by Arnold.

. . .

  IX. Why did he maintain such close relationship with Haug, Lange,
      and Eckerlin that they even came to visit him at Barr, and he
      visited them, and they stayed with him and Ruopp as long as
      two weeks?

      They were not with him long, but stayed at the farm of
      Mr. Gambh at Barr.

. . .

  XVI. Why did he praise Eckerlin on February 10, 1705, as a godly
       and well-read man, from whom he could learn much and to

whom he would go if it had not been forbidden to him?
At that time he did not yet know of Eckerlin's errors, which
are rightly to be detested.

. . .

February 19, 1705.[35]

Interrogation of Pastor [John Frederick] Ruopp, M.A., of Gottesweiler.

I. Whether he approved of Pietistic conventicles such as were
held by Kraft, Eckerlin, and Haug?
There must be a differentiation made between those held
regularly where anyone can come, both men and women,
and those which take place occasionally. As for the former,
he does not approve of this, especially when they occur in
violation of the city magistrate's prohibition. As for the
latter, which take place accidentally, he could not condemn
them. When he was further asked whether the conventicles
held by Kraft, Eckerlin, and Haug were not formal meetings held at regular times, he had to admit after a long
digression that they were to be so classified, and therefore
to be considered as forbidden.

. . .

V. Why did he remain on such intimate terms and familiarity
with Eckerlin, a follower of Weigel and a fanatic, who is called
a brother by the fanatics here and in Germany?
He does not approve of the Weigelianism and fanaticism
with which Eckerlin is supposed to agree, and had not
known that Eckerlin was given to such.

VI. Why did he recommend to the Burand woman in her melancholy to go to Eckerlin, who treated her with Weigelian
methods, and not to a preacher?
He asked that the woman herself be questioned about this
matter. He referred her to the pastor who heard her confession, but also said that Eckerlin was a devout and experienced man in the cross, who could be of service, which
the late Dr. Salzmann had also testified to him.

. . .

XII. Why did he not discourage his brother Fröreisen, the shoemaker, who had been at all of the conventicles at Eckerlin's house, and often visited him [Ruopp] and related everything to him, from such meetings and religious conversations?

His brother Fröreisen was at the conventicles in Eckerlin's house only twice, and as they did not do anything wicked, he did not discourage him.

. . .

XXV. Whether he was with the company at Oswald last year? Who was present? What did they do?

He admitted that he, his brother, and Eckerlin were at Oswald and sang a few hymns with one another from the hymnal which Eckerlin had with him. He also confessed that occasionally when he came to the city he visited Eckerlin.

1705.[36]

EXPULSIONS

Strassburg Pietists Expelled

The hearings were followed immediately by punishment. As had become usual for cases of this kind, banishment was the sentence imposed. Extracts from the city records describe the expulsion of Haug, Röderer, and Eckerlin. A letter from the royal palace at Versailles to the Strassburg city council ordered that the Pietists be expelled.

Saturday, February 21, 1705. [John] Frederick Haug was led out of the city by the guards [*Fausthämmer*—armed with the battle-ax] and exiled for ever by order of the honorable town council.

Monday, March 23, 1705. The Reverend John George Röderer, M.A., was notified by order of the honorable town council that he must leave this city and its dominions without delay and must never set foot therein on penalty of certain and drastic bodily punishment.

On the same day, Michael Eckerlin, the capmaker, in consequence of the former decision, was led out of the city by the guards [*Fausthämmer*], and expelled for ever from its dominion.[37]

King Orders Expulsion

To the Strassburg City Council.

Your letter of the second of this month was returned to me, from which the king has seen that, following his orders, the person named Haug was expelled from Strassburg. This was for having been the pastor in the assemblies held in the village at the home of the person named Klein, a farrier. He was condemned to the penalty to which they have been sentenced. Their homes have been taken away to guard against this activity, which is forbidden under penalty of corporal punishment.

This is the case of the last-named person, Eckerlin, a tailor, who had been reprimanded in the month of March, 1701, for having dared to dogmatize, and who had been prohibited from repeating the same under penalty of exemplary punishment. He has transgressed again. His Majesty approved of his being put into prison and finds [it] good that he be expelled. This is also true for those named Ruopp, minister of Gottesweiler, and Röderer, minister of Barr in the dominion of Strassburg, who have been remiss in their duties by being leaders of the sectarians.

From Versailles, March 17, 1705.   de Chamilladt[38]

PIETISM IN BASEL

One of the eight at the first baptism of the Schwarzenau Brethren in 1708 was Andrew Boni (1673-1741). He was born on March 30, 1673, the son of Andrew Boni and his wife Anna, whose maiden name was Hämer. He was confirmed into the Reformed Church in his birthplace of Frenkendorf near Basel on Palm Sunday, 1690.[39] Following in his father's footsteps, he became a weaver, and migrated to Heidelberg as a journeyman. On December 12, 1702, the Heidelberg city council noted that "Andrew Boni, linen weaver by trade, born in Frenkendorf in the Basel area and of Reformed faith (and his wife Marie Sarah, born at Seltz) was accepted and admitted as a citizen on the condition that he produce his birth certificate within three months to prove his vows."[40]

One month later, he was awarded the title of master weaver: "A piece of workmanship made by Andrew Boni, local citizen and linen weaver, was presented to the sworn-in masters of the linen-weaver guild, Jacob Moser and Christopher Hammann, and was found acceptable."[41] However, his wife soon died, and he returned to Switzerland. He proceeded to introduce the radical Pietist and Anabaptist doctrines which he had learned in the Palatinate, and was investigated in the summer of

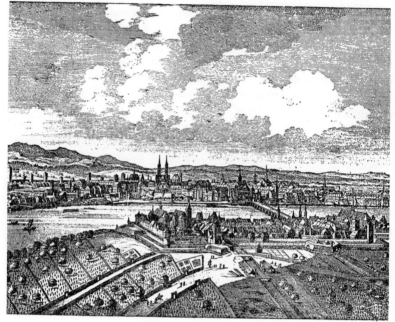

A View of Basel in 1702
An engraving by Peter Schenk, from W. Hadorn, *Geschichte des Pietismus in den Schweizerischen Reformierten Kirchen* (Konstanz and Emmishofen: 1901).

1705 by the authorities. The local pastor complained that Boni refused to bear arms and appear at drills, rejected the swearing of oaths, and did not attend holy communion.

The Basel clergy examined Boni on these points, and recommended that he be further instructed. Boni said that since he was returning to Heidelberg in any case, instruction was unnecessary. His second Heidelberg sojourn lasted over a year; then he reappeared at his home. He began holding meetings and preaching radical Pietist and Anabaptist views. The local authorities soon denounced him to the Basel city council.[42]

Andrew Boni Denounced

Honorable . . . Sirs and Lords:

. Your Graces' subject, Andrew Boni the younger, linen weaver of

Frenkendorf, left here more than a year ago and lived in the Electoral Palatinate. He returned to his parents this fall in said Frenkendorf. He has stayed there to date, and has dared to spread his Anabaptist sect secretly through nocturnal conventicles. Especially his brother Martin has been initiated in and infatuated with these errors. Your Graces can see this, among other things, from the enclosure and the accompanying booklet which Andrew brought with him from the Palatinate.

If this evil is not checked in time, it is to be feared that this false teaching will spread in all directions and may infect many more. This is because it has a good outward appearance and meets with rather favorable response, as is known, among the common people. I have therefore deemed it my duty to issue this obedient report to Your Graces and humbly leave it to the discretion of your most wise opinion. I write this with God's strong protection, and remain . . . ,

Liestal,   your humble and obedient servant,
November 26, 1706.   Bernhard Strübin, mayor.[43]

Frenkendorf Pastor's Statement

The following is the enclosure mentioned above, which was submitted by Pastor Meyer of Frenkendorf, Boni's home.

Some time ago upon the order of the authorities, Andrew Boni of Frenkendorf was separately examined and his case was discussed because of his Anabaptist errors both by the entire honorable clergy and His Excellency Dr. Antistes. Although he had left his parents again more than a year ago and lived in the Palatinate, he has now come here again. Since fall he has been secretly and without my previous knowledge at his parents' in Frenkendorf. Far from having turned from his false opinions and accepting better information, he not only still tries to make disciples through nocturnal conventicles, but also has misled his brother Martin Boni on a new, dangerous error concerning infant baptism. (It has not been possible to turn the latter from these errors to date, although he swore the yearly oath last year and takes communion for outward appearances because he is afraid of punishment.)

Last Sunday, the twenty-first, Andrew Boni stood sponsor at the holy baptism of a child of his cousin Jacob Boni. He appeared without the customary side-arms [bayonet] and the bouquet on his hat, which are usually worn. After the baptism was completed, he asked me to show him where in the Holy Scriptures infant baptism and the provision of godparents is commanded, pulling out his New Testament, which he always carries with him. He said that Christ has given us sufficient information about everything necessary for salvation and has not withheld anything. He did not find anything about the above practices in the New Testament. He asked what could it benefit the child that the ritual is read to him, for he cannot understand it anyway. Upon his request, I gave him all necessary information in a friendly manner. However, he did not want to accept this. He insisted on the letter, and had all of the usual Anabaptist excuses ready to answer all arguments:

The words which institute baptism refer to adults. They must first be taught and only afterwards be baptized. Infant baptism is not included in those entire households who received baptism from the holy apostles, because in Acts 16:34 it states explicitly that the baptized rejoiced after they had received baptism. This could not be said of children. When the Lord says, Mark 10:14, that the little children be permitted to come to Him, it does not mean that they should be baptized. Some say [infant] baptism was introduced instead of circumcision, when one circumcised the children on the eighth day. This was valid under the Law, but we live under grace. It is useless to say that baptism is shared with the infants as a sign of the covenant of God, because they do not understand it. He maintained these opinions persistently.

The following Monday, the twenty-second of this month, his mother came to me in Liestal along with one of her friends. She made clear the displeasure she had for the stubbornness of her children. She said that they, and especially her husband, often got into bitter arguments with them. Not long ago the older [son] called back in anger to his father as he was leaving them: "Now the devil can't help but reveal himself!" She requested of me, however, that I should not take the matter further. Within three weeks her son would go away again with a companion. (Her son did not always stay with them, but stayed for a time in Bern, where, among others, the wife of a pastor who had left the church gave him one *Reichstaler*.) His mother also showed me a booklet which she had found after her son had left. She had gladly sent this to the mayor yesterday upon his request. The point of the booklet was that the authorities could neither expel people who erred in matters of faith nor coerce their consciences. They must rather tolerate them in the Lord, and use only the punishment of excommunication.

She also said that the older [son] was a close friend of a Palatine preacher named Mr. Preuel. Her younger son, Martin Boni, often visited a tenant in Basel, a stocking-stretcher, born in Turn, who resides outside of the city at the Black Star. I have considered it most necessary to report all this the day before yesterday to His Excellency Dr. Antistes, because it is to be feared that through them still others might be infected and incited.

Jacob Maximillian Meyer

November 26, 1706.   Pastor in Frenkendorf."

Boni Brothers Arrested

Upon receipt of the report from Frenkendorf, the Basel city council ordered the Bonis to be questioned by another government body, the Council of Seven. Swiss city government was in the hands of councils of varying sizes, with the smaller councils acting in executive capacities. John Berchtold was the stocking-stretcher of Turn, mentioned in Pastor Meyer's report as being often visited by Martin Boni.

Minutes of the Small Council.
November 27, 1706.
Andrew and Martin Boni, Anabaptists.
. . .

[Resolution.] These two Anabaptists are to be brought here in custody, and questioned by the Council of Seven. They are to be interrogated separately about the identity of their followers. . . ."[45]

Boni Brothers Questioned

Hearing of the Boni brothers.

According to Your Graces' decision, my highly esteemed sirs, the Council of Seven, summoned before them at the city hall yesterday morning, John Berchtold, the stocking-stretcher from Turn, now residing here, aged thirty-six years. . . . [He was examined.]

(Concerning the imprisoned Anabaptist brothers Andrew and Martin Boni from Frenkendorf.)

Hereupon, the above-mentioned gentlemen went to the inner Spalen-Tower. They first questioned the older brother, Andrew Boni, aged thirty-three years.

How long had it been since he had returned? The latter said that he returned to this district last fall, and had left here one year ago from last summer. He also admitted that he had previously seen the pastor and the clergy, who admonished him to conform to our laws. But as he had found that such was against his conscience, he left here after the clergy had given him two weeks to think it over.

Upon being asked why he had returned to this district, he answered that his brother, Martin, had written him that he should come. He had returned because he loved his brother. In addition, the country should be free and open for all people. Even if one were expelled, he could still return if he had not done anything evil.

Upon being asked whether he had held meetings with other people since his return to this district, he replied with *yes*. Some of the people had sent for him, and some of them had come to him.

Upon being asked who those were who sent for him, he answered that this was up to his free will to say or not. If he did say it, he would indeed be a traitor, for he would cause them misery. He was obliged to speak with all who desired it. However, he had not spoken with everyone who had sent for him because he did not have the time. He did not know what else could have hindered him.

Upon being asked who those were who came to him, he answered that he would not say.

Upon being asked where they had had their meetings, and whether his father and mother had known about this, he said that when people came to him, they spoke with each other openly. His father and mother had always opposed him, and they were sorry enough about it.

Upon being asked what his intention was, whether he had in mind to remain in this district, he answered that he had no certain home but wherever the Lord let him stay, there he remained.

Upon being asked whether he knew the man who distributed some of their books around the district, he answered with *no*.

Upon being asked whether he had given books to those with whom he associated here or at his home, he admitted this and testified that they had been books which contained rules on how a Christian should live. He had only one copy of the kind of booklet, of which one had been sent here from Liestal. He still had two different booklets, one of which was at home and the other he had with him. He pulled this out of his sack, and it now lies in the office.

He claimed to know nothing about John Berchtold's belonging to their sect, but said that the latter was afraid and had expressly said that he would have nothing to do with them.

After this, the younger brother, Martin Boni, about twenty-eight years old, was summoned. He was asked when his brother Andrew had come here. He answered [that it was] last fall. He had written him that he should come because he loved him.

Upon being asked whether Andrew had instructed him, he admitted this and testified that previously he had lived like an animal for the day alone. He had . . . glutted, swilled, danced, and pranced. The pastor had known about it, but had not prevented him from doing so.

Upon being asked whether they had had secret meetings, and if so where, he denied this.

Upon being asked who had come to see his brother and him, he answered, no one especially.

Upon being asked to whom then his brother had gone, and by whom he had been called, he answered, to the friends. They certainly would not ask him further.

Upon being asked who then these friends were, he answered, the Bonis, of whom there are many there. He did not want to name any by their Christian names. He further testified that when these friends came to them it was not expressly because they had told them to come.

Upon being asked whether he knew John Berchtold, he answered with *yes* and testified that he had become acquainted with him through John Müller, an Anabaptist who had visited him on his journeys up and down the country. The first time that he went to Berchtold's home it was with this Müller; he had since then been at his home several times. He hoped that he was not himself an Anabaptist, but desired to lead a pious life. As this Berchtold had the reputation of being pious, he had visited him several times, and they had talked with each other.

Upon being asked whether he and his brother wanted to stay in this district or not, he answered, yes, if they could.

Upon being asked whether he knew of anyone who had sold certain books at Pratteln about a year ago, he said that he had already been asked about that at home; he did not know anything about him, however.

Whereupon the examination was closed.

Read December 1, 1706.[46]

Basel Clergy's Report

The Small Council also asked the Basel clergy for their opinion of the brothers Boni. Noteworthy is the fact that although condemning the Bonis' stubbornness, the clergy themselves criticized the shortcomings of the church and the government which gave rise to the Pietist protest. The council then passed the sentences: expulsion for Andrew Boni and compulsory instruction for Martin Boni.

December 12, 1706

The report of the clergy concerning Andrew and Martin Boni, Anabaptist brothers of Frenkendorf, reads as follows:

Respected Sirs . . .:

In obedience to Your Graces' order, we have summoned before us the two brothers, Andrew and Martin Boni from Frenkendorf, as well as John Berchtold of this city. First, the brothers were questioned concerning several points mentioned in the protocol as well as about their doctrines and faith. The older [brother] Andrew especially answered very arrogantly, unreasonably, defiantly, and wickedly, with complete denial of all proper respect and honor. He was also asked to tell why he blurted out the following un-Christian words against his old father, to whom he owes, next to God, his life and everything else (seeing that according to the Fifth Commandment he should honor him greatly): "Now the devil can't help but reveal himself."

He herewith called his [father] a man possessed of the devil, that is, a child of the devil. He was asked whether he thought that he had done right in so doing. He said that his father was an angry and greedy man, and had at that time burst out at him in rage: "I wish that I would not have to have you in my sight any longer!" Anger comes from the devil. A Christian has to speak out plainly without equivocation, which he did at that time. He did not admit that he uttered these unreasonable words in bitter anger himself, and repaid invective with coarser invective against the rule of the holy gospel.

When we questioned this Andrew Boni about his doctrine and faith, he absolutely rejected infant baptism. He called our worship services and the partaking of holy communion as is usual among us human inventions and coercion, because those who do not wish to attend the public meetings are expelled from the territory.

He said about the office of preaching that it was not instituted by Christ, but rather that the present-day preachers were servants of men, hirelings, and preachers for pay. Every single Christian who received the gift of the Holy Spirit is allowed to rise up in the congregation and teach.

Concerning the authorities, he maintained that it was indeed necessary to have authorities in the natural state, as such people understand it, among the un-reborn, non-Christian, and servants of sin. However, the reborn, who are in a state of grace, sin no more, and therefore need neither judge nor authorities. He then tried to claim that a person could achieve perfection and complete freedom from all sin in this life through the grace of God. For himself, he does not consider that he is completely perfect, but he does not doubt that through the Spirit working in him he would soon attain perfection.

To summarize, one and a half years ago this person was similarly examined about his faith and called to account. At that time he offended only in three points: on taking oaths, whether a Christian could swear these; on the organized church, whether this should consist only of saints with no offending sinners—blasphemers, gamblers, Sabbath-violaters, usurers, drunkards, etc.—to be tolerated therein; on the sword, whether a Christian should be given it, and whether force is to be driven out with force. We now find that as he has now resided in the Electoral Palatinate for another year, he has absorbed all the other errors of the Anabaptists, enthusiasts, and fanatics. He holds so obstinately and stubbornly to these doctrines that, although he is defeated and done in with God's Word, he still remains firm in his opinion. When he has no other refuge, he answers that he believes firmly in his doctrine. He is completely assured of it through Scripture as well as through the inner instruction of the Spirit. He needs no other instruction, etc.

Concerning his brother, Martin Boni, however, as he is simpler, more ignorant, and humbler, it seems to us that if he were further spoken to with kindness and lenience, by authority of the Holy Scriptures, he could perhaps still be led again upon the right path. This, especially, because he does not completely reject good instruction, but rather shows himself willing and grateful to accept this.

We find that the only cause of such division in the churches, in which such people are greatly involved, is the offensive sin which is common in city and country and which goes unpunished. This is especially furthered when the preachers, in their places of service, do not oppose this with seemly zeal, but rather practice themselves what they condemn from the pulpit; they seek more for themselves than for Christ. Martin Boni introduced many complaints along this line against his pastor. This, we say, is the only cause which leads to such dangerous schisms in the Christian church. When, on the one hand, the judges do not deal out appropriate punishments for open sins, and, on the other hand, the preachers let everything take its own course, or participate themselves in it, this kind of fanatic finds easy access among the simple people. They try to make themselves important, and raise themselves above others through the appearance of humility and piety. They try to convince the people that the class of authorities as well as the office of preachers are unnecessary and degenerate. In order to meet this problem it is most necessary that we for our part recognize this, and that this stone of offense be removed from our midst as far as lies in our power.

Finally, John Berchtold was also summoned and spoken to. . . .

This is the report which we were to make about these three persons in response to Your Graces' order. We leave it to the high prudence and foresight of your discretion [as to] what is to be done further in this matter. We herewith commend Your Graces to God, the Almighty, for further blessed government, and commend ourselves to continued favor with the authorities. In the name of the assembly of deputies and servants of the Divine Word in the church and universities,

Done December 9, 1706.   John Rudolph Zwinger, D.D.

Boni Brothers Sentenced

[Decision of the council.] Andrew, the older brother, is to be immediately brought here in custody. He is to be expelled after he has been made to vow to stay away from this territory forever on penalty of punishment by the pillory. The younger [brother] named Martin shall be tolerated longer, because there is still some hope for his conversion. He must, however, present himself from time to time to the pastors to be instructed. Berchtold must in the future avoid meeting with such suspicious people.⁴⁷

Andrew Boni to City Fathers (1)

Andrew Boni wrote a letter to the city fathers of Basel after his release, attempting to explain that he had not meant to give his word not to come back. His position on the relationship of the state to individual conscience is in the Anabaptist tradition and is similar to that used by Brethren through the years. The council did not seem to be open to this kind of witness, and ordered Boni's immediate arrest if he ever re-entered their jurisdiction.

[To the mayor of Basel.]
Much grace and peace from God our Father through our Lord Jesus Christ. Amen.
Dear Mayor and Servant of God: Gracious Sir:
Your sentence has banned me forever from this city and district. Mr. Lang, who was sent to me, obliged me to promise not to return to this district or city. I told him that I could not promise that. I have, indeed, done nothing wrong. After the conversation had lasted a while, I shook hands with him, and said, "I will commend it to God." Upon that, they led me away. Right away I regretted this in my soul. I said to the attendants that they should take me back to the tower again. I had done wrong in promising, although I had only said these words — "Well, I will commend it to God," which those who heard it will truthfully testify. But immediately I regretted this in my soul.

Therefore it was impossible for me to go away. Instead, I returned to the tower in the city, and I said there, as mentioned above, that I had regretted it. They said that I must go to the courthouse. They would not let me back in. At the courthouse, I spoke first with a gentleman who lives upstairs; he was in his nightgown. I told him that I regretted that I promised not to return, and that I had done nothing evil. He said, "I advise you to leave. You are a miserable person. Do you really want to force the authorities to punish you?" I said, "No. I want to bear willingly and patiently whatever the authorities will impose on me." He said that I should go to the prison keeper; he would register me.

Upon this I went away again. As I left, a maid came and called to me that I should return. A clerk was there; he asked me what my business was. I told him. He said that he would tell this to the alternate councilor. Then a gentleman with a yellow wig came. I told him how much I regretted that I had promised that I would not return to the district or the city, even though I had only said that I would commend it to God; he had taken that as a promise. This alternate councilor became very angry with me and said, "Do you want to be beaten with switches?" I said, "Whatever the gentlemen impose upon me." He said that I should get out of there. I then thought that I had repealed my mistake, and could now go in the name of the Lord.

This, my dear mayor and servant of God, gracious sir, I wanted to inform you of for the sake of my conscience, and for your further information about my faith. I believe in and confess such authorities as the holy Apostle Paul describes in the thirteenth chapter of his [letter] to the Romans. He says there: "For rulers are not a terror to good conduct, but to bad" [verse 3]. This authority is from God in so far as it is like the love of God in the Fifth Book of Moses [Deuteronomy], chapter seventeen, and punishes the wicked and protects the good. Where there is such an authority, I know that it will tolerate me. If disobeying the orders of men means opposing God's ordinances, then the apostles also disobeyed (Acts, the fourth chapter, nineteenth verse): "Whether it is right in the sight of God to listen to you rather than to God, you must judge."

It is therefore evident that I know what man's commands are. They are that to which they want to force me. I know they are, for in the New Testament, I know, nothing is forced. "For Christ is the end of the law, that everyone who has faith may be justified" (Romans 10:4). Christ says in John 7:38, "He who believes in me, as the scripture has said . . . ." Paul says to the Galatians in Galatians 1:8: "But even if we, or an angel from heaven, should preach to you a gospel contrary to that which we preached to you, let him be accursed."

This is the confirmation of the truth. I hope it will be sufficient, for "the just shall live by his faith" (Habakkuk 2:4; Galatians 3:11; Hebrews 10:38; and Romans 1:17), and as Saint Paul says to the Romans in 8 [verse 33]: "Who shall bring any charge against God's elect? It is God who justifies."

May the grace of our Lord Jesus Christ be with you, dear mayor. Amen.

(Andrew Boni, the expelled
(Read on December 29, 1706.)   Anabaptist from Frenkendorf.)[48]

Boni's Arrest Ordered

Minutes of the Small Council.

December 29, 1706.

Andrew Boni, an Anabaptist from Frenkendorf.

A letter was read which was sent to the council from Andrew Boni of Frenkendorf, the Anabaptist who was recently expelled from the city and district. He testifies that he has regretted his promising to avoid this area, even though he did not really promise this, but only said that he must commend it to God.

[Resolution.] All officers are to be written to about this Boni, and also preparations are to be made here, that in case he sets foot anywhere in our territory, he is to be detained. He is to be brought here in custody. The mayor of Liestal is also to be ordered to forbid the relatives and acquaintances of this Boni from accepting any letter or writing from him. If he should stay in the vicinity it is to be reported.[49]

Boni Arrested

Four months later one of the provincial governors, at Waldenburg, about twenty miles southeast of Basel, reported to the Basel council that he had taken Boni into custody.

Honorable . . . Sirs:

On the basis of your order of December 29, 1706, that the subject Andrew Boni of Frenkendorf, who was expelled because of his Anabaptism, should be arrested and returned as a prisoner, I took him in custody at Oberdorf. He had stayed there overnight at a bathhouse with a woman from the Bern area. The latter was taken to the border, because she seemed to be mentally confused. I am sending the above-mentioned in safe custody to Your Graces. I commend Your Graces to the protection of the Most High. . . .

Waldenburg,   Your humble and obedient servant
April 22, 1707.   John Buxtorff, governor.[50]

Andrew Boni to City Fathers (2)

Andrew Boni wrote another letter to the Basel authorities while a prisoner in the city. He called upon Basel to repent because of the rapidly approaching "day of the Lord," using both prophetic and apocalyptic terminology.

Much grace, mercy, and peace from God, the Father, through our King, Jesus Christ. Amen.

Favorable, Gracious Sirs and Lords, and the entire Honorable and Wise Council of the City of Basel:

I pray heartily and humbly to God through Jesus Christ that you will be patient with this, my poor and simple letter. Hear it simply, then judge it in simplicity according to the love of God and your neighbor. May the God of peace give His grace and mercy through Jesus Christ. I know through the goodness of God that all depends on this alone. The dear God has brought me here again, and once more into the bonds of my gracious lords, for as long as the dear God intends, for which I am obliged to thank Him. This, inasmuch as everything works for the good for those who love God.

I came here not through my own will, but rather through God's will and out of love for God and my neighbor. I also came because of the request in letters from my neighbors. Therefore now hear the words which God will give me to write, miserable creature that I am, through His goodness. I do not hesitate to write that this will be for the good of you, your city, and district of Basel. O Lord, help me; let it succeed! Amen.

After Moses, the holy man of God, was frightened by the wild complaint of the people of Israel in the wilderness, he spoke to God: "If thou wilt deal thus with me, kill me at once, if I have found favor in thy sight, that I may not see my wretchedness" [Numbers 11:15]. God told him to choose seventy men from among the elders of Israel. He would then come and take from the spirit of Moses and lay it upon the seventy elders. They should then bear the burden of the people so that Moses would not bear it alone. This then happened, and the seventy prophesied. There were, however, still two men who had remained in the camp. The spirit rested on them and they prophesied. When Moses was informed about that, he said: "Are you jealous for my sake? Would that all the Lord's people were prophets, that the Lord would put his spirit upon them!" (Numbers, chapter eleven [verse 29]). The same wish that Moses had, the Lord God promised through the holy prophet Joel in the second chapter.

The pastors have long known this and have prayed for it, but unfortunately with irreverence. They still do not know what it means when they pray during the religious instruction of the children: "Pour over us thy spirit of grace and prayer. Pour it especially over the present dear youth, the sons and daughters who are thy servants and maids, so that they may prophesy and attain thorough instruction about their eternal salvation. Do this so that they are not continually tossed and swayed by all sorts of evils, but rather are upright in faith and love, and grow in all things toward Him who is the head, Jesus Christ."

I am assured before God through Jesus Christ that no human nor any devil can lead me away from this thorough instruction. Yes, I say this from the witness of the Spirit of God, which He (through His eternal love which He has in the Son of His love) imparted upon me, a godless sinner. This happened after I had become obedient little by little to the disciplining Spirit of the Father through [His] goodness. Disobedience is sorcery and sin, for the saving grace of God has appeared to all men. It disciplines us so that we may deny all ungodly nature and worldly lusts, and instead live for the chaste and righteous God, and a pious life in the world, and wait for the coming of our Lord Jesus Christ.

Oh, that all men knew or wished to know in what kind of a time we live! Oh, if they would only open their eyes and see how God gives many people over to the sword (Jeremiah, the twenty-fifth chapter, and Ezekiel, the twenty-first chapter). Yes, if one reads these chapters and reflects a bit, and also [considers] the prophecy of Jesus Christ (Luke, the twenty-first chapter, and Matthew, the twenty-fourth chapter), [it will be seen] as I for my part cannot see anything in it but that the day of the Lord is approaching mightily. Injustice has already long had the upper hand. However, blessed are they who endure this, and those on whom injustice is wreaked, but woe to those who inflict it. The plagues are coming and will be transferred from one people to another, namely, those plagues of which all the prophets, apostles, and Christ prophesy, as well as the revelation of John. The child of destruction will and must be revealed, which the Lord will kill with the spirit of His mouth. An end will be put to him through the appearance of His second coming (Second Thessalonians in the second chapter).

"Turn away from man in whose nostrils is breath, for of what account is he?" (Isaiah, in the second chapter [verse 22]). Christ says in the twenty-fifth chapter of Matthew that those who have done good to His brethren have done good to Him; and those who have done evil to His brethren have done evil unto Him. He bids them go away into everlasting punishment, but the righteous into life eternal. Oh, therefore, may indeed every man see to it that he does not oppose those who love God. I do not seek the favor of any man. "Cursed is the man who trusts in man and makes flesh his arm, whose heart turns away from the Lord. . . . Blessed is the man who trusts in the Lord, whose trust is the Lord" (Jeremiah, in the seventeenth chapter [verses 5 and 7]).

Yes, it is good to trust in the Lord and not depend on men. It is good to trust in the Lord and not depend upon princes, especially in these last terrible and disturbed times, when wrath will come over the godless and unbelievers. Yes, the people are afraid on earth, and they are distressed in fear and expectancy of the things which shall happen on earth. For this reason the fig tree blooms, as Christ says in Luke, in the twenty-first chapter, namely, that He has already started to pour out His Spirit. Christ says to His own to lift up their hearts for their salvation nears. "And this gospel of the kingdom will be preached throughout the whole world, as a testimony to all nations . . ." (Matthew 24:18 [14]). There will be many Johns, who will say, "Repent, for the kingdom of heaven is at hand" [Matthew 3:2]. But it seems to me that scarcely a fraction will come from the universities, for the school of Christ is very humble. Jesus did not choose any theologians to be apostles. Further, the prophets, Moses and David, were only common people, namely shepherds. Oh, if only people might read in the prophet Isaiah in the sixty-second, sixty-third, sixty-fourth, and sixty-fifth chapters, and in the prophet Zechariah from the ninth chapter to the end of the prophets.

What a wonderful time it will be for those who give themselves to God and renounce all that is worldly and temporal. It seems to me it is also the time about which it is written: ". . . the heavens and the earth shake" [Joel 3:16]. Oh, that the hearts of all the people may be moved so that they respond to the friendly invitation of our dear Savior, Jesus Christ, when He says, "Come to the wedding; all is ready." Then the Spirit and the bride can speak, and whosoever hears it shall say, "Come!" Whosoever thirsts shall come and whosoever wishes to shall receive the water of life without cost. To attain this there is no better means than that which the dear God himself makes clear in the prophet Joel in the second chapter, where he says: ' "Yet even now . . . return to me with all your heart, with fasting, with weeping, and with mourning; and rend your hearts and not your garments. Return to the Lord, your God, for he is gracious and merciful, slow to anger, and abounding in steadfast love, and repents of evil. Who knows whether he will not turn and repent, and leave a blessing behind him . . . . Blow the trumpet in Zion; sanctify a fast; call a solemn assembly; gather the people. Sanctify the congregation; assemble the elders; gather the children, even the nursing infants. Let the bridegroom leave his room, and the bride her chamber. Between the vestibule and the altar let the priests, the ministers of the Lord, weep and say, "Spare thy people, O Lord, and make not thy heritage a reproach, a byword among the nations. Why should they say among the peoples, 'Where is their God' " ' Then the Lord became jealous for his land, and had pity on his people" [verses 12-18].

Now I ask the honorable and wise council, as well as all men here in this city and district of Basel, whether anything is more necessary than just this. The people will soon not know what they will do because of arrogance and godlessness. Greed, usury, luxury, and pride are so terrible and have so taken the upper hand that all people could not bewail it sufficiently even with tears of blood. I do not mention such other lusts as glutting, swilling, immorality, and lewdness in cursing and swearing, quarreling and fighting, and in lying and betraying. Yes, with my clumsy hand I can hardly describe enough the sins and vices of this city. In sum, they all reach to heaven.

God intends to punish them, if they do not turn to Him with all their heart, and pray as mentioned above.

Whoever wants to, can test this to see whether I lie or not, and whether I have taught of God or of the devil. It does not come from me, and men cannot give it to me, much less take it away. Therefore I have given myself over to the eternal God, in whom is all love, mercy, peace, and rest now and in eternity. Therefore it is not surprising that Paul says: "Who shall separate us from the love of Christ? Shall tribulation, or distress . . . ?" and so forth in the eighth chapter of Romans [verse 35]. Now, may the God who made and created all —and also maintains all, and repays each one according to the works which he has done during his life, be they good or bad—be given praise, honor, and thanksgiving through Jesus Christ for ever and ever. Amen.

(Read in part, April 27, 1707.) [Andrew Boni][51]

Boni Again Examined and Expelled

Boni was brought before the Small Council for examination. Following the examination, he was punished by being placed for a time in the stocks or pillory and was then expelled once more from his native Basel.

Examination of Andrew Boni.

Andrew Boni, expelled Anabaptist of Frenkendorf, aged thirty-four years, has been imprisoned in the Spalen-Tower and was examined by the Council of Seven.

Why did he return here contrary to his promise and vow? He said that he had made no vow, but rather had said that he would commend it to God.

When he was asked whether he would then remain away if he were again expelled from the territory, he said that he could not promise that!

On being asked who those were who had called him into the territory again, he said that he did not wish to say. On being asked where he had been in the meantime, he said, at Bern. He would not tell with whom, not to his enemies.

On being further asked whether he did not feel obliged to tell the authorities the truth, he answered, yes, except when it would bring hardship to his neighbor who loves God. As far as his own body was concerned, he did not mind what happened to him.

When he was asked for what purpose and end he had come here again, he answered, from love for God and his neighbor. He referred thereby to a booklet which he surrendered (enclosed with this).

As nothing more could be done with him, the prisoner was released from the questioning, and ordered sent back to his previous place of custody.

. . .

[April 27, 1707.][52]

Minutes of the Small Council.
April 27, 1707.
Andrew Boni, the Anabaptist.

Andrew Boni, an Anabaptist from Frenkendorf, who was expelled under penalty of the pillory on December 11, 1706, was caught at Oberdorf several days ago, arrested, and later transferred here in custody.

[Decision of the council.] He should be placed in the pillory, and again expelled forever under penalty of beating with switches.[53]

II. Formation

The Lord then showed these persecuted exiles a place of refuge, or a small Pella, in the county of Wittgenstein. There lived there at that time a lenient count and several awakened countesses. Freedom of conscience was granted at Schwarzenau, about one hour distant from Berleburg. Therefore, although Wittgenstein is a poor and rugged land, many different kinds of people gathered in Schwarzenau. This otherwise little-noticed village was in a short time greatly changed, so that in a few years it was known far and wide. Those who came together there because of persecution were at first called "Pietists," although they differed from one another because of various opinions and also through diverse customs and habits. They themselves, however, called one another "brethren."

—Alexander Mack, Jr.[1]

THE BIRTH OF THE CHURCH

As seen in the testimony of Martin Lucas and the Diehl brothers in the Heidelberg hearings, the Pietists knew of two areas where free exercise of religion was granted—the counties of Wittgenstein and Marienborn. Although otherwise a little-noticed and ill-favored land, the territory of Wittgenstein, which was divided into two parts, Sayn-Wittgenstein-Berleburg, and Sayn-Wittgenstein-Hohenstein, became known far and wide because of its policy of toleration. Bounded to the north, west, and south by rough hill country, its secluded location was favorable for this policy, so unusual in that era.

At that time the Wittgenstein counts were responsible only to the imperial government, although there was a feudal relationship with the prince of Hesse-Darmstadt. As the imperial organization was weak, and its bureaucratic machinery ponderous, the repeated complaints of neighboring counts about the toleration extended by the count of Sayn-Wittgenstein-Hohenstein, Henry Albert (1658-1723), were not taken up until 1720, after the Brethren had left earlier in the same year.

Schwarzenau, a small village previously consisting of a manor house erected as a residence in the late sixteenth century for the widowed or dowager countesses of Sayn-Wittgenstein-Hohenstein at Laasphe, a mill, and a few houses, was greatly enlarged when it became the gathering place for religious refugees forced to leave their homes in other parts of Germany. They even came from as far as Switzerland, the Netherlands, and England. Located in one of the most beautiful sections of the Eder valley, it came to be known by them as the "Valley of Peace" *(Friedenstal)*. Most of the settlers built rude houses or huts in the hills surrounding Schwarzenau. One group of homes was built in a valley above the village which came to be called "Valley of Huts" *(Hüttental)*.

The father of Henry Albert, Count Gustav, had married a French Huguenot daughter of one of France's most distinguished families— Anna Helena de la Place. In 1685, when Louis XIV repealed the Edict of Nantes, which had guaranteed toleration to French Protestants, the Huguenots were forced to choose between renouncing the faith and fleeing the country. Among the thousands who fled, a group came to Schwarzenau upon the invitation of Count Gustav. Although they were of Reformed faith, as was the county of Wittgenstein since 1555 (confirmed in 1574), this reception was an important first step toward the later granting of virtual freedom of conscience.

Schwarzenau

Photo by M. R. Zigler

Count Henry Albert, although nominally remaining Reformed, was himself inclined toward Pietism. This can be seen in a letter of his written to his brother August David in Berlin, on May 1, 1700, containing glowing praise of Hochmann. His four younger sisters—Amalie, Anna Sophie, Henriette, and Louise Magdalene—were completely taken with the new teachings, and all eventually married Pietist commoners, much to the horror of their relatives. Although under pressure from all sides, Henry Albert maintained the policy of toleration until his death in 1723.

One probable reason for his tolerance was a desire to attract hard-working settlers to his thinly populated and poverty-stricken territory. Harshly ravaged by both friend and foe in the Thirty Years' War, the territory was badly depopulated. Settlers were given nearly all of the privileges of subjects in return for a yearly tax. They were freed from the usual responsibilities and given the count's land on lease.[2]

This is a description of Schwarzenau by a contemporary, the separatist John Christopher Edelmann, from the year 1736.

"As I was traveling through Schwarzenau, I remembered that I had heard a great deal in Jena and other places about the Pietists at Schwarzenau. At that time I considered everyone who was given the name of Pietist as better without exception than those called orthodox. . . .

"Nevertheless, I was happy to come this close to this village. It lies one and a half hours from Berleburg in a pleasant valley, surrounded by delightful hills and forests, through which runs the Eder River and other cool brooks. The village belonged to the count of Wittgenstein, and was in actuality a widow's residence for the dowager countesses of Wittgenstein. Before the strangers settled there (most of whom had been driven from other places because of their Pietism, and found there complete freedom of conscience) they must have lived as if in a cloister in this solitude because there were only the manor and a few small houses to be seen.

"At that time, however, the village had been very extensively built up by all kinds of people who sought something better there. For people who loved solitude it was most delightful to live there. Only a few houses were located closely together, and it is surprising that those houses which were isolated were not plundered by robbers for a considerable time. However, when they found out that wealthy people were among them, they appeared on the scene and the residents had a miserable time afterwards. . . ."[3]

Photo by Grobbel

The "Valley of Huts" Above Schwarzenau

Preparation

Among the radical Pietists who found refuge in Wittgenstein were some who, although they had broken with the established church, felt the need for some organization in order that Christ's commandments could be followed completely. A particular concern was their state of unbaptism, for they rejected the infant baptism which all of them had received as members of the Reformed or Lutheran churches.

Hochmann von Hochenau to Grebe and Mack

Two of this first Brethren group, George Grebe and Alexander Mack, wrote to Hochmann, whom they considered their spiritual guide. He was at that time in prison in Nürnberg, having been arrested for preaching there. From his answering letter it can be seen that they had asked him for his opinion of their desire to be baptized in the manner they considered apostolic—trine immersion. His response was one of cautious encouragement, warning them to "count the cost." This is the first known expression of the theme which was to become so important for the early Brethren and their descendants.

To George [Grebe], gunsmith, and Alexander Mack at Schwarzenau.
From the prison in Nürnberg, July 24, 1708.
Remember Jesus Christ, risen from the dead. 2 Timothy 2:8.
In this Jesus Beloved Brother:
    I have received your dear letter of July 4 from Schwarzenau. You
evidently do not know of the arrival of my letter which I sent to you
some time ago, enclosed in a letter to Brother Peter Gilbert from the
Palatinate (who was a butcher, and is now residing in Marienborn).
He was to have received this from Brother Christian Erb at the
Ronneburg [Castle]. I do hope that you will receive the same safely,
and will have delivered the enclosed to the Brethren Meusli and John.
    Concerning the content of your letter, may this serve as an answer.
I am still held in arrest to this date by the local authorities, and therefore cannot yet go to you. Although I have applied in writing for my
release to the local authorities, I have not yet received an answer.
Therefore I must await with patience and resignation what God will
do with me in this case. I am at least still firmly resolved to remain
true to my God, and not to make a profession of any sect but only
to Christ, the Son of the eternal and living God, to whom I have here
publicly confessed myself. Come what may, I know with certainty
that the truth of Christ is on my side and that my Immanuel himself
is contending for me.
    Concerning, then, your intention on baptism, I want to write to
you my simple opinion according to my conscience before God. I am
still firmly convinced that the water baptism of children has no
foundation in the Scriptures, because Jesus nowhere commanded that
children be baptized, much less did the apostles ever baptize children.
It can be proved incontestably from the Scriptures, however, that Jesus
has expressly commanded that adults, who have become His disciples
and followers through true repentance and faith, also be baptized with
water after His own example (as He was baptized by John only as an
adult) in the name of the Father, the Son, and the Holy Spirit. Now
if God the Lord should lead some of His faithful witnesses to baptize
in water also, and should He plant in the hearts of His children
through His Spirit [a desire for] such an outward water baptism (by
being immersed in flowing water as Jesus was when He went into
the Jordan) and to be baptized or immersed, I will not let myself be
against it.

A View of the Town and the Castle of Laasphe
A lithograph from P. Herle and Company, Paderborn.

However, this would need to be carefully tested before the countenance of God to see if this conviction is really from God, and if such souls are also resolved through God's grace to suffer and dare all for it, and yet remain loyal to Jesus Christ. From such actions at the present time will inevitably follow nothing but the cross and misery, as the anti-Christ will still rage against the members of Jesus Christ. One must, therefore, first carefully count the cost, if one will follow after the Lord Jesus in all the trials which will certainly follow from this. Without this true following of Jesus Christ, the water baptism will help little or not at all, even if it were to be performed on adults after the example of the first Christians. God does not look on the outward but rather on the inward—the change of heart, and the sincerity of the heart.

I have the same opinion concerning the Lord's love feast—the foundation must be based on the love of Jesus and the appropriate community of members. I will not oppose it, if they want to hold the outward love feast in the memory of the Lord Jesus, as it corresponds with the Scriptures in every respect. Where the love of Christ unites the hearts inwardly and they are impelled by the laws of Christ— when they are willing thereby to sacrifice their lives for Christ and His church, and desire to proclaim the death of Christ with heart, mouth, and deed—in sum, where they pledge and bind their properties and lives to Jesus and His church, I shall not be against it. When, however, only an outward, legalistic work is made of it without the spirit of Christ and love prevailing and ruling in the hearts, then I can in truth not think much of it.

We see that it is often held in the sects of today, and still Christ is not recognized in their hearts. Where, then, there is a righteous and inward being which is given over to God for life and death, then the outward form might also well be held after the example of the first Christians and the apostolic church. It will also have its blessing from God. Where, however, there is no love of Jesus in the hearts, then I consider all of the outward form to be pure hypocrisy, which cannot possibly be pleasing to God. It may then be said, as the Lord said in Isaiah 29 [verse 13], ". . . this people . . . honor me with their lips, while their hearts are far from me . . . ." This happens today in the large church gatherings of all sects, and still Christ and His spirit are not recognized.

Dear brethren, you know that it has always been my teaching that I have ever aimed at true surrender to God and Christ, but that I have not discarded the outward if the inward is first there. Test what I here write and do that which you find before God with sincere hearts. I will not stand in the way of the impulse of your consciences, when it is purely divine and has God singly and alone as its aim. This I do advise before God—that you not exclude from love others who do not look on this as you do, because promptings in this matter are varied. No one can rule over the conscience of others. Rather, we all stand under the ruling of our Lord, Jesus Christ, who called us all with His precious blood not to slavery but to freedom. May Jesus bless you and baptize you with fire and with the Holy Spirit so that you might remain steadfastly loyal to Him.

It is certainly worth the effort to love Jesus above all, and risk all for His sake, cost it what it may. My heart can find peace only in the single-minded love of Jesus. He who has once had a taste of what it means to love Jesus will find little appetite in the manner of this world. May the Lord Jesus do with me further according to His will, because I have resolved through God's grace to be loyal to my Jesus whatever might be done to me.

I have set out in the service of my all-merciful Lord Jesus Christ, and I will remain with Him because I can certainly find no better Lord no matter where I may go or turn. He has been my King up to now, and will be my King in the future. I owe Him the greatest service because of His power over salvation. After I have endured a brief time here, then I will rule at the appropriate time with Jesus in the eternity of eternities. Then there will be eternal joy about our heads, joy and bliss will seize us; pain, fear, and sighs will depart from us; and God will wipe all tears from our eyes.

Even though I cannot be with you in person, I am with you in spirit, and rejoice over all the goodness which God grants you. The time may still come that I will be released from this Babylonian captivity, and we can meet each other in mutual blessing. I embrace you in the spirit of Jesus and remain the loyal brother and intercessor before God for you and all sincere children of God.

                                                            Hochmann.

P.S. Dear Brethren George [Grebe] and Obededom [Alexander Mack]: I would prefer that you do not let this letter, which I have written to you according to my conscience, be read by all, but only by those who can bear and understand it. It could be that some, who do not understand the matter clearly, might judge from it that I want to advise and encourage you to something new and sectarian, which is farthest from my mind. You yourselves know that you wrote me about this first. I can only answer you according to my conscience. You well know that I respect no coerced arrangement, but rather leave all souls to the spirit of Jesus. I embrace you both warmly, yes, all brethren, in the love of Jesus, and remain your loyal brother before God.[4]

First Eight Brethren to Palatine Pietists

About the same time one of the group was chosen by lot to draft an open letter telling of their concern. This was then circulated among the Pietists in the Palatinate. This important document throws a clear ray of light upon the motivations behind the decision of the early Brethren to perform the first baptism. The unknown writer, undoubtedly one of the first eight, described how they had been led to this decision. He related that the visit of two "foreign brethren," probably English Baptists or Dutch Collegiants, was the occasion on which the concern and desire for baptism (which had been in the hearts of several unknown to one another) had become articulate. A strong appeal was made for their Pietist brethren to join with them in the baptism to which they felt called because of their desire to follow Christ's example and commandments in all things. Here, as in all of the original documents, the emphasis is upon obedience, not upon baptism as such.

To All Those Beloved Called in Christ Jesus. Greetings!

Under the providence of God, in Christ Jesus the beloved, I announce and make known to the brethren beloved in God the wonderful divine ordinance which has revealed itself among brethren through their manifest confession about the true baptism. According to the Holy Scriptures, Jesus Christ, our Savior, received this true baptism from John the Baptist. When John, however, refused, our dear Savior said, ". . . for thus it is fitting for us to fulfil all righteousness" [Matthew 3:15]. After he had been baptized, a voice from heaven called, "This is my beloved son, with whom I am well pleased [Matthew 3:17]. Listen to him" [Matthew 17:5]. John bore record saying, "I saw the Spirit descend as a dove from heaven, and it remained on him" [John 1:32].

I must first describe the beginning, when all of us, in varying numbers of years ago (indeed, one experienced a strong agitation of the heart already five years ago) expressed to several brethren: "You men, dear brethren. We must be baptized according to the teachings of Jesus Christ and the apostles." However, when this was opposed, it was passed over, but was not completely erased from our hearts. At various times I had an occasion to admit or realize before God and my conscience that it would still occur, and I was assured of it in my heart. In the past two years the other brethren were moved in their consciences that they must be baptized, but none of us knew of the others' concern. Quite by accident, when two foreign brethren visited us, that which was in our hearts was revealed. Our inner joy increased and we were strengthened in the Lord not to be negligent, and to come together in the fear of the Lord. Each one revealed and opened the depths of his heart. As we found that we all agreed with one spirit in this high calling, we have decided to announce this to our beloved brethren through an open letter. This is to see whether they also find themselves convinced in their hearts to help confirm this high calling to the pride and glory of our Savior Jesus Christ, and to follow the Creator and Fulfiller of our faith. We drew lots, and the lot has fallen on the most unworthy.

Dear brethren, please have patience with this simple letter, as the dear Savior and Redeemer has patience with all of us, and hears and sustains us in His long-suffering.

I also want to remind the dear brethren that we must publicly profess that which Christ Jesus taught and did without hesitation or fear of men. We need not be ashamed and must above all suffer and endure all things with rejoicing.

"Joy! Joy! More joy! Christ prevents all suffering. Bliss! Bliss! More bliss! Christ is the sum of grace!"

Concerning baptism, Christ, the first-born, is our forerunner, of whom the apostles and many thousands testified with their blood that Jesus Christ was the Son of the living God. Now Jesus did not only teach, but also acted and commanded, saying to His disciples: "Go therefore and make disciples of all nations (and make known to them Jesus, the Son of God, that they may believe on Him, that He is the same), baptizing them in the name of the Father and of the Son and of the Holy Spirit, teaching them to observe all that I have commanded you" (Matthew 28 [19, 20]). Dear brethren! What is then better than being obedient and not despising the commandments of the Lord Jesus Christ, the King of all Glory? This, especially as we have left all sects because of the misuses concerning infant baptism, communion, and church system, and unanimously profess that these are not according to the teaching of Jesus Christ. We profess that they are rather man's statutes and commandments, and therefore do not baptize our children, and testify that we were not really baptized.

We should, however, remind ourselves of our baptismal covenant, and profess at the same time that it is man's commandment and teaching established after the statutes of the world, and does not follow simply the teaching of Jesus Christ. Oh, beloved brethren in the Lord, we will not be able to meet the test at that time when the Lord [*Hausherr*] will come and require from us the obedience which He has commanded of us. We have been unfaithful servants, as we knew, recognized, and professed the will of the dear Lord. Oh, there is still time today, dear brethren, before the sun of justice sets and the time breaks upon us of which Jesus says that one can work no more! Is it not highly necessary that we go to meet the Son of God on the holy path, and kiss Him, before His wrath is kindled?

Dear brethren, we cannot err, as He—the Way, the Truth, and the Eternal Life—goes before us, and His teaching, namely Jesus Christ's, is sealed by His blood. His disciples have loyally followed Him and sealed it with their blood. Saint John faithfully explains to us in his second epistle that many deceivers have come into the world, and gives us the sign that whosoever does not remain in the teaching of Christ has no God. However, whosoever does remain in the teaching of Jesus Christ has both the Father and the Son. When we consider the eternal providence of God, which stands so clearly in the written teaching of Jesus Christ despite all controversy, does not this also seem a great miracle, that the almighty God so cares for us that we have a sure guide, and that a light always appears for us in the darkness? May God be eternally praised and glorified for His goodness, grace, and mercy, which He still evidences even to this hour.

In the second chapter of the Acts of the Apostles, it says that the multitude was so convinced by the sermon of Peter that they spoke, " 'Brethren, what shall we do?' And Peter said to them, 'Repent, and be baptized every one of you in the name of Jesus Christ . . . ,' " and it is added, "For the promise is to you and to your children and to all that are far off, every one whom the Lord our God calls to Him" [Acts 2:37-39]. Now the apostles remained single-mindedly obedient and did not lay any emphasis on whether the Holy Spirit came to the persons before or after the baptism; rather, they remained firmly by the commandment of their Father and baptized those who had shown themselves repentant. This needs little proof, dear brethren, as the entire New Testament is full of it. It can, however, easily be seen that this is no slight or poor matter which can be taken lightly. It cannot possibly be that all obviously disorderly persons are accepted for baptism, when it is known that they are without true remorse and repentance.

There is also an exact relationship and brotherly discipline, according to the teaching of Jesus Christ and His apostles. When a person does not better himself, after faithful warning, he must be expelled and cannot be treated any more as a brother. We are truly assured that our Lord Jesus Christ, who at that time was given power and might in heaven and on the earth, is the initiator of our action, and will know how to carry it through wisely, and also provide here the one and the other to whom He will entrust wisdom and understanding. The ways of the Lord will then be orderly prepared, without giving offense and annoyance to the God-loving brethren and sisters. For the world, however, Christ and His disciples are a stumbling block and an annoyance, and it takes offense at the Word on which they are founded.

Dear brethren, it will certainly not require much more proof, as each one who is from God will be taught everything by the anointing, and will well understand the importance of baptism. Paul writes, Romans 6, "Do you not know that all of us who have been baptized into Christ Jesus were baptized into his death? We were buried therefore with him by baptism into death, so that as Christ was raised from the dead by the glory of the Father, we too might walk in newness of life" [3 and 4]. This is then the covenant of a good conscience with God, as Peter writes in First Peter 3:21 and explains very clearly that as the great flood cleansed the first world, so they have explained baptism, that from now on, all of the old sins and uncleanliness shall be washed away through baptism. For as a person is cleansed outwardly through water, so is the inner person cleansed through the blood of Jesus Christ in faith. The Holy Spirit gives His testimony thereto. These are the three witnesses on earth, of which St. John speaks (1 John [5]:8).

I am quite convinced that you, dear brethren, are more familiar with the Holy Scriptures about this than I am, concerning Jesus Christ's teaching, action, life, and conduct. Your hearts will be, with ours, so mightily convinced that if an angel came from heaven and proclaimed something different we would not accept it. I do not doubt that some one could ignore this ordinance, and consider it unnecessary without the loss of his salvation if grounded in God. I also do not doubt that some out of folly for their own opinions may fail to do as our Lord Jesus Christ has done. But as Christ our head and keeper lowered himself into the water, so must we of necessity, as His members, be immersed with Him. Moreover, we do not write one point which is not from the teachings of Christ and His apostles out of the freedom of conscience which each one has. It may be that God has revealed to us, where possibly presumption is practiced. We live in the appearance of good and simple work and wish to eat our own bread in quiet conduct according to the teaching of St. Paul, the apostle. Where, however, God places different work on a brother, which may well be harder than physical work, then each one should attend to his own work to which God has called him, in the fear of the Lord. That I would like to have someone to be as I am, is very deceptive, for each should live according to his calling.

So then, if some more brethren wish to begin this high act of baptism with us out of brotherly unity according to the teachings of Christ and the apostles, we announce in humbleness that we are interceding together in prayer and fasting with God. We will choose him whom the Lord gives as the baptizer as God will reveal to us. If we then begin in the footsteps of the Lord Jesus to live according to His commandment, then we can also hold communion together according to the commandment of Christ and His apostles in the fear of the Lord. We now wish from the bottom of our hearts, grace, peace, and love for all brethren, from God our Father in Jesus Christ, His beloved Son, through the Holy Spirit. May the triune God seal, strengthen, found, and confirm His eternal truth in our hearts, that we may highly respect all that which is commanded through God. Let nothing depart from our hearts, but rather let us think upon it, talk about it, and also tell our children, that they also learn to observe the commandments and witness of God. Yes, the Lord God of our fathers, the God of Abraham, be praised, the God of Isaac, and of Jacob, be highly exalted, and His name be glorified to the end of the world. Amen.

[Summer, 1708]   [One of the first eight][5]

THE FIRST BAPTISM

Alexander Mack, Jr., Describes the First Baptism

Alexander Mack, Jr., described the actual events of the first baptism in the preface to the first (1774) American edition of his father's writings. Using papers left by his father and Peter Becker, the younger Mack told of the preparation—how the group earnestly studied the Bible. They also searched the latest investigations of church history to learn about the practices of the early Christian church, which they were eager to imitate as closely as possible.

Certain details were deliberately omitted, for example, the name of the person who baptized the leader, Mack, before the latter baptized the others. They wished to avoid human error, such as honoring men rather than God. They were not interested in the acclaim or recognition of the world. The baptism must have taken place sometime between early August and late September of 1708.

It soon became evident that the words of Christ in Matthew 18 [verse 15] where He says, "If your brother sins against you, go and tell him his fault, between you and him alone," and so on, could not become a real Christian custom, because there was no organized Christian church [*Gemeinde*] there. For this reason, some returned to the churches from which they had separated themselves. They could not subject themselves to a stricter Christian discipline, and the all-too-great freethinking there seemed more dangerous to some than the churches which they had left.

Therefore, some felt powerfully drawn to seek again the footsteps of the first Christians. They passionately yearned to avail themselves in faith of the ordained testimonies of Jesus Christ according to their right value. At the same time, it was emphatically opened to them in their hearts how necessary is obedience in faith if a soul wishes to be saved. This opening brought them immediately to the mystery of water baptism, which seemed to them a door to the church after which they yearned. However, there were great differences of opinion among the Pietists about baptism, which sometimes grieved the truth-loving souls.

Finally, in the year 1708, eight persons agreed together to establish a covenant of a good conscience with God, to accept all ordinances of Jesus Christ as an easy yoke, and thus to follow after their Lord Jesus— their good and loyal shepherd—as true sheep in joy or sorrow until the blessed end. These eight persons were five brethren and three sisters, as follows: first, George Grebe, from Hesse-Kassel; second, Luke Vetter, also from the state of Hesse; the third was Alexander Mack, from Schriesheim in the Palatinate between Mannheim and Heidelberg; the fourth was Andrew Boni, from Basel in Switzerland; the fifth, John Kipping, from Bareit in the state of Württemberg; the three sisters were: first, Joanna Nöthiger, or Boni; second, Anna Margaret Mack; and third, Joanna Kipping. These eight persons united with one another as brethren and sisters in the covenant of the cross of Jesus Christ as a church of Christian believers.

They found in trustworthy histories that the early Christians during the first and second centuries were planted into the death by crucifixion of Jesus Christ, according to the commandment of Christ, through trine immersion in the water bath of holy baptism. They therefore diligently searched the New Testament, and found that everything agreed with this perfectly. They therefore had an ardent desire to be furthered through this means, practiced by Christ himself and commanded by Him, for the fulfillment of all righteousness, according to His saving counsel.

This problem then presented itself. Who should perform this good work on them outwardly? One among them who was their leader in their meetings had visited in heartfelt love from time to time various meetings of the Baptist-minded [Mennonites] in Germany. Most of these admitted that immersion in water was indeed correct, if one wished to practice it in holy baptism out of love for Christ. However, they also tried to prove along with this that sprinkling with a handful of water was also good enough, when otherwise everything else was right. This, however, did not satisfy the consciences of the eight.

Therefore they appealed to him who was their spokesman to immerse them upon their faith after the example of the first and best

Christians. As, however, he considered himself to be unbaptized, he wished first to be baptized by them, before he should baptize others. Therefore they agreed to unite in fasting and praying in order to obtain a good solution to this matter from Christ himself, the founder of His holy ordinances. He wished to be baptized by the church of Christ, and the others shared this desire. They were strengthened in this impasse by the words of Christ where He so faithfully speaks: "For where two or three are gathered in my name, there am I in the midst of them" [Matthew 18:20].

In their trust in God's dear and certain promise they drew lots with fasting and praying, to see which of the four brethren should baptize that brother who so ardently desired to be baptized by the church of Christ. They promised one another never to reveal who the first baptizer among them was, so that no one might have cause to call them by someone's name. They found such folly reprimanded already by Paul in his writing to the Corinthians.

After they were thus prepared, the said eight went out to the water called the Eder in the solitude of the morning. The brother upon whom the lot had fallen, first baptized that brother who wished to be baptized by the church of Christ. When the latter was baptized, he baptized him who had first baptized, and then the other three brethren and the three sisters. Thus all eight were baptized in an early morning hour. After they had all emerged from the water, and had dressed themselves again, they were all immediately clothed inwardly with great joyfulness. This significant word was then impressed on them through grace: "Be fruitful and multiply" [Genesis 1:28]. This happened in the said year, 1708. However, they have left no record of the month of the year, or of the day of the month, or of the week.[6]

Account in the Ephrata Chronicle

A later description of the first baptism is found in the history of the Ephrata community, the famous monastic center which resulted from an early split in the church in Pennsylvania. The account in the *Ephrata Chronicle* [*Chronicon Ephratense*] was published in 1786 although written earlier. It varies somewhat from that of Alexander Mack, Jr., which may be explained because of the intervening years and because it was based upon secondhand testimony. Inasmuch as the *Chronicle* was written to justify the Ephrata group and their own particular doctrines, such as the importance of celibacy, their description must be used with some caution.

It is still fresh in the memory of all that with the beginning of the present century, important changes in the realm of the church took place in many lands, especially in Germany. A great many people, of all stations, separated themselves from the common forms of worship, and were in general called Pietists. But as only the three known church-parties were included in the religious peace, the Pietists everywhere began to be proceeded against with much severity. On this account many of them returned to the church, and were therefore called Church-Pietists. Most of the rest went to the districts of Marienborn, Schwarzenau, Schlechtenboden, etc., whose rulers had themselves been awakened, and so granted them asylum and liberty of conscience.

From among the Pietists gathered in that region, two congregations were soon formed whose principles were radically contrary: namely, the Community of True Inspiration and the Schwarzenau Baptists. As the relations of the superintendent [Conrad Beissel] were intricately involved with these congregations, they will often have to be referred to. The Schwarzenau Baptists originated in the year 1708. The persons who at that time were the pathmakers amid much opposition were Alexander Mack, their teacher, a wealthy miller of Schriesheim on the Bergstrasse (who devoted all his earthly possessions to the common good, and thereby became so poor that at last he had not bread enough to last from one day to the next), his companion [*Hausschwester*], a widow Nöthiger, Andrew Boni, John George Höning, Luke Vetter, [John] Kippinger, and a gunsmith, whose name is not known. These eight united with one another, chose one of their number by lot as a baptizer, and then, according to the doctrine brought from heaven by Christ, baptized one another that same year in the running stream of water that flows by Schwarzenau. Who their first baptizer was has never become known.

From these eight persons are descended all the various kinds of Baptists among the High Germans in North America, who now are scattered from New Jersey to Georgia; but whether they were the first who restored immersion, as a candle to its candlestick, in Germany, is a question demanding closer investigation. It is asserted that the godly

Hochmann agreed with them on the subject of baptism, but as they carried the matter out while he was under arrest, he could not afterwards insist upon it any more; probably, too, their sectarianism was a hindrance to him. Certain it is that God was with them at that time.

Neither was there any difference between them and the congregation afterwards founded at Ephrata, except with reference to the Sabbath, and it is affirmed that Alexander Mack once publicly declared: "We now lack nothing any more, except the Sabbath, but we have enough to bear already." They had their goods in common, and practiced continence, though, it is said, they did not persevere in this zeal longer than seven years, after which they turned to women again and to the ownership of property involved therein. And this is very likely from the fact that, afterwards, when the great awakening in Conestoga took place, during which similar circumstances arose once more, they always declared that if it were possible to live in that way their fathers at Schwarzenau, who for a time had the same earnestness, would have succeeded in it. Thus they made their faithlessness the criterion according to which they would judge God's guidance, which was the very source from which afterwards arose the division between them and the community at Ephrata.[7]

THE REACTION OF OTHER SEPARATISTS

HOCHMANN'S OPINION

Hochmann was released from his one-year-long imprisonment in Nürnberg in October of 1708 and returned to the Marienborn area. He soon heard of the action of Mack and the others and was immediately asked for his opinion. Two letters, one to Count Frederick Ernest von Solms, an "awakened" ruler, and the second to Christian Liebe, reveal an unwillingness to judge the Brethren, but strong emphasis against making outward baptism a necessity for everyone. His attitude about the Brethren was later to become more negative; their action had the effect of making his teaching less radical.

Hochmann von Hochenau to Count von Solms

To Count Frederick Ernest von Solms.
Jesus Christ yesterday, today, and the same in eternity.

In this Jesus Dearly Beloved Count:

Praised be the Almighty God, who has released me again from imprisonment according to His eternal love and placed me in that freedom of conscience wherewith Christ freed me! I can again testify about Christ and publicly proclaim His name to my brethren! I am actually appointed thereto by God, in so far as it is indeed fitting and right that I should dedicate and consecrate all of my life-energies to Him, who has prior claim upon me because of the work of creation, as well as the right of the salvation—"for all that is consecrated to God" or "the practices of the world need not be joined in any longer." God has so led me from the world through His mighty arm that I cannot possibly return to it. The manner of the world seems too disgusting and foolish to me that I should cling to it and abandon Jesus, the eternal and living fountain.

Concerning the requested comment on the baptism, my impartial opinion is that nothing can truly change the heart except when Jesus himself baptizes the innermost depths of the heart with fire and with the Holy Spirit. No outward element is capable of transplanting men from the darkness to the light and from the power of Satan to God, but rather the true spiritual power from above is necessary for this. When, however, the heart is right, and Jesus has taken possession of it with His love, and one wishes in Christian freedom to have outward immersion performed on him, I cannot understand why such people are so persecuted for it. They are, indeed, not doing anything else but what Christ did in the Jordan, and what the early Christians did without exception. In Acts 2:41 it says specifically, "So those who received his word were baptized."

This is certain, that baptism practiced in infancy and without the child's having come to the age of discretion, and therefore not having yet been taught about the Christian faith, cannot be maintained from the Holy Scriptures, if one examines the matter without prejudice. Also there is neither an express mandate, nor any examples available, that the apostles baptized children. I have found this in impartial examination of the truth. If then someone in adult years has reached the point of receiving the true baptism of the spirit within himself, and, after sincere prayer and self-sacrifice to God in Christ, knows that he has received it (if it is not forced upon others as an absolute requirement for salvation) then I cannot possibly find it right that such people are so zealously attacked. Love must rule in all things. In Christianity there is no place for either enforcing or preventing that one has to omit this or that. Rather, everything must be left to Christian freedom, as Luther himself taught from the beginning of the Reformation: Whether to baptize or not to baptize must be left free.

It is the same case with the communion of the Lord. If two or three have become one heart and one soul in the love of Jesus, and can risk life and death together for the sake of Christ and the church, who will deny them the outward breaking of the bread? Just as Peter says of baptism: "Can anyone forbid water for baptizing these people who have received the Holy Spirit just as we have?" (Acts 10:47). The same is true of feet-washing. If the members of Christ wish to wash one another's feet in Christian freedom, out of love for Jesus and sincere humbleness, who will deny it to them, for Jesus has indeed specifically commanded it (John 13 in entirety).

To sum up, my feeling is briefly aimed therein that one must seek Jesus in one's heart as the only true foundation of salvation and the heart must be completely purified through the true living faith in Jesus. In case it is wished to perform in true singleness of heart also those outward actions which the first Christians did in addition to these inner unmovable bases, I cannot consider this a mortal sin, if one only remains in impartial love toward those who cannot feel in their minds this necessity for these outward acts. The freedom of Christ suffers neither force nor laws.

I cannot approve at all that a political magistrate wants to use violence against these people, and visit those with persecution who wish to practice such outward ordinances of Christ among themselves. As soon as God led me in this county, and I heard of the baptism, I brought the matter before God in prayer, and therefore came to the conclusion that I should remain in impartial Christian love with all, the baptized as well as the nonbaptized. Both parties sincerely love and seek after God. Love improves more than zeal. The more we remain in love, the more pleasing we become to God, who, indeed, is even kind to the ungrateful and wicked. . . .

Finally, this must remain immovably with us, to love Jesus above all, and to deny everything, should it be even entire kingdoms, for the sake of uniting ourselves with Christ. For what will it profit a man if he gains the whole world, and forfeits his life? Or what shall a man give in return for his life? (Matthew 16:26). May Jesus bless My Dear Count, and give him the grace that he may concern himself about his poor soul, which Jesus purchased with His dear blood, more than about the manner of this world, which is indeed wicked and seems to be predestined from God to be full of confusion. . . .

In haste,   Your loyal advocate before God
Eckartshausen, November 2, 1708.   Ernest Christopher Hochmann.[8]

Hochmann von Hochenau to Christian Liebe

My Dear [Christian] Liebe, Beloved Brother in Jesus:

May the eternal love of Jesus fill your heart, and make it ever ready to praise and honor God and the Lamb, inwardly and outwardly.

Concerning the matter of the baptism, it is my impartial opinion that baptism by fire and spirit must take place in every Christian. Where this does not occur in the soul, the outward water baptism alone without the inward one can make a Christian of no one. Before God in Christ, only the new creature has value. In faith working through love is found the entire essence of Christianity. Indeed, I believe that where one is outwardly baptized, even as an adult, that cannot possibly help one to salvation, if the person has not been inwardly sanctified in the body, soul, and spirit of Jesus.

If, however, this has happened, and the person wishes to have himself also baptized outwardly, then I will not oppose it, although one must inwardly take care that one is impelled to do this by the Divine Spirit. Along with this, I maintain that one cannot possibly force this outward baptism on everyone, but rather each must be left free to act as he is led by God. Then one will remain in love, also toward those others even if they are not baptized outwardly. Outward baptism without the inner baptism of spirit and fire will not unite the hearts. It is only the spirit of love which can make two to be one.

It is the same with communion. When this is held by living members of Christ in truly united love, then I will not oppose it. To the contrary, in so far as they wish to ally themselves with me in life and death for the sake of the name of Jesus, I will take communion with them. However, without the inward alliance with the spirit of Jesus, the outward will avail little or nothing at all. We see, indeed, that persons of all sects practice the outward communion and yet do not have the love of Jesus in their hearts. It is true that the first Christians observed the Lord's supper almost every day. They were, however, of one heart and soul. Where this is not the case, and it is not like the first Christians, there will be little power present.

I will commit the brethren who were baptized to God, and will not judge them, for they have done nothing unscriptural. If their motive is from God, they will be able to endure all trials, for they will not escape opposition. I want to advise warmly, however, that they do not begin a sectarian spirit against others who are not inwardly impelled to the outward baptism, as it usually happens with such matters. Love must rule in all things. I have nothing against anyone who has himself baptized out of love for Jesus, and takes outward communion. Where, however, this is done without love, I see little value in it. When the inward life is upright, indeed there can also be the outward form, but the outward without the inward is nothing.

I hope soon to speak with you personally, and to kiss you in the love of Jesus. Brother Christian [Erb] has received your letter and greets you warmly with me.

Hochmann.

I greet all brethren in God.
[c. November, 1708][9]

GICHTEL'S COMMENTS

John George Gichtel (1638-1710) was a Lutheran lawyer who became a follower of the teachings of Jacob Böhme, the shoemaker-philosopher. He lived very ascetically in Amsterdam, from where he conducted a heavy correspondence with his followers, who were called the "Angel Brethren" [*Engelbrüder*], and who considered themselves to be the "priesthood of Melchizedek." In four of these letters written in late 1708 and the spring of 1709, Gichtel refers to the Brethren. His sharp critique is an indication of the attitude of other separatists, who attacked one another as vigorously as they did the established churches.[10]

Schwarzenau Anabaptists' Activity

I have already received information from Heidelberg about the Schwarzenau Anabaptists. Also two of the "Euchites" from Laubach

have visited me and eaten with us. Their (Anabaptists') praying is only selfishness and not of God's Spirit. They yell so loud that one's ears hurt. They were incited therein by K. and H. [König and Hochmann?].¹¹
December 7, 1708.

Schwarzenau Anabaptists' Baptism

One must strive and overcome, if one wishes to be crowned. The natural water is of course not sufficient for the rebirth. It has to be the water of the eternal life, which Christ alone can give. The good souls in Schwarzenau, who have themselves baptized in the natural water, are not deeply enough grounded. We see here sufficiently that the Anabaptists are not any better for having been baptized as adults. Rather, some baptized infants surpass them in good lives. Time will reveal their error to them.¹²
December 10, 1708.

Schwarzenau Anabaptists' Zeal

P.S. After ending this [letter] I have received a detailed report about the new Anabaptists in the Schwarzenau area. They also observe feet-washing and communion, but refuse to let anyone participate who has not been baptized by them with water. And because all new sectarianism produces zeal, this is also true with them. When, however, this fiery ardor has burned down, then the zeal will lessen of itself.¹³
April 20, 1709.

Schwarzenau Leader Shares Means

M. has also visited us, who likewise has traveled here from Schwarzenau. ... There is an Anabaptist there [Mack?] who has some means which he shares, and in this way makes disciples. These allow themselves to be baptized in water. As long as the money lasts, his disciples will be united. When it is all gone, then this edifice will also fall.¹⁴
May 21, 1709.

LADY VON CALLENBERG AND GEORGE GREBE

Lady Clara Elizabeth von Callenberg (1675-1742) was born in Rothenstein, two miles from Kassel. When the Swiss Pietist Samuel

König visited Hesse after being expelled from Bern, she was "awakened"
(c. 1700) and soon left home with her four other sisters. They stayed under
way with George Grebe, a member of the Pietist group at Kassel, who
was the court gunsmith.

They later fell in with the notorious Eva von Buttlar group, which
was to the Pietists in Wittgenstein what the New Jerusalem of Münster
had been for the Anabaptists of the sixteenth century. After this group
was dispersed, she stayed with her brother-in-law until 1703, when she
returned to her home near Kassel.

In 1706 she again came into contact with Grebe, and finally in 1709
she sought his hospitality at Schwarzenau, where he had migrated earlier.
The description in her biography of this visit reveals a glimpse of the
home life of the early Brethren.[15]

As the five young Ladies von Callenberg now (c. 1700) had
arrived in Kassel, after they had left their parental home in order to
establish themselves in Saxony, they stopped at the home of a rich
man named George Grebe. He was also a Pietist and court gunsmith,
whom they already knew. The nobleman at whose house their brother
had stopped off sent them his compliments immediately, and invited
them to his house with the plea not to bring upon themselves the
disgrace of staying with a commoner. They sent him a message,
however, that they thanked him, but that they felt completely content
at the home of this smith, their brother in Christ Jesus. . . .[16]

She [Clara Elizabeth] thought about nothing else except bidding
farewell to the world forever, and dedicating herself to God alone.
She began again [c. 1706] to meet with some of her old friends, who
were pious and honest people, especially with the gunsmith Grebe.
She received many letters from him and, through him, also from other
devout people. They gave her courage to re-enter the path of godliness
with complete trust in God, to give herself anew to God, to follow
His promptings, to return to Him with love and trust as did the
prodigal son. . . .[17]

She resolved then [c. 1709] to betake herself to Schwarzenau, to
which she had an inner calling, and to live there in solitude and have
nothing more to do in the world except serve God. She had been
informed that one could live in that place in complete freedom of
conscience and that many devout souls were there. Among others there

was the gunsmith from Kassel whom she knew, who had also betaken himself there. . . .[18]

She arrived safely at Schwarzenau then, in 1709, and stopped off with the good gunsmith George Grebe, who had a small hut there. He received her with great love. He was very poor and his wife in childbed. As he had only one room, he sheltered our Clara in the attic under the roof, where she climbed every night like a hen. The poor accommodations which she had with these good people, however, were made pleasant through the courage and solace which God deigned to plant in her heart, as well as through the kindness and love with which these good hosts served her. She therefore was full of joy and pleasure to be finally in the "desert" for which she had so long sighed.

Her arrival at Schwarzenau was suspect in the eyes of many of these devout people, as they did not know the disposition of her soul, and only judged her according to the appearance of outward things, which gave cause for this distrust. But it pleased God to teach these people better through her conduct. When she arrived at Schwarzenau, she had only one *Taler,* that was all. Moreover, she started to spin industriously to earn her bread.

Lady Dalwig, who was with the dowager countess at Berleburg, and who knew her [Clara Elizabeth], invited her for a visit, after she had stayed with the smith Grebe for three weeks. She then went there.[19]

THE REACTION OF NEIGHBORING RULERS

The exciting events in Wittgenstein did not go unnoticed. Henry Albert's brother-in-law, Count Charles Louis of Sayn-Wittgenstein, began a violent attack upon the Wittgenstein ruler. Particularly incensed by his sisters-in-law having married commoners, he compared the Brethren with the fiery Anabaptists at Münster. Although his details about the baptisms in the Eder are probably exaggerated, his polemics reveal the seriousness of the step which the Brethren were led to take.

Called a "zealot against this brood of Satan" by his assistant, von Rauchbart, Charles Louis literally bombarded the imperial government and other rulers with complaints. He wrote repeatedly to the imperial solicitor (who was the law-enforcing agent) at Wetzlar and Vienna; to Henry Albert's liege lord, Ernest Louis of Hesse-Darmstadt; to Henry Albert's brother August David in Berlin; to Count Gustav of

Waldeck; to the counts of the Wetterau Collegium; to Prince Alexander of Nassau; to the prince of Darmstadt; to the prince of Hesse-Kassel; and to Henry Albert himself.[20]

Count Henry Albert completely rejected these attacks, and claimed his right to tolerate religious dissenters if they were otherwise harmless and pious. As an immediate count of the empire, he would not take dictation from his peers. In a letter to Charles Louis, Henry Albert claimed that several other German provinces tolerated religious dissenters. His letter was printed in a pamphlet published by his sisters as a defense against the earlier publication issued by Charles Louis, in which they were attacked because of their association with Pietists. Most of Charles Louis' letter of reply to Henry Albert is also given below.

Count Henry Albert to Count Charles Louis

[Your Excellency; Gracious Lord:]

. . . In the meantime I have been informed of your letter to the prince of Hesse-Kassel, written at Korbach on July 5 [1709] . . . in which you completely overstepped your bounds and had the impudence to defame me before the entire Holy Roman Empire. You used very strange expressions, claiming that I protected a Quaker and fanatic pack at Schwarzenau, who were not to be tolerated by any mediate or immediate estate of the empire in their territories, but rather must be exterminated by banishment from the empire with fire and sword. This was on the basis of some ill-chosen imperial decrees that had previously been issued against rebellious subjects. You claimed that you were inclined, as well as obliged, to incite the imperial solicitor's office against me. . . .

Whether I otherwise have the power to tolerate this or that so-called Anabaptist and [other] religious opinion in my county (as is done by other estates of the empire in Hamburg, Altona, Kleve, in the Palatinate, Neuwied, East Friesland, the Duchy of Moers, and other imperial estates) you may investigate only when you can show authority and instruction therefor from the emperor and the entire empire. In the meantime no one will convince me that it is my responsibility and office as ruler to persecute with popish reprimand these or those persons who allegedly err in religious matters and ideas, which is contrary to all reason, the manifest prohibition of Christ, the principles of the Protestant church, and natural duty. Or, on the other hand, that I should tolerate obvious adulterers, fornicators, murderers, blasphemers, drunkards, and other criminals who are subject to the imperial decrees and jurisdiction, Jews and associates of Jews, treat them as Christian brethren, and let them go free with the excuse of human frailty. I remain otherwise,

	your
Wittgenstein,	Henry Albert
August 20, 1709.	Count of Sayn-Wittgenstein-Hohenstein.[21]

Count Charles Louis to Count Henry Albert

Honorable Count, Most Honored Friend, Beloved Brother-in-law and Cousin:

My Dear Prince is aware that it is common knowledge throughout the empire that fanatical and heretical people of low and knavish extraction and unknown vagabonds gathered as a pack from all kinds of places have established their residence in the Schwarzenau area. ... Moreover, they have separated themselves from the three churches established in the Holy Roman Empire—the Catholic, Lutheran, and Reformed—apart from which no others are to be tolerated according to the Peace of Osnabrück of 1648, article seven in entirety. In their rejection of the most holy sacraments, condemnation of the established office of preaching, and overthrow of all divine and human order, authoritative Christian church constitution, republics, and law and order, they seem, in sum, to be repeating the history of Jan van Leyden, Knipperdölling, and Thomas Müntzer and consorts. The latter had caused the Holy Roman Empire great and manifold evil through their gathering as a pack, but through the unanimous co-operation of the imperial estates they were finally exterminated with the aid of God (imperial decree of 1535).

My Dear Prince is further not unaware that Castell had a child several years old who died before being baptized, and has another still living who is almost three years old and has not yet been baptized. Further, many other people live in infamous scorn of this most holy sacrament. They not only withhold it from their children, but also deny the validity of the baptism of those who received it in their infancy. They call it most blasphemously only a wash-water, and therefore do not hesitate to renew it. They call the most holy communion a swine's feast and a cold broth, which one makes of bread and wine in one's mouth. Yes, they completely discard the above-mentioned ministry.

Such people are not to be tolerated in the Holy Roman Empire according to the imperial constitution, an authentic extract of which may be found in Enclosure A. Rather, they are to be sought out by the imperial solicitor and exterminated with fire and sword. Also all immediate and mediate estates and subjects are completely prohibited from tolerating such unscrupulous false teachers under penalty of loss of land and people, as is shown in the above-mentioned enclosure.

My Dear Prince is aware that in pursuance of this, the imperial solicitor denounced this pack as early as 1703, and specifically My Dear Prince and the countess of Berleburg as hosts, helpers, and defenders of these horrible fanatics. Although the solicitor's intention could not be carried out at the time because of the adjournment of the most praiseworthy Supreme Court, according to definite announcement it will very soon come to pass. My Dear Prince's connivance up to now has been taken rather amiss by the imperial government. Our further silence in this matter could likewise be prejudicial for us. Recently a certain prince, who is dissatisfied with our house, has declared that if we do not check this menace, which is ruining religion and land, and show some zeal in avenging the dishonor brought upon our house through these rabblelike family-defamers (both male and female), he as well as some other neighboring counts will not only co-operate to disturb this evil but will also by no means consider and treat us as cousins any longer.

We are finally resolved in the name of God to hinder this by virtue of our Christianity and our duty as an immediate count of the empire and to comply with the imperial constitution, considering it necessary for the salvaging of our honor against further dangerous affairs. Moreover, we are resolved to show our displeasure to the entire world through our judicious zeal to seize all ways and means of checking this evil.

We have had the sad experience to this date that My Dear Prince has not only shown far too much patience, but also has not hesitated to defend these people and give them all possible assistance. . . . We cannot help requesting My Dear Prince as a friend and cousin to deign to consider the following: (1) Whether this fanatical movement intends to maintain itself stubbornly although it is clearly forbidden by the imperial constitution, and already accused by the solicitor, which action will soon be reactivated. (2) Whether My Dear Prince will not be the chief victim of this, and even be in danger of losing land and people. (3) Whether the neighboring imperial princes and estates, some of whom are related, will not consider ways and means of taking revenge upon those who dishonored our families. (4) That we and our friend and beloved brother-in-law, My Dear Prince's brother in Berlin, may be forced, under such circumstances, to denounce this to the emperor and his solicitor, in order that we may not place ourselves under suspicion and make ourselves liable to the same punishment. (5) That these fanatics will completely destroy the entire land, hunting grounds, forests, and everything else; we, as co-investors, are greatly concerned that further deprivations stop. . . .

I am certain that if My Dear Prince will take the above and its consequences under careful consideration, he, as a count of the empire who loves religion, God, justice, order, and honor, will finally see to it that ways and means are found to interrupt this. My Dear Prince should no longer listen to his wicked councilors but reject them. They are seeking to influence My Dear Prince by all manners and methods, but when it is too late, however, they will not be able to help him out of this against the imperial laws and constitution.

If this does not happen we will be truly sorry that My Dear Prince as our dear cousin and brother-in-law should fall into such misfortune. This would also force us and other relatives, who love religion, justice, and honor, to try to bring into effect the imperial constitution against him because of our duty. We hope for something better for him, and have considered it our duty to have this sent again.

We remain My Dear Prince's humble and willing cousin and friend

Korbach,
August 29, 1709.

Charles Louis
Count of Sayn-Wittgenstein.[22]

Count Charles Louis to Imperial Solicitor

When Charles Louis received no satisfaction from his brother-in-law, he complained to the imperial solicitor at Wetzlar, calling on him to take action against the Wittgenstein count. The message was delivered by one of Charles Louis' officials, von Rauchbart. The answer of the

The Castle at Berleburg in Wittgenstein

lawyer, Dr. Martloch, requested more definite evidence. The latter's appeal for "adequate means" may be an example of the corruption which is known to have existed in the imperial offices. The response by the count of Sayn-Wittgenstein was the so-called Enclosure Q, which was a long bill of complaints against his relatives in Wittgenstein. Only those points directly dealing with the Brethren or other religious dissenters are here repeated. It is not always clear whom the vindictive count is attacking, but there are unmistakable references to the Brethren.

[Honorable Sir, Imperial Solicitor:]

. . .

We learned to our great delight about your most praiseworthy zeal in particular, in presenting a complaint a year ago before the most praiseworthy Imperial Supreme Court (as befitting your office) against the notorious so-called Pietists and Anabaptist fanatics who began at that time to gather as a pack in the Berleburg and Wittgenstein areas. Further, we have seen that a harsh mandate was issued especially directing the dowager countess of Berleburg to cease tolerating these people, not only from the published mandate, but also from a special report. We had fervently hoped at that time that this evil, which is disturbing the religious system, and the imperial lands and people, would be completely done away with by this action. We had hoped that the above-mentioned Wittgenstein and Berleburg rulers, our cordially beloved cousin and brother-in-law and female cousin respectively, would apply this to themselves.

It had been our hope that they would expel those people who have fallen under the imperial ban, by virtue of their duties as estates and members of the empire, according to the constitution and the Imperial Court regulation through the Peace of Westphalia—in particular to the sharp mandate of the most praiseworthy Supreme Court, in compliance with the reminder of the imperial solicitor. We were informed to our great sorrow that this pack, particularly under the leadership of the fanatics König, Baudner, Hochmann, and Castell, increases from day to day.

. . .

Not only do they deny the validity of this [holy sacrament] to those who were baptized as infants, and most blasphemously call it a poor wash-water, but they also persuade them to be rebaptized. Consequently, many people, both adult men and women, have bathed naked in the River Eder flowing there, and have instituted that as the true and rightful baptism. Also many Anabaptists from the Palatinate and other foreign places have established residence there. . . .

A great number have established residence at the estate of Homrighausen in the county of Berleburg, and especially at Schwarzenau and Elsoff in the county of Wittgenstein, which belongs to my beloved brother-in-law, Henry Albert. They have built hermitages in the wilderness, and live in such a blasphemous way that they are ruining the territory and its people, etc. I ignore the fact that they will cause, through their wicked conduct, if the imperial solicitor is not successful in bringing the praiseworthy imperial constitution into effect on behalf of the empire, the entire land and its people to be subject to the imperial ban and other imperial laws, especially to the harsh punishment dictated by the statutes of the most praiseworthy Imperial Supreme Court.

Partly as a Christian, partly as an imperial count who seeks to save his noble house from such family dishonorers, partly because of being a co-investor . . . , and partly as the senior member of the house, whose further silence and the consent implied thereby would be not unjustly taken amiss by the entire world—we have considered it most urgently necessary to shift this heavy blame from our shoulders and profess our sincere zeal before the empire. We have also sent a cordial exhortation to our above-mentioned brother-in-law advising him to tolerate these fanatics no longer (which we can deliver to the imperial solicitor through [von Rauchbart], who will deliver this letter). This has not been effective, as it seems that the said Count Henry Albert has rejected all friendship with us on account of these fanatics until we cease agitation against them, as can be seen from Enclosure T.

Therefore we wanted to inform the imperial solicitor of our displeasure and zeal to profess this before the whole world. We wanted to remind him of his duty through this denunciation, not doubting that he will continue his most praiseworthy zeal against these sectarian rabble-rousers, at the re-opening of the most praiseworthy Imperial Supreme Court, which will soon take place, God willing. We remain, obliged for all services, . . .

Wildungen,
November 14, 1709.

[Charles Louis,
Count of Sayn-Wittgenstein.][23]

Dr. Martloch to Count Charles Louis

Most Honorable Count of the Empire, Gracious Lord:

Your Excellency's letter dated Wildungen, November 14, of the current year, about the Pietistic fanaticism sent to the imperial solicitor, was delivered to me by [von Rauchbart] in the absence of the above. Upon the latter's suggestion I broke the seal and ascertained the contents with proper respect. The imperial solicitor's office had taken up this matter before in order to counter properly this evil with appropriate means, and expected everything else but that its intention on such an important matter could be hindered.

Therefore, I will not neglect, as far as lies within my power, to proceed with this matter once again as soon as it is possible in the court, with all appropriate zeal and earnestness. This could be done if adequate means were placed in my hands. I have made arrangements in this regard with the said [von Rauchbart]. To this end, it would be good if suitable denunciations of these excesses and frivolities could be submitted from various places. I humbly commend myself herewith to the grace of Your Most Honorable Excellency.

	Your Excellency's humble and obedient
Wetzlar,	Francis Sigismund Martloch
December 10, 1709.	Lawyer of the imperial solicitor.[24]

Count Charles Louis to Dr. Martloch

Honorable, Most Learnéd Doctor:

We have learned from your letter to us of December 10 as well as from von Rauchbart's oral report that you would consider it helpful if denunciations (similar to that which we have published about the notorious Anabaptist fanatics) were issued from other places where these people have infiltrated into churches, schools, and police systems, and have caused confusion. Further that the imperial solicitor should be given one or the other special reports and factually based information by which the later prosecution by the solicitor against these godless false teachers could be aided and facilitated. This will be resumed following the re-opening of the most praiseworthy Imperial Supreme Court, which will soon occur, God willing. We found great pleasure in his most praiseworthy zeal, and wish, first of all, before God, every rewarding success for this most necessary and beneficial work. This is so that the honor of the holy Name may be saved from this infamous rat-rabble, and many poor souls may be freed from these dangerous coils of Satan. Likewise, that the pure doctrine and true faith might grow and blossom unhindered in the future.

For these reasons we have resolved before God to give the imperial solicitor all the assistance in our power in order to facilitate this most necessary work. This is not only to help the solicitor, but also to enable other noble houses dishonored by these frivolous seducers also to assist the imperial solicitor in his most praiseworthy intention at every opportunity. Therefore, we have wished to add some other facts to the other information, as shown in Enclosure Q. We assure you that if a commission were sent to the Wittgenstein and Berleburg areas on behalf of the empire, and if the false teachers were arrested and imprisoned separately, and the matter sharply investigated—if the chancery officials, pastors, schoolmasters, jurymen, common people as well as those persons named in Enclosure Q, and the misled people belonging to this pack, were examined—many more scandalous and godless matters and gruesome excesses would be found. We leave this to the discretion of a high imperial commission.

We remain herewith, the doctor's most cordially inclined

Wildungen,   Charles Louis,
February 5, 1710.   Count of Sayn-Wittgenstein.[25]

Count Charles Louis Denounces Wittgenstein

Enclosure Q

Herewith is presented a factually based report, for the information of the imperial solicitor, about the pack of fanatics, the so-called Pietists and Anabaptists, notorious the world over, and gathered from all sorts of places in the Wittgenstein counties. This will serve the legal proceedings of the praiseworthy court, which will—God willing —soon convene.

In the first place, it is known all over the empire and to the imperial solicitor that already many years ago all sorts of vagabonds under the leadership of the enthusiasts Hochmann, Baudner, König, and Knecht—all under the appearance of special piety—gathered as a rabble and spread about many dangerous and peculiar religious doctrines in the counties of Berleburg and Wittgenstein. They led such

God-displeasing and scandalous lives before men that the honorable solicitor was right to submit—by virtue of his office—an official complaint to the worthy Imperial Supreme Court in the year of 1703 in accordance with the imperial constitution. The Imperial Supreme Court adjourned, however, and the imperial solicitor was hindered in prosecuting the instituted process for the duration of the absence of the Supreme Court. Therefore, this dangerous rabble took advantage of this opportunity masterfully, and, under the leadership of the above-mentioned and other subversives who joined them later, so multiplied that now the entire Berleburg and Wittgenstein counties are filled with such people, and they now consist of many hundred families.

Of these people it is known that they: (1) live in gross contempt of God's holy Word, the office of preaching or ministry, and public services of worship, inasmuch as they not only organize private meetings, or as they call them, exercises, where males and females are permitted to teach whatever the Spirit moves them to after the manner of the Quakers and the Anabaptists, but also undertake all sorts of infamous, scandalous, and blasphemous matters. This is testified to in writing from a credible pen published to the world several years ago, the so-called *New Disorder of the Contemporary Pietists* [*Neuer Unfug der heutigen Pietisten*] giving the example of the arch-blasphemer Mother Eva [von Buttlar] and her godless following—Ichterhausen, Winter, Biedner, Baudner, Appenfeller, and consorts, including Lady von Callenberg. This is also known about Berleburg, where they gathered together in the castle as well as on the Homrighausen estate, and in Schwarzenau in Wittgenstein.

(2) Further, that they not only discard the merits of Christ, and the holy sacraments as means of our salvation, along with the Schwenkfelders and the Anabaptists, but also, in rare contempt of the same, deny the baptism of their infancy. They do not shy away from renewing this with the notorious rebaptism. Therefore, many adult men and women were baptized in the Eder River flowing there at the instigation of Anabaptist rabble gathered there from Holland and England, as well as those resident there. This they claim as the true bath or rebirth. (Recently a man seventy years old was rebaptized without any clothes on in the above-mentioned river and nearly drowned.) They withhold this most holy bath from their children; many examples of this are known. . . .

Yes, there are indeed found among these misled persons many who have forbidden their children as old as six, seven, eight [years], or even older, to be baptized. This could be attested to by the people in the Schwarzenau and Berleburg areas. In particular, the miller in Schwarzenau has not let his children be baptized. [The same is true of] very many farmers at Beddelhausen and Elsoff. The former tenant at Schwarzenau, named Holl, from Ernsthausen, now resident at Elsoff, should be strictly examined, as he also allowed his child to reach the age of six before having it baptized.

(3) They not only abstain from the most holy communion of our Lord and Savior Jesus Christ, but also revile it most blasphemously as a swine's feast or cold broth, which one makes of the bread and wine in one's mouth. Some of them maintain that this sacrament can bring no salvation, but is rather a symbol of Christian brotherhood. Therefore they prefer to receive the *agapé,* as they call it, in their secret meetings. As, however, they commit nothing but scandalous acts in those meetings and the redeeming ordinance of the Savior and the benefit of this most holy sacrament are soiled by their blasphemous conduct, they are justly to be classed with those about whom the Spirit of God testifies —Jude, verses four, twelve, thirteen, and sixteen. They are therefore to be placed in a class with the Anabaptists on this point. . . .

(4) The secular authorities, governmental regulations, constitutions, the republican administration of justice, social rank, honors, positions, respect for parents, respect of wives for husbands, considerations for the family—all this they discard. They teach that one is bought dearly, and should not be a servant of men. Therefore it is not necessary to obey godless authorities and parents. The [offices of] emperor, king, elector, prince, count, and other stations of nobility and honorary positions, and even civil services, cannot be entered by the Christian with a good conscience. In Schwarzenau alone there are over three hundred families and in Berleburg not many less. . . .

They also reject all courts and court proceedings. In other words, they sing the same tune on this point as the Anabaptists. . . . Instead of God's Word they emphasize all sorts of heretical and forbidden books—Theophrastus Paracelsus', Cornelius Agrippa's, and Jacob Böhme's—as is well known. . . .

These and similar excesses occur daily in horrible examples under the disguise of piety. One will find many of the same, if the entire ministry, schoolteachers, chancery officials, and civil servants in the towns and villages, mayors, jurymen, town officials, and common people were sharply examined. This is left to the discretion of a higher commission. May the great God give His grace, to the honor of His most holy Name and to the well-being of many poor souls, that the truth may be revealed, justice furthered, and wickedness hindered and punished.[26]

Landgrave of Hesse to Count Henry Albert

Charles Louis' strategy of bringing pressure upon Henry Albert by denouncing him in various quarters resulted in a reproach from Henry Albert's liege lord, the landgrave of Hesse.

Ernest Louis, by God's Grace, Landgrave of Hesse, Prince of Hersfeld, Count of Katzenelnbogen, etc.

First, our friendly greetings, etc., honorable and dear nephew and loyal vassal.

The Lord Count [Henry Albert] is quite familiar with the fact that various enthusiasts, fanatics, and godless sectarians not only stole into the county of Wittgenstein several years ago but also were further tolerated and granted protection. This, despite the fact that the Lord Count has not only, by this violation, brought a very disadvantageous disgrace upon himself and his territory, but, moreover, he can be held strictly accountable for this by the Holy Roman Emperor, and the entire German nation, as well as, in particular, by us as his liege lord. We therefore have graciously made this known to the Lord Count, and well-meaningly wish to remind him by no means further to allow or to tolerate the above-mentioned vicious and most scandalous pack, but rather to expel them expeditiously from his territory. He should never permit the like to infiltrate into his county, much less defend them. In which gracious expectation we remain with favor and good-will,

Darmstadt,	the Lord Count's well-intentioned uncle,
November 25, 1710.	Ernest Louis.[27]

Count Henry Albert to Landgrave of Hesse

In reply to the letter from the landgrave of Hesse, Henry Albert clearly stated his right in religious matters to answer only to the emperor, and defended the Brethren and others in Wittgenstein as devout and orderly people. His reference to the prompt suppression of "evil instruments" mingling among them is an allusion to the scandalous activities of "Mother" Eva von Buttlar and her group.

Your Highness, etc.; Gracious Lord, etc.:

. . . I read the [letter of Ernest Louis of November 25, 1710] with the more astonishment as, on the one hand, the above-mentioned statements are imputations the like of which I never expected from Your Highness. Those who have so "kindly" reported them to you will have to give an even more serious account of themselves before Your Highness than that with which I am ungraciously threatened. This is because they cause . . . such an ungracious, and undeserved, reference to and [threatened] harsh application of the highly forbidding imperial statutes, with no more basis than an unproved fact. On the other hand, it seems incomprehensible that I am accused of protecting, as you called them in your above-mentioned letter, a fanatic, enthusiastic, and godless pack, against which one or the other imperial statute is supposedly zealously aimed.

It is known all over the nation that the house of Wittgenstein was raised to the dignity of princes, and made an immediate estate of the empire with the ruling prerogatives appertaining thereto. Among which is the direction of religious matters [*regale circa sacra*] according to the very wisely written decisions left to us by the Lord Landgrave Philip the Magnanimous, of which one of the most eminent ones is that none of the Protestant estates will either question or wish to be induced to forfeit this right by this or that unfounded allegation. In addition we have the right of toleration of one or more subjects who do not agree with the authorities of other counties on this or that point in matters of conscience, but are otherwise leading quiet lives. This is the chief part of the former right, and is in conformity with the Word of God as well as the principles of the Protestant faith and imperial edicts.

I am not obliged to give account in regard to this to Your Highness but to His Imperial Majesty and the empire. This has been firmly covenanted and acknowledged by numerous confirmations and grants of privileges. If I should give account to you I would be allowing my rights to be infringed upon, and would be committing myself to an authority who was not competent.

However, out of the respect in which I otherwise hold Your Highness, I will assure you that I am, in fact, not aware of one single person in my territory whom I would be obliged to expel from it under the imperial statutes in question. Some have settled on my land already years ago and have led quiet lives to this date, out of a pure desire to lead lives pleasing to God. They have turned away from the masses of the worldly minded, the entirely rational faith, and the godless, sectarian, and quarrelsome mania of branding dissenters as heretics. It is most unlikely that Your Highness would consider such people as being banned by the imperial statutes, as it is known that Your Highness as a Christian has tolerated such people in his own territory up to the present.

Moreover, it cannot be unknown to Your Highness, that, whenever the devil tried to mingle in among them, and strengthen his hand with evil instruments, I very soon put a stop to it. I have imprisoned and properly punished such subjects as soon as they could be proved guilty of this or that criminal act. Whether I am to be blamed for doing this will prove itself in due time and in the correct place, if necessary. I trust I shall not come off with less honor than if I had threatened one or the other for this or that point of conscience, or if I had enforced the papal bull and declared their open prayer meetings criminal. Although it is traditional, and now a custom to punish the evil found in all kinds of sinful conventicles, and otherwise punish the bad morals that are really contrary to the imperial decrees, but, more important, against Him from whom all authorities derive their power to check this evil, Your Highness will doubtless approve my tolerating the others. This is the dutiful reply which I owe to you. Wittgenstein, January 7, 1711.   [Henry Albert][28]

Christopher Seebach's Statement

One of the most articulate separatists in Wittgenstein was Christopher Seebach. He became notorious by publishing numerous books containing his radical religious views. The archives of Wittgenstein contain a statement sent to the Wittgenstein clergy in which he criticizes pastors who obtained their offices corruptly. Seebach was expelled from Wittgenstein in March of 1719, probably because of his notoriety. It is also possible that the coming of Henry Albert's brother, August David, played a role. The latter, formerly a high official at the court in Berlin, fell from favor and was forced to return to Wittgenstein and content himself with the administration of part of that tiny county. He complained about the damage which the settlers were causing to the forests and game.

May God give the honorable inspector and the entire clergy of the county of Wittgenstein much grace and peace.

The inspector and the clergy can perceive from the enclosed letter that I am resolved to present a petition to the Roman emperor via the public press, as well as to the Imperial Court at Wetzlar and all of the Protestant estates of the realm. Into this petition I wish to incorporate the following points: (1) whether a disciple of Jesus Christ ought to consider those who purchased their offices with money to be Protestant preachers and servants of Jesus Christ, or whether he should not rather be able to apply the following texts to them: "I did not send the prophets, yet they ran" [Jeremiah 23:21]; and "Your silver perish with you . . ." [Acts 8:20]. I want to testify with a sincere heart to His Imperial Majesty and all Protestant estates of the realm, that my purpose is not at all to slander some one among the clergy, or to chide. Rather, if it is demanded of me that I should profess a certain church, then I am forced to reveal the outrages which prevail among the churches.

One of these many outrages is this, that some among the clergy purchase their positions with money. The word of the Lord Jesus is clear enough, when he says: "Truly, truly, I say to you, he who does not enter the sheepfold by the door but climbs in by another way, that man is a thief and a robber" [John 10:1]. Where is a text in the Scriptures that implies that money is the door through which one may enter the sheepfold of Christ? God in heaven will one day reveal it before the eyes of the whole world that such preachers did not go through the door, but rather climbed in elsewhere, and hence, according to the testimony of Jesus Christ, were thieves and robbers. Therefore it happens that such a false, godless, and devilish life is led in the very midst of the so-called Christians. For how is it possible that thieves and murderers could bring their wards to the path of salvation!

(2) I wish to plead with the Imperial Roman Majesty, as well as with the Imperial Court at Wetzlar, and all Protestant estates of the realm, that they reconsider, for the sake of God, whether the present

way of proceeding coincides with the example of the apostolic church. There it says: ". . . the weapons of our warfare are not worldly . . ." [2 Corinthians 10:3].

But in the present day, they come with soldiers and baptize children who expressly declare that they do not wish to be baptized. A servant of Jesus Christ understands very well that the word of Christ when he says, "Let the children come to me, and do not hinder them . . ." [Matthew 19:14], could not possibly mean [to] take soldiers with you and baptize the children with force. Never did John the Baptist or a disciple of Jesus Christ baptize anyone with force. But why is it then that they must come with soldiers in our day? The answer is that we have the kind of teachers who did not enter through the right door, but rather climbed in elsewhere.

These points I intend to present publicly to the entire Christendom. I thought, however, it would not be inopportune if I first communicated them to the honorable inspector and the entire clergy of this county. I remain, herewith, the obliging servant of the honorable inspector and the other honorable clergy,

Christopher Seebach.[29]

Alexander Mack's Land Contract Renewed

An indication that Henry Albert was successful in continuing his policy of toleration is the renewal of Alexander Mack's land contract on April 23, 1719. Mack is expressly promised freedom of conscience, a most unusual privilege in that day.

Copy of June 4, 1733.

We graciously permit Alexander Mack to own and reside in his small house and garden at the *Behälterchen* close to the Berleburg path at Schwarzenau. As heretofore was the case, he is to have peace and is not to be molested by anyone. He shall retain his freedom of conscience which I already granted him earlier. He shall, however, pay a tax of 30 *Albus* (in words: thirty *Albus*) yearly for house and garden. Certified by my personal signature and accompanying seal. Wittgenstein, April 23, 1719.

Henry Albert,
Count of Sayn and Wittgenstein.[30]

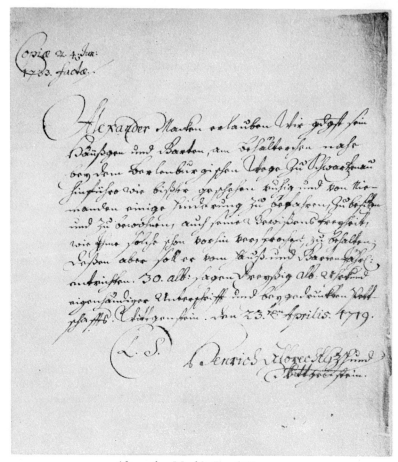

Alexander Mack's Land Contract

TENSION WITH THE INSPIRATIONISTS

The Community of True Inspiration, or Inspirationists, represented a problem for the Brethren in Wittgenstein. The movement stemmed from the radical developments in France after the revocation of the Edict of Nantes. Repressed Huguenots who sought shelter in the hills of the Cevennes fought back against their oppressors. Among these "Camisards" in this state of terror, some broke into prophetic outbursts accompanied by convulsions.

After some of the prophets escaped to England they went to Germany, where the Pott brothers of Halle received the talent of prophecy. Eberhard Louis Gruber (1665-1728) and John Frederick Rock (1678-1749) became the leaders of the movement, with the real beginning in Germany occurring in Marienborn in 1714. As will be seen, the great alarm which they caused in that area was the reason for the authorities taking sterner measures there, which resulted in the Brethren group having to leave.

The elder Gruber, a learnéd and devout theologian, as a separatist had posed the questions that Mack answered in his *Basic Questions,* published in 1713 [see page 325ff.]. After criticizing the Brethren for their sectarianism, he was drawn against his will into the new sect. He organized a Schwarzenau meeting of the Inspirationists in 1715. This meant that two young and zealous movements were trying to convert the yet-undecided separatists in the Wittgenstein and Marienborn areas at the same time. A clash was inevitable. Several fragments from the voluminous Inspirationist publications indicate the friction between the two groups.[31]

Rise of the Brethren

[1772 Publication]

He (Eberhard Louis Gruber, M.A.) migrated from Stuttgart in 1707 with Brother John Frederick Rock, a pastor's son. Both settled in the Ysenburg area, where they had freedom of conscience. At about the same time, other "awakened" and persecuted persons had founded their own church fellowship to teach, to baptize adults in flowing water, dipping them under water, and to hold communion among themselves. These were called "Dippers" [*Tunk-Täufer*] or New Baptists [*Neu-Täufer*]. From them come the Seventh Day Baptists in Pennsylvania.

These were forerunners, and did not wait for the correct time, which God had planned, to gather and prepare a congregation from among the sinners through His prophetic Spirit.

Paul Giesbert Nagel[32]

Decline of the Brethren

[1713 Publication]

. . . the New Anabaptists, who have corrupted themselves by their outward ceremonies, incite themselves further to prayer and outward exercises. Many of them have turned away from these scanty precepts to the informal worship of the New Testament. Others, especially their leaders, have revealed to the world by their blasphemous inconsistencies that they have only shells, and are even losing their outer virtue and insights more and more.

[Anonymous][33]

Mack Fails in Attempted Exorcism

[1748 Publication]

. . . Mr. K[ayser's] intended proof, page 47, has turned out badly. The evil spirits disfiguring themselves in all manner even as angels of light may and can call themselves as they will—this does not harm the Inspirationists. It is surprising that not one person considering himself to be a learnéd theologian or famous mystic has attempted to drive out the spirit of Inspiration, or even that of a false Inspirationist. Name-calling is easy, but to free a person really possessed or captive requires more.

A certain leader of a sect (A.M.) [Alexander Mack] tried his luck once with an inspired person, E. C. W. [Mrs. E. C. Wagner]. He came to grief, however, as the true Inspiration spirit did not leave her (only long afterwards because of some disloyalty). Rather, he had humbly to receive his lesson from this spirit, and drop the attempt at exorcising it.

John Adam Gruber[34]

Mack's Death Predicted

[Undated manuscript]

. . . Soon after this, an announcement of the coming death to a blasphemer Alexander Mack, and the one who is closest to him, and Andrew Boni, all three from the so-called New Baptists [*Neu-Täufer*] or Dippers [*Tunk-Täufer*].

Ursula Meyer[35]

III. Expansion

After this [the baptism] the above-mentioned eight persons were more and more powerfully strengthened in this newly begun obedience in faith to witness publicly about the truth in meetings. The Lord especially imparted His grace in them, too, so that more became obedient to the faith. Therefore, in the space of seven years, namely by the year 1715, there was not only a large church fellowship at Schwarzenau, but there were also lovers of the truth to be found here and there in the Palatinate. Especially at Marienborn a church fellowship gathered, because when they tried to gather in the Palatinate, they were persecuted and moved to Marienborn. When the church fellowship there then became larger, they were also persecuted, and came together at Krefeld under the king of Prussia, and found refuge there.

From time to time, the Lord awakened several co-laborers during these seven years, and sent them out into the harvest. Among these were: John Henry Kalcklöser from Frankenthal; Christian Liebe and Abraham Dubois from Eppstein; John Naas and others from Nordheim; and Peter Becker from Düdelsheim. To these associated themselves John Henry Traut and his brothers, Henry Holzapfel, and Stephen Koch. Most of them went to Krefeld during these seven years. However, John Henry Kalcklöser and Abraham Dubois went to Schwarzenau, as well as George Balthasar Gansz from Umstadt, and Michael Eckerlin from Strassburg.

—Alexander Mack, Jr.[1]

THE MARIENBORN AREA

Wittgenstein was not the only area which allowed comparative freedom for religious dissenters. Ernest Casimir of Ysenburg-Büdingen (1687-1749) is well known for his edict of 1712 promising religious freedom to artisans and others who would settle in his territory. His policy was expressly aimed at building up the county, which was heavily damaged in the Thirty Years' War. The example of nearby Hanau, where French Huguenots had already greatly expanded commerce through their skills, was not lost on him. This edict is one of the earliest public offers of tolerance in Germany.

Ernest Casimir Issues Edict

We, Ernest Casimir, Count of Ysenburg and Büdingen, etc., etc., announce and make known to all: it is obvious that there are not only many plots in the outlying villages which were deserted in the ruinous wars and have remained unbuilt to date, but also that an area within the town walls so large that a whole street could be built thereon lies idle for building. We are therefore very much interested in seeing construction on such empty plots, and in order that foreigners might come in and be induced to build houses, we have after due consideration resolved to grant the following privileges and freedoms to those who wish to build. We make this known by means of this public charter.

I

Some honest people avoid migration to a county because they are not members of the established church of that county, and therefore fear a coercion of conscience. We are convinced from the nature of the religion of the Kingdom of Christ and the spirit of man, as well as from the Holy Scriptures and the example of the great church Reformation and decisions arising therefrom, that the power of the authorities does not include matters of conscience. We therefore wish to grant everyone complete freedom of conscience. None of our subjects or foreigners and settlers in our county, who profess another than the Reformed faith, or even who profess no outward religion at all because of their scruples of conscience, will be caused difficulties or annoyances, if they behave honorably and virtuously and in a Christian manner in their civil conduct toward the authorities and subjects.

II

Impartial justice shall be administered to each and every one, and all those building outside of as well as inside the town are to enjoy all privileges and rights which the older citizens and residents have.

III

[New residents] and their heirs are herewith, by virtue of this charter, freed from the compulsory labor and serfdom usual in this county. These duties shall be completely annulled and retracted as far

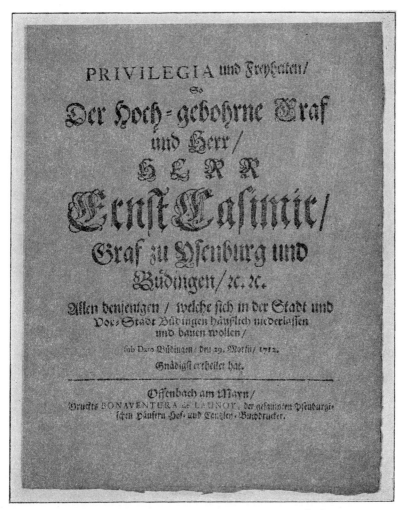

First Page of Count Ernest Casimir's Edict of 1712

as the new builders are concerned. All may freely leave here again
and resettle here or outside of the county.

IV

Just as local residents have all of the building [wood] and firewood necessary for the whole year free of charge from the large forests assigned to the town, so the new arrivals shall enjoy the same privileges. The same is true of the privileges of hunting, pasturage, and brewing, as well as the citizens' privileges of livelihood, commerce, trade, and in particular the obtaining of civil property—in sum, all legal rights which the citizens have enjoyed to date.

V

In addition, whoever wishes to build may have the wood at no cost, and can also have stone free of charge from the quarry near the town, as well as lime at a very low price, namely, an eighth-measure for one half of a *Guilder*.

VI

All new two-storied buildings shall enjoy ten years of inviolable exemption from all taxes and requirements.

VII

After the years of exemption have expired, each new resident shall pay his share toward the common expense, on the basis of his property, just as the old residents, but shall not pay the authorities more than a reasonable ground-rent.

VIII

In order that foreigners might have some information about the character of this county, the yield of vineyards, tobacco, wonderfully fine fruit and vegetables, wool, etc., is sufficient for a large number of new residents. This can be seen from the fact that the population was previously two to three times as large as it is now.

IX

As many vineyards now lie barren, those who request it shall be given the use of some at no cost. It is well known that a good healthy wine grows here.

X

It is our intention that primarily artisans should be attracted here and manufacturing established which is here lacking. Because of this want, our money has been previously drained from the county. We therefore wish to grant artisans who build or otherwise establish residence here special privileges and freedoms, and to take due care of their comfort and convenience.

XI

They will be pleased to learn that all victuals and foodstuffs here are available at low prices, to which end the recently re-established weekly market will contribute.

XII

Especially all wool manufactures can be practiced here with good effect, as a large surplus of very good, soft wool is available in the county. This must now be exported to foreign countries via Frankfurt

Ernest Casimir I, Count of Ysenburg and Buedingen
Courtesy of Dr. Karl Dielmann, Fürstliches Schlossmuseum, Büdingen.

because of the lack of factories here. In addition, the town is equipped
with a fulling mill.

XIII

Moreover, the fact that wood may be had at very cheap prices (a
cartload of wood will be delivered to the door for a *Kopfstück,* or at
the most six *Batzen*) is a great advantage for those factories which
require quantities of wood.

XIV

Furthermore, there is a shortage of armorers, cutlers, coppersmiths,
pewterers, beltmakers, ropemakers, glovemakers, and metal workers in
all Ysenburg. Such trades can be practiced here to good profit.

XV

Especially tobacco-dressers could make great profits here, because
large quantities of tobacco are grown here, which to date have been
exported in a raw state to foreign countries.

XVI

Similarly, all kinds of artists could make a living here, such as
printers, bookbinders, painters, wigmakers, goldsmiths, watchmakers,
sculptors, etc.

XVII

If any of the artisans has reservations about entering a trade guild,
he will not be forced to do so. Otherwise, however, they shall be
granted the citizen and guild privileges without charge and without
deposit of any fee.

XVIII

If learnéd persons and those who can live from their capital wish
to settle here, they shall enjoy every freedom and our special protection.

XIX

We also intend to establish a mail coach to Frankfurt for further
convenience, and see to it that the highway passes through here, as
was previously the case.

XX

There is also located here a hospital with considerable income, and
now the entire noble family of Büdingen is resolved that an orphanage
should be established here. Therefore, those who might be reduced to
poverty through misfortune may be comforted that they or their
surviving orphans may be admitted therein.

XXI

On the other hand, we have issued a regulation that no street begging is permitted so that our citizenry is not annoyed by that.

XXII

Parents have the convenience that their children can be instructed free of charge in the public county school. Those who wish to study may progress far enough in order to be admitted to the universities and enter academic studies.

XXIII

Those, then, who wish to migrate here have no customs fees or imposts to pay for their household furnishings, merchandise, and other goods, but rather shall be completely freed from all such expenses, and therefore not be burdened in any manner. On the contrary, they shall be assisted with all aid and encouragement. To certify and verify the truth of this we have personally signed this and have given our seal.

Büdingen   Ernest Casimir
March 22, 1712.   Count of Ysenburg and Büdingen.[2]

Palatine Dissenters Settle in Marienborn

From 1707 to 1714, expelled Pietists from the Palatinate found an asylum in Ysenburg-Büdingen. Most of them settled in that part of the territory known as Marienborn. The ruler of the Ysenburg-Büdingen-Marienborn territory was Charles August (1667-1725), an "intelligent, well meaning, and active" man, whose devout Reformed faith made him conscientiously concerned about the religious beliefs of his subjects.[3] The names of those from the Palatinate who were accepted as settlers [*Beisassen*] were entered into the government records; an example of this is the entry for John Naas, John George Schmidt, and Julian Stumpf, which follows.

Extrajudicial minutes.
May 18, 1711.
John Naas, John George Schmidt, and Julian Stumpf, born near Worms, are permitted to reside as settlers at Düdelsheim. The condition is that each pays two *Reichstaler* a year, that is half a *Reichstaler* every quarter in advance to the administration [*Kellerei*]. Further, they must strive toward honest and quiet conduct, and should not cause inconvenience to anyone.[4]

The Manor of Marienborn in 1736

Courtesy of Herr August Scheid, Büdingen.

The tolerance of Charles August was strained by the coming of Alexander Mack and other Brethren from Schwarzenau, who proceeded to baptize some of the Palatine settlers. The count's position was that everyone was free to conduct his own devotions in his own home, and he did not object to small private gatherings. Public religious exercises such as the baptisms carried out by the Brethren created excitement and were rightly to be repressed. The remarkably complete collection of documents available at Büdingen provides a detailed picture of the expansion of the Brethren in the Marienborn area.

THE FIRST BAPTISM

The councilors of Charles August of Ysenburg wrote to the pastor and the local official at Düdelsheim, a nearby village, to investigate a report of the baptism of one of the settlers there. Their reply, based upon the testimony of several local eyewitnesses, is the most complete description known of an early Brethren baptism. The mother of the baptized was then ordered to leave the territory, and Alexander Mack was told to stay away in the future.

Information Requested

To Pastor Rosa and Deputy Administrator Winter, Düdelsheim:
First our friendly greetings, honorable . . . sir and friend respectively:

We do not wish to withhold from you the fact that the right honorable, our gracious lord, His Grace, has been informed among other things, that some foreign and alien persons are said to have dared to rebaptize in broad daylight one of the settlers residing at Düdelsheim or elsewhere. These baptists had equally little direction from God as from the civil authority to do so. They are therefore by no means to be permitted, on the one hand, to perform such a baptism, and on the other hand, to receive such a baptism. This, especially because all kinds of confusion and disorder arise therefrom. We are justly eager to check this at the beginning, so that other truly God-seeking souls, who live more quietly and peacefully in all honor and piety, might by no means be led astray or disturbed by such heretical people. Therefore, you are to inform yourself in detail and report here fully without delay, giving the people involved, place, and date, and other data. We remain, your cordial councilors of the count, etc.
[Marienborn], August 31, 1711   Ysenburg councilors.[5]

First Baptism Described

Honorable . . . Sir Councilors:

Reverend, Honorable and Dread Sirs:

We will obediently report without reservation in response to the order received on the thirty-first of past month about the baptismal act in the water here, which we were diligent to investigate in detail immediately. We learned that this was carried out on the twenty-first of August in the Seeme brook in the woods. It was seen by some subjects, named John Fegebrandt, John Ernest Lüder, John George Nantz, Christopher Krafft, etc. A person named Alexander Mack, born at Schriesheim near Heidelberg and usually residing at Schwarzenau but now staying with Jacob Bossert at Himbach, performed this act. The other men who allegedly attended the baptismal act are by name: the above-mentioned Jacob Bossert, settler at Himbach; Martin Lucas, buttonmaker of the upper village [Düdelsheim], and Daniel Ritter staying with him. The women were: the baptized, known under the name of Eva Elizabeth [Hoffmann's] daughter from Himbach; the others supposedly attending the act were the sister of the baptized, and the wives of Jacob Bossert, Martin Lucas, and Daniel Ritter.

These are the circumstances of how the baptism was carried out: they knelt around an oak tree with lifted hands, and prayed. The baptizer, however, went at once into the brook, measuring the depth with a stick. He then said, "Come in." The person in question (who looked as if she did not want to go into the water but was held to it by the others) entered the water and knelt, resting on her heels. The baptizer then began to question her: "If you are willing to renounce the world and the devil and your own flesh, then answer with 'Yes'." She answered, "Yes." He then grasped her braids and dipped her three consecutive times under the water with these words: "I baptize you in the name of God the Father, the Son, and the Holy Spirit." After this he went with her out of the water and said, "Now your spirit and faith are strengthened." She went to the tree where the other women held a linen sheet around her on one side.

While she changed her clothes, they all sang the last verse of the hymn, "Lord Jesus Christ, Turn Toward Us" [*Herr Jesu Christ, dich zu uns wend*]. After this they kissed one another and went to the house of the buttonmaker, Martin Lucas.

After this dutiful relation of the above, I remain, reverend, honorable, and dread sirs,

your humble and loyal servant,

Düdelsheim,   J. L. Winter

September 1, 1711.   Louis Herman Rosa, local pastor.[6]

Widow Hoffmann and Mack Expelled

Minutes, September 4, 1711.

Inasmuch as Eva Elizabeth Hoffmann allowed her daughter to be baptized by Alexander Mack on the twenty-first of last month in the river at Düdelsheim, according to the reports submitted by the honorable Pastor Rosa and Deputy Administrator Winter, the above-mentioned women were summoned today. After they had appeared, the illegality of their action was made clear to them. Then the official [*Keller*], Quans, told the mother that because of the above-mentioned situation, as far as she was concerned, the [count's] protection was withdrawn by virtue of the decree of His Grace of July 14, 1710. She must therefore betake herself from the territory. It shall also be made clear to Alexander Mack that he should avoid this territory. To this end, all of the villagers were ordered that no one is to shelter him, under penalty of arbitrary punishment.[7]

Alexander Mack to Count Charles August

Mack's appeal to the count on behalf of the widow Hoffmann is the only original letter written by the leader of the early Brethren to have been preserved in Germany, as far as is now known. It is in its own right an important statement of Brethren belief.

Gracious Lord and Count:

An order has been published by the chancery of the lord count, first, that Eva Liz [Eva Elizabeth Hoffmann], a poor widow, must leave the territory together with her daughter, and that I too must leave the territory of the gracious lord, anyone sheltering me overnight to be fined five *florins*. I find myself impelled, therefore, to write

A House in Himbach Where Pietists Gathered

these few lines to the lord count, to ask him to reconsider seriously before God, the judge of the living and the dead, whether this proceeding is according to the will of God, who established the authorities to punish the wicked and protect the good.

In the first place, Eva Liz was indeed at the chancery and was examined; however, she was not found guilty of any misdeed for which the authorities and justice had the right to persecute her. In the second place, I was not even examined, let alone asked what my faith was, much less found guilty of any misdeed. Such a procedure, firstly, is counter to the Jewish law, John 7:51, where Nicodemus says: "Does our law judge a man without first giving him a hearing and learning what he does?" Yes, it is also counter to the Gentile justice, Acts 25:16, where Festus says ". . . it was not the custom of the Romans to give up any one before the accused met the accusers face to face, and had opportunity to make his defense concerning the charge laid against him." Yes, I will not mention anything about Christendom, that a Christian could, through the spirit of Christ, do such a thing.

Now I will freely and publicly confess that my crime is that Jesus Christ, the King of kings and Lord of lords, desires that we do what we are doing—that the sinner shall repent and believe in the Lord Jesus and should be baptized in water upon his confession of faith. He should then seek to carry out everything Jesus has commanded and publicly bequeathed in His Testament. If we are doing wrong herein, against the revealed word of the Holy Scriptures, be it in teaching, way of life, or conduct, we would gladly receive instruction. If, however, no one can prove this on the basis of the Holy Scriptures, and yet persecutes us despite this, we would gladly suffer and bear it for the sake of the teachings of Jesus Christ.

Therefore we would only appeal to the Supreme Judge, Jesus Christ, who will judge rightly on the day of revelation, and repay everyone according to his works, without regard to persons. Then Jesus will say, Matthew 25 [verse 41], to those on the left, "Depart from me, you cursed," because they had not fed His flock, and as the text continues. Oh, what will He say to those who have persecuted unjustly and without giving a hearing! They will have to say, "Oh, mountains, fall on us, and, hills, cover us, because we cannot stand before Him who sits on the throne." Therefore I am making my humble appeal to the gracious lord that he might test according to the

Holy Scriptures and investigate thoroughly everything that now goes on in his territory. For he, too, has an immortal soul, and will have to give account one day before Jesus, the supreme liege lord, by whom he was placed in authority in his territory, about the way he governed his territory—whether it was according to sacred order or not.

The whole earth is the Lord Jesus'. He has final power over all the elements. He who molests His members molests Jesus himself. How can it be justified when members of the Lord Jesus are prevented in their wish to baptize themselves in water after confession of faith, and to testify that Jesus is the true prophet to whose teachings they willingly submit; this, when they reject and abjure the devil, the world, and all evil, and lead exemplary lives before God and man. How can the poor Baptists help it that it is such an unusual performance, and that because of the harmful and [later-]introduced infant baptism, the true baptism of repentant sinners after their confession of faith commanded by Jesus has become so strange and obscure that even the chosen ones are almost offended and repelled by it?

It is probably not unknown to the lord count that for some time infant baptism was testified against publicly and in books, and that it is still being testified against in his territory from the public pulpit. Should there then be no baptism, because infant baptism is invalid? Far be it, for Jesus commanded it very earnestly, Matthew, chapter 28, and Mark, chapter 16 [verse 16], and said: "He who believes and is baptized will be saved. . . ." What Jesus has ordained cannot be intentionally changed or broken by any person without loss of eternal salvation. If, however, true baptism brought no cross with it, but rather a good life, honor, and comfort as does infant baptism, the learnéd theologians would undoubtedly know how to support it from the Holy Scriptures. As, however, true baptism brings with it all sorts of contempt, and one cannot be a friend of the world at the same time, they say, against their own consciences, that it is an outward work not essential for salvation. Meanwhile, they allow the poor Christians to proceed under great difficulty, while they follow along living very

On the two following pages
A Letter of Alexander Mack to Count Charles August
This is the only known extant letter written by Alexander Mack, Sr.

Gnädiger Herr und graf

Alexander Mack

comfortably with a doctrine which indeed keeps them from and avoids the cross.

I do not wish to annoy through writing too much, but rather close herewith, and leave it to the judgment of the lord count. As far as I am concerned, however, I do not complain at all about having to leave the territory, because I had planned to leave anyway. But because of Eva Liz, who is a poor widow, I humbly ask again that a little more consideration be given her. Should I, nevertheless, enter the territory again, I offer to defend my faith, if it is desired. If I can be shown by the learnéd theologians to be in error in some points, I will be happy to be instructed. If it is not possible, I ask again for understanding, for there has otherwise been much disorder in this county already.

I wish, meanwhile, for the lord count blessings from God and grace and divine light for his government, that he, too, may attain a good standing under the Kingdom of Christ. I heartily wish this for him, and remain his humble,

Written the fifth of the   Alexander Mack,
Fallmonth [September], 1711.   a member of Jesus Christ.[8]

THE SECOND BAPTISM

Second Baptism Reported

Hardly one month later, the Düdelsheim official reported a second baptism, this time of four persons, again performed by Alexander Mack. The authorities ordered the expulsion of Mack again, and the banishment of those baptized.

Honorable . . . Sir Councilors:
My Especially Most Gracious and Dread Sirs:

This morning at the break of day four persons—namely, Esbert Bender, from Dillenburg; Augustine Pfeil, from the county of Moltzungen near Kassel (staying here with John George Nantz); a woman [staying] with the commonly called Eva Elizabeth at Himbach; and the widow Geyer staying with John Weiszheim here—were baptized in the brook in the woods by the Baptist Alexander Mack. Present were Martin Lucas and his wife, Ritter and his wife, and the woman commonly called Eva Elizabeth and her daughter. The baptized were summoned and have all admitted the deed. I therefore obediently wish to report this herewith to the reverend, honorable, and dread sirs, and await with due respect further instructions. I remain, as always, commending my reverend, honorable, and dread sirs to God,

Düdelsheim,   your obedient and loyal servant
October 13, 1711.   J. L. Winter.[9]

Mack and Others Expelled

To the Deputy Administrator Winter at Düdelsheim.
Our etc.

We learned from his report that day before yesterday at the break of day, four persons—namely, Esbert Bender, Augustine Pfeil, the widow Geyer, and another woman staying at Himbach—were baptized by Alexander Mack in the brook at Düdelsheim. This was in the presence of Martin Lucas and his wife, as well as Ritter and his wife, and Eva Elizabeth and her daughter. Further that these baptized persons were summoned, appeared, and all confessed the deed. We have noticed the above in your letter of day before yesterday.

We, as well as the right honorable, our gracious lord, Count of Ysenburg, are firmly decided by no means to allow such actions to take place and be carried out in this territory, nor to tolerate such persons, the baptized as little as the baptizer. As, moreover, this Alexander Mack was already ordered last month, September, to stay away from this county, you must immediately notify this Alexander that he must leave within twenty-four hours and never return, making clear that should he ever violate this again—which we hope not—he will be expelled by the executioner. The above-mentioned persons—those who were baptized by him, and those who were present—must vacate the territory within eight days. You are to inform them of this immediately, and after this time has elapsed you are to resort to the usual means of enforcement if necessary to carry this out, without asking for further instructions. We remain,

Marienborn, October 15, 1711.   [Ysenburg councilors][10]

Official Reprimanded

The councilors reprimanded their official at Himbach for not having executed the order of expulsion upon the widow Hoffmann,

After receiving his excuses, the councilors again ordered that she had to leave immediately.

To Keller Quans at Himbach.
Our etc. etc.

Our honorable and gracious lord, Count of Ysenburg, has learned with displeasure that Eva Elizabeth Hoffmann has remained and resided to this date in the district of Eckartshausen. You have, of course, not only been ordered orally but also in writing on the tenth of last month, September, that this woman was not to be tolerated, but to be sent out of the territory. We inform you again at the special request of His Grace that you must carry out this order within twenty-four hours, using the usual means of enforcement, if necessary, to get rid of the above-mentioned Eva Elizabeth. You are also to report why you did not comply with the previous order. We remain,
Marienborn, October 15, 1711   [Ysenburg councilors][11]

Official Defends Himself

[To the councilors]
Honorable . . . Sirs:

I herewith wish again to inform obediently the reverend, honorable, and dread [sirs] (as already done on September 3 at my regular day of appearing at the chancery) that Eva Elizabeth Hoffmann was told, immediately after my receiving the oral order from the chancery, that the count no longer wished to tolerate her in this county, because she had violated the gracious lord's regulations. I personally explained and made clear to her for the second time, after receiving the written order from the count's chancery, that she must leave immediately inasmuch as she had brought it on herself through her act of disobedience.

She replied to this that she had received a batch of wool from Hanau to spin, and she would certainly be permitted to spin that first. She had been very quiet according to her promise, and had not sinned against the gracious lord, for she had not forced her daughter to have herself baptized. I said that I could not help her. She must obey the lord's command, and see for herself where she could go. I sent word to her later that I was surprised that it was taking so long until she left. The answer came to me that she had not yet been able to convert everything into money. She said that she still had beets and other crops in the fields, which she first wanted to dispose of for money, and gave other similar [reasons]. I pointed these out to Councilor von Boltzing ten or twelve days ago.

Therefore I have obediently complied with the order of the lord's chancery as a final enforcement was not mentioned therein. I did not wish to proceed with it on my own authority. As the gracious lord has expressly ordered it, I will obediently and humbly obey. As there are more of the same who were baptized, I will obediently wait for more specific instruction as to how I should proceed with them. I remain, and that with proper respect, your honorable and dread [sirs']

Himbach,	most obedient and loyal servant
October 15, 1711.	A. Quans.[12]

Widow Hoffmann's Expulsion Reordered

[To Quans]

First our friendly greetings, dignified, especially dear friend:

You are aware of what went on and was decided at the last consistory concerning Eva Elizabeth Hoffmann: that she induced her daughter to be publicly baptized by a person named Alexander Mack in the river near Düdelsheim. As she acted contrary to her written promise, protection is now to be withdrawn from her by virtue of an enclosed government decree of July 14 of the past year.

You are to carry this out. She is to be informed immediately that she is no longer to be tolerated in this territory for that reason and must betake herself elsewhere.

We remain,

Marienborn, November 10, 1711.   [Ysenburg councilors][13]

The Third Baptism

Almost a year went by before the third known baptism occurred. Again Alexander Mack came to the Marienborn area to administer the baptism. This time he had to pledge by shaking hands not to return, which promise he kept. The persons baptized and those attending were to be examined.

Third Baptism Reported

Honorable . . . Sir Councilors:

I herewith obediently report to the honorable and dread [sirs] that the wife of John Henry Diehl here wanted to go with some local people to Schwarzenau to be baptized there. This was reported to me day before yesterday by her husband, who urged me to prevent her strictly from this. I therefore warned her on the basis of the lord's orders.

Last night the Baptist Alexander Mack arrived here. As soon as I learned of it, I had him informed that he must live according to the orders of the count, my gracious lord, and should not try to perform any baptism here. He then sent word that he had not come here for that reason, but rather to visit good friends. As it had been late the foregoing night, he had only wanted to stay overnight and leave again very early in the morning, that is today.

However, this morning it was reported that Alexander Mack, in violation of the lord's orders, baptized last night at the Lindheim boundary John Henry Diehl's wife Marie Elizabeth, John George Schmidt, and John Naas' wife from here, as well as Julian Stumpf's wife from Stockheim. This was in the presence of John Naas, John Henry Traut, [Jacob] Bossert, and two other men and women including Peter Becker's sister-in-law (staying with John Ochsenhirt) and another unmarried woman from Schwarzenau.

I therefore summoned John Henry Diehl's wife again, and accused her of disobeying the lord's command. She answered that she must obey God more than the authorities, whereupon I later released her. I made clear to Alexander Mack that he was to stay here in the inn until I received further orders from the gracious lord about him, as to how I am to proceed further. I request the same quickly. I remain, as always, your honorable and dread [sirs']

Düdelsheim,	most obedient and loyal servant
November 5, 1712.	J. L. Winter.[14]

Mack Expelled for the Third Time

To the Deputy Administrator Winter.

Our etc.

Dignified etc.

We have learned from the contents of your report under yesterday's date about Alexander Mack and the baptismal act carried out by him. We have also humbly reported this to the gracious lord. The gracious lord, His Grace, stands by the previously issued order, and is satisfied with your conduct in carrying out these orders. You are further specifically ordered to convene the presbytery of Düdelsheim and order the said Alexander to appear before them.

You are to tell him that the most gracious count, His Grace, does not wish to interfere with anyone's conscience or to impose this or that tenet. However, disorder and other inconveniences arise from this God-displeasing baptism. Moreover, this Alexander had previously been strictly forbidden to re-enter the county. Therefore he, Alexander, must immediately leave the county, first, however, promising by the shaking of hands not to come again. The gracious lord, His Grace, will consider him an unrepentant, disobedient and even perjurous person, in case he is caught in the act [of coming again], and will punish him accordingly.

You are to have all of the foreigners and inhabitants of Düdelsheim come together (although without using force) and order every one of them, on pain of the count's displeasure and arbitrary punishment, against providing shelter for or accommodating Alexander Mack, should he dare against all hopes to re-enter the territory. Further, all those who were baptized, or who were present, should be informed at their homes that they should remain near at hand for two weeks, as the gracious lord, His Grace, has mercifully resolved to bring the Baptists to account for this baptism. You are to report the carrying out of the order immediately, and again in some days, that this examination had taken place at the appropriate time. Wherewith we remain your well-disposed, . . .

[Marienborn], November 6, 1712.   [Ysenburg councilors][15]

A Hearing Is Ordered

To the Deputy Administrator Winter at Düdelsheim.

P.S.

Also etc.

You are to announce to the baptized persons at Düdelsheim that they are to appear at the chancery a week from day after tomorrow, Thursday, that is December 1. We remain, as in the letter,

Marienborn, November 22, 1712.   [Ysenburg councilors][16]

One of the Marienborn clergy called to participate in the hearing was Samuel König (1670-1750). König was himself a former radical Pietist, having been expelled from his native Bern in 1699. He associated with Hochmann in Wittgenstein around 1700, and finally settled in Büdingen in 1710. He was understandably in favor of mild treatment of the Brethren and found little wrong with their baptisms. He wrote to the count requesting that he be excused from the hearing. The count, however, in his reply denied this request.

Inspector König to Count Charles August

Honorable Count, Gracious Lord:

I received day before yesterday a letter from Your Grace's councilors in which I am asked and directed to appear at the consistory for the interrogation of those people newly baptized by Alexander Mack. After I had considered this matter somewhat, and had pondered over it in the fear of the Lord, the desire arose within me to explain my attitude to Your Grace with this letter as follows. As these people look upon what they have done as a matter of conscience, and consider it a commandment of God which they should and are obliged to obey, a consistorial hearing may be neither good nor fruitful. Rather, these persons would consider this as a type of persecution and an offense to their consciences. In my humble opinion, I would think it more likely that friendly persuasion and private conversation to warn these people against partisanship and sectarianism—encouraging them to true nonpartisan, brotherly love in Christ for all believers and God-fearing people, whether they are rebaptized or not—would find better reception in their hearts. Moreover, this is also actually more in conformity with the tender spirit of Jesus Christ and with brotherly love, which is the Christian's highest commandment.

If there is anything wrong with this type of baptismal act, it is that their baptism is commonly not a sacrament of unity and brotherly fellowship with all believers and God-fearing people but rather a sacrament of separation and partisan spirit. Nevertheless, friendly and affectionate persuasion will accomplish and avail more against this than harsh methods or punishment. I also want to appeal to Your Excellency, gracious count, to spare these poor people from banishment, as they are not accused of any crime. This would please the dear God, and be in conformity with the benevolent love and mildness of a wise

The Castle of Buedingen

Christian sovereign. Besides which, banishment or exile is a type of punishment which was never practiced or permitted by God our Lord in His most holy Law, nor was it ever used by the ancient saints, wise men, God-fearing sovereigns, judges, or kings mentioned in the Holy Scriptures. It was, however, used by some godless people, an example of which is the seventh chapter of Amos, verses twelve and thirteen. It is least of all used against people who can be accused of no crime.

I ask, finally, that Your Excellency, the gracious count, might be so kind as to excuse me from the said hearing, and receive not ungraciously my sincerely intended letter. I remain, with cordial recommendation in the eternal mercy of God, that He may powerfully govern Your Grace's heart to the good of all,

	Your Excellency, the gracious count's,
Büdingen,	loyal and humble servant,
November 25, 1712.	Samuel König.[17]

Count Charles August to Inspector König

To Inspector König.
Charles August, Count, etc.
Our etc.
Reverend, Well-learnéd, Dear, Devout and Loyal [Sir]:

Your letter of yesterday's date has been delivered. We have noticed therein what you well-meaningly wish to remind us of concerning our policy toward those persons that have been rebaptized. Our intention is merely directed to the end that the spoiled cravings of the spirit, which always desire something new, be quieted and corrected. We can in this way lead sick souls nearer to God. For this reason, we have approved of the calling of a meeting of the consistory to consider sufficient means for their correction, as well as to apply them. We give thereby the assurance that the benevolent way of governing has always been the most pleasant to us.

Notwithstanding this, the leading astray has become too great. Nothing is availed through continued connivance, and the work has to be begun sometime. The good souls are to be exhorted in love to guard themselves from evil, as well as to bear in mind carefully that through their conduct (which is not according to Christ's commandments) neither should annoyance be caused, which we otherwise

gladly bear for the sake of the teachings and the name of Christ, nor outward unrest among my native-born subjects. Duty and natural gratefulness demand this from them. There will be n ore to say about this upon your arrival. We remain,
[Marienborn], November 26, 1712.   [Charles August][18]

Consistory Recommends Mercy

The report of the consistorial meeting, owing to the influence of König and others, recommended that no severe action be taken against the Brethren.

In the presence of the illustrious sirs (Councilor Metting, Inspector König, Assessor Janovy, Pastor Diehl from Eckartshausen, Pastor Rosa from Düdelsheim, and myself, Secretary Geyer) was related that which had taken place in connection with the baptized, that they were summoned here on that account; and that in which our most gracious lord, His Grace, had ordered them to be instructed.
Whereupon the following has been approved:
(1) that our most gracious lord, His Grace, is to be requested humbly that the revocation of protection be as yet deferred, so that the hearts of the zealots might not be moved to think that they were being persecuted for the sake of Jesus' name. Moreover, this conforms with Gamaliel's attitude. This baptism is in itself no more objectionable than infant baptism. It is recommended that each pastor, as the occasion presents itself, explain that to his congregation, so that it will not seem so strange to the subjects in the future. In this way, the most gracious lord, His Grace, may not have to fear further untoward action in this regard on the part of his subjects. Otherwise concerning rebaptism such Anabaptists are tolerated in many places. It is not now such a novelty as it used to be.
Further was approved:
(2) that they should be told, with forbearance, what we thought of their baptism—what reasons they may have had to adopt such, and, however, also explain what division results therefrom and to what degree such division is to be condemned because of its effect. They are also to be admonished not to lay too much emphasis on baptism but, to the contrary, to show all others most brotherly friendship, because through these heresies the love in many hearts has grown cold.

And further, [the consistory]
(3) wishes to explain to them that they have been accepted under the protection and have been maintained with the condition that they not cause the gracious lord, His Grace, inconvenience. They had promised this but up to now it has not been observed, etc. Whereupon, the above-named baptized persons who were present at the baptismal act recently, and were themselves rebaptized, were summoned by name and were spoken to.

Marienborn, December 1, 1712.[19]

The Fourth Baptism

A year and a half went by before the fourth and last baptism was reported in Marienborn. The fact that two of the baptized, Peter Becker and his wife, were subjects of the count rather than settlers, as had been those previously baptized, caused considerable excitement. John Naas carried out the baptism in the presence of several witnesses.

Fourth Baptism Reported

Honorable . . . Sir Councilors:

I should obediently report to the reverend, honorable, and dread [sirs] that recently the local Anabaptists baptized three persons in the water here, near the Düdelsheim woods. The one was [Gottfried] Neumann from Himbach, the others, however, Peter Becker and his wife, subjects from Düdelsheim. There was caused a great scandal among the community, and there are those who are willing to level a complaint. I have felt impelled to report this obediently to the reverend, honorable, and dread [sirs]. I remain with due respect, reverend, honorable, and dread [sirs],

Düdelsheim,	your humble and obedient servant
May 15, 1714.	John Louis Wiszkemann.[20]

More Information Requested

To the Deputy Administrator Wiszkemann.

The gracious lord, His Grace, was humbly informed of your report of the fifteenth of this month concerning some persons who baptized and were baptized in the Düdelsheim area in violation of

the lord's prohibition. Therefore the most gracious lord has most graciously ordered that you should at once inform yourself exactly who the baptizers were, as well as the baptized and those found present at this act. You are to send in a report about this. Peter Becker and his wife, however, are to be ordered to appear at this chancery tomorrow. We remain etc.,
Marienborn, May 15, 1714.   [Ysenburg councilors][21]

Participants Named

Honorable . . . Sir Councilors:

In response to the order of the honorable and dread councilors, I most obediently report that [John] Naas, here, performed the baptismal act upon Peter Becker and his wife. Those present were John Henry Traut, the sackmaker; John Jacob Koch; Daniel Ritter and his wife; John Henry Holzapfel and his wife, and the Benz woman, all residents here.

I remain herewith your honorable and dread sirs'
Düdelsheim,   humble and obedient servant
May 16, 1714.   John Louis Wiszkemann.[22]

Expulsion Ordered

The harsh order given below was drafted by the councilors, and demanded the immediate expulsion of all concerned. However, the count held up the order and arranged for another hearing by the clergy and his officials.

Order to the Deputy Administrator Wiszkemann.

The gracious lord, His Grace, has been again informed to his great displeasure from your report that some [persons] in this county have baptized and been baptized in the presence of others, against the lord's issued prohibition. Great disorder arises through this, and such persons do not live up to their promise to live quietly and in seclusion. The deputy administrator is herewith ordered: to summon the baptizer Naas before him, and to tell the former that he has to leave the county for ever within forty-eight hours; to order the foreign settlers, who were present at the baptism, and others who adhere to the same and are of the same opinion, to betake themselves from the county within eight days, and to stay away for ever; to announce to the resident subjects who attended the baptism, that they should refrain from similar undertakings in the future, and conduct themselves peaceably, failing in which they will suffer the same penalties as the others. After the above-mentioned time has elapsed, you are to proceed to carry out this order with the usual means of enforcement, if necessary, without further requests for instructions, and report about it. [Marienborn], May 16, 1714. [Ysenburg councilors][23]

Neumann Questioned

Another of the baptized, Gottfried Neumann, was questioned about the baptismal act.

In response to the chancery order of yesterday's date concerning the settler Neumann from Bergheim, who was recently baptized at Düdelsheim, this serves as the required report that the above-mentioned appeared today, upon a previous summons. He gave the following information:

(1) John Naas, resident of Düdelsheim, had baptized him;

(2) those present were Daniel Ritter from this place, also the two sackmakers there, Peter Schilpert, a linen weaver, John Henry [Holzapfel], a shoemaker, and still others, whose names he did not know;

(3) the place where he was baptized is behind the woods in the brook there [Düdelsheim];

(4) he is ready to betake himself from here; however, he hopes that the gracious lord will mercifully grant him some time in addition, if it is not possible to leave strictly within the eight-day period. He was permitted to remain according to the above order, until notified to the contrary.

Himbach, May 17, 1714. [Quans][24]

NEUMANN'S REACTION

Gottfried Neumann, who was baptized along with Peter Becker, was a former Lutheran theologian from Leipzig and later a teacher at Halle, who went to the Marienborn area when he became a separatist. After a period of searching he was attracted to the Brethren who were meeting there, and was baptized. He described this in a letter to the Pietist leader, August Hermann Francke of Halle, on March 18, 1719. Neumann was the first in the area to be converted to the new Inspirationist movement. He describes this and his leaving of the Brethren in his letter and also in a printed testimony. He eventually joined the renewed Moravian church under Count Zinzendorf and became one of their outstanding hymn-writers.[25]

Gottfried Neumann to August H. Francke

Most Honorable, Most Esteemed Professor:

. . .

At this time a special awakening arose in the hearts of many among the friends in this land, who did not wish to remain longer in such division and indifference. They therefore began to unite in prayer and edify one another from the holy Word. They were called New Baptists because they practiced, among other well-seeming ordinances, baptism of adults by immersion. They were mostly single-minded and good souls. They displayed at first a great earnestness and zeal in their behavior and conduct, through which many were moved and were drawn into their circle. Finally, they were also able to affect me through their affectionate and humble manner, and through their strong "magic," they induced me to be baptized.

I can, however, hardly describe to you, dear sir, with what fear and darkness my soul was filled and surrounded, when these people led me to their baptism. I would have turned back along the way, if I had followed the resisting impulse of God. And what floods of temptations came over me inwardly and outwardly after this baptism! I believed that I would have sunk and perished therein if the mercy of my God had not sustained me and led me through. These temptations made me call out and cry unto the Lord, who inclined toward me in mercy and protected my soul from their sectarian spirit. He later revealed this to me and gave me courage and faith to witness earnestly against their false righteousness and sectarianism which showed themselves more and more during the short time that I associated with these people. I also influenced many others to change their minds.

Hardly was half a year gone when this last unusual awakening through the Inspiration broke to the surface in this land (which beginning is dealt with in the *Experience-filled Testimonies* [*Erfahrungsvolle Zeugnisse*], published in 1715. I was the first at this awakening to see these wonderful workings and movements in Hanau, and at the same time received a strong indwelling of the spirits. . . . Finally after two days of struggle and deliberation (of which there is a printed testimony) I was drawn into these things through special occurrences, and accepted and confessed the matter as divine. I have spent almost four and one-half years in this highly unfortunate economy and tested and learned to know various actions of the Spirit and the powers. . . .

Ronneburg,   Your humble and obliging servant
March 18, 1719.   Gottfried Neumann.[26]

Neumann's Statement

Various Experience-filled Testimonies: Gottfried Neumann.

. . . A year had now gone by since the love of God had gripped me anew, and I had to bemoan sincerely the backsliding on the part of myself and others. As at that time a new earnestness and zeal was awakened in my soul, I searched with great longing for fellowship with brethren with whom I could unite in common prayer and love. As is well known, among the separatist friends in this county [Marienborn] everything was in complete division and little single-mindedness was found among them. I could not achieve my aim there. However, I happened once to visit a meeting of the so-called New Baptists who had come together in a fellowship for just the same reason. I saw that they strove to edify one another, which moved me and caused a closer association and fellowship with these people.

Although others had made them very suspect to me because of their sectarian spirit, I had to trust them in the hope that through persevering, united prayer and struggle, all impurities would be taken away by and by, and love would be brought more pure and complete to the fore. To this end I also purposed to do all I could to banish the differences which had come between the Baptists and the other separatist friends which made a wall of division between them, and to erect a harmonious union in love. However, I found later to my great sorrow that this split and division among the children of one Father was hardly possible to be healed, and that human efforts were of no avail if the Lord did not himself make a new creation through His Spirit.

I saw clearly enough that, on the one hand, there was great decay and that most involved themselves again in the things of the world and strove for the comforts of the flesh; on the other hand, I also perceived that sectarianism and pharisaism tried to lay hold of the hearts and thereby hinder the blessing and growth in love. On this point I had all I could do to prevent my being swept along in the same pharisaical sectarian spirit which has a good outward appearance. Thus I lived some time with continual sighing, pressed under a heavy burden until finally all my strength expired. . . .[27] [He then met the Inspirationists, who tried to convince him to join them.]

I tried nevertheless, then, to justify myself somewhat, and to defend the Baptists in this or that point, although I already knew that they were not free from the accusation of sectarianism. As I was then talking about this with another brother who traveled with the Potts, the eldest [brother], John Tobias Pott, was seized with a strong convulsion and utterance about the Baptists and especially about those who called themselves the leaders and teachers among them. I was so completely overwhelmed and convinced by this that I had to clap my hand over my mouth. I had nothing further to criticize, because all this, which was delivered with great emphasis and spiritual power, had lain dormant within me for a long time. It was now completely revealed and discovered at one blow. . . .[28]

EXPULSION OF THE BRETHREN

The baptism of Peter Becker (1687-1758), his wife, and others, who were subjects of the count, whereas those baptized previously had only been settlers, was the occasion for harsher measures. More influential in the change of policy, however, was the rise of the Inspirationists. In their dramatic prophecies, they denounced the wickedness of the authorities. It is understandable that this kind of religious expression created more excitement than that of the Brethren. The latter were quiet and well-behaved, and were considered by the authorities to be troublesome only because of their belief in the necessity of baptism by immersion.

Lists of those professing the Brethren faith were drawn up by the officials. Adherents were summoned before the government authorities, who gave them two alternatives: if they refused to confine their religious expression to devotions in their homes, then they must leave.

Düdelsheim Anabaptists Listed

List of the Anabaptists in the Düdelsheim district.
Düdelsheim, May 18, 1714.

Residents of Düdelsheim:
  Balthasar Traut
  John Henry Traut
  Daniel Ritter and his wife
  Julian Stumpf
  John Kring and his wife
  John Naas and his wife
  Peter Schilpert
  Henry Holzapfel and his wife
  Jacob Koch
  Anna Marie, a widow
Subjects who were baptized:
  John Adam Schneider and his wife
  Peter Becker, his wife, and his wife's sister
  John Henry Diehl's wife
Residents of Rohrbach:
  John Schmidt
  Barbara, a single person[29]

Brethren Listed

List of Our Names.
  John Naas, his wife, with five children.
  Jacob Preisz, his wife and son.
  John Henry Traut, two sons, one daughter, and son-in-law.
  Julian Stumpf with three children.
  John Keim, his wife, and two children.
  John George Schmidt, his wife and six children.
  John Jacob Koch, and John George Koch.
  Daniel Ritter and his wife.
  Peter Becker and his wife.[30]

Eckartshausen Brethren Summoned

Honorable . . . Sir Councilors:
  In response to the count's chancery order received under today's

date, I have ordered all of the so-called Baptists residing in the district of Eckartshausen, namely:

> John Jacob Preisz ⎫
> John Preisz ⎬ of Himbach
>
> Michael Wagner ⎫
> John George Bauer ⎬ of Bergheim

and the two recently baptized, [Gottfried] Neumann and ——— Höcker, to appear day after tomorrow, Thursday, at eight o'clock in the morning at the count's consistory at Marienborn. At the same time, I requested Pastor Diehl to come to the same place on the above-mentioned day and hour. I herewith obediently report this and remain in the meantime, with due respect,

Himbach,
May 22, 1714.

reverend, honorable, also most dread sirs,
your loyal and obedient servant
A. Quans.[31]

Names of Marienborn Brethren Submitted by the Group
(See page 183)

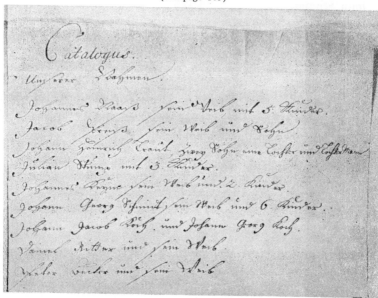

Brethren Activity Forbidden

To Deputy Administrator Wiszkemann at Düdelsheim.
Etc. etc.

The honorable and gracious lord has had made clear and had explained in all earnestness the following to all of the so-called Baptists who reside in this county, when they appeared here today upon summons: His Grace will respect their full freedom of conscience in the carrying out of their devotions in private meetings in their homes in a quiet way, and will otherwise leave them in peace just as other subjects and those taken under protection. He will, therefore, tolerate their further stay in this county on this condition. However, he positively cannot permit the Baptists to organize a new sect or church congregation and to presume or dare to practice their faith publicly. This is just as little permitted as baptism or rebaptism; it is in fact absolutely forbidden. This with the addition that in case they do not intend to conform to these requirements, it would be best for them to betake themselves out of this territory to avoid further annoyance, etc.

We have wanted to give you, herewith, this report so that you will pay close attention to these Baptists. If they do not conform to the above-mentioned order of his lordship, you are to report it here immediately and await further instructions on the matter. Should they, however, prefer to leave the county, you are to administer speedy and impartial justice, if they have legitimate claims upon the subjects for conversion into cash.

We remain herewith,

Marienborn, May 24, 1714.　　　　　　[Ysenburg councilors][32]

Brethren Decide to Leave

Honorable . . . Sir Councilors:

Upon receiving the most gracious order of the most and right honorable, most gracious count and lord, I have announced to the strangers who have adhered to the Inspirationists at Rohrbach and who have frequented their gatherings (except for Stäb, who is absent) that they must remain quiet or leave the territory within a week. It seems, however, that they will not submit to keeping quiet. In the meantime I ordered the village mayor to watch them and keep me informed of everything.

The Baptists have decided to leave, and the subjects who accepted their belief intend to do so also. However, as they cannot arrange their affairs so quickly, and the weather is too bad to travel in, they have asked if His Grace would graciously permit them to remain until the trade fair, allowing them to live according to their consciences and to continue their meetings until then.

Otherwise, they humbly express their gratitude for the merciful protection enjoyed up to the present, and wish His Grace God's mercy and His mild paternal blessings. I therefore obediently request further orders, reverend, honorable and dread sirs, and remain,

Düdelsheim,   your most humble and obedient servant
March 12, 1715.   J. L. Wiszkemann.[33]

Charles August Demands Compliance

[To Deputy Administrator Wiszkemann]

It has come to our attention that much disorder has been caused by strangers who sojourn in our land without our permission, as well as by settlers. We therefore hereby order our deputy administrator Wiszkemann in Düdelsheim to make emphatically clear to those strangers as well as to the so-called Inspirationists who were previously accepted as settlers, that they are to betake themselves out of the territory because of the terrible noise and disorder which they have no intention of stopping. He should have the other settlers appear before him, who are here in the territory with permission, under the condition that they conduct themselves very quietly without having a following or forming a church fellowship. He should confront them with their recent conduct which is not according to their promise and the conditions under which they were accepted into the territory.

At the same time, he should explain to them that if they have no intention to live in the future as mentioned above—to conduct themselves in that way, obeying the regulations of the county, especially concerning infant baptism, funerals, and marriages, and serving God in quiet without great excitement and noise—and to subject themselves to the above-mentioned regulation, protection will be denied to them. Otherwise, they would have to leave the territory within two months, during which time they are to refrain from all private meetings.

Those, however, who wish to stay in the territory under the above-mentioned conditions should perform statute-labor or give the money equivalent just as the other subjects, in addition to their fees for protection and settling, in return for which they are to enjoy the same benefits in common which the other subjects enjoy.

Marienborn, March 22, 1715.   Charles August of Ysenburg.[34]

Passport Issued to Brethren

Faced with the decision of abandoning their faith or losing their place of refuge, the Marienborn Brethren chose to migrate. The passport issued to them stated that the government considered them to be of irreproachable character, except for their Anabaptist views. It recommended that all assistance be given to them.

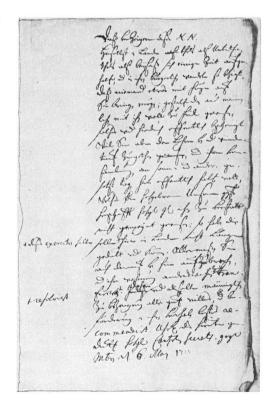

A Draft of the Passport for the Marienborn Brethren

The bearers of this, ——————————, have resided in this territory for some time, some as subjects, and some as settlers. They have so conducted themselves in their civil lives that no one can reasonably bring anything against them. As everyone has been completely satisfied with them, this is hereby publicly certified. They have taken up the teachings of Anabaptism, and desire to hold their gatherings here publicly on Sundays and other specified days, which the honorable count, our gracious lord, had not intended to permit. Because of this religious activity it has not been possible to tolerate them longer in this territory. As they are resolved to leave here and transfer their residence elsewhere, we therefore warmly recommend to everyone to aid them in their undertaking as evidence of our good will.

Certified below by the government official of our most gracious count.

Dated Marienborn, May 6, 1715.[35]

Becker Given Certificate

Official records contain details on the sale of land and the dates of leaving. An example of this is the following item concerning Peter Becker.

Büdingen Diary.
June 27, 1715.

Peter Becker of Düdelsheim, who desires to leave this county, is granted a certificate of discharge [*Ledigschein*] in the usual form, without cost, under the date of the twenty-fourth of this month.[36]

THE LOWER RHINE AREA

In addition to Marienborn and Wittgenstein, there was a third island of toleration in the Germanies—the city of Krefeld. For hundreds of years an insignificant town, it was the location of the settling in the seventeenth century of numerous Mennonites driven from their old homes, who introduced the textile industry and made Krefeld one of the most prosperous commercial cities of Germany in the following century. From 1600 to 1702 it was ruled by the Dutch House of Orange, which maintained a policy of toleration. Under the Prussian rulers

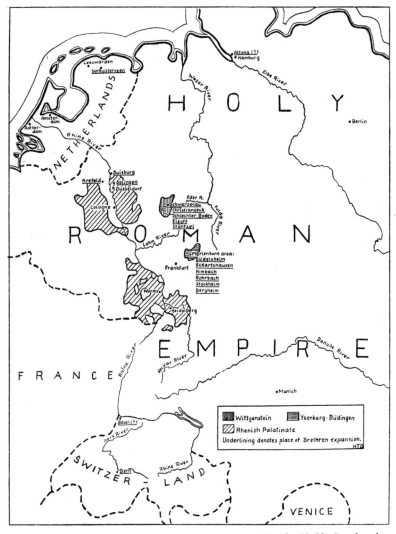

Map by Hedda Durnbaugh

Brethren Expansion in Western Europe

after 1702 the Mennonites enjoyed virtual equality with the Reformed church.

Religious refugees from all over the Holy Roman Empire flocked to the city in the Rhine valley northwest of Düsseldorf. It was from here that the thirteen Mennonite-Quaker families in 1683 left for Pennsylvania, where they founded Germantown near Philadelphia. Hochmann had visited Krefeld as early as 1705. Whether the Marienborn Brethren migrated to Krefeld because of this connection is unknown. They undoubtedly knew, however, that they would find tolerance there because of their similarities with the Mennonites, who received them cordially.

The Berg area across the Rhine from Krefeld was also a center of radical Pietistic activity. Hochmann's message there met with great response. When the Brethren from Krefeld visited the hilly district in their missionary zeal, they found a field white for harvest. Solingen, where the world-famous steel was made, was the scene of greatest activity.

JOHN LOBACH

Perhaps the outstanding figure here was John Lobach (1683-1750), who has left a record of his youth and the fierce struggle within himself culminating in a Pietistic conversion. Typical is the almost morbid sense of sin about relatively trivial matters, reminiscent of St. Augustine in his *Confessions.* Part of his autobiographical writing is here included, as a significant description of a conversion to Pietism.[37]

Excerpts From Lobach's Autobiography

A New Sign of the Divine Miracle of Love of this Time . . .

. . . I was born on June 11, 1683. My father begot me with sinful seed and my mother conceived and gave birth in sin. In my third year of age, I had a fear of hell, with which, without doubt, my parents had threatened me, when the wicked seed of the serpent moved in me. Once this was so strong in me that I wanted to shoot to death a wagoner who was loading the bread baskets. As this was impossible, I shrieked and screamed and pretended to be sick out of sheer wickedness. Then they tried to free me from this fear, in that they said that there was no hell in the place where we were going to move. I could not believe this at all, however.

My mother taught me to pray several little prayers from the manual, and to repeat these regularly mornings and evenings. If this was neglected once, then I would pray my little prayer twice. If I did not say my hymn-prayerlet, then the fear of hell was with me. From the sixth year of my life on, my parents sent me to the Latin school until my thirteenth year, on the advice of good friends. In this time I learned so much Latin that I could speak it well. However, the arrogance that grew within me over this is indescribable, nor can the godlessness which the youth in school displayed well be described.

Although one can learn something from Latin, Greek, and Hebrew (which are in themselves very good), the fear of God is little considered in the learning of these languages, and is even forgotten. On the contrary one learns pride most of all. When a youth learns a little Latin, then he must wear a fashionable coat when he walks in the streets or goes to school or church. If he goes on further to the higher schools [universities], then he must strap a sword at his side. With this, he can carry on with the others all kinds of mischief which they are taught by the devil—dueling and fighting, yes, even murder, of which there are more than enough examples.

For my part, I admit that when I think of the tricks and sins which I committed at school with my fellow students I have to marvel at the great patience and forbearance of God that He does not cause the schools to sink into the depths. O God, what sins, scandals, and vices occur in the world! They are not only committed by the young people in these schools, but even seem to be concentrated there! In the Latin school I was also to learn the Lutheran catechism. When, however, our Reformed pastor realized that, he gave me (in great blindness) the advice that I should come to him every Saturday, which I then did. He taught me to dispute against the Lutherans, and gave me a booklet which was anti-Lutheran.

Is it not a ground for bewailing and complaining that people dispute and quarrel about which is the best church? Each person considers that denomination to be the best into which he was born. Later I often wished that the Reformed pastor had taught me to fight against the sins which were in me and in my body—against the lust of the flesh, lust of the eyes, and the pride of life. But unfortunately, these three "daughters" are so well liked and esteemed by all men in all churches that no one cares to quarrel with them, to conduct a war or even to argue against them. They are left in peace, and grow in the esteem of most people.

As at that time I understood Latin rather well and otherwise conducted myself according to the fashion of the world, many people advised that I study and become a preacher. I also believe that, if my father had not lacked money at that time, he would gladly have purchased with money the gift of preaching (as is practiced today) for me. It is only natural of people that they wish their children to achieve offices and high honors. If someone can perform in the pulpit with the appearance of piety, and deliver a memorized oration or sermon, then everyone thinks that his is the voice and power of God. It is actually nothing else than empty and proud words, because there is nothing in it (2 Peter 2).

From the thirteenth year on, my father transferred me from the Latin to the French school. After I had studied French for half a year, God visited me with an illness. This caused me to lie for about five or six weeks in a daze, completely without reactions. I felt little, even no thoughts at all, about my soul. Those who visited me did not ask me about it, either. Oh, miserable state in which I lay! Oh, blindness and darkness in which I was at that time! I did not know what I was doing. I lay imprisoned by the devil. I was dead to the good. My free will utterly hated God's judgments. How would I have fared if I had then left this world, and should have stood before the Judge at that day (before whom old and young are revealed and must receive their sentences according to how they had behaved during their lives—whether good or bad)?

But God had patience with me. He helped me to recover, and restored my health to me. However, here the wicked proverb proved to be true: "When the sick person recovers he is worse than before." My life and conduct were simply wicked, vain, and perverse from my youth, and one sinful act followed another. My father's birch drove me to be good, but I did this against my will only because of fear—to avoid punishment. My parents made me read the gospel on Sunday, not because of love for it, but to keep up appearances. Often I turned two pages at once without being noticed, just so I could finish quickly, although I had great fears about this in my conscience. I could indeed conceal my trick from my parents, but a judgment voice of God spoke to me in my heart that "all is revealed and discovered before my eye." However, I did not obey this voice, but rather piled the mountain of sins higher and higher.

After this, I had to learn my father's trade. As we were together once in our workshop, we spoke with each other about the rebirth—that without this no one could enter the Kingdom of God. Then one asked the other, where, actually, could such a reborn person be found. We decided upon the preachers. When we considered, however, their lives and conduct, yes, even their sermons, we concluded that they were certainly as much minded after things of the flesh as we and other people were.

Then my father said that he remembered a preacher who had always spoken about rebirth and renewal, and showed the people life as it came from God, such as he had otherwise never heard preached. At this time, we firmly resolved to read the Bible in the future, and began to study the Bible and to pray in the morning before we started work. . . .

We also attended church more regularly and paid more attention than previously. However, we heard neither counsel nor answer from the watchmen who were supposed to and wanted to watch out for souls. They bothered little about damage to our souls. Rather, they were unexperienced in the true ways of God. In addition they were quite slow, lazy and silent on discipline, as Isaiah also said about his time (56:10, 11), "They are all dumb dogs; they cannot bark, dreaming, lying down, loving to slumber. The dogs have a mighty appetite; they never have enough. The shepherds also have no understanding; they have all turned to their own way, each one to his own gain, one and all." May the almighty God convert them and us!

I was zealous in reading the Bible at first, but before I came to the end, I again became careless, indolent, and lazy. My father died in 1702 because of an unexplained accident in a far-off place [see page 276]. This caused great grief and mourning for my mother and me. In the meantime, the audacity of my old Adam gathered enough steam to erupt. Up to this time I had never been in taverns or the inns with godless company. Now I gradually joined in with sinners. They enticed me and I freely followed them. I made my mother very unhappy, however, when I went out on Sunday and did not come back until very late at night, or not at all. The devil and my companions had brought me so far that at that time I did not consider it a sin.

At that time most people, yes, I daresay, all, praised me and said only good things about me. But the judging voice of my God told me the contrary, and continually accused me and frightened me. I often went with this company to court the girls, as is the heathen custom in this land which the devil introduced. In the evenings, or at night, I often went home alone, and had at that time many strange thoughts, which frightened me in the extreme. Among other things, I often thought what it would be like if I married and begot children, and one or more of them would not be saved, etc. This caused an indescribable fear.

I often worried about myself—whether I was really chosen by God as a receptacle of His grace. I then resolved to convert myself to God, and to improve my life. But then this thought came to me: Why do you need to be more devout than others? If you are chosen by God for eternal life, then you cannot be lost. If you are not chosen, then do not trouble yourself with trying to lead a better life. You are and will remain lost and damned.

Often I wished: "Oh, if I just had never been born!" I spoke to God: "Why did you not let me die in my mother's womb, or in my childhood, when I had not sinned so much? Oh, woe is me," I also thought to myself. "Oh, if I had only been an animal, then after death everything would be over. But now I must be rejected by God for ever and ever because of my sins, and tormented by devils in the eternal unquenching fire." Such thoughts made me so afraid that I often could not go to sleep because of them.

Often when I came home from the inns, and lay down in bed, the cursing and swearing, the vile and useless words came to my ears, and rang so loudly that I could not go to sleep because of them. Then I also thought: "If God now takes me from the world, then hell would be revealed in me, and I would be given to the loathsome devils." I then remained in the power of the spirits of hell in indescribable fear. Yes, they swarmed around me like bees. However, I kept all this to myself in quiet. Also I had no one to whom I dared to reveal my heart's innermost thoughts. . . .

Further, my God frightened me at night with dreams of such nature that I could not forget them the next day. However, I did not yet turn steadfastly to God, but rather went according to the custom of the world and served vanity, but often with great discontent. The more I sought the world, the more God opposed me with misfortune, loss, and calamity. I experienced only a curse with my trade instead of a blessing, so that the work often turned out badly and was in vain. I also had to run continually after the merchants and my difficult trade. The more I worked, the more I got into debt. In sum, I experienced that everything is cursed with man, as long as he does not live according to the commandments of God (Deuteronomy 27). Thus, my poverty and misfortune at work were a serviceable means for my conversion.

Previously, I had clothed myself above my station, as the world does, though we had debts in many places. Rather than let my poverty become known, however, I dressed myself even better, to retain my reputation and other advantages.

Despite this God the Almighty still pursued me to capture my soul. I finally became tired and bored with further efforts in things of the world, and of running after them. Only then did I turn to God. I prayed to Him, and often spoke to Him in my heart: "Lord, I see that all racing and running after the world and earthly things is not blessed because of my sins. Oh, Lord, if only it were not too late for my conversion. Oh, I fear that it is too late for me. The door of grace is closed for me, because I often sinned wantonly and against my better knowledge."

This doubt was with me for some time, and I had little courage to approach God. I had committed very many sins against the Holy Majesty. Once, as I was alone in the garden, and was engrossed in these doubts and timid thoughts, behold, God spoke through His Spirit to me in these words: "If a man parts from his wife, and she leaves him and takes another husband, he may take her again! You, however, have sinned with many lovers, but come again to me, saith the Lord." As I considered these words in my heart, I spoke, "Oh, Lord, what am I, and my house! You could well expel me with your foot of revenge as I have indeed sinned with many lovers."

Hereupon, it was assured me, however, that He does not wish the death of sinners, but rather that they turn to Him and live. In this was my heart touched by the Word of the loving God, that I also believed that Jesus Christ was a Savior of all men, but especially of those who believe in Him. Here fell at once the false, perverse, and godless assumption which I had previously made about the choice of grace—namely, that God in His wisdom in eternity chose only some for eternal life, but let most men remain in their sins, and passed them by with His grace so that they were created for eternal damnation.

I was emphatically instructed and strengthened by God through His Word against this, my absurd and satanic doctrine. Afterwards, my heart was much pierced and smitten by the arrow of the love of God, when I thought about my sins and the transgression of God's commandments. Once during the church Mass, I went to the solitude of our garden. As I had the late Neander's hymnal with me, I opened it, and found the hymn "So Must I Then Endure Still More" [*So soll ich denn noch mehr ausstehen*]. I especially noted therein the second, third, and fourth verses. I had to weep bitterly over these and could not help pouring out my heart before God with a loud voice.

I began to confess with a sorrowful heart all the sins which I had ever committed. My God also held the Ten Commandments before the eyes of my spirit as a clear and bright mirror. I was earnestly convinced that I had transgressed against all of these commandments, and therefore still remained under the curse. Even though this had not happened in a manner punishable by the courts of the world, I indeed experienced at this time the spirituality of the law and its severity. Such things at which the world would only laugh awakened in me the greatest sorrow. For example, that I, especially while attending school, occasionally had stealthily stolen fruit from my neighbor's trees for pleasure. . . .

I experienced then finally a living solace and assurance in my soul that if I now began a new life and put away the works of darkness, Jesus would cleanse me from all sins with His precious blood with which He had purchased me as His own. He would grant me the Holy Spirit to assure me of the inheritance of the saints. Then, I surrendered myself to Jehovah, and promised to serve Him from then on. I also prayed earnestly that he would powerfully lead me, so that I might follow Him with pleasure and joy. Whereupon, it seemed to me then at first, the path was very easy that I had allotted myself. I thought that if I then only led a quiet, devout life, people, when they saw this, would praise it and would also turn to the Lord.

However, I soon experienced the opposite—namely, that he who turns from wicked men is the prey of everyone. But this had to happen so that I would avoid the world and its company more and more, and seek quiet solitude. . . . I therefore went on with a fearful and sorrowful spirit for about three years. I could not weep about [and repent of] my great and various sins which I had committed before the Holy Majesty of God. . . .

As I now was laid low in this condition [of illness] but remained patient, not only the rough worldlings but also my own friends opposed me. They first said this and then that about me. One said that the devil had caught me in his temptations. The other shook his head, and said, "If he is devout, why does such a thing happen to him?" Several said that I was insane, and had lost my mind. Still others advised my mother to take away my books, for I brooded too much and confused myself therein. She should take care that I was not left to myself, otherwise I might inflict injury upon myself. I, however, thanked my Abba [Father] that He did not let me be tempted beyond my strength. . . .

I lay ill for over half a year. During this time I was considered worthy to observe heavenly things continually. I heard the voice of the Almighty speak like heavy thunder and the roaring of much water. I was so encouraged thereby to watch over my soul that I could sleep neither day nor night. Yes, I was made a watchman and seer for the present-day Christianity. I saw its abominations and horrible murders, its apostasy, and saw how Christianity—a devout city—began to become a harlot. Yes, it became a treacherous anti-Christian harlot who imprinted her marks on the great and the small, the rich and the poor, and has seduced the kings to strife and ruinous war with her golden Babylonian chalice. Oh, what a lamentation one wants to sing and profess about you! Christianity, you fallen harlot! Oh, how miserably it will befall you, when the Lord will visit you because of all of your wickedness and misdeeds!   The End.

J. L. [John Lobach][38]

HOLDING OF CONVENTICLES

Lobach's Life Described

The description of John Lobach's life is continued in a statement written by a close friend. His narrative begins with Lobach's experiences with the local Reformed clergy after his Pietistic conversion.

Note. What here follows about the late John Lobach has been

composed by one of his intimate friends and near relatives after his death. [Noted by William Weck.]

They loyal young champion, J. L. [John Lobach], who described above his own first years of awakening, progressed in the grace of God, and became a shining light, as it were, of the local congregation. This was even admitted by the preacher at that time, Mr. Hackmann. It happened, through God's wise providence, that Lobach and some of his friends had to endure all kinds of mockery because of their progress and confirmation in Christianity. The preachers, especially the above-named Hackmann, became their persecutors. The latter had at first joined with them and had even defended them publicly from the pulpit.

When, however, the rumor grew loud in the surrounding territory that the above-mentioned preacher wanted to become one of them, and preached pietistically, two preachers (presumably sent as spies) came unexpectedly to church one Sunday. They seated themselves exactly opposite from Preacher H[ackmann]. When he saw them, he permitted himself to be seized by the fear of men, and diverted from the path of truth. He now again swung to the other extreme, and began to criticize that which he had previously found good. From that time on, he was cold toward J. L. and the others, and flared out at them with coarse, worldly zeal. This occurrence he recognized, lamented, and repented of in his last years of life. He also then reconciled himself in love with J. L. Because of this, the special details of his persecution will not be mentioned here. Also the awakened ones at that time might not, perhaps, have remained within the bounds of deserving respect toward the preachers. They may have attacked the outer degenerated church system too violently.

In the meantime, although the said J. L. had recovered somewhat from his lengthy physical illness and melancholy, he was not yet able to carry on his usual trade. He therefore occupied himself with teaching children. He held a school for children at the woods [*zum Busche*] and I do not know where else. He not only conscientiously taught the children the usual subjects, but also daily admonished them to be good, and instructed them in the Christian doctrines. I still recall that he did this especially among the children of his relatives and sisters. This was possible because God gave him at that time great energy, courage, earnestness, and loyalty. He had a special talent in speaking and praying. He indeed retained these gifts for many years, and was occupied in winning souls for the Lord Jesus, and visiting the sick and the poor. He spread his good seeds everywhere, and went about doing good.

He must have been a blessing for many souls then, because he and his friends held meetings with great earnestness and zeal on Sundays, not only in Wald, but also now and then on farms, in Solingen, and here in the parish. Usually a large number of people came together, among whom were many eager and awakened souls. They were abused, oppressed, and hated by the preachers and other children of the world, the more so as some of them had separated themselves from the organized church, because of the bad behavior of the preachers.

In the meantime there came a witness of truth, Ernest Christopher Hochmann von Hochenau, who was hated by the world, but much loved by God. He was a nobleman, both outwardly and inwardly, and an ardent lover of God and his neighbor—a faithful solicitor for the bridegroom Jesus Christ. The latter taught from time to time with great power and admonished the people to repent. Many were touched and converted through this, and occasionally miraculous things happened with this dear man. It would take too long to relate them fully here. This impartial friend of God was especially envied by the learnéd men, and was called, as was customary, perverse and a false teacher. Thus disgrace and persecution were increased because of this for the souls who were awakened and inclined toward the good.[39]

John Lobach to William Hoffmann

A collection of the letters of John Lobach was made after his death and circulated among Pietist groups. One of the first in the collection is his letter to William Hoffmann, a Pietist leader who is best known for his influence in awakening Gerhard Tersteegen, the famed German Reformed mystic and hymn-writer. Lobach's letter provides a vivid description of the conventicles and the reaction of the clergy.

Dearly Beloved Brother W[illiam] Hoffmann:

After Brother Baus and I had returned from Mühlheim and told our fellow members about your love, faith, and meetings, we gathered in the name of Immanuel on the next Saturday, September 13, in Solingen at the *Kirchhof,* the home of the widow Katterberg, whose son is very zealous in the work of the Lord. After we had sung the Twenty-fifth Psalm, the said Peter Katterberg implored God with a reverent prayer that Jehovah-Immanuel might be present at our meeting and penetrate our hearts with His holy presence and fear, and pour therein His spirit of grace and prayer. This was a plea that we would speak and repeat through His sweet lips the words which Jesus spoke to the apostles and to His people when He was on earth, through His spirit in our hearts and souls.

After this we opened to the fifth chapter of Matthew and read it. We then began to speak among ourselves, and to listen with joy how one contributed his talent, and another a different one, to the good of all and the honor of God. It would become too lengthy to write very much about this. In brief, we united ourselves in Jesus, our heavenly King, Prince of Life, the Initiator and Fulfiller of faith, to look constantly upon Him when we were persecuted, reviled, and hated for the sake of His righteousness. We expected that we would be accused of all kinds of evildoing when we tried to live up to the good, which is what happened.

All three of the preachers and the elders came in where we were as we were speaking and meditating. They began to shout at us: "What! What! What are you doing here? Do we not have churches and houses of God for this?" Thereupon the said Peter Katterberg gave them a modest and fitting answer, which, however, the preachers did not accept. They quashed all of our speaking and answers, raged at us, and threatened us violently because we were beginning such a disorder. We replied to this, however: "You are resisting in us the order of God, as we have a command that we should exhort one another daily— in season and out of season. You are hereby publicly informed that we do not fear your defiance, if we follow after the good. Therefore, you will exert yourselves to no avail in hindering a work such as this, which is from God."

Nothing we said helped a bit, nor had any validity with them. Only what the preachers said was valid, as if it were spoken from heaven. They shouted, saying to us: "Phooey! That you should gather like this; that you dare to try to teach. God has established us as the servants of the congregation. Why do you not come to us? Why do you not come tomorrow, for that is the Lord's Day?" We answered, "We have the command from God: 'Today! Today! While you hear the voice of the Lord.' If we are still alive tomorrow, we will also come to the Lord our God then." I cannot possibly describe the great blindness of the learnéd men and the Pharisees of today. I also said to them, "I have never found more perverse people, who resist the good more, than among the scribes of today."

Therefore, let us pray together in faith with united power, for these poor and miserable people who consider themselves rich. May Jehovah open their eyes and enlighten them that they might fall off of their prancing steed of selfishness and call unto the Lord, "Lord, where are you?" that they may avoid perishing as blasphemers. They blaspheme about that which they know nothing about, but only through natural comprehension. I suggested to them that they should attack sometime the gatherings in the taverns just as they have attacked us. I assured them that they would be better able to defend that before God than this, where they dared to quarrel with the invincible God.

As for the rest, I commend the matter to my dearly beloved Abba and Father, and am assured that He will himself end this to His praise and use, and to my salvation and that of all of His children. May He give us patience and faith to the very end!

September, 1713. John Lobach.[40]

Henckels Questioned

The minutes of the Reformed consistory at Solingen show the action taken by the church to try to check the Pietist movement.

Solingen consistory minutes, September 7, 1713.

[John Frederick] Henckels appeared, and after many questions and answers about the private conventicles, he was asked: (1) Whether he was willing to cease holding private meetings, and especially those on Sundays? Answer: he could not bind his talent to bear interest at any given time or day, but when the opportunity arose, he would be ready to use it in order to lose no time. (2) Whether he intended in the future to conform to the attendance at the public worship services? Answer: when God impelled and held him to it.[41]

Consistory Warns of Pietists

Solingen consistory minutes, December 7, 1713.

This decision has been drafted, and was announced from the pulpit on three consecutive Sundays as follows:

The fanaticism and the so-called Pietism have not only become common in this territory here and there, but are also trying to penetrate into our own congregation. Because of this, however, we are obliged to be on guard against this pernicious movement, by virtue of the Word of God, the responsibilities of our office, the church discipline, as well as many resolutions pertaining thereto of the district and synod, especially that of the last-held general synod at Duisburg. This was strictly enjoined there to the congregations of the four united territories; we must prevent it everywhere, notifying the official authorities about it, if necessary. This so that this evil does not make further inroads, but, on the contrary, so that the so-dearly purchased doctrine of truth in waiting upon the Word of God, the holy sacraments, and otherwise all other good order, shall be maintained.

The local consistory, therefore, to the honor of God, and for the good of all upright Christians, has to warn this congregation well-meaningly, to beware of the false teachings of such a pack of agitators and dissenters, to desist from contact with them, and to avoid all meddling. The congregation is also to invite loyally those who have strayed to return to the bosom of the true church (outside of which there is neither redemption nor salvation), so that it is not necessary to resort to other means. Moreover, they are to pray publicly for such mistaken people, and to make them known to the congregation by name. After this, they are to cut them off as dead members, and cast them out.

For the time being, it has been decided that in case some of these transgressors die in the near future, they are to be buried without the least of the usual church ceremonies, such as tolling the bell, singing, or preaching (for they highly blasphemed all their life against such ceremonies and everything that pertains thereto). . . .[42]

The Coming of the Brethren

The Lobach biography quoted above also describes the coming of the Brethren, and their success in attracting John Lobach and some of his friends to their movement. Besides the six who were later imprisoned because of their new faith, some women were also baptized. It is significant that women played a role in every area of Brethren expansion.

Solingen Group Baptized

It further came to pass that some Anabaptists who had been persecuted and expelled in the South [*Oberland*] because of their practice of baptism came to this area. They made the acquaintance of the awakened, and also attracted various souls to themselves through their earnestness and zealous love. They taught them that it was absolutely necessary that they be baptized as a symbol of their conversion, and thereby become separated from Babel. Because these dear souls here were without exception unexperienced children of grace, and had been rejected in part by their own, some of them let themselves be brought to the point of baptism after many prior struggles and trials. These were namely, J. L. [John Lobach] with five other brethren, and also some women. Through this means it happened that the hate of the preachers and also other people increased, which God permitted for a holy purpose, and they were considered disloyal heretics. They were severely denounced and persecuted, and it shortly thereafter happened that they were actually imprisoned. They were taken to Düsseldorf, which W[illiam] Grahe has further described, as follows later [*A Faithful Account,* see page 241ff.].

Many remarkable things occurred before this, however, wherein could be noticed the folly of the preachers and other people still in the darkness, as well as the steadfastness and joy of heart of the persecuted friends. God did not look at their weak understanding, but at the sincerity of their hearts. He especially supported them with His grace in their oppression. Many people were much impressed, convinced, and made favorable to them through their calm suffering.

After the six unmarried brethren were finally freed from their imprisonment, they went to Krefeld. They were well received there by good-hearted friends, especially among the Mennonites. They dedicated themselves to quiet and devout lives, worked industriously with their hands, and earned their livelihood. They also continued to hold their communal meetings, breaking of bread and feet-washing, according to the ordinances of Christ. This was because several awakened souls from the Baptists had established their residences there, most of whom also lived devout lives. Some of them, including also their leader [*Lehrer*], John Naas, later migrated to Pennsylvania, as did also our friend W[illiam] Knepper. Jacob and William Grahe married in

Krefeld, as did our friend [John Frederick] Henckels, who, however, moved to Holland.[43]

Reformed Synod Asks Investigation

The baptism of the Solingen group was soon brought before the synod of the Reformed Church, who viewed the Brethren activities with concern. In the Lower Rhine area, the Brethren were commonly referred to as *Dompelaars,* a Dutch term meaning "Dippers" or "Baptists."

Minutes of the General Synod of the Reformed Church.

The General Synod learned to its great sorrow that some people formerly holding to the Reformed Church had themselves baptized in running and other waters by certain so-called *Dompelaars* now staying in Krefeld. As the synod had so wished, the preachers in Krefeld informed themselves concerning the teachings and manner of worship of these above-mentioned *Dompelaars,* and had zealously opposed their innovations which are so damaging to the church of God. The synod therefore recommends to the honorable preachers of the Moers District to interrogate these *Dompelaars* about their teaching, and to inform the Secretary Mann thereof, so that the latter can most respectfully submit this matter to His Royal Majesty.

July 9-16, 1716.[44]

KREFELD

With John Naas, Peter Becker, and Christian Liebe as its leaders, the Brethren church fellowship at Krefeld expanded vigorously. Although their message particularly attracted Mennonites to their fold, they also made inroads among the established Reformed Church. The zealous Brethren proved to be a major problem for the Mennonite congregation at Krefeld. The Mennonites had many similarities with the new group, and the mode of baptism—whether by aspersion (sprinkling) or immersion —seemed to be the chief point of issue. According to one scholar, one of the Mennonite lay preachers, Gossen Goyen (1667-1737), was baptized by immersion in the Rhine in 1724. Whether or not Goyen was actually baptized by the Brethren, he was very close to them, helping to free Christian Liebe from the galleys and visiting the imprisoned Solingen Brethren.[45]

Mennonite Minister Defends Aspersion

Another preacher, Jan Crous, preached a sermon in 1716 in which he presented the orthodox Mennonite viewpoint. The following is the outline of part of the sermon preached by Jan Crous after conducting a baptismal service by aspersion, as was the usual Mennonite practice.

. . . We want now to give public testimony of our faith, etc.

Note. Witness given of the necessary points, etc. Also the things on which differences exist such as nonresistance, oath-taking, baptism, communion, church discipline, in which the one is more insistent than the other, etc.

But, as time allows, to say something more about baptism: (1) what it is, (2) on what persons, what they must be like, (3) the method and manner, whether by aspersion or immersion.

We affirm: it is evident in the Holy Scriptures, as in history, that they immersed in the earliest times, etc.

But it is not evident from the Holy Scriptures that they always did this, as can be seen in certain situations, that is, several thousand in one day, and the prison keeper in the night, etc. That they must have gone to the water, but also have respected aspersion, etc., and that shortly after the apostles, a church father said that God wants mercy and not sacrifice, that in the cold countries aspersion causes less damage to our bodies, etc., and was used at that time, etc.

Still we will gladly tolerate in this those who prefer immersion, etc.

We wish, however, that they will likewise tolerate our method of aspersion. That we are satisfied with this baptism and consider it as good as immersion has various reasons, but principally the following two bases:

(1) Immersion is nowhere specifically commanded. If that were necessary, would then our Lord Jesus have left his church in blindness on that point, more than the Jews were in earlier times, where everything was prescribed and said in great detail, where, when, and in what manner they had to do things, etc.? That the Lord would also have said this, etc.

(2) As the ceremonies are not the essence of the worship itself, but only symbols which portray something greater, one must not look

so much at the symbol but at the thing itself. Water does not wash
the sin away, not even a Jordan. Rather, the essence of the thing
which is being symbolized is what matters, etc.

Palm Sunday, April 5, 1716   (Jan Crous)⁴⁰

Hochmann von Hochenau to Gretchen Hendrichs

Brethren activity was not only attacked by the official church
authorities and opposed by their Mennonite brethren, but also by Hochmann, their former mentor. The latter wrote to a friend, Gretchen
Hendrichs, in Krefeld, who had asked his opinion on the baptismal question. He advised against it and belittled Brethren practices. Hochmann was
keenly disappointed by the Brethren movement, which he looked upon
as sectarian and divisive.

Remember Jesus Christ who is raised from the dead (2 Timothy 2:8).
In this Jesus Dearly Beloved Sister:

I have received your letter along with the token of your love.
Just as I praise and glorify Jehovah, who is the foundation and life
of all things, for His granting the pure and white linen, I likewise
wish from the bottom of my heart that God might grant that you may
clothe yourself with beautiful and pure silk for the white and pure
linen which you have sent. (The silk is the righteousness of the
saints, Revelation of John 19:8.)

This is to answer your request about the dipping: I consider this
unnecessary if one has already been baptized, be it as a child or in
adult years. I was baptized as a child by Lutherans, had a Roman
Catholic mother, and even had Roman Catholic godparents. Even
though I did not understand the matter at all at the time, I was already
truly baptized with water. I was truly offered up to God the Father,
the Son, and the Holy Spirit in water baptism. Although this or that
abuse crept in, God cannot hold that against me . . . .

Further, at my infant baptism the devil and all his works were
renounced, at least outwardly, on my behalf by my godparents. I was
dedicated to the triune God in His presence. Therefore, in my adult
years when I learned to understand the matter, I repeated my baptismal
covenant before the countenance of God in His presence and that of
all the holy angels. I renounced anew the devil and all of his system
on my own behalf and again offered myself to the triune God with

full understanding. I gave myself completely in His possession, so that I desire to be no other's than the triune God's now and in eternity.

As then the essence of baptism is based on the above, for my part I consider the repeating of water baptism to be unnecessary. Rather, I would pray to God that He might baptize me from day to day, ever more and more, with His Holy Spirit and with fire—that He might give me the grace to remain true to Him until the end in the baptismal covenant, renewed before God's countenance, but without repeating the outward immersion. It was not necessary to join that party or sect for this repetition of the baptismal covenant before God's countenance, or to listen with others to their rather coarse, or also subtle, sectarianism. I would become through this more confused and separated from my baptismal covenant rather than be strengthened or made firm in the essence of this baptismal covenant, which exists in the true uniting with God.

I therefore live in freedom from all scruples of conscience in respect to baptism. As I have been made righteous through faith, I have therefore peace with God, through our Lord Jesus Christ. Let others dispute and quarrel about baptism as long as they wish. For my part, I refuse to be drawn into a quarrel about it with any person, lest I lose on that account my inner peace, in which, of course, the essence of baptism lies. Rather, I remain directly under Christ and enter through Him into the true fellowship of all the saints who are already one in the triumphant as well as militant church on earth. I love all true believing members of Christ, be they baptized in childhood or in adult years, or even if they have never been baptized with water at all, but are reborn through the water and spirit from above.

I believe, with the dear Peter, that God is truly no respecter of persons, but rather that among all kinds of people those who fear Him and work righteousness are acceptable to Him (Acts 10:31-35). Whoever, then, is acceptable to God and Jesus Christ, the highly praised Head of the congregation, and who is received in His heart of love—how can I dare to reject him and to ban him . . . ?

I admit that I do not respect any banning which is not exercised with the approval and complete consent of Jesus Christ, who was raised to the right hand of God. The other kind of banning I consider a sectarian, presumptuous imitation of the letter of the Scripture, because the life of the spirit and power is lacking. Therefore it has so little power and influence on the souls. Those people in our area who have been banned recently testify that they have had more peace after their banning occurred than before they were banned.

I maintain that no person can place me in the ban except myself. It is hardly possible of my Jesus, that He would wish to place me in the ban. Rather, He assures me that He will love me to the end. I can place myself in the ban if I separate myself from my Jesus through willful, knowing, premeditated and stubborn sin, and, like Demas, again learn to love the world. That is the ban in which no one except myself can place me through my stubborn wickedness. God will, however, protect me from evil, so that I do not separate myself from my most beloved King Jesus. I do not have the slightest reason to do this, because I am assured that I would not be better off under any lord in heaven or on earth than under Jesus. He has written down my name in His hand, according to His prophecy, as He says: "Fear not, little flock, for it is your Father's good pleasure to give you the kingdom" [Luke 12:32].

To say something further about baptism, I consider that those who were once baptized with water, be it in childhood or in adult years, have no need of the dipping. Only confusion and disorder in the congregation will come from it. The kingdom of anger and rage will be furthered, rather than the Kingdom of Christ, which is a kingdom of peace and love. I do not wish to be used for this purpose. If, however, there is someone who has never been baptized— neither in childhood nor in adult years—and he feels himself compelled in his conscience to the outward water repentance, I cannot see why this conscience cannot be tolerated, if he absolutely insists that he be baptized by immersion in the water of a river in the name of the Father, the Son, and the Holy Spirit. I will not make for myself the least scruple about it, because one must accommodate and tolerate weak consciences, especially in such matters which are not wicked in themselves. God himself allows us our weaknesses.

However, it should be made perfectly clear to such people that they should by no means get the idea of considering themselves better because of this outward dipping than other people who were not dipped. Otherwise this dipping would be a snare, a fall, and a matter of pride for them. That which is highly esteemed among men is abomination in the sight of God (Luke 16:16 [15]).

A person who has not been baptized at all but is truly humble would be much more preferable to me than such an arrogant saint who insists only on dipping and despises others on that account. He who evidences spiritual arrogance is far removed from the true essence of baptism, which consists of the humility of the heart. Finally it remains in the end as Paul says in Romans 2:28, 29, "For he is not a real Jew who is one outwardly, nor is true circumcision something external and physical. He is a Jew who is one inwardly, and real circumcision is a matter of the heart, spiritual and not literal. His praise is not from men but from God." This can be applied in all respects to baptism.

If only the sons of men would give up disputing, fighting, and quarreling, and truly take the word of the Lord Jesus into their hearts and souls, as He said in Luke 10:42: ". . . one thing is needful. Mary has chosen the good portion, which shall not be taken away from her." This one necessity, however, lies in the innermost unity with Jesus Christ. One must continuously penetrate into His heart of love and take of its abundance of mercy and more mercy for the growth of the inner man. When a person becomes accustomed to this, he forgets all quarrel and strife. It is most distasteful to him when he hears that others spend their time with this, and forget the best in the process, namely, union with Christ. From Him must be born faith, and love for all men, even for enemies.

So, dear sister, I have herewith tried to answer your request about the dipping. If you can agree with it, that is good. If, however, you do not understand this as I do, then we will still want to bear with each other in love, and only follow after "what makes for peace" (Romans 14:19). What I have here written, you could share with others, so that they might not become taken with the dipping, and in that way create disunity and sectarian partisanship among the good friends at Krefeld.

I greet all of them especially warmly. May Jesus himself enlighten each heart at Krefeld with His spirit, light, and power, that they might learn to recognize that about which the essence of Christianity is principally concerned. This is, namely, that one becomes a new creature before God, as Paul says, "For neither circumcision counts for anything, nor uncircumcision, but a new creation" (Galatians 6:15).

May the Lord Jesus make us and all the friends (both men and women) at Krefeld such new creations that we can one day appear with great joy before the judgment seat of our Lord Jesus, and hear Him say to us: "Come, O blessed of my Father, inherit the kingdom prepared for you from the foundation of the world" [Matthew 25:34].

I greet all of the Mennonite ministers [*Lehrer*] warmly, and wish them from my heart the spirit and power of the Lord Jesus. If they only direct their entire congregation to the new creation, then the real improvement from within, or inwardly from the heart, will arise from the hearts of their hearers. This will certainly not come about through the outward dipping as the good Alexander Mack believes. There are people in this area who have been baptized already at least two or three times, and still little know what the essence of the new creation is. Hardly are they baptized, when they are placed in the ban because of their unchanged characters. This could not happen if the outer dipping had as good an effect on the souls as they maintain.

For my part, I will remain with Jesus, whose yoke is easy and whose burden is light. The local Baptists' strict law and human yoke is completely intolerable to a spirit made free by the blood of Christ. At times, it goes even further than the Mosaic Law. If, however, people do not take up the easy yoke of Christ, and will not hear the sweet voice of Jesus in their hearts, then let them take up their intolerable yoke upon themselves. Let the people sound their rough voice of thunder from the mountain of Sinai.

Please greet Dr. Lange at Nollenhof warmly as well as Morbek at Kleve from me. You may communicate this letter to both of them; perhaps they will appreciate it. I greet the friends at Hüls very warmly in the love of Jesus, as well as those at Michelshof. This letter may be read to anyone who you think can understand it. It has been written according to my conviction after the truth, and will be effective on the consciences of those people who make room for impartial truth as it is before God and Jesus. I commend you to God and to the word of His grace, and remain in sincere love for God,

> your loyal brother and advocate before God,
>
> Ernest Christopher Hochmann von Hochenau.[47]

Friedensburg [no date]
Nathaniel greets you all warmly.

Duisburg Consistory Questions Krefeld Brethren

Three Brethren members from Krefeld went to nearby Duisburg, where they baptized several people in the Rhine River. For this they were haled before the Duisburg consistory, sharply questioned, and finally released. The Reformed synod of the Kleve area took the matter up again. They were concerned because the new group was making inroads among their members.

Duisburg consistory minutes.
January 25, 1717.

¶1. Judge zur Meyede and Mr. Ryss were absent.

¶2. It has been found necessary to summon the so-called Baptists to appear, because they have started to cause here diverse disorders. They have held a love feast at the Mennonite Winand's, administered communion along with feet-washing in their manner, and even dared to baptize here in the Rhine some simple-minded or stubborn people, and consequently have caused an extraordinary crowd to gather and noise among the young people and others through this unheard-of undertaking.

¶3. All three presented themselves: the first said that his name was John Naas, and [that he] was born near Worms. The second was named Schilpert; the third's name was Hekker [Höcker?] and [he was] from Dillenburg.

¶4. It was wished to be known with what purpose and with what authority they had come to this place and ventured these absurdities in which they were apprehended. The answer received was that they acted upon an inner impulse and call, and had also been invited by some of the local inhabitants.

¶5. It was further asked and answered:

(a) To which church they formerly belonged? Answer: They had resigned from the Reformed Church.

(b) For what reason had that occurred? Because of the godless way of living of the Reformed, by whom they were even persecuted because they had wanted to lead more holy lives.

(c) What grounds could they give for their way of baptism? It is said: "Go therefore and make disciples of all nations, baptizing them in the name of the Father and of the Son and of the Holy Spirit" [Matthew 28:19]. Infant baptism was introduced

by the Pope and was anti-Christian. Furthermore, in the first
three centuries after Christ's birth nothing was heard of any
infant baptism.

(d) It was replied to them: on the first point, that it applies to
adults, for neither at that time nor now would anyone have
found it wise to steal the children from their parents and baptize
them against their [parents'] will, but rather the adult must
become willing to do so through reasonable instruction. They
[the Baptists] had, in fact, not instructed any of the baptized, and
had not even examined them for they baptized one person who
was in complete ignorance, and another who did not even believe
in the triune God. The latter they tried to deny, at first, but
later when it was suggested that they be put to the test, they
finally admitted it. They had to use the absurd excuse that they
[the baptized] would learn later.

On the second point it was shown to them that up to the present
time no Antichrist had ever lived. On the third point, however, it
was explained to them that one would be happy to demonstrate the
exact opposite to them in Tertullian, Irenaeus, Cyprian, etc., and this
preferably if they would bring someone who understood the Latin
and Greek languages.

The opportunity was taken therefore to expound to them with all
emphasis the unshakable bases of infant baptism, with its inestimable
advantages and holy propriety. An endeavor was made to convince
them with mildness and modesty. They were, however, so irresponsi-
bly stubborn along with their scandalous ignorance (they were so
confused they continually blushed for shame), that they broke out
with the reckless words: "God forbid that we allow ourselves to be
persuaded to infant baptism; that would simply be wasted effort, etc."

¶6. After they had been dismissed and the consensus taken, they
were again admitted, and the following sentence passed with unanimous vote of the clergy and elders: they must once and for all spare
the city and congregation their teachings, feet-washings, and holding
of love feasts and communion. This, partly because they were found
completely unversed, partly because they had freely admitted having
separated themselves from our church, partly because they not only
misled and baptized separatists but also Mennonites, and therefore
could not hide or sneak through among the latter. Otherwise one

wished them warmly, that the Lord might through His infinite goodness grant them enlightenment and mercy, for their restitution and
sincere conversion.

¶7. The meeting was closed with prayer.[48]

Kleve Synod Expresses Concern

Minutes of the Kleve Synod.
May 25-28, 1717.

The synod finds [it] most painful that the so-called *Dompelaars*
and Baptists at Krefeld not only still continue in their false teaching
and suspicious meetings, but also induce many to rebaptism and
thereby to belittle and even to despise the sacrament of infant baptism.

Some time ago they incited this kind of disorder even in Duisburg,
and refused to submit to any church or consistorial discipline. They
are being defended and assisted in this irregularity in punishable
manner by some of the Reformed in Krefeld and Duisburg.

Further, the Pietists imprisoned in Düsseldorf [the Solingen
Brethren] and many others holding to them are introducing all sorts
of pernicious tenets, and proclaim themselves to be ministers [*Lehrer*],
to the affront of the public preaching office. In no manner do they
permit themselves to be induced to abstain. Therefore the synod
begs most humbly that it may please His Royal Majesty to consider
most mercifully issuing appropriate decrees to hinder such separatistic
people completely and to abolish this disorder which has infiltrated
into the church.[49]

Brethren Marriages Recorded

Two entries in the Mennonite church book record marriages of
Brethren couples. In both cases John Naas, who is listed as the
teacher or minister of the group, appeared as sponsor.

January 9, 1717.

John Preisz from Hanau and Marie Odelia from the Upper
Palatinate. 1. 2. 3. [bans]. As witnesses have appeared John Jacob
Preisz, the cousin of the bridegroom, and John Naas, minister of the
so-called *Dompelaars,* who certifies that if the parents of the bride
raise any objections, their congregation will stand good for everything.

April 29, 1718.

William Möller, from Mettmann in the Berg area, and Jacobina de Turck from Frankenthal. 1. 2. 3. [bans]. The bridegroom hereby certifies that the minister at Mettmann, Merkes, refused to give him a permit [*Lastbrief*] only because he [Möller] has adopted the religion of the local Baptists. In order that no weighty objection might be brought to prevent this marriage, either from the side of the [family of the] bridegroom or from [the family of] the bride, John Naas, minister, in the name of their congregation, has here stood sponsor.[50]

Brethren Listed in Krefeld Census

A census taken in Krefeld at about this time listed the names of four Brethren. Two of the four were on public relief, evidently resulting from the migration.

The following persons are only residents because they were too poor to purchase their citizenship rights, which amount to four and a half *Reichstaler*.

[Name]	Trade	Parents	Man	Woman	Children	Relatives
. . .						
Luke Vetter	on relief	—	1	1	4	—
. . .						
Peter Becker	serge weaver	—	1	1	—	—
. . .						
Martin Lucas	buttonmaker	—	1	1	3	2
. . .						
Daniel Ritter	on relief	—	1	1	—	1
. . .[51]						

Krefeld Pastors Report

The pastors of the Krefeld Reformed church were asked to report at a special meeting of the synod whether they had carried out the instruction of the previous synod on investigation of the Krefeld Brethren.

Important in their statement is the assertion that the Brethren were tolerated by the city officials, under the lenient Prussian rule.

Minutes of the Extraordinary General Synod. February 16, 17, 1718.

Both local [Krefeld] pastors Püll and Sarn were requested to appear before the council upon the reading of ¶44 [see page 204]. After they had appeared, they were asked whether they had complied with the instructions of the said paragraph. Had they informed themselves about the doctrines and conduct of the so-called *Dompelaars* living with them? Why had they not sent Secretary Mann a report about it as requested? The above answered that the former had been carried out. The *Dompelaars* turned in a creed in reply to several questions put to them. The Reverend Timman of Homberg, the president of the Moers District, who was to forward it to Pastor Mann, had had the creed for a long time. They complained a great deal about their correspondent—that he had tried to make them look suspect through a critical statement at the last general synod, without having had the slightest authority.

They reported that those people had not stolen into the community, as the pastors had been reproached, but rather that these people were tolerated with the knowledge of the bailiff.

Resolution: on the first point, Pastor Püll is directed to write to his president that the latter might send the creed of the so-called *Dompelaars*, which was presented by them to Secretary Mann in the next mailing. On the second point, Secretary Mann is to confer with the moderators, after receiving the said creed and answer, and to decide whether to take it up with higher places or not.[52]

Swiss Separatist Describes Brethren

An excerpt from a letter by the Swiss separatist, Nicholas Tscheer, written from Germany, critically described the Brethren as one of the three new Pietist sects along with the Gichtel group and the Inspirationists.

Letter from Nicholas Tscheer to the friends in Switzerland concerning the present state of Pietist groups in Germany [from Krefeld in 1719].

. . . The third party [besides the Inspirationists and the followers of Gichtel] who have erected a new household and wish to increase their numbers are the Schwarzenau Baptists. Their foundation, as is well known, rests on the mere letter of the Scriptures, and is an imitation of the early Christians. The spirit will not co-operate on this basis, however. As they had completed their harvest in Marienborn, the Palatinate, Schwarzenau, and around those areas, they came here to this district. They have recently publicly baptized six people in the Ruhr, . . . which [act] caused great excitement.

They have a great zeal to impress their beliefs upon the conscience of men through the authority of the Holy Scriptures. They are gathering a great number of poor people, who, of course, are little changed by the baptism, love feast, and other ceremonies unless they had a good foundation before. Unbelief, materialism [*Bauchsorg*], poverty, jealousy, and other forces of wickedness break out from time to time, and cause division and unrest.

These people consider and attack the Inspirationists and other Pietists as imposters.[53]

Poem Mentions Dompelaars

An unusual reference to the Brethren is found in a description of the principality of Moers in which Krefeld is located. It occurs in the Dutch translation of an earlier Latin quatrain describing the religious groups represented in Krefeld. In the Dutch version, the *Dompelaars* are substituted for the Quakers of the original.

(1) [Original Latin quatrain written by the principal of the Moers *Gymnasium,* Cruse, in 1724-25]

> Papa, Moses, Pennus,
> Calvinus, Menno, Lutherus
> una in Creyfelda
> varium cantant alleluja.

(2) [Dutch translation by Peter van Sarn, Reformed pastor in Krefeld]

> Reformeerden en Papisten,
> Lutheranen en Mennisten,
> Dompelaers en Abrams Soonen
> t'samen nu in Kreyfeld woonen.

(3) [English translation]

> Lutheran and Mennonite,
> Catholic and Israelite,
> Calvinist and New Baptist
> All in Krefeld now exist.[54]

IV. Suppression

Although, on the one hand, they found favor with God and the people, [on the other hand] they also encountered enemies of the truth. Now and then persecutions occurred for the sake of the Word. Some endured with joy the confiscation of their property. Others, however, had to endure bonds and imprisonment. Some spent only a few weeks, but others several years in the prisons. Christian Liebe had to spend several years locked to the galley, pulling the oar in the midst of criminals. All were freed with clear consciences, however, through the miraculous providence of God.

—Alexander Mack, Jr.[1]

As has been seen, the Brethren movement met with varying degrees of opposition wherever the Brethren found themselves. They were fortunate in their choice of a century. At an earlier date the same activity would have been punished with execution by burning at the stake or drowning, which was the sentence passed upon thousands of Anabaptists in the sixteenth century, or harsh imprisonment resulting in death, suffered by hundreds of Quakers in the seventeenth century. By the eighteenth century, the Enlightenment had progressed far enough that the usual punishment for religious dissent came to be banishment. As far as is known to us, no member of the Brethren group was martyred for his faith.

This is not to say that the Brethren did not experience suffering for their beliefs. Two episodes stand out in this respect—the sentencing of Christian Liebe to serve as a galley slave, and the imprisonment of the Solingen Brethren. In each case, there exists a surprisingly well-documented story of the imprisonment and the release. The efforts of the Dutch Mennonites, the Swiss Pietists, and others present nearly classic examples of assistance to those repressed for religious reasons.

CHRISTIAN LIEBE

The narrative of the Liebe imprisonment begins in the year 1714, when the Brethren leader made a journey to Bern, in Switzerland. The

Bernese government had been trying for generations to stamp out the Anabaptists. In 1711 there had been a large forced migration to the Netherlands. Some of those who left with this exodus returned to the Bern area, largely owing to the split between two leaders—Jacob Amman, whose followers were the Amish, and John Reist. The Reist faction, which returned, was considered especially incorrigible by the authorities, who decided to send four members of the group to the galleys. This was the situation when Liebe was arrested in Bern.[2]

CONDEMNED TO THE GALLEYS

Christian Liebe Sentenced

Minutes of the Bern City Council.
January 6, 1714.

Memorandum to the honorable members of the Anabaptist Commission. Christian Liebe, the Baptist minister from the Palatinate who came from outside Switzerland into the area of authority of the city council, had to admit that his purpose was to visit the local brethren, to minister, to solace, and to baptize someone if the occasion arose. He was not unaware of the published government prohibition of such activity. Therefore the honorable council and the high council and officials have approved that this foreign minister should not be given any less punishment than the local ministers, who were sentenced two weeks ago. Therefore the council and the mayor have resolved that this Christian Liebe should likewise be sent to the galleys along with the other ministers imprisoned here. They hereby inform the honorable members of this with the friendly request that the above-mentioned should be transferred at the right time to the officials, together with the others. In the meantime, however, they should arrange that he be put with the others.

Also: Memorandum to inform the sergeant of the court of the above with the order to put the prisoner with the others until the appointed date.[3]

Departure Ordered

Secret Minutes of the Bern City Council.
July 26, 1714, in the presence of the Senate.

Memorandum to the sergeant of the court and to the court clerk.

The report has arrived that His Royal Majesty of Sicily is willing to accept the six Anabaptists and thieves condemned to the galleys. After the royal order is received, they will be met at Ouchy on the fourth of next August. Their Graces wish to order you to forge chains on these six persons as necessary, and to transport them safely to Lausanne. You are to send them with an escort of about twelve fusiliers [infantrymen] at the break of day, taking care to go unnoticed. They are then to be turned over to the provincial governor on August 2. For this purpose the leader of the escort is to be given the enclosed passport and the letter to the provincial governor. In addition you are to impress strictly upon the escort and instruct them that these said galley slaves must be safely turned over to the provincial governor on the above-mentioned day with no danger of their escaping. You will know how to take all necessary measures, chaining as well as others, to this end.[4]

Aid for the Prisoners

Liebe and the others were sent off on the lengthy and painful journey over the mountains. They were taken to Turin to spend the winter, where they were imprisoned in a vault with ninety criminals and vagabonds. They had to do hard labor outside every day.

However, there were those who interested themselves in their fate. Several Pietistically inclined members of the Swiss aristocracy took up their case. The Mennonites in the Netherlands and northern Germany soon heard of the plight of their brethren and submitted an appeal to the Dutch government, the Estates General. The Dutch Mennonites had for many years assisted fellow believers in countries where there was suppression. The correspondence between the Swiss and the Mennonites reveals the story of the release of the prisoners.

Von Wattenwyl Summoned

Gabriel von Wattenwyl, a member of one of the leading Bernese families, was reported to the Bern city council by the Anabaptist Commission as the person who was interceding for the prisoners.

Minutes of the Bern City Council.
December 18, 1714.

Memorandum to the honorable members of the Anabaptist Commission. From the presentation and submitted statements and letters

A View of Bern in the Early Eighteenth Century

From W. Hadorn, *Geschichte des Pietismus in den Schweizerischen Reformierten Kirchen* (Konstanz and Emmishofen: 1901).

the honorable council members have learned who the persons were who have written to Colonel Hackbrett and also to the Baptists here on behalf of the Baptists sentenced to the Sicilian galleys. They have also learned with regret that this evil of Anabaptism has not only broken out in the country but also in the city, so that the council will have to take remedial steps, in the former place as well as in the latter. As Their Graces find that this matter deserves more investigation, the honorable council members wish to request the honorable members to summon Mr. Gabriel von Wattenwyl before them.

They should try to learn whether he has written this letter of his own motivation, or who has advised him thereto. Also, who is to pay the official ransom or liberation money? Further, why has he so lightly ignored his oath of allegiance which he made by giving his hand, and patronized these Baptists who are so dangerous to this country, against the clear content of the oath? They should also take appropriate steps to discover the patrons of the Baptists and bring them to account for it, and present them with their statements about this before the chamber. This with the understanding that in case the honorable chamber feels this business is of such importance and weight that it is too difficult for them, Their Graces leave it to them to decide whether it should be brought before the honorable city council and officials. To which end Their Graces hereby return your presentation and submitted statement.[5]

The Mennonites in Amsterdam appealed to their government as soon as they heard of the sentencing of the five as galley slaves. The Estates General sent a strong letter of intercession to Bern, calling for revocation of the order. The Dutch reminded the Bernese authorities that both governments had joined in protesting similar punishments of their Reformed brethren by Catholic powers. The Bernese council replied two months later offering to release the prisoners under certain conditions.

Dutch Mennonites Appeal

Most Powerful Estates General of the United Netherlands:

The Mennonites or *Doopsgezinde* Brotherhood of this country wish to express in all humbleness and due respect that they, as petitioners, are very grateful to Our Most Powerful Lords for the letters of intercession sent to the Canton of Bern some time ago. They were sent in order that the canton might cease prosecuting and persecuting the brethren of the petitioners who live under the jurisdiction of the above-named canton. The petitioners had hoped that the previously mentioned letters of intercession had been well received by the above-mentioned canton.

However, they learned with sorrow and grief that once again a great number of their brethren had been put into the prisons of Bern. Five of them were sentenced to life imprisonment as galley slaves. To that purpose they had to walk chained hand and foot to Turin. When they arrived there, they were put into prison again in the fortress in order to be shipped to the galleys of Sicily during the coming spring. Their names are: John Lüthi of Lützelflue, Peter Wüterich of Trüb, Joseph Probst of Lambertsweil, Christian Liebe from the Palatinate, and John Baumgarten of Trüb. The latter died while at the fortress of Turin.

Therefore the petitioners again request letters of intercession from Our Most Powerful Lords to the Canton of Bern, in order that the above-mentioned brethren [in Bern] of the petitioners might be set free and might exercise their faith in peace and quiet. Further, that the above-mentioned four prisoners at the fortress of Turin—the fifth having already died—might be recalled from there and restored to freedom.

The petitioners are also requesting that their previously mentioned brethren might obtain permission to sell all their goods and property within two years and migrate from there to the Palatinate, Alsace, or the Netherlands, in case that the above-mentioned canton will not tolerate them in their territory. Also that Our Most Powerful Lords might please commission their consul Runkel to use his good offices (because such could be used profitably) toward obtaining the discharge of the above-mentioned Mennonites, for those imprisoned at Bern as well as those at Turin.

January 22, 1715.　　　　　　　　　　　　　　Cornelius Beets.

(Request of the Mennonite Brotherhood for letters of intercession.)[6]

Estates General Intercede

[To the Canton of Bern.]

Noble, Most Honorable, Wise and Prudent Sirs, etc.

The complaints, which the good inhabitants of our state, the

Mennonite or *Doopsgezinde* Brotherhood, have made concerning the severe procedures that are being taken against their brethren in the praiseworthy Canton of Bern, have induced us to intercede for them anew with Our Dear Sirs hoping that our intercession for these good people with Our Dear Sirs will be successful.

The complaints of the above-mentioned Mennonites or *Doopsgezinde,* who live in our state, consist of this, that they have learned with great sorrow and grief that again a great number of their brethren in Our Dear Sirs' territory have been put into prisons and that five of their number were sentenced to lifelong labor as galley slaves. For that purpose they had to walk to Turin, chained hand and foot, where they were again put into prison in the fortress, in order to be transferred to the galleys of Sicily in the coming spring. The names of the above-mentioned five condemned men are: John Lüthi of Lützelflue, Peter Wüterich of Trüb, Joseph Probst of Lambertsweil, Christian Liebe from the Palatinate, and John Baumgarten of Trüb. The last-named died at the fortress of Turin.

The Mennonites or *Doopsgezinde* who live in our state are submissive and obedient to their authorities in matters which—according to their consciences—do not conflict with the holy Word of God. They do not fight; they have love one for another, and are peaceable in their Brotherhood. When we consider this conduct and conclude from it that the conduct of their brethren in Our Dear Sirs' canton [must be similar], we cannot help having compassion with those poor people. They suffer such severe punishment only because they want to serve God in a clear conscience according to their understanding of His will out of His holy Word, which they have made the basis of their faith. Even though they err in understanding, they much rather deserve compassion than such severe persecution—especially from Our Dear Sirs, who would agree with us that faith is a gift of God, who has reserved for himself alone the judgment over men's consciences. Moreover, Our Dear Sirs have often complained along with us about and protested against the persecution in other places, which our own Reformed brethren have had to suffer for professing their church up to this very day.

We shall now leave it up to the wise and enlightened judgment of Our Dear Sirs what strong arguments would be raised by the enemies [the Catholics] of the true Reformed church, to justify their persecutions, if they are able to confront us with such a living example of a Reformed government which proceeds so severely against their subjects (because they do differ from them in some points, yet on the other hand make the Word of God the rule of their faith) or if they should find some of those poor people on the galleys because of the profession of their faith—about which we complain so much when our Reformed brethren are condemned to the galleys for conscience' sake. We hope that Our Dear Sirs in reflecting upon this will be moved to have compassion for these people.

We very cordially request that Our Dear Sirs might be pleased to release those of the above-mentioned persons condemned upon the galleys who are still living and set them free, as well as the other prisoners. If Our Dear Sirs cannot approve of their returning to Our Dear Sirs' territory to live there quietly, would they please give them permission to sell all their property and to move elsewhere. Thus Our Dear Sirs will certainly in this do a deed worthy of Christian love and tolerance. We shall be pleased to remember our sympathy as much as possible and consider this a token of pleasant friendship which we shall recognize at every occasion as committing us in the future to the sustenance of every good and friendly relationship. Noble, most honorable, wise, prudent sirs, etc.

The Hague, January 22, 1715.   [Estates General][7]

Bern City Council Replies

Most Powerful Sirs, . . .

First, our friendly greeting and [expression of] readiness to serve you.

Our Most Powerful Sirs' most honored letter to us of the twenty-second of last January has reached us in good order, etc. It was your intention upon the request of your Mennonite congregations to recommend to us by your efficacious intervention the further toleration of the Swiss Baptist-minded [*Taufgesinnte*] in this country and the revocation of the sentences passed. We do not intend to voice a protest against some of the greatly detailed matters contained therein, because we remember quite vividly what Our Most Powerful Sirs communicated to us on March 15, 1710, on the same matter, and what we replied to that on April 26 of the same year.

On this point we only refer to the credentials which Our Most

Powerful Sirs later issued to your consul, Mr. Runkel, on December 30, 1710, and the negotiations we had with him at that time after they had arrived. Already at that time we showed mercy to the Baptists here, who had deserved punishment a long time previously, out of pure regard for the weighty intercessions of Our Most Powerful Sirs. In addition, we permitted them to be taken into your noble country by virtue of the agreement made with Mr. Runkel on February 11, 1711. The Baptists were permitted to take all their money without paying any fees, and also all of their relatives.

Likewise, it is no less hard for us to make a definite promise this time to Our Most Powerful Sirs, as much as we would like to do so. The reason for this is that all the kind means employed have availed nothing and a considerable number [of Baptists] whom we had thought to be still in Holland hurled themselves into our country again. Our Most Powerful Sirs will please be informed from the enclosed printed poster made public on May 24, 1714, our reasons for carrying out the more severe punishment with which they had been threatened for a long time. . . .

In order to demonstrate candidly our special respect for the intervention of Our Most Powerful Sirs on behalf of [the Baptists], we shall, on our part, be willing and inclined to condescend to this: if the Mennonites will provide Our Most Powerful Sirs with sufficient guarantee that those Anabaptists who are still at Turin will never enter our dominion again, and send someone with such a guarantee here, we shall once again be willing to provide him with a letter or recommendation to His Royal Majesty of Savoy to set them free. We would thus turn them over to the Mennonite Brotherhood without repaying their expenses, as well as all of those who might actually still be in our country. At this point we want to call your attention to the fact that they are, for the most part, without funds as their means have been consumed by their maintenance. . . .

Mayor
and Large and Small Councils
of the City of Bern.[8]

March 27, 1715.

De Treytorrens to Gossen Goyen (1)

Nicholas Samuel de Treytorrens (died 1728), a nobleman from Cudrefin, in western Switzerland, who may have joined the early

Brethren movement, became involved in the effort to free Christian Liebe. In his letter to the Mennonite minister in Krefeld, Gossen Goyen, the details of this intervention are given.

Beloved Friend and Brother in Christ, Gossen Goyen:
As a greeting I wish you and all of your family grace and peace of Jesus Christ. Amen.

Several days ago, as I was getting ready to travel again to Schwarzenau, I received a letter from a friend at Bern. He informed me that he had received a letter from the Palatinate, written by the mother of Brother Liebe, who is on the galleys. The letter also contained a petition to the local authorities here asking for the liberation of her son. [My friend also informed me] that he had been successful in submitting the petition in her name. Both the Small Council and the Large Council of the Canton of Bern decided that, if the above-mentioned Mrs. Liebe sent someone here, they would give him a letter of recommendation to the king of Sicily. In this letter they would consent to and request that the above-mentioned Brother Liebe might be released, stating that they would give him a full acquittal, provided that he would never come again into the territory of Bern. The same friend immediately reported all this to the mother in the Palatinate. He added—without having asked me— that in order to gain time and save much expense, she should merely forward by mail the commission to receive the letter of recommendation and take it to Turin to me, because I had been interested in the prisoners already last summer, and was at the present time still in the country. When I learned about all this, I went to Bern myself, where I am still, in order to get more information about this matter and to wait for the commission from Mrs. Liebe, which has not arrived as yet.

In the meantime I have talked to several good friends in Bern, especially with the dear friend Mr. von Wattenwyl. He has also been concerned about the imprisoned brethren. I wanted to find out whether it would be possible to help the other three poor brethren who are on the galleys along with Brother Liebe, and to set them free also. Therefore they thought it good and feasible for me to write to you, namely, that you should inform the friends and brethren of the congregations at Amsterdam by express mail, of the following:

upon receiving a letter of intercession from the Estates General, which had been granted upon the petition of the Dutch Mennonites, the Councilors of Bern wrote, several months ago already, concerning the liberation of the brethren who are in slavery. They would permit their release if the Mennonites in Holland guaranteed that they would never return into the territory of Bern, and if they paid all the expenses which the king of Sicily might demand. If they grant a letter of recommendation concerning this to the above-mentioned king, someone from Holland should come on behalf of the *Doopers* [Dutch Mennonites] in order to further their discharge. Those in Amsterdam will surely have seen this in the answer to the Estates General.

Therefore the friends here are of the opinion that, as the prisoners are willing to commit themselves in writing never to enter the Canton of Bern again—unless with permission of the Bernese councilors or through a special command of God—the friends in Holland could well guarantee for this in their commitment. They should also request the Estates General to answer the councilors of Bern to that effect. As it was decided in both the large and the small councils that they would promote the releasing of the prisoners from their chains on this condition, they ought to do still more, yes, even release all the imprisoned friends, women as well as men—about forty persons in all—who are imprisoned at Bern, as they offered in their reply to the Estates General.

For the present, Brother Liebe is the only one to be set free, provided that he is still living. As the king of Sicily has undoubtedly bound himself to liberate all the brethren as soon as the councilors of Bern request it, the friends here are of the opinion that this could be done at the same time if the friends in Holland requested the reply of the Estates General to the councilors of Bern immediately. They should also let Mr. Daniel Knopf at the Bank of Bern know about this, and forward him everything in order that he might get information from the council what the outcome of all this would be. Or [they suggest] that a friend from Holland should even come here to promote this, which I would very much appreciate.

It would be very difficult for me to travel to Turin and probably even farther by myself. However, out of love toward Brother Liebe, and particularly if the others are included and can be released also through the above-mentioned means, I shall gladly undertake this journey regardless of hardship, danger, or expense as far as possible.

My dear friend can now discuss this with the friends, and do your best as quickly as you can. In the meantime, as soon as I shall have received the letter of commission from the mother of Brother Liebe, and after that, the letter of recommendation from the councilors of Bern to the king of Sicily, I shall start on my journey to Turin—God willing—for winter is almost here.

I would have traveled to Germany again a long time ago, if I had not been waiting for the Estates General to answer the reply from the councilors of Bern. Since I agreed to do this, we have all been wondering why the reply from the Estates General has not yet arrived and why our friends at Amsterdam have not urged the Estates General to reply. For now, as a pious bailiff has taken the place of his deceased predecessor in Bern, the matter could have been carried through quite smoothly, if the Estates General had only persisted. When you do me the favor of writing to me again, please let me know what kept the Estates General from replying.

One of the most eminent city councilors of Geneva has had a letter written to the friend Mr. von Wattenwyl stating that a certain archbishop from England had inquired of him what the outcome of the suit was against the imprisoned brethren at Bern as well as against the others that had been condemned to the galleys. The archbishop stated that he had already a great sum of money to ransom them, if that was possible, and if he could learn where they now were. God be praised for the love which He puts into the hearts of men for the poor prisoners. I hope that God will speedily rescue them from their slavery. But it will hardly come about through money and ransom, for the king of Sicily has committed himself in writing to the councilors of Bern to release them only when the Canton of Bern demands it. Therefore it is unlikely that he would release them for money on the intervention of others; it is necessary to go first to the councilors of Bern [to ask] for their freedom. May God add His blessing and guidance to this matter. Amen.

I greet you cordially along with your wife and children. I also greet our congregation as well as yours, especially Brother Naas. Please inform me how you and they are getting along together. It is my heartfelt wish that everything will very quickly come to true unity. Amen. In the meantime I am asking you to remember me in your prayers and remain your friend and servant,

Bern, October 5, 1715.　　　　　Nicholas Samuel de Treytorrens.[9]

De Treytorrens Imprisoned

The city authorities were not happy with the interest shown by De Treytorrens in the Anabaptists. He was imprisoned and questioned by the Anabaptist Commission.

Minutes of the Bern City Council.
November 2, 1715.

The Anabaptist Commission has placed in the arrest of the ecclesiastical court a certain De Treytorrens of Cudrefin, who maintains false beliefs and tenets; he also allegedly wrote a despicable tract, of which a copy has been sent to Mr. T. von Buren. The above-mentioned is to be examined on account of his actions and the findings to be brought again to Their Graces, the council.[10]

De Treytorrens Banished

Minutes of the Small Council.
November 9, 1715.

Memorandum to the honorable members of the Anabaptist Commission. The council has decided upon your presentation concerning the fanatic or Anabaptist Nicholas Samuel de Treytorrens of Cudrefin, that he should be banished from the city and country as an undesirable guest, after he first compensates for the expenses of his imprisonment, as far as he is able. The reverend sirs will report to Their Graces, the council, about this, in order to transfer this De Treytorrens to the sergeant of the court and court clerk for banishment.[11]

De Treytorrens to Gossen Goyen (2)

In a second letter to Gossen Goyen, De Treytorrens continued his account of his efforts to free Liebe and the other galley slaves. As has been seen from the official records cited above, he was banished from the city, but not before his request was granted. Mentioned in the letter is the possibility of his publicizing the story of his treatment by

LETTRE MISSIUE

Ecritte au Chef de la Chambre de Religion dans la Ville de Berne en Suiſſe, par vne perſonne du Pays.

Oꝛ

Eſt repreſenté le procedé rigourreux tenus jusques icy par LL. EE. dudit Berne & leurs Chambres de Religion , envers leurs pauures Sujets Anabaptiſtes , Pietiſtes & ſemblables , & auſſi envers l'Autheur de ladite lettre & autres.

Imprimé cette Année 1 7 1 7.

Title Page of the Third Section of the Book Written by
Nicholas Samuel de Treytorrens
Courtesy of the Bürger Bibliothek, Bern.

the Bernese authorities. He did carry out his project with the book, *Lettre Missive* . . ., printed in 1717.

Beloved Friend and Brother Gossen Goyen:

As the councilors of Bern have issued to me the letter of recommendation to the king of Sicily soliciting the release of our imprisoned brethren, I shall now set out on my journey to Turin in a few days. I thought that you, my dear friend, might appreciate learning what happened to me in Bern when I attempted to obtain the above-mentioned letter. . . .

After taking this upon myself out of love, I traveled to Bern and went at once to the head of the council. I handed him another letter from Mrs. Liebe, in which she humbly expressed her gratitude to the authorities for granting her petitions, asking that they might give me the letter of recommendation to the king of Sicily to further the matter. The mayor was very friendly to me, and said that I should come again in a week. He wanted to have this letter read to the council. When I came back to him, he was even more friendly than before and said that the councilors had sent an order to the Anabaptist Commission to make out this letter for me at once. I was to go to the president of the commission, who would give me everything and tell me how to go about it. Then he wished me a blessed journey.

When I appeared before the Anabaptist Commission on the day appointed by the president, he asked me what I wanted. I answered that he was acquainted with it already—I had come for the letter of recommendation on behalf of the imprisoned slave, Christian Liebe, at Turin. He then said to me that I was to have it; the government had ordered him to give it to me. I then said that since I was going to take this long journey to liberate Christian Liebe by authority of the said letter, this would be a good opportunity to liberate the other poor fellow prisoners from such great misery too. There were only two of them left; they were even subjects of this country. So it had come into my mind that I would like to make a small petition out of love for the other prisoners, which I would communicate to them if they thought it feasible. They could kindly have the said petition read to the council. I wanted, however, to leave them full liberty to do whatever they thought best in this matter.

Upon this they became so angry against me for having interested myself in those poor prisoners that they spoke harshly with me, even saying that I must be of the same opinion as those people. They began to question me about religious matters, and then they had me put in severe arrest on bread and water. The jailer was forbidden to let anybody visit me. As, however, they had kept my petition and the letter of commission from Mrs. Liebe, they had to present them to the council. When those were read to the council, they were so greatly moved by this petition that they immediately ordered the liberation of the others. They were to be included in the letter of recommendation together with friend Liebe.

In the meantime I was brought before another religious commission and examined about religious matters. They could not find anything to accuse me of, and had to certify that they thought me to be a pious, honest, and just man, who was seeking God with all his heart and had the foundation of the true fear of God and piety in his soul. They could find nothing wrong with me except that I was somewhat melancholy, and had a few wrong opinions; they wanted to exhort me to abandon those. So then finally they asked me whether I could not accept all of the ordinances of their church concerning the inward as well as the outward matters. I then answered that I was very impartial to all devout and sincere souls in the sects; still, if one had to observe the outward forms of worship, I would much prefer to observe those instituted and taught by Christ and His apostles than the ones that were introduced later by poor, blind men. That was only just and natural. Upon this they had me taken back to my prison.

Several days afterwards I had to pay twelve *Reichstaler* for expenses, in which was included one *doubloon* paid to the office for the forwarding of the letter of recommendation. Afterwards they had the sergeant of the court pronounce the verdict: I was banned from this territory forever, etc. They did not require me, however, to take an oath on it. They granted me only four days' time to carry out the commission concerning the letter of recommendation from Bern, which Colonel Hackbrett was to give me, along with other instructions to the court at Turin, as well as to say good-by forever to my relatives and to make arrangements for my few belongings with them as best I could. So then, after those four days I betook myself to Neuchatel, where I am still. I am only waiting for a friend from Bern to bring me the letter of recommendation and other instructions, which had not been finished when I left. Then I shall set out at once on my journey by myself to Turin.

Many friends and also others have been astonished about the way the councilors of Bern proceeded against me—that my imprisonment should cause the liberation of the others and that the councilors had to give me their commission even though I was put under the ban. May God, who gave His blessing to the outset of this undertaking, likewise bless the conclusion of it to the praise and glory of His name. Amen.

It is not known, however, how large a sum of money the king will demand for releasing the imprisoned brethren. I will perhaps write to the dear friends in Holland if it should be more than I can pay myself or can receive from the dear friends in this area. I hope that they will do their best. It could well be that I shall travel yet this winter to Sicily, where the prisoners are, if the king will give me an order to release them. We would stay there until spring, when there should be ships from Holland, and we could all embark and go to the dear friends in Holland. God will arrange everything.

I commend myself and all these matters to your prayers. I am enclosing a copy of the petition which I handed in to the councilors of Bern. It may well be that some day I will have to put the proceedings of the Bernese against me and other brethren, as well as many other things before their eyes, in print. For the rest I commend you and your dear ones as well as all the other brethren and sisters of your congregation as well as ours to the merciful love and grace of God, especially Brother Naas, if he is still there, and others. I commend myself to the prayers of all of you. I remain your loving friend and brother in Christ Jesus.

Neuchatel, November 20, 1715.   Nicholas Samuel de Treytorrens

[P.S.] I visited and consoled the imprisoned brethren and sisters here in Bern, of whom there are still about forty. I recommended them to the Bernese friends. They are calm and confident—thanks be to God. If you want to write me, you can address it to: Monsieur Nicholas Samuel de Treytorrens at Turin, care of Monsieur Thallian's, banker at Turin, next to the palace of the prince of Cavingnand.
December 7, 1715.

P.S. After I had written this letter, two weeks passed until I received the letter of recommendation from the Bernese friend. The devil almost prevented it because of a conspiracy of the king of Sicily against the Bernese, which he had plotted but was discovered in. Therefore, if I had not been promised the letter before that, perhaps I would have never been able to obtain it. However, as this was already known everywhere, and as I had already paid one *doubloon* for the dispatch of it, they had to let it go through. Day after tomorrow I am to get the rest of the commission, as the friend who is to forward it to me wrote me from Bern, because he saw it at the colonel's. As I shall soon depart in the name of the Lord, pray for me that God may bless me and protect me. Amen.[12]

Christian Liebe to Dutch Mennonites

At this time a remarkable letter was sent by the three surviving galley slaves from Palermo to their benefactors in Amsterdam. Christian Liebe was undoubtedly the author of the moving letter, which reached Amsterdam by most indirect means. The address on the outside of the letter read: "The gentleman is requested to forward this letter to that good friend in whose name he wrote on behalf of us prisoners to Leghorn and later to Palermo. He may open it, whether he be in Amsterdam or elsewhere. Express! Express!"

In God Dearly Beloved Friend:

It must have been two days ago when a merchant of Palermo came with a captain from Leghorn to us prisoners on the galley ship. They said that because of our letters they had instructions to set us free, but they had not yet been able to carry it out. We told them that nothing could be done here or at Turin with the king but only in Bern with the authorities. So they said I should write this to Amsterdam. I wanted to make this somewhat known to the dear friends, because while we were still at Turin we learned from a certain gentleman that a letter had come from Holland to Bern from the Estates General on behalf of our liberation. The matter then came before the council and the mayor in Bern in Switzerland, who had sentenced us to the galleys, and it was decided that the Baptists condemned to the galleys might be released. This was on condition that the Estates General would guarantee that the Baptists would not return to Bernese land and territory after they are freed.

We have hoped that they would do this because we would be

willing to promise the government at Bern not to enter their territory again after we are freed unless we had liberty to pass through like others. Therefore we think that if another letter were written from the Estates General appealing to the government at Bern, the result would have the blessing of God. However, they should do whatever love teaches them to do.

We are greatly obliged to God and to the dear friends in Amsterdam, whom we shall repay as our strength allows. I have already written to them once, but do not know whether they have received it. I reported therein that already one of us has died here because of much grief and strenuous traveling, and one a year ago at Turin. There are only three of us left, who warmly greet the dear friends who are concerned about us or ask about us in love. We ask, too, to write to us, if they so please and to let those at Krefeld know that it is permitted for them to write to us. Let the dear friend Gossen Goyen know that we are still minded to hold out through the teachings of Jesus Christ. May God grant us strength, life, and blessing. May God be with you. If we should not see or speak with each other in this world, may then God prepare both of us for His eternal Kingdom, where we can see one another with joy. I have written this out of love; I hope you will not take it amiss. Please forward the enclosed note to the dear friend Gossen Goyen in Krefeld.

Palermo,	I remain your faithful servant
November 16, 1715.	Christian Liebe Peter Wütrich
	Joseph Probst[13]

Galley Slaves' Condition Described

The merchant from Palermo mentioned in Liebe's letter was a Mr. Teissier, who was acting on behalf of the Bernese friends. His report was forwarded to the Mennonites at Amsterdam.

Concerning the five Swiss about whom I have been fully informed, three of them are still living and the other two died—one at Turin and the other one here. The ones still living are the following: Christian Liebe from the Palatinate, Peter Wütrich, Joseph Probst. The one who died at Turin was John Baumgarten, and John Lüthi died here. They are well treated on the galleys by the admiral, and do not have to work. I have attempted to have them unchained so that they might go about freely on the galley, but I did not succeed. It was feared that His Majesty of Turin might show displeasure about this, knowing that they had been sent there by His Majesty and were sentenced for life imprisonment with the express order (for their own reasons) that nobody was permitted to speak with them, so that I was not able to speak with them personally.

They now have in their hands the forty gold coins [*pistols*], which had been deposited and transferred to Vienna by that friend, from which they have taken small amounts from time to time, according to their needs. It is no use to think about obtaining their liberation here, under whatever pretext it might be. His Excellency, the commandant, cannot take any steps in this matter as yet, so that one will have to approach His Majesty of Turin mentioned above on that, which I can do. I shall always keep them recommended to Captain Vincento Li Cascio, who is first officer on the same galley ship and is dependent on our house. Would My Dear Sirs please give me for my guidance the order to replenish their fund as soon as the forty *pistols* or their other money is consumed. This will serve My Dear Sirs [as information] that, when their comrade died, they were ordered to bury him and to officiate themselves. That is all that I can report to My Dear Sirs about this.

Palermo [1715]   [Mr. Teissier][14]

Daniel Knopf to Dutch Mennonites (1)

Daniel Knopf, the friend of De Treytorrens in Bern, carried on the correspondence with the Dutch Mennonites after De Treytorrens left for Sicily. Knopf had earlier been active in the Pietist movement in Bern before 1700. He enclosed copies of the official correspondence to a Colonel Hackbrett, who was charged by the Bernese council with effecting the release of the remaining prisoners.

Mr. Peter Apostool in Amsterdam.
My Dear Sir and Friend:

The letter from the deputies of the Mennonite Brotherhood in Holland of November 22 reached me in good time, as well as the enclosed copy of the letter sent by the Most Powerful Estates General to this canton of October 30. In replying to this, I should like to say, first, that I am quite willing and inclined to oblige My Dear Sirs and friends in this regard, and to be of some help and comfort to those prisoners as far as I can.

Furthermore, I report that Mr. De Treytorrens has now filed a second petition here in favor of Christian Liebe on behalf of the latter's mother. In doing so, instinctively motivated by love and compassion, he interceded also for the other friends imprisoned on the galleys. Upon this, the commission appointed for this matter issued an acknowledgment and forwarded it to Colonel Hackbrett as of November 1, as my dear friends will see from the enclosed copy (Number 1). However, the realization of this order was somewhat delayed, because the said Mr. Hackbrett hoped that this government would itself dispatch a letter to the king of Sicily to expedite this matter and have it delivered to him. I approached several influential persons concerning this. However, the government here considered it better not to write to the king himself, but rather to issue an order in regard to this to Colonel Hackbrett and leave the matter up to him. This was then done on December 3, a copy of which is enclosed (Number 2) [see next document].

Upon this, the said Mr. Hackbrett composed a letter to Commandant Lanfranqui, secretary of war of His Majesty of Turin, and sent it to me on the seventh of this month. I forwarded it to Mr. De Treytorrens at Neuchatel, where he has stayed for several weeks. According to his letter of the ninth of this month, he has departed from there. May God be with him and bless his undertakings. Messrs. Malacrida and Company, by whom I am employed, wrote to Mr. Peter Thallian at Turin that he might provide the necessary money for him. Since they have no correspondent at Palermo, they asked Mr. Bocier in Geneva to take the necessary steps there in this matter with his correspondent, Mr. Teissier, in order that there might be no lack of money. I wrote Mr. De Treytorrens that he should find out who the archbishop was about whom he reported.

As far as the rest of the prisoners here at Bern are concerned, I have learned from the secretary that the authorities were inclined to set them free provided that they would promise not to enter this territory again, etc. This secretary turned the letter from the Estates General of October 30 over to me in order for me to translate it into our language. Please extend my humble salutation to all of the

deputies. I close herewith, commending my dear friend to the grace
of Jesus along with cordial greeting. I remain,

My Dear Sir and friend's
Bern,   obedient servant and friend
December 14, 1715.   Daniel Knopf.[15]

Galley Slaves' Release Arranged

Minutes of the Bern City Council.
December 3, 1715.

To Colonel Hackbrett, temporarily in Lausanne. We have received
an intercession from the powerful Estates General of the United
Netherlands, and especially humble petitions from relatives on behalf
of the Baptists who were sent to the galleys of the king of Sicily a
year ago. They ask that we might be content with the punishment
which these Baptists have already suffered, and that we release them
from the galleys. Out of respect for the above intercession we have,
insofar as it is in our power, graciously granted this to the said galley
slaves and their relatives, in the hope that this punishment on the
galleys will have had its effect on them and that they will never
again set foot in this territory.

As it was possible to turn them over previously through your
arrangement, we wish now to ask you to solicit at the court of His
Royal Majesty and all favorable places at court the liberation of all
those now living and to take all appropriate steps for their release.
For your information, the Mennonite congregations in Holland as
well as the local bank have offered to advance funds or reimburse you
for all of the money necessary for their release, which may be requested. You will know best how to arrange this and act upon this
information. God be with you.[16]

King of Sicily Agrees

The representatives of the king of Sicily responded to a letter
by Colonel Hackbrett, which had been forwarded through De Treytorrens, by offering release on generous terms.

Dear Sir:

I have received, sir, a letter of the seventh of last month, in which
you have taken the trouble to inform me of the mercy which the

council of the state of Bern has granted to the five galley slaves who at present are on the galleys of my lord, the king of Sicily. In this letter you state that you have been requested to ask His Majesty on their behalf for the release of the above-mentioned.

I regret that a journey which I was obliged to make for several days to Turin has hindered me from the pleasure of taking the matter up more promptly, as I would have desired, at your commission. I have not failed after my arrival here to present this to His Majesty, who is willing to permit this, if a small indemnity is required for the [short] time which the said galley slaves have been detained on the galleys. He has ordered me to write by the first regular mail to the viceroy of Sicily, who engaged them in the first instance, who is to produce them, and have them sent to Nice. From there they are to be escorted to the frontier of this state, or to Savoy, or to the Buche d'Aoste according to where the gentlemen of the state of Bern will desire him to put the galley slaves at their disposal. His Majesty takes pleasure in adhering to their request at present. Just as he herewith takes pleasure in receiving this request about the galley slaves, so will he also on all other occasions.

I shall take care to inform you of their arrival in this state on this side of the sea, in order that you can inform your sovereign-authority for their disposal as may be wished. I remain with all possible respect, sir,

your very humble and obedient

From the chase,	servant,
January 10, 1716.	Lanfranqui.[17]

Daniel Knopf to Dutch Mennonites (2)

In two final letters from Daniel Knopf to the Mennonites at Amsterdam, the good news about the release of the prisoners is related. A remarkable example of international and interconfessional aid was thereby completed.

Highly Esteemed Sirs, Beloved Friends:
Since my last letter of January 19 I have been hoping to receive soon more news to report to you, dear sirs. I had hoped all the more after I had received a letter from Mr. De Treytorrens of February 15 from Nice, in which he informed me of his safe arrival there. He

also mentioned that they had given him reason to hope that the prisoners in question might yet arrive at Nice during the month of February.

Therefore I have been waiting for letters from one mail delivery to the next, especially as I had received a letter from you, dear friends, of March 13. The reason why I did not answer it before now is that I received a letter from Mr. De Treytorrens a week ago. He reports that to date he has been waiting in vain for the arrival of our friends from Sicily, because no ship from there has landed since then on account of the hazardous winds. Now I am confident of receiving soon the news of their safe arrival at Nice. In that case I shall not fail to communicate this to you, dear friends, immediately. I have received letters directly from the friend Jan Frerickson since then.

Finally, you, dear sirs and true friends, are all greeted and commended to the grace of Jesus.

Bern,   . . . Your humble servant and friend
April 25, 1716.   Daniel Knopf.[18]

Daniel Knopf Reports Release

Highly Esteemed Sirs, Beloved Friends:

My last letter was written on April 25. I hope that it has arrived safely. Since then I have received a letter from Mr. De Treytorrens dated April 8 from Turin, in which he reports the happy news that he and the prisoners in question have arrived there safe and sound after their discharge. They are about to continue their journey under the kind hand of God to Geneva, from there to Newcastle (or Neuchatel), and then to Germany. Doubtless he will write to you, dear friends, in person, yet I did not want to fail to tell you of this report immediately. I am praying to God that He might be with them on their journey and protect them from all evil.

Bern,   Your obliging servant and friend
May 20, 1716.   Daniel Knopf.[19]

THE SOLINGEN BRETHREN

On February 1, 1717, six Brethren from Solingen and their landlord were marched off under heavy guard to be imprisoned in Düsseldorf. Their crime—being baptized by the Krefeld Brethren. Nearly fifty years later the youngest member of the group, William Grahe, wrote down their experiences in Düsseldorf and in the fortress of Jülich where they were sentenced to hard labor for life. This narrative was highly cherished in Pietist circles and copied many times. It was often read in their meetings as an example of loyalty to the faith.

Max Goebel, the Reformed church official who wrote the standard work on nonchurch religious activities in Germany during this time, said of the Solingen Brethren and Grahe's story: "Their further fate and four years of hard imprisonment and their eventual release from the fortress at Jülich have been described so exactly and completely, so faithfully and warmly, that I feel I must present here this story in its entirety and unchanged." He devoted twenty-five full pages in his third volume to publishing this document.

There are two known handwritten copies in Germany—one in Krefeld and one in Bonn. A Dutch version taken from a privately owned copy was printed in a Mennonite periodical in the Netherlands in 1861. An incomplete excerpt was published in a German newspaper in Krefeld in the late nineteenth century. The following translation is based on both manuscript copies, which have minor variations.[20]

THE PRISON EXPERIENCE

William Grahe Describes Imprisonment

A faithful account of the seven persons imprisoned for the truth and for the sake of Christ, named:

1. John Lobach;
2. John Frederick Henckels;
3. Jacob Grahe;
4. William Knepper;
5. Luther Stetius;
6. William Grahe;
7. John Carl.

These seven persons named were taken from the town of Solingen to the prison at Düsseldorf on February 1, 1717.

Collected and written by William Grahe in Krefeld, 1763.

Soli Deo Gloria!

[To God alone the glory!]

As we seven men named above, who had learned to recognize

The Reformed Church at Solingen-Wald

the suppressed truth according to the understanding of the first
Christians, also endeavored to live in harmony with this as far as
faith and mercy had appeared in us, we were arrested in the town of
Solingen by the local judge. We were bound two by two around our
arms; John Carl, as the seventh, had one of his arms tied to the other
with a rope behind his back. We were thus led away to Düsseldorf,
which journey we passed mostly in singing. As we were led away,
we were all overwhelmed with mercy and joy, so that we praised and
glorified God for His mercy that we might now endure something for
His pure truth. We sang the hymn: "O Jesus, My Bridegroom, How
Happy I Feel!" [*O Jesu, mein Bräutigam, wie ist mir so wohl!*]. The
excitement among the people was also very great; yes, there were
many so awakened and impressed by the matter that it was with them
as Paul said about the Galatians: "What has become of the satisfaction
you felt? . . . you would have plucked out your eyes and given them
to me" [Galatians 4:15]. We prisoners were accompanied by shouts
of rejoicing and went to Düsseldorf, singing most of the way.

Most of the armed guards who were with us to escort us went
home, considering it unnecessary to go along and watch over such
peace-loving and cheerful persons, so that we seven prisoners had
only seven guards. They were like that dean of Flanders, as he once
went out to seize the so-called heretics or devout Christians. He met
a captain of the militia [*Land-Capitain*] in an inn, who had many
soldiers with him in order to catch thieves and similar criminals. The
captain came to him and asked how he, the dean, could go to seize
people with so few men. The dean gave him to understand that there
was no danger, as he seized only single-minded and devout people,
who did not defend themselves. The captain replied, "You want to
seize the good people, and I the bad. Who will finally be left?"

We arrived then at Düsseldorf as prisoners in the evening, and
as it was dark, we were taken to the prison without any crowd gathering. We were surprised that we were put in such a nice prison. We
stayed there together until February 4. In the afternoon the jailer
came, and announced that the judges [*Herren*] were coming to examine us. The seventh, namely John Carl, who had come along, was
released after paying a fine. The six of us, however, who were to give
account of ourselves for the first time before men in high places, had
for that reason a considerable inner struggle. Despite this, as soon as

each one came to the chamber or room where the gentlemen were, we experienced truly there what Jesus says: "Do not be anxious how you are to speak" [Matthew 10:19], and immediately all fear fell away. We were all able to give account of ourselves with cheerful spirits.

I went in with confidence as the first, and all fear fell from me as if a heavy coat were taken from me. I said: "Gentlemen! I wish you all much mercy, peace, and blessings from God. I am ready to hear what you have to say to me." They thanked me first for my wish, and then said that we had been accused of beginning a new doctrine. Therefore it had been necessary for them to seize us. We answered them that we were surprised that they considered this a new doctrine, for what we had taught and done is nothing else but what Jesus taught and commanded us to do, which is completely based on the Holy Scriptures.

We also told them to search the Holy Scriptures carefully and they would then find that this was nothing new. We further said that men had strayed far from the truth and the right way, so that it was indeed very necessary to seek anew for the former way—which was the good and rightful path—in order to walk therein. We had intended to do nothing else, and also had done nothing else except what was based on the Holy Scriptures. If we were therefore looked upon by the judges as criminals, we were, despite that, innocent, and we remained unafraid. The judges replied that they had seized us because we did not remain in one of the three established churches. Whereupon we said that they might send a request to where we had lived and investigate to see if anyone could present or bring a complaint against our lives and conduct, as we were minded to live with and to treat all men in peace. The judges said that they had nothing against our lives and conduct, only that we must abide by one of the three churches. We were to think this over.

After that we were visited on the following day by a Jesuit father named Bramer. He came to us in a very friendly manner, flattered us greatly, and asked why we had been imprisoned, and who had been the cause of it. We answered that we did not worry about that; that we were here in the hand of God, and nothing could happen against His will! The said Jesuit asked us what our doctrine and way of life were. "Oh," said he, "that is all fine and very good; you have acted correctly and appropriately, for the life of the world is so wicked that one might well wish to better himself. Only one thing astonishes me greatly—that the Protestant preachers have accused you because of the baptism, for your way of baptism can be proved by the Holy Scriptures but infant baptism not at all." We replied to this that we were also astonished that the authorities wished to arrest us against the teaching of the Holy Scriptures. "Yet, dear people," said he, "there are other teachers in God's church. The point of contention is the church's traditions, because therein is infant baptism established."

We answered: "We hold that the Holy Scriptures are sufficient and more important than tradition. It is enough for us that our teaching and faith are grounded according to Holy Scripture on the rock of salvation, Jesus Christ." Finally, after a long conversation which he flatteringly conducted, he said, "It is all well with you; insofar as you strive to change and improve your lives it is very praiseworthy; you lack just one thing." We asked him what that was. He said that we must return to the fold of the true church of God. We then answered: "We strive to be members of the universal Christian church on earth." He said, "Yes, the Roman Catholic Church." We answered him that we could hold alone to Holy Scripture, which was sufficient for our guide and compass. He remained outwardly friendly to us and left us with a cordial wish. However, after he closed our prison door behind him he said outside, "If the prisoners are thus treated—namely, if they are together in one room, so that one can talk with the other, it will not be possible to convert them." He then arranged with the authorities, the next day, that we were separated from one another, each by himself, and in addition, that there was one empty cell between each one and the next, so that we could not speak with each other.

Moreover, at that time it was very cold, so that some had to get up during the night to keep warm by walking up and down. We had meanwhile often been visited by the Jesuit father, Bramer, who had completely forgotten his first assumed friendliness. He had told the authorities many bad things about us—that we prisoners were stubborn blockheads who could not be converted, and that we should be treated more harshly. After we had been there for several weeks, we were taken two by two and asked whether we had thought better of it. We answered that the grace of God had appeared to us and had called us to leave the vain world, and to surrender ourselves to God

Aufrichtige Nachricht.

von denen

Um der Wahrheit und Christi
willen in Verhaft genommen
sieben Personen:

1) Nahmens Johannes Lobach.
2) Johann Friedrich Henkels.
3) Jacob Grah.
4) Wilhelm Knepper.
5) Luther Stettius.
6) Wilhelm Grah.
7) Johann Karl.

Diese sieben
benannten Personen sind den 1ten
Febr. 1717 von der Statt
Solingen nach Düsseldorf in
Verhaft gebracht worden.

The Title Page of William Grahe's "Faithful Account"
Courtesy of Dr. J. F. Gerhard Goeters, Bonn.

with all our hearts, to love Him alone, according to the gospel of Jesus Christ. There was no need for us to reconsider this. They said further that we would be given six more weeks to reconsider and to accommodate ourselves to one of the three churches. We answered that we needed no time to reconsider concerning the three churches or choose which was the best, for one condemned the other. The Protestants say about the Catholics that they have an anti-Christian doctrine, and that the Pope is the Antichrist; on the other hand, the Romans even say of the others that they are of the devil. Thus simple people soon will not know where they should turn. It is better that we hold to the Holy Scriptures, to the rock of our salvation, Jesus Christ. The judges responded: "Yes, yes! That will do. We shall see what you will do." We then returned to our prison. In the month of April a rumor arose that we were to be flogged. We readied ourselves for it, although our friends told us that we should prepare ourselves and make ourselves ready for even more and harsher punishment.

This crisis passed away until in the month of May the privy councilor and chief magistrate himself came to each of our cells and said: "You will be given three more days to think better of it; otherwise you must expect whatever may happen to you." We answered little, only this, that nothing could happen to us unless it was God's will. In the meantime, a hard trial came for us, because the rumor spread that three of us, namely the three older ones, were to die, and the three younger ones were to be flogged, or even sent to the galleys. Moreover, several people came—even John Stetius—who said that the executioner had said that whenever he was to execute someone he always had some prior indication such as that the execution sword rang by itself at night. This had recently happened to him. So it was that we had to endure the fire of trial in various ways. The loving God gave us, however, courage and confident hearts always, for which we gave thanks to Him. At this time there were other unusual circumstances which were also written down. The jailer was so treacherous, however, that he often opened the door unexpectedly and called for us to appear before the judges immediately, and then he stole everything. He treacherously stole many important things from me in this way. One day, after we had just left our cells, I found my knife which he had stolen from me secretly. I had received it from a friend shortly before, because the jailer had previously taken away all of our knives, and had given us wooden ones in their place. We had to eat with those until friends secretly brought us others.

The Jesuit father, Bramer, wasted all of his efforts on us. The last time that he came to us, and as he was about to leave soon after, I, William Grahe, asked this Jesuit whether the Holy Scriptures or Bible described the way to salvation? He answered, "Yes, certainly!" Then I said, "I believe that too. We are therefore agreed on this point." I said further: "You have often come to us in order to convert us to your faith, in which, however, much is contained that cannot be found in the Bible. I ask God that He will save me [from that]. Consequently there is no hope for unity in that way. But since you admit and hold, as well as I, that the way to salvation is sufficiently pointed out in the Bible, I could then find a means by which we might agree. Namely, each of us must discard all of his knowledge—that is, I will discard my knowledge, and you must discard all of your religious conclusions and formulas. We will then study the Holy Scriptures, praying to God with sincere and simple hearts and minds that He might give us His spirit so that we might understand the Holy Scriptures rightly, and then the Holy Scriptures will show us the way. If you can be of the same mind with us on this and be content, then we could take hope that we could agree with you." He recoiled, spit in front of himself, and said to us: "What? Should I now begin again, after I took this path thirty years ago? Phooey!" and went away. I called after him: "Then all your efforts are in vain!" On another occasion, when he asked Luther Stetius what he thought of the Pope, Stetius answered: "The Protestants say that he is the Antichrist. We will leave it at that." That priest [*Pfaff*] finally stayed away and considered us stubborn heretics who must be punished with all severity, which he also faithfully informed the authorities.

It happened at that time that a man and his wife were brought as prisoners who were supposed to have associated with criminals. They were then tortured, first the wife, who had thumb-irons screwed on, so that she screamed piteously. When she was freed from them, the husband was brought to the rack. The torture chamber must have been directly under our prison, for we could hear everything. He had the thumb-irons and the so-called Spanish boot screwed on at the same time, so that the man moaned and screamed so much that it was unbearable for us to hear it. After they had tortured him long enough, he was brought to an adjoining cell, and we were taken before the judges. They took us to the torture chamber, where the executioner stood in the door. This was to frighten us so that we were to think that the same thing would happen to us that had happened to the others. We, however, had to arm ourselves with faith and hold fast to our hope in Him who was able to make us strong even to stand steadfast against the Antichrist and devil; we experienced this at all times to the praise of God. We then came before the judge, who only asked us, as often before, whether we had reconsidered. We answered as before and were again taken to our room, so that we thanked the merciful God and Savior that we were saved from the terror of torture.

After this a Lutheran preacher came to us, who was supposed to demonstrate his skill. He was much more moderate than the previous one, and sought to persuade us to join one of the sects. When he, however, failed to accomplish anything, he also stayed away. After this a Reformed [preacher] came, who showed himself even more lenient. He promised us great things, and rejoiced that there were people who strove for betterment. If we would only go to church, then we would bear great fruit; we were also to have complete freedom to speak in the church. When the preacher preached something [wrong], then we should tell him about it. As we answered him modestly, he deluded himself that he had already ensnared us with his cleverness, and wrote immediately to many preachers, that is, Knevel, Ovenius, Hackman, and also to others, so that six preachers came to us in the prison on May 15, 1717. Ovenius asked: "John Lobach, why did you come here into prison?" Lobach answered: "So that your villainy might be revealed." They presented such untimely assumptions that all their hopes dissolved into water. Nothing of which the first preacher had spoken was mentioned at all.

Pastor Ovenius, as chairman, began to speak first. They had learned from their colleague that we were minded to return to our former church. For that reason they had all come together here in order to hear what we had to say about it. We answered that this was more than we were aware of, for we had never mentioned such a thing or given such to be understood. We had only said: "If the Reformed conducted themselves according to the Heidelberg Catechism, and if only the infant baptism, swearing of oaths, and the sixtieth question [on justification by faith] were different, we could then soon agree with you. As that was still far in the future, you have not been wise in expecting that of us." They then got over this into a state of confusion and all sorts of argument, so that nothing came of all this. In the meantime the room had become so crowded with people that they extended past the doorway, and the preachers wanted the door shut. Finally, they went away in disgust, and each of us returned to his own cell, so that we were left in peace by those learnéd theologians.

In the meantime, the rumor mentioned above—that some us were to die and some of us were to be sent to the galleys—lasted for a time. Some of us really endured the agonies of death. John Lobach's mother resolved to follow her son herself unto death, as he had to sacrifice his life for God for the sake of the truth. This crisis passed, however, through special providence so that we were left in peace most of the summer. We spent the time in reading and writing, and also many hymns were composed. That we read and wrote so much came about because various people sent us all kinds of communications which we were to answer. One of the first to come into our hands was a message seven quires long. It was composed in a rather sermonizing style, and the authors prided themselves on their accomplishment. It was, however, without power or savor. We answered this by giving our convictions in brief. Later came an inquiry covering twelve points or questions which we also answered. This was, however, along with the previously mentioned, taken away by the jailer and lost. There was also a creed composed in a simple manner, and the same was put into rhyme by W[illiam] Knepper, who also composed about four hundred hymns there.

It happened once that the jailer refused to bring us any water, so that I, W[illiam] Grahe, received no water from him for five weeks. The idea was that he would deliver to us old, stale beer for which we would have to pay the price of good beer. I could enjoy or use water better than that beer. In the meantime a well opened itself in my room, because when it rained the water often fell through the eavestrough past my window. I fixed a little board so that it was held tightly between the bars, and placed a vessel on it. In this way I could catch enough water to pass quantities of it in a narrow glass through a hole made in the wall near the floor to a brother who was next to me in another room. One time another brother who was far from me was very thirsty. He made a small trough which he could cut an inch thick and push through the thick boards and also receive water from another brother. Finally the jailer saw that he could not torment us in this way and brought water again on his own accord.

We sat in prison until in the fall, without being molested very much. Our case was then taken before three universities. The Roman [Catholics] recommended in their bloodthirsty manner that we be executed, the Lutherans the galleys, and the Reformed hard labor at Jülich. We were then condemned to hard labor for life at Jülich. The appointed day came, although the jailer had not told us, even though he knew about it already. He had concealed it from us with the intention that when we had to leave immediately without warning he could fall heir to everything which remained in our rooms.

However, one of my relatives came to the prison and called me by name. When I looked out I was asked whether I knew that we were to be taken to Jülich very soon. The armed guards had already appeared at the prison. I then called all of my fellow prisoners to pack their things quickly, as we had to leave immediately. We could call to one another, for if attention was paid, one could hear and understand everything even though every one had a wall between himself and the next. Therefore we quickly packed everything that could be taken along, and in such manner that it could be easily carried. When the jailer came, he said: "You must leave immediately; come out at once!" When he saw that each of us had his baggage and pack on his back ready to carry, he ground his teeth in rage, pounded his hands, cursed, and asked who had told us. We must be unusual people to learn everything in advance. He received, by the way, my straw bedstead and some earthen pottery as a souvenir, and also from all of us our names and some poems written on the walls of the prison.

We then had to hurry away in the afternoon with forty-eight guards at about three o'clock on December 1, 1717. They took us as far as the Rhine, but we crossed over with only twenty-four [guards]. We had to stay overnight at the first village. It was strange for us to be among such sinister creatures, after we had lived in peace for ten months. It took three days until we arrived at Jülich, because we were not used to walking in our imprisonment or in prison, and we were unable to walk far.

It so happened as we were walking along toward Jülich that some of us with a few guards had gone ahead, and some others had lagged behind a good two thousand yards from each other, so that I walked alone in the middle of a field far from both parties, and had no guards with me. A man came from the side of the field and fell in beside me. He saw then the first group going along with the guards and asked what kind of people they might be. Then I said that I belonged to them too, and explained the situation to him. He was astonished that I was walking along alone and had no guards with me. I answered him that they did not worry about our running away. That was not necessary for us, for we did not fear any man, because Jesus, His truth and teaching were our protection and solace. I had many opportunities to escape; if I had just stopped in a street, I would soon have been forgotten and lost sight of. I could have gone wherever I pleased, but the love of the truth and for my brethren kept us together. We finally came together again and went along as a group until we came to Jülich, which was on the third day following our departure from Düsseldorf.

We were then placed in the prison called the "Bacon Pantry" [because of the many rats there]. There were twelve other prisoners there, mostly very wicked people. We had only one *stiver* of money among us. We were not given anything to eat, contrary to the usual practice with prisoners, because bread day had been the previous day. We therefore had to trust to the merciful providence of God. We came to the Bacon Pantry at about ten o'clock and at twelve o'clock the other prisoners ate. Their behavior seemed so disgusting to us that we had no desire to eat with them. However, they did not offer us anything anyway. We resolved to fast if the dear God so desired, but at one o'clock a soldier came to the grating, or bars, and said that he came from Düsseldorf. There John Stetius, Luther Stetius' father, had spoken with him. He had told him that he had a son in the prison where the soldier was stationed. He had requested him to tell us at once that we should have whatever we needed brought from the canteen-owner [sutler]. The soldier went at once to the canteen-owner, and returned immediately to us, and asked if we wanted to have a noon meal; if so, he would bring us whatever we said. We answered that it was up to him; so he brought us a lentil soup, meat, butter, and bread. We refreshed ourselves after our strenuous and exhausting journey. We thanked the dear Father for His goodness and . . . care, that we were treated in such a miraculous manner.

It was Saturday when we came to Jülich; therefore, we could rest on Sunday. On Monday we had to go to work with the other evildoers to the ramparts of the castle. After we had pushed wheelbarrows for a while, we were ordered lowered in a large bucket forty feet deep in the ground. Four of us spent most of the winter working underground, and pushing wheelbarrows. The dirt was wound out of the hole by others. After being there for several days we were visited by two brethren, Christophel [?] and [Stephen] Koch, and, soon thereafter, by Christophel and William Müller. They paid for that which we had received from the canteen-owner and arranged some other matters. Soon afterward there came three other friends, namely Hubert Rahr, John van Emrath, and Jan Crous. They showed themselves very obliging to us and also to the commandant. Shortly thereafter, Brother [John] Naas with someone else visited us, and also had complete freedom to talk with us. They could not stay with us very long, however.

We received, like all prisoners, five and a half pounds of bread every four days. When we came first into the Bacon Pantry, the other prisoners demanded an initiation treat. We said such foolishness was quite godless. But we could protest all we wanted to to no avail, and criticism helped not at all. They said even if our Lord God himself came here, He would have to provide an initiation treat. We then had six quarts of beer brought for the men, and they were satisfied. When they noticed that we had no lice, some of them put them in our bedding and clothes. We also sang in prison, until a corporal came and forbade us that. They also sent word to us and demanded that we give them our books. We, however, answered that we owed and were ready to render obedience to our authorities in all just matters, but in this case we need not obey. If they had the church histories looked into they would find that such a thing was never demanded by Christians but was rather considered a great sin, although committed in the time of the persecution by the heathen. They then sent for them with this pretext that they just wanted to see the books once; then we should get them back again. Therefore we sent the same, that is, five Bibles, to them, but never recovered them until we were freed.

It happened once, after we had been in Jülich for some days, that some officers and two Capuchin monks came. The Capuchins began at once to argue with us, and soon asked whether we could do miracles. We asked one of them in return whether he could work miracles. He said, "Yes, through God's grace I have worked miracles." We said that true believers never praise their own miracles. He said that he had the true faith: "We! We are the true church of God!" He said that he had the true faith, and that they, in the Roman Church, had the true faith. That had been attested to by the cats and donkeys with Anthony of Padua. We replied: "Oh, a poor proof!" We said further that he should ask God that he might be given a new heart and light and His Spirit, or else we feared that he would be sadly betrayed by his imagination. He was as far from the true faith and the church of God as heaven was from the earth. He then burst out in anger and said to the one who was speaking with him: "You lie like a scoundrel!"

He was also told that he was certainly a wretched person to have such a terrible way of speaking, and to have such poor knowledge of God, of Christ and His truth, and of himself. If he did not completely change, then, we feared that he would have little share in Christ and His grace. Then he said: "What, should we not be saved? Then God could not be a true God—indeed, God would be an unjust God if we were not saved." Almost all those who were with him were shocked, including the Catholics, and shook their heads. We did not wish to speak with him further and said he did not deserve an answer, as we had never heard such rough talk before. We then turned away from him. He went away and blasphemed. He had made himself loathed by his own people, as even the Catholics complained greatly about him—that he was so rough and had spoken so godlessly.

It happened around New Year's that gypsies came into the area; forty of them were imprisoned in Jülich, and put into the Bacon Pantry. The other prisoners had to be placed elsewhere. We were separated. Lobach and Jacob Grahe were placed underneath the gate named Paradise with four others; W[illiam] Knepper and John Frederick Henckels were placed in the salt-chamber with some others; Luther Stetius and I with four others were placed above the guardhouse, with two peasant jurors who had been brought to Jülich tied to horses' tails by riders. While we were there the other prisoners treated us meanly. We had made a three-legged stool, and when we came from work at noon or in the evening they always ran ahead. They would take our stool and let us stand by them, until we went to work again. Then I thought of this trick: I made a stool from four old barrel staves which they were unable to use. When I wanted to use it, I put it together— which they could not accomplish. Therefore they had to leave it to me, because when I stood up, it fell apart.

After we had lived above the guardhouse for some time, the gypsies were taken away, and we (Luther Stetius and I) with the other prisoners were taken back to the Bacon Pantry. The other four brethren, though, stayed where they were. It happened around Candlemas [February 2] that Luther Stetius' father came to Jülich. He requested of the commandant that we be released from the Bacon Pantry and we then joined Jacob Grahe and John Lobach. It so happened that Knepper and Henckels had two other prisoners with them; those two fought with each other and hurt each other seriously, and ruined and broke Henckels' and Knepper's belongings. That gave the opportunity for both of these brethren also to come to us under the gate called Paradise. Therefore all six of us were together. We had our dwelling in this prison for about nineteen months. This dungeon was four feet deep under the ground, with walls about ten feet thick. On the inside of the light slit there was a heavy iron grating, in the middle another, and on the outside the opening was only one foot high and one and a half feet wide. The grating was so narrow that a rat could hardly creep through. Around Candlemas the sun shone through, but only for three to four weeks. In the summertime when we wanted to sew we had to light a candle.

We always had our work to do. In the spring we had to work outside of the town by the mill pond, first here, then there. As we were working there once, a Capuchin monk who saw us asked us various things. When he failed to get his way, he said that he had good advice for us. He would give us only half a pound of bread and half a quart of water a day and have us beaten daily; we would then soon be converted! Once John Lobach and I had to haul trash in the town. As it was almost evening, Lobach wanted to buy something, and had to go through the town a short distance. The guard went with him, and they passed a house where the town commandant was standing. He said that that could not be done, and ordered another soldier to take Lobach and the guard to the castle as prisoners. When I joined Lobach later, he said that now he had been arrested twice over. The outcome was not serious, except that the soldier who had been Lobach's guard had to stand three extra watches as punishment. We paid for this, however, with twenty-two and a half *stivers* (three shillings), and after that they trusted us more.

They often let us go into the town by ourselves to buy what we needed. I have gone outside the gates without a guard and been seen by the commandant, but I had asked him about it while working. I also went for water more than a quarter of an hour in distance outside the town. Once I and Jacob Grahe worked outside of the town walls. When evening came and we wanted to return to the town, we had lost our guards. We looked for them a long time, and then decided to return without them. We then found one guard in a dry ditch; perhaps he did not want to go to the town, but we called him and then he went with us; so we came back to town. They trusted us even that when only two of us were in the town they would not be deserted by the rest, which was our idea also.

The treatment we received depended on who the guards and officers were that guarded us. Of all the work we had to do, the worst was that in October 1718. In the mornings when the frost lay on the ground, we had to dig out the muck from the town moat, often standing in water to our waists. This was so the soldiers could not desert. This work lasted fourteen days. The other prisoners could not be forced to do this even with blows. The extremely hot summer of 1719 followed, and we all became gravely ill and many were lame.

I must report something about our housekeeping methods. Besides the food which we received every four days, each of us contributed one *stiver* for the daily maintenance. When all six of us were together, we kept house, and cooked barley, peas, and lentils. If we bought two pounds of barley for two and a half *stivers,* they would last three days, or we could cook them for three meals; two quarts of peas, costing four *stivers,* lasted also three days; and two quarts of lentils, the same. We were quite content with this. Each took turns cooking, and all had their regular turns.

Most of us learned how to make buttons (which John Lobach knew, and from whom the others probably learned it [footnote of the

copyist]). In the summertime, we could not work much at that, however, because we had to work from five o'clock until eleven, and from
one to seven. We had two rest periods of half an hour each at about
eight o'clock and four o'clock, but that did not help much. Therefore
we could not do much buttonmaking in the summertime, but in the
winter when the days were short we could earn quite a bit by doing
that, and with the profits we were able to buy what we needed for
our maintenance. In addition, good friends sent us various things, so
that we were not in want of anything. We had to praise therein the
merciful providence of the benevolent God. We also learned how to
make our own clothing so that we were not dependent on anyone for
that either.

On June 24, 1718, the captain of the guard sent us two letters
along with white paper and ink, and said that we were to answer the
letters. They were from two Franciscan monks from Altenhofen.
They wrote us very flatteringly and called us "dear brethren" and
"children of God" and other fine names. They wrote that they had
heard of us that we wanted to improve our lives, which was a very
good thing. They were also two brethren of one faith, one mind,
one trade—in sum, were in all things one. They wanted to tell us
that if we wanted to convert people, we should betake ourselves to
God's church, travel with them to England, where the heretics lived,
and then we could convert the latter. We answered, however, that
we were most astonished at their expressions, that they thought that
they could deceive us with such complimentary words, calling us "dear
brethren" and "children of God," and yet in spite of that consider us
outside of the church of God. They were, therefore, very much
mistaken on that point; that which they considered the church of God,
we deemed to have strayed in the most part from the teachings and
simplicity of Jesus Christ. As long as they were not of a mind to leave
a church like that, and to obey the gospel of Jesus Christ in humbleness,
we could not accept them as "dear brethren." There was no point in
their writing us further in that vein. We heard nothing more from
them.

At the beginning of the year 1719, the Brethren John Naas,
Alexander Mack, Fischer from Hall [Halle?], and Eckerlin came
and visited us. Whenever we had visitors, the canteen-owner went to
the commandant and secured permission for us to have our meals at

One of the Gates of the Juelich Fortress

his place. This was profitable for him, and it cost us and our friends plenty. We had to accept it, though, because in this way we could often be together for half a day, which otherwise would have been impossible. We were visited so often that the people of Jülich were astonished that we had so many acquaintances, and that we showed such warm love for one another. They clapped their hands and said that such a thing was not common among them. We must indeed have something special. Once two brethren came, namely John Weck and Clemens Knepper, who went to the general and requested that two of us might go home for several days, and they would take their places in prison for that time. The general replied, however, that he could not grant that, for he was not our judge, but the servant of the judges.

I have mentioned before that the Romans said of the Protestants that they were of the devil. This I myself heard from a Capuchin, who wanted to convert a Lutheran corporal. The corporal did not respond; so the Capuchin said: "Why do you hesitate so long? It is true that the Calvinists and the Lutherans are all of the devil." At this time there was a prisoner named Jacob who was a Catholic. He was otherwise a cunning scoundrel, but after he had observed us for some time, and had seen that we sat quietly by ourselves when we had a rest period, he began to join us. He acted as if he wanted to begin a new way of life, and discarded some of his rough habits, and stayed with us a great deal. We tolerated him, and let him come to us without hindrance.

This the others could not bear. He was denounced, and soon a Capuchin came to us on the ramparts, just as it was a rest period, and Jacob sat with us. He spoke to us with great solemnity, saying: "I order and command you not to talk with this Jacob, but rather let him go," and made a long oration. We replied to him, however: "We do not know you. Who gave you authority to give us orders? We ignore your orders. If Jacob wants to sit or stand with us, we cannot prevent it. If you have the power to command that Jacob should not associate with us, that we must accept." This method of conversion worked so well with this Jacob that he did not come to us any more, but resumed his former bad habits, and conducted himself most godlessly. It was better for him to do that than to improve his wicked life, because sins, no matter how great, can be forgiven by the priests.

About the same time, the dear friends, Peter [text incomplete] came to visit us, and we again had freedom to refresh ourselves at the canteen. It also happened once that as we were working on the ramparts it rained so hard that we all went into the hut where the dirt was hoisted up. Many Catholic prisoners and a Lutheran dragoon named Maurice from Herbeth were standing there. Luther Stetius and I were also inside. The Catholics talked about us, and one of them said: "One can clearly see that the Catholic Church is the best, for such people as those cannot be found in it." Then said Maurice in his peculiarly dry manner of speaking: "That you may well say, for the Catholics are all so impenitent that they cannot improve their lives!" The others were so ashamed and embarrassed that no one gave an answer to this. There was a long silence. We had to force ourselves not to be tempted into laughing about his remark, because of the clever jibe and expression of Maurice, who was otherwise no saint, but had studied as a youth.

Once when the general had some gentlemen from outside of town with him, namely the mayor of Altenhofen and the Privy Councilor Deroc from Düsseldorf with still others, they had the desire to see us. They had us come to them on the ramparts and argued for a long time with us. Deroc said: "You should perish here like animals." (The same Deroc, however, at the time of our release, supposedly spoke rather in favor of than against it.) We answered him: "Men have power over us no longer than God permits." Many mocked us; many sympathized with us. General Hackhausen, especially, was never harsh with us. Once he said to us as he was coming along the ramparts: "How are you, dear people?" We answered: "Fine, Your Excellency." He waited a while longer to see if we had anything to say. It was very unfortunate that he was away from Jülich most of the time.

In the year 1719 there was that intensely hot summer. At that time many died in the fields in the area of Jülich from the heat. For four weeks in June we had to weed out the grass from between the stones in the castle square, where there was no shade. Once a corporal with four soldiers went to the castle chapel to escort the priest with the so-called monstrance. Our guard said that we would have to fall on our knees when they came. We replied that if we were willing to do that we would not need to be in prison. We would not even take our hats off. The soldier was very much perplexed. Finally he had this idea: he said that we should go off to the side until they had come out and had returned again. We said that we would gladly do this. Thus we escaped from the burning rays of the sun for a time. We went into an old chamber until the priest was in the chapel again.

When this work was over, we had to work outside of the town. To come at eleven o'clock noon to our dungeon, which was like a cellar with walls (as previously mentioned) about ten feet thick, we had had to walk for half an hour. We would become very hot, and our blood thin. As we then came into our cold dungeon, our systems were completely changed, and then the blood became thick. Because of this we all became sick, and had much pain in our feet and legs. They sent a doctor to us, but he said that he could not help us as long as we stayed in that dungeon. So two of us were taken at once to a cell above the guardhouse, and two others also the same day. I said that we were all sick, and could not take care of ourselves, and that the others should join us; so we were all placed together in the cell above the guardhouse. We were there for seventeen weeks and were ill most of the time. Most of us were near death, and had to reckon with that possibility. Some had scurvy so badly that their gums grew over their teeth, but the surgeon from the artillery had some good medicine for that. So all of us recovered with God's blessing, but I was crippled for a long time.

Finally we were improved enough that some of us could go to work again. As the town commandant then saw that the location above the guardhouse was advantageous for us, he wanted us to give him a gift of a linen sheet costing five *Reichstaler;* otherwise we would have to return to the old dungeon under the gate. It was not our intention to buy any alleviation with gifts; so we had to leave again immediately. At this time Jacob Grahe was very ill, and could not stand to do much work because of great pains in his head. We had to let our things go, until he was better again. After being in the old dungeon again for some time, we were visited by Gossen Goyen and Jacob William Naas. They received permission to sleep with us in the dungeon, which was dangerous for the captain of the guard to grant. Gossen Goyen asked us why we were in this old dungeon again. After much questioning he finally learned from someone that we had refused to give the commandant a present. They spoke to the latter without our knowledge and sent him something. After fourteen weeks, we were put in the cell above the guardhouse again.

Shortly thereafter, we had to work on the tower of the castle, one hundred twelve steps high, clearing off wood and carrying away trash. Some of us got swollen legs from this. Once Luther Stetius and I had to roll heavy stones along the wall, where one could have easily fallen from the high tower wall into the abyss. At Pentecost, the rough lumber framework, weighing two thousand pounds, was to be erected on the tower. About twenty men were working on it. The carpenters could not handle it, and the heavy construction collapsed and injured many people. It struck my head and I immediately lost all feeling and consciousness, and lay there as if I were dead. Luther Stetius came to me, cried out and wept, and thought I was going to die. After a few minutes, however, I regained consciousness and feeling, and could see again and talk a bit. I saw Luther Stetius standing over me in sorrow and full of sympathy. I said to him brokenly, for my tongue was completely stiff, that it was not as bad as he might think, but my back hurt me terribly. He should lay something under my back, which he did right away. The heavy wood had fallen directly on my head, but as a small pile of wood had been lying near by, the entire fall was broken. Otherwise I would have been completely smashed. My back was very badly crushed, though, and my shoestrings were in pieces and my feet injured. I could not remember how that had happened.

The falling of the structure caused great alarm, and many people came running to where we were. The injured were carried away. It took four people to carry me, first down a ladder, and then the one hundred twelve steps. Two men had to clasp hands and let me lie on my back on their arms; otherwise I had unbearable pain. I then lay benumbed for five days, so that they hardly dared to move me. The surgeon put salve on my back and laid a plaster on it. After several days I was improved enough to stand up a little. When my old friend and landlord, John Carl, heard of this mishap, he said that now nothing could prevent him any longer from visiting me. He then came to us, and when he saw me in the back of the dungeon in my wretched condition, he went past all the brethren and threw his arms around me like Joseph with Jacob. He wept on my breast for a long time, so that he could not speak for tears. Then he kissed all the brethren and spoke with them. We refreshed ourselves and rejoiced in the Lord.

We were also visited at that time by John and Gilles de Koker, whom we did not then know. They looked at our work in the dungeon, namely that of buttonmaking, and asked if we made buttons. We said yes, that when we were not working on the ramparts, or after work or on holidays, we made buttons. They looked at some of the forms, and laid a gold coin [half a *pistol*] under a form, which we found only after they had left.

After being back in this cell for barely ten weeks, we had an order that we had to be separated from one another, and were not to talk to one another. Yes, even if one met another on the ramparts, he had to go right by with the wheelbarrow. We were not allowed to walk or stand together, and we all had to go in haste to other cells. Jacob Grahe remained in this cell; Henckels was placed in the zoo; John Lobach, under the gate where we had been together for nearly two years; Luther Stetius above the salt-chamber; Knepper in the salt-chamber, and I, W[illiam] Grahe, since I was not yet well, in the Bacon Pantry with other prisoners, who were to take care of me. I had to lie there between two others who were as full of lice as an ant hill. Each morning I had all I could do from six o'clock to ten o'clock to kill the lice and fleas. I was also maltreated in other ways. After twenty-six days, some brethren managed to arrange that I was relieved of this misery, and was put into another small cell next to Luther Stetius. It was seven feet wide and seven feet long, but was big enough for me. There was a chimney opening for a stove in it, and the corporal gave me permission to build a fireplace, which I did, so that I could cook for Luther Stetius and myself.

At that time, the elder William van der Leyen with his son-in-law, von Löwenich, and Captain Salbach, with the lieutenant of the guard, visited us, and asked me whether I had recovered from the fall on the tower. I took the opportunity to secure permission from the captain and the lieutenant of the guard that the other prisoners might bring me stones and lime. I built a chimney which was as good as any mason could have built. Finally I regained enough strength to go to work again. It was odd—the order had been given that we were not even to walk, sit, stand, or work together, but then the general-commandant ordered all of us to sit together around a large rock and break up bricks, as though they were mocking the order of the priests.

In the meantime steps were being taken to free us. This came
about without our knowledge as follows. There was a merchant of
Elberfeld, Rütger Schleiper, by name, who happened to be traveling
in a lighter with some gentlemen from Holland. The latter had
conversed among themselves about the state of religion of the time,
and remarked to one another that matters had been changed, under
God's mercy—one did not hear of persecution on religious grounds any
longer. They thought that everything was now in a state of decent
peace and tolerance. Then Schleiper spoke to them: "I beg your
pardon, sirs, but it is not entirely as you think. There are at this
moment six persons in Jülich, who have been in prison for about three
years already for the sake of their religion." The Dutchmen said that
they had not known about that. One of them, named De Blois, a
theologian [*Licentiat*], later spoke privately with Schleiper and asked
him what the prisoners' situation was. He wanted to have a complete
report about them. Then Schleiper said that although the prisoners'
home was barely three hours distant from his, he could not give complete information about them. In order to satisfy their interest, he
would like to recommend a certain person who knew much more
about the six. A resident of Krefeld, named Hubert Rahr, had much
contact with the prisoners and he could give them a detailed report.

De Blois wrote to Hubert Rahr that he had learned that six men
had been imprisoned at Jülich for three years because of their religion,
and that he would like to have detailed information about it. Rütger
Schleiper enclosed an envelope explaining how the matter had come
up, and asked Rahr to see to it that De Blois received an answer.
Hubert Rahr then wrote us that there was someone who wanted very
much to know about our imprisonment—the cause of it, and how long
we had been imprisoned. This we answered briefly, not knowing its
significance until later when we were freed. We sent the answer in
faith to Hubert Rahr, who forwarded it to the De Kokers in Rotterdam, who, in turn, delivered it to De Blois. Then these gentlemen
took it before the Dutch Estates General. The Dutch government
wrote to the Elector Palatine. The latter replied that he would release
us, but this promise was not fulfilled, for we remained in prison.

It happened that about this time someone of us wrote from the
prison to the De Kokers in Rotterdam, who were astonished to see
that a letter was still sent from the prison. They went at once to

Licentiat De Blois and showed him the letter. De Blois went immediately to the Estates General. At that time there was an ambassador of the Elector Palatine in the Hague, who had urgent business to transact. The Pensioner Fagel himself went to the ambassador and told him that he should write his lord that as long as the six prisoners in Jülich were kept in prison his petition would not be heard. So the ambassador had to write to Mannheim that the Estates General insisted in all earnestness on freedom for the six prisoners and that he could achieve nothing as long as they remained in prison.

A letter was then sent to Düsseldorf that they should send a commissioner to Jülich to see that the six prisoners were freed, and that the privileges of the craftsmen's guilds were not infringed upon. The general was also written to at the same time, that he should inform us that we were to be released. The general himself (who otherwise gave orders to the highest officers) wanted to have the privilege of bringing us the good news. He came to us while we were working and said, "Dear people, you can now be happy. You will soon be released, but because of your trade, instructions must first come from Düsseldorf." I was somewhat sick that day, and had not gone to work, but had remained in bed to sweat a bit. At four o'clock I heard the brethren at the door, and the corporal said, "You must be very pleased that you will be released now." When I heard those words I leaped out of bed and was completely well again, so wonderful was it to regain freedom. I can testify in all honesty, however, that the wish that I were not imprisoned did not come into my mind once while in prison. But thanks be to God that He had maintained and protected us, and poured His grace upon us.

We now had to wait for three weeks until we learned what was to become of us. During this time we made ourselves ready to depart. We sewed and mended whatever we could, so that we had everything clean and in good shape. Commissioner Ceres was later surprised when he had all of us before him and had seen all of us. He said to the last one, that is, Jacob Grahe, that we did not look at all like prisoners, but rather like townspeople. He expected us to look ragged and tattered. We had learned, however, that a Christian must be honorable in all things wherever possible, and that only a lazy person has to have torn clothing. As we had the opportunity to mend everything ourselves, we thought it proper to do so.

After three weeks a commissioner named Ceres came from Düsseldorf, along with John Hoppe, a friend and merchant from Solingen, and Clemens Knepper. The corporal came and took us away from the dungeon in haste; his intention was to take some of our things which we did not have time to make secure. We were taken to the parade ground, where we had to wait for a long time to see what would happen to us. We were treated as though we had first to go through a trial. Finally they called us, one after the other. They began with the youngest and followed through to the oldest. I was then the first to be called to the main guardhouse.

After I had paid a fitting salutation to the commissioner, I said: "I ask the commissioner for permission to sit down, because my legs have become so weak in prison that I cannot stand very long." He said: "Yes, yes, just sit down." Then he asked: "Why have you been in prison so long?" I replied: "We have been wondering, too, why we have been kept in prison so long. We have never harmed anyone." He asked: "Are you not tired of being in prison?" I answered: "That would soon be found out, if the prison gates were left unlocked. But as long as God intends that we be imprisoned, we accept it as being from the hand of God." He asked how long we had been imprisoned, and why, and what we believed and taught. I answered him on all these points. He was a poor theologian, however. He asked me how old I was. I answered that I could not tell exactly, but that I recalled that I had asked my mother as a child how old I was, and she had said eight years old. According to this, I was now twenty-seven years old. He then had taken down: "Age twenty-seven, according to mother's statement."

He asked what trade I had. I answered the sword- or knifemaking trade. After questioning me for an hour, he asked: "If the Elector Palatine granted you the great mercy of releasing you from prison and banishing you from the territory, would you swear under oath neither to carry on your trade nor to teach it outside of the territory?" I answered: "I am not in a condition to carry on my trade, as you can well see, and have no intention to do so. Therefore I can easily make this promise. Concerning the oath, however, the commissioner will well know, or be reminded, that we swear no formal oaths. But on this point we are willing to give our pledge and shake hands on it, which is as binding with us as a formal oath." Therefore I had to give this pledge and shake hands on it. Then they wrote something down for me, and read it to me. I was with him for one and a half hours and then was allowed to leave.

After I had been dismissed from him, I was not permitted to return to the other brethren, nor tell them what had happened to me, but rather had to go another way. Neither could I speak with John Hoppe or Clemens Knepper, who were standing on the parade ground. They thus proceeded with us as if we were being examined by the court. Luther Stetius was called in after me and briefly asked what his trade was as I had been. His response was the same as mine. After he had given his pledge and his hand on it, he was also released. The same occurred with Henckels and Lobach. William Knepper was a weaver; so he did not have to promise anything.

Jacob Grahe, however, as he was asked whether he would promise not to carry on his trade or to teach others, happened to remark: "If the Elector Palatine demands it, I will do it." His case was left unsettled, and he had to leave without the process being finished. We then had to wait for five more weeks in prison because of this technicality. As he said, "If the Elector Palatine demands it," the commissioner thought he had first to inquire of the Elector Palatine whether that was his will. The commissioner said to John Hoppe that he could release the five, but because Jacob Grahe had said: "If the Elector Palatine demands it . . . ," he had to stay in prison until word came from the Elector Palatine. John Hoppe thought that it would cause great criticism and disapproval if one remained in prison. It would be better if all six stayed together until we were all freed at the same time. We were then returned to prison, and kept under stricter guard than before. We could not understand this procedure, for we did not know the reason at that time. It was for the best, however, that we stayed together.

Finally the day for our release came—November 20, 1720—after we had been in prison for four years less two months and ten days. The count of the castle had a document which he read to us, which sounded as if we had promised under oath never to set foot again in this county. We protested against it, but he said that he could only read what was written. We thought that it would not be of importance. We were therefore free. They did not say when or where to leave, and let us do as we pleased. We distributed our household furnishings among the other prisoners and said good-by to our acquaintances. Many rejoiced with us, yes, even officers and priests clapped their hands and wished us much blessing upon our freedom.

As some of us were not able to walk, a horse and wagon were hired, and the driver loaded the rest of our belongings on it, and the weaker ones of us also. John Hoppe and Clemens Knepper were with us and arranged for everything. We left Jülich in the evening. In the morning of the next day we were at an inn, and an old farmer, with his cap under his arm, thought we were monks because of our beards. We came to a wide but shallow stream, and William Knepper carried three other brethren across. I sat on the wagon. In Erkelentz, the commandant did not want to let us through, until John Hoppe persuaded him. We finally arrived at Krefeld on the third day. John Hoppe went ahead of us as our protector; we followed, and then came Clemens Knepper. We stopped at Hubert Rahr's home, where we were welcomed with the greatest joy by all of the brethren.

Praise be to the loving God for His boundless mercy![21]

From the Letters of John Lobach

The collection of letters of John Lobach previously mentioned contains several letters written during the imprisonment of the Solingen Brethren described above. Three letters sent to Lobach's mother are given below, the first of which was written while he was expecting to suffer the death penalty.

John Lobach to His Mother (1)

Most Dearly Beloved Mother:

Grace and peace from God and Jesus Christ and abundant solace through the working of the Holy Spirit. I, your imprisoned son, wish in the Lord that you might be strengthened by this in your sorrow and hardship which you have, as I know, on account of me and my imprisoned brethren. Yet I am reassured in my soul that some day you will receive a thousand times more joy and comfort for all your sorrows if you will only follow our Lord Jesus in the denying of your own will and by freely taking His cross upon yourself. Oh, would to God that I could describe to you the great love of God to the degree in which I have partaken of it, especially in this my imprisonment. Then I would know that you had great joy instead of sorrow.

It has been rumored that I and Brother Henckels should be sacrificed. Do not be alarmed at this; rather rejoice with us in the Lord and remember that mother in the Second Book of Maccabees, chapter seven [verses 22 and 23], who watched her seven sons being martyred in a very cruel manner in a single day. Yet she suffered it with great patience for the sake of the hope which she had in God. Thereby she became so encouraged that she comforted one son after the other with a valiant heart and said to them: ". . . it was not I that gave you life and breath, and it was not I that brought into harmony the elements of each. Therefore the creator of the world, who formed the human race and arranged the generation of all things, will give you back again life and breath in his mercy, as you now are regardless of yourselves for the sake of his laws."

I know that my death will cause much grief and anguish, pain and sorrow, but I also know and am reassured that the merciful Father will not let the innocent victim perish, but will assist the widows and orphans. He wants to be their judge, their husband, and their father. Only keep praying and calling upon Him and live worthily according to the gospel of Jesus Christ. Oh, do not let yourselves be seduced by sweet and glib words, which Satan's apostles have taught, who seem to be devout in outward appearance and assumed godliness. Oh, beware therefore of the scribes and the leaven of their doctrine. However good they may appear to be, their doctrine grows and hatches nothing but basilisk eggs. If one eats them one must die. ". . . and from one which is crushed a viper is hatched. Their webs will not serve as clothing; men will not cover themselves with what they make. Their works are works of iniquity, and deeds of violence are in their hands. Their feet run to evil, and they make haste to shed innocent blood; their thoughts are thoughts of iniquity; desolation and destruction are in their highways. The way of peace they know not, and there is no justice in their paths; they have made their roads crooked, no one who goes in them knows peace (Isaiah 59:6-8)."

Even though they live in this world in a temporary Sodomite peace, in voluptuousness, pride, abundance, and without sorrows, as the righteous who have been made righteous in Jesus and His blood, let us then not sin on account of this or enter into their ways. I know that they will work on you with beautiful, glib words and will attempt to deceive you about the cross of Christ. For whoever does not take Christ's shame and cross upon himself, even though he may speak in the tongues of angels and give his belongings to the poor, there is no love of Jesus in him and he is still a non-Christian, even if a thousand people, yes, if the whole world, tells me what they will. I know now through the grace of God that I walk in Jesus' path, and I know in whom I believe and who it was that effected and began this faith in me, namely Jesus Christ, the solace of my soul, who is my own.

He who is my dearest spiritual Friend and Brother has visited me here in my imprisonment quite faithfully, has gladdened my heart and refreshed me, so that often the time passed too quickly. Oh, should not His love, which He poured through His spirit into my heart and the hearts of my brethren, oblige me to suffer death willingly for the sake of His gospel and His truth! For His love is stronger than death and His zeal is as sure as hell. Its ardor is fiery and a flame of the Lord that even many waters could not quench nor the floods drown. And if a man would give all the money and all the goods of the world for this love, it would avail nothing.

Now then, may the merciful God pour His love into your heart, dear mother, through His Holy Spirit, that you may easily overcome your grief and hardship. Yes, I am reassured of it in my soul, that you will congratulate me on my martyrdom through the love of Jesus, because you are convinced that I and my imprisoned brethren are not suffering for misdeeds but rather for good deeds and for the sake of the gospel and a saving doctrine. Therefore call to me as did the mother mentioned above as she was about to lead her last son to martyrdom, when she said: "Do not be afraid of this butcher, but show yourself worthy of your brothers, and accept death, so that by God's mercy I may get you back again with your brothers" [verse 29]. Oh, think of the inexpressible joy and eternal glory which we shall experience together with all the other elect who have come out of great affliction.

Oh, dear mother, brothers, sisters, and sisters-in-law with your children, do let us all carry the cross and passion of our Lord Jesus. Through this He was to enter into His glory. Let us too strengthen and encourage one another to do so, as long as we live. Yes, even if we should suffer the greatest agony, pain, and misery that has ever been endured by a creature in the whole world, it would have to be considered a trifle, yes, even nothing at all, as compared to the eternal joy and glory which we shall enjoy in infinite eternity. There, God himself will wipe away our tears and clothe us in the white silk of the righteousness of Jesus Christ, compared to which all the decoration and splendor of this world is nothing, yes, will have to be considered as filth. Then, in place of all the tears which we have shed here for our sins, we shall be given pearls and jewels. Then we shall partake of the indescribably and unutterably glorious wedding feast on Mount Zion, together with Abraham, Isaac, and Jacob, and all of the saints. Then it shall be as the mouth of the Lord says in Isaiah 65.

I am glad to give myself up to death for the sake of Christ, who gladdens my heart whenever I remember that this death opens the door for me to eternal bliss, and at the same time closes it on all suffering for ever. I consider myself as nothing other than an offering for my God and shall endure gladly and willingly whatever pain and suffering they may inflict upon me, which I shall not feel nor perceive. Jesus will reassure me through the joyousness of His Spirit with His promise and transfer me to the place of bliss through His crucifixion. Indeed, consider what the unbelievers, who became disobedient to the gospel of God, will have to suffer when the just Judge on His appointed day will come with a burning fire to take revenge on all godlessness, and make them drink from the chalice of His grim wrath, and pour out His wrath with all the other plagues upon them. When I think of this, I should rather choose to drink a thousand times from the cup of suffering of which Jesus and so many holy martyrs have partaken. For in faith I can already see the bottom of the chalice, of which I am to drink, and I see that it is pure and clear. But all the earthen vessels will be set aside for the godless, and especially for those who harrassed us and persecuted and killed the witnesses of the truth, and they will suffer unbearable pain in the bottomless pit where there burn fire and sulfur. Yet, as long as I breathe, I shall by grace not cease to pray and intercede with my Father for all those that hate and persecute me, be they known or unknown to me, that He may not store up their sins until the awful day of His revenge.

I herewith wish to forgive all of my enemies from the bottom of my heart for everything where they intended harm to me, or where they reproached, reviled, slandered, or called me a heretic out of wickedness. Oh, you who were ill disposed to me! Why should I not wish you well and wish you God's blessing? I call heaven and earth as my witnesses, who will give testimony on that day of revelation along with your consciences, that I have forgiven you from my heart. Recognize, repent, and bemoan your misdeeds not because you have offended me or any other man, but because you have offended your God and Creator, and have crucified Jesus, His Son, in His members. You certainly know that whatever is done to His members, be it good or evil, is received by Jesus as if it were done to Him. He will not leave unrepaid good or evil. The good which is done in His name for the least of His members, even if it be a drink of cool water, He will not leave unrepaid. On the other hand, whatever evil is done will also be repaid. When one of the least of these is annoyed, God will not let it go unavenged. He will not have His anointed ones laid hands on. Whosoever lays his hands on them lays his hands on the apple of God's eye.

Therefore, the Lord, my God, has kept me to this very hour as if I were the apple of His eye, so that I have met with no harm from my enemies. Even though they have reviled me, this was immediately forgiven them in my heart, for in this way I achieved honor and grace with God. Oh, if men only knew how much better and richer treasures are the shame and cross of Jesus than all the treasures and honor of the world, they would not be ashamed of the shame and cross of Christ. They would rather praise and glorify God for it along with me.

That men have reviled me was for my own good, because they drove me thereby to the Source, and chased me to God, the well of my life. Therefore, I again forgive all of my enemies, because they have caused me no harm. I will, in my weakness, remain constant in prayer with the Father as long as I live that He may not store their sins until the end, but rather let them recognize their sins in this life, so that they also might achieve, in this time of grace, repentance and forgiveness through Jesus Christ. My Savior taught and commanded us to love our enemies, saying: "Love your enemies and pray for those who persecute you" [Matthew 5:44]. Therefore I shall also love my enemies with a fervent love from my heart, and share with them a blessing from the living spring of the heavenly blessings. I wish from the bottom of my heart that they might change their minds while it is still "today," and might wash and cleanse their hearts. I wish that they might be given the grace of Jesus Christ more abundantly than I have experienced. I wish that they might grow and increase in grace in learning His will, and that they might see the light of His countenance and look to the bright light of the gospel of Jesus Christ. I wish further that they might live unencumbered with the children of God in one spirit, and in one soul, and stand together with the militant church of Jesus Christ here on earth. They might thus fight for the faith of the gospel, so that they might overcome themselves and might receive the fulfillment of the faith, the salvation of their souls. Amen.

I implore all of them, who have offended me and the members of Jesus Christ, if they cannot yet understand or comprehend this, to beware in the future through the grace of God from judging and deciding, and to learn from the counsel of Gamaliel in Acts 5:38, 39: ". . . keep away from these men, and let them alone; for if this plan or this undertaking is of men, it will fail; but if it is of God, you will not be able to overthrow them. You might even be found opposing God!" I am therefore assured that they will later realize that this is not a foreign doctrine, but is rather the doctrine of Jesus Christ, which brings salvation to all men who let themselves be led by the guiding of the Father, and follow the Lord Jesus in His commands. Those who do His will will recognize that this doctrine is from God.

When I read this to my imprisoned brethren, they desired from the bottom of their hearts that this might be written also on their behalf to their wives, children, fathers, mothers, sisters, brothers, and relatives, and also to their enemies.

Your son whom you love,

Düsseldorf,   John Lobach

from the new fortification,   (and Jacob Grahe, John Frederick

April 20, 1717.   Henckels, [William] Knepper)

From our imprisonment from which God will soon deliver us.[22]

John Lobach to His Mother (2)

To Tringen Kohl, widow of Peter Lobach.

I must take this opportunity, my beloved mother, to send my warm greetings to you, and to wish you with weak sighs grace upon grace from the abundance of Jesus. I am happy that you are still well and in good physical health.

Brother Knepper suffers now daily from chills. Brother Henckels' legs are swollen, but not as much as usual. Brother William Grahe still has pains in his legs. Therefore, the other three of us, that is Brother [Jacob] Grahe, Stetius, and I go to work, but the others stay in the prison.

This, dear mother, is a token of the love which I have for you. I assure you that I would be completely willing from my heart to take care of you in your old age, if it is the will of our Father in heaven. Yet, I do not doubt that our God and Creator, whose creation and children we are, will take care of you and be able to nourish you. He will certainly do this if we approach Him with our whole hearts and put our entire trust in Him. He always has intended well with us, even though we sometimes think that He has hidden His countenance from us. Eventually, everything which has seemed a hindrance to us will prove to work out for the best. Amen!

I greet you and embrace you often in spirit, and wish you the grace of God from the riches of our Lord Jesus. Amen.

Jülich, from the castle,	Your dear son
April 20, 1720.	John Lobach[23]

John Lobach to His Mother (3)

To Tringen Kohl, widow of Peter Lobach
Dearest Mother:

I must take this good opportunity to send you again in my own hand warm greetings and my wishes for God's blessing. May the Lord our God bless these in your soul with His grace and spirit. Sixteen days ago I learned from the brethren in Krefeld, and from the letter of my brother, Abraham, that you were recently in Krefeld, and were still in good health. This pleases me greatly. The more you learn to be willing to accept God's will, and be content with everything just as the Lord provides, the more He will be with you.

On the eleventh [of this month] all of us were separated. The two sick brethren had to suffer the most because of this. Brother Henckels was placed with nine other prisoners, and Brother William Grahe with thirteen in the Bacon Pantry. The general had to carry out the order of the Elector Palatine commanding this. William Grahe spoke to him after a few days had passed, and the general told him that he had had no pleasure in doing so, but he had to carry it out. He also permitted Brother Henckels to stay in the house of the canteen-owner until he is well again, because the prison in which he was placed was always full of tobacco smoke.

I was very sorry for the Brethren Henckels and William Grahe, that they always had to be in the company of such coarse men, and that they could not be cared for in their weakness any longer. But I know that my tears on their behalf have come before God so that He will not lay more upon them than they can bear. Brother Jacob Grahe also became weak on Saturday. It is as if it were a fever, as he says. Yesterday it was a little better, and I do not know how it is today. We must commit each one to the mercy of God. The Lord has been with us, which is our greatest solace and peace in the present situation.

To the only good God and loving Savior be praise, honor, glory, and thanksgiving in all eternity,

Jülich, from the castle,
June 24, 1720.

your obedient son in the
grace of the Lord
John Lobach.[24]

John Lobach to John Weck

A fourth letter from the collection of the Lobach correspondence is addressed to John Weck, Lobach's brother-in-law. We learn from this that Lobach's mother had come to nurse him back to health in the prison, but had fallen ill herself. The note, written by William Weck, John Weck's son and the compiler of the collection, adds the tragic information about the death of the mother.

To John Weck.

My mother and I send our greetings and best wishes to you, dear brother-in-law John Weck and sister Anna Catherine. I want to inform you that my mother is well, thank God. As far as I am concerned, I am still rather weak. I have fever every day, but it has abated somewhat, so that it is milder and easier to bear than when my sister was here, and than it was earlier.

My dear mother desires that you go to our house in Wald and take from the chest the largest cloth, two shirts, an apron, and some other things which you know about. Please send these to Gottfried Teschenmacher in Elberfeld, who will forward them here.

I and my dear mother send herewith warm greetings to you, my dear brother-in-law, sister, and children. Greet also Tringen for us, and our tenants at Wald, also my cousin William, and Henry and Adelia. Tell them how mother and I are. As for the rest, we send greetings to all good friends and acquaintances who fear the Lord. You have probably learned from the wife of Brother Grahe that my mother and I have moved out of the dungeon to another room.

I close herewith, and only remind you that you might earnestly and wholeheartedly seek and learn to love the Lord, our Creator, Father and the Source of all good, from whom we enjoy all good things. We can do nothing more precious nor more glorious here in this life than wholeheartedly seeking the sole source of our being, from which we come. The Scriptures say also that those who seek the Lord shall praise and rejoice in their hearts. Therefore, one can imagine what great joy, and what a secret, glorious, and blissful life those souls will experience here in this lifetime who find their God and Savior Jesus in their inner hearts and have fellowship and friendship with them. Think further on these things. I remain,

> your dear brother-in-law

August 1720   John Lobach.

P.S. Please send our warm greetings from my mother and me to my sisters Wilhelmina and Christine, along with their children.

Note [by William Weck]. The mother of the late John Lobach had gone to Jülich to take care of him in his illness at that time, as we see from the above. After he improved, his mother fell ill with a fever, and her son had to take care of her. She died in the prison. It should be noted that several years earlier Lobach's father, Peter, died in prison in Bonn. It was a period of war, and the French often raided and looted this area. The old Peter Lobach, who was an old, honest, loyal "Nathaniel," went along once to cut down trees to block the roads against the French. While they were felling the trees, some French cavalrymen came along and tied the old Peter Lobach and some others to their horses, and dragged them to Bonn. There he became ill with dysentery, and died in misery. He was buried behind a wall, outside of the city, if I am not mistaken.

When Peter Lobach's wife heard that he was ill, she immediately went to Bonn. When she asked the sentry about her husband, she was given this answer: "The devil has already taken him." She then went to the other prisoners, and one said, "Tringen, he is no more. We have just buried him." She rejoiced that she did not find her husband in misery. In the light of this, it can be imagined how this dear woman must have felt when shortly thereafter her son John was taken to prison in Düsseldorf. Oh, how wondrous are the ways of the Lord! This dear Mrs. Lobach has had to endure a great deal besides this way of the cross.[25]

Intervention by the Estates General

As recorded in the narrative of the Jülich imprisonment, the Solingen Brethren were released through the intervention of the Dutch authorities. Some details on how this took place are found in official records of the Estates General, the Dutch governing body. The visitor De Blois signed the first appeal for their release, which was also supported by the Dutch Mennonites.

Appeal Made to the Estates General

To the Most Powerful Sirs . . .

All of the friends of John Lobach, John Frederick Henckels, Jacob and William Grahe, William Knepper, and Luther Stetius living in this country, want to bring to your attention, in all humbleness that the above were sentenced to hard labor for life by His Highness, the Elector Palatine. All six of them come from the district of Solingen in the Berg area and are at present relegated to imprisonment in the fortress of Jülich. They must push the wheelbarrows on the fortification but are allowed nothing but water and one and a half pounds of bread a day for their subsistence. [They will not be released] unless they renounce their private opinion that when a person has reached a competent age he must be baptized upon his faith. After they had been accused solely for this reason by the Elector Palatine, the above-mentioned six wretched persons (though they were otherwise of the Reformed faith) met with the misfortune of being taken as prisoners from their homes on February 1, 1717, to Düsseldorf. There, after a strict detention of ten months, they had to suffer the above-mentioned sentence.

Since then they have been in a very sad and miserable state, because they are emaciated by illness, continuous fatigue, and other hardships. If the petitioners had not found an opportunity to provide them with some subsistence, these unfortunate people would soon have sunk into their graves through failing health and pain. Therefore, the petitioners, who find themselves pressed in all things by love, took heart to appeal to Our Lords' well-known benevolence and mercy. This, especially since His Majesty of Great Britain has similarly paid attention with pity and compassion to these most unfortunate people, and has graciously agreed to grant his mighty intervention. The petitioners most humbly pray and implore that Our Lords add what they think right and to that purpose send orders to their ambassador at Heidelberg to employ his good offices in conjunction with those of His Majesty of Great Britain toward the liberation of these six innocent persons from their aforesaid slavery. This is under the condition that, as soon as they are free, they immediately leave the county and territory of His Highness, the Elector Palatine.

Done by

December 9, 1719.　　　　　　　　　　　　　G. de Blois.[26]

Dutch Ambassador Reports Efforts

The Dutch ambassador to the Elector Palatine was instructed to secure the release of the Solingen Brethren. His communications to the Estates General describe his efforts in carrying this out. Of interest is the fact that other Protestant powers also interested themselves in the prisoners.

My Lords:

. . . I do not know whether My Lords will approve of this following step [made] in compliance with My Lords' resolution of the ninth of the last month of last year, and upon a request of all of the friends of the six imprisoned subjects of His Highness, the Elector Palatine. The latter are natives of the district of Solingen in the Berg area and [are] now imprisoned at the fortress of Jülich. Should I further continue to urge unilaterally that they be discharged? Several ambassadors, with whom I discussed the matter, expressed their displeasure that I should try apart from the other ambassadors, all by myself, to prescribe to His Highness, the Elector Palatine, in what way he should make his rebellious subjects obey, who hold an opinion that cannot be tolerated in the empire. [They did it in] such a way that I cannot conceive that my further efforts can be of any avail. I am awaiting My Lords' further resolution upon this. . . .

I remain in utmost submission and loyalty,

My Lords'

Heidelberg,   humble and most loyal servant
January 20, 1720.   P. de Spina van Grotenhage.[27]

Dutch Ambassador Reports Again

Most Powerful Sirs:

. . .

While this was being written, the privy councilor and vice-president of the government, Baron von Ullner zu Dieburg, came to take his leave out of respect for My Lords before continuing his journey down [the Rhine] tomorrow or the day after at the latest. He will reside at the court of My Lords as a minister extraordinary for the sake of settlement. I took at this time the opportunity to speak with His Honor about the discharge of the six prisoners at the fortress of Jülich, who have been condemned by His Highness, the Elector Palatine, to hard labor for life. They work with the wheel-barrows at the fortification (which is made stronger than ever by this network of moats) and are allowed only water and one and a half pounds of bread a day to sustain them, if they do not renounce their private opinions.

Although his [Ullner's] father-in-law is governor of the above-mentioned fortress, he expressed a great aversion against being involved in such an odious matter so shortly before his departure. He did not want any of the other countries, much less the ambassador of Great Britain, to intercede together with me for the six prisoners in order that they might be liberated. . . .

Your . . .

Heidelberg,   most humble and loyal servant
February 13, 1720.   P. de Spina van Grotenhage.[28]

Palatine Representative Reports Pleasure of Dutch Government

After the representative of the Elector Palatine informed the Dutch government of his sovereign's decision to free the Brethren, he was able to report back to Germany the pleasure of the Dutch government. It will be recalled from William Grahe's narrative that the Dutch refused to transact any diplomatic business with the representative until the prisoners were released. Thus ends another instance of aid for Brethren oppressed because of their beliefs.

Princely Elector, Gracious Lord:

I informed the Pensioner Fagel several days ago of the issuance of Your Electoral Highness' gracious edict of the twenty-sixth of last month. This states that the Anabaptists, who up to now have been imprisoned at Jülich and condemned to hard labor, are to be released and expelled from Your Electoral Highness' entire territory, because of highest innate clemency and special respect for the intercession which the Estates General have sent. Upon hearing this he showed himself to be delighted, because the relatives of the said Anabaptists in this country have often submitted appeals on their behalf. He intends and promises that this will encourage him to be useful to Your Highness in return in order to deserve this graciousness.

. . .

The Hague,   Your humble and obedient servant
October 8, 1720.   Francis, Freiherr von Ullner zu Dieburg.[29]

V. Emigration

This congregation of Baptists at Schwarzenau expanded greatly. A branch of it settled in the Marienborn district, but was persecuted there three times, and finally found a refuge in Krefeld in the year 1715. Here a division took place. Some say it was with reference to the question whether one might marry out of the congregation. Others maintain that the occasion of it was the marriage, contrary to the teaching of Paul (1 Corinthians 7), of a single minister of theirs by the name of Häcker. If this be so, there must still have been a considerable measure of awakening among them at that time, and their error consisted only in making a law out of the teaching of Paul, which it was not meant to be. In the year 1719 a party of them arrived in Pennsylvania with Peter Becker, who afterwards became their leader [Lehrer].

—Ephrata Chronicle[1]

SCHISM AND EMIGRATION OF 1719

The Krefeld Controversy

The decade 1719-1729 brought great changes for the young movement. A quarrel in the church fellowship at Krefeld has traditionally been given as the impetus for a mass migration of Brethren to the New World. The core of the migrating group were the Marienborn Brethren, of whom Peter Becker was the outstanding personality.

George Adam Martin, a member of the Brethren in Pennsylvania, included the story of the Krefeld schism in a long autobiographical section of the *Ephrata Chronicle*. His motive for writing was to explain his reasons for leaving the Brethren fellowship and joining the Ephrata community. He had not been at Krefeld himself during the time in question, and evidently received information of it from John Naas. Certain details of his account are undoubtedly incorrect, but the general picture is probably accurate.

Martin Writes in Ephrata Chronicle

Wondrous things also happened to Christian Liebe, who also was a preacher among them. He was taken prisoner in Basel [Bern], where he had been engaged in divine affairs, and was sold into the galleys, but ransomed after two years. At last he settled in Krefeld, where he and the above-mentioned J. N. [John Naas] superintended the congregation, until they at last fell out with each other, because J. N. publicly called him a comfort-maker [*Pilvenmacher*] before the whole congregation, and then left. Christian Liebe tried to continue his ministry in the congregation, although everything wasted under his hands; the Brethren who had been prisoners withdrew, the whole congregation was abandoned and everything was ruined. He himself became a merchant, and even at last a wine merchant, and married outside of the congregation, against their own rules. Not a branch is left of their Baptist business in all Europe. . . .

If God had not spared a branch of the root of Hochmann von Hochenau, the whole brood would have died at birth, like the Baptists of Münster. This innocent branch was P. B. [Peter Becker], who was a spiritual son of Hochmann, but was baptized, and came to live at Krefeld. Here he energetically exercised the gifts he had received from God, in singing and fervent praying to the benefit of the congregation—although he was otherwise no orator, and led a quiet life. Soon after he had to experience what he had not expected, for his spiritual father had taught him peace and love; but here he heard much quarreling and strife, which soon deeply grieved him. It happened that a young brother, Häcker by name, who had studied, and who was a warmly awakened person and an intimate friend of the said P. B., wanted to marry the daughter of a merchant, who also had been baptized into the congregation, but still served the Mennonites as preacher, because they did not wish to lose him, and gave him a yearly salary of eight hundred *Guilders*. This man was glad for such a son-in-law, and married them with great pleasure, not thinking that it would produce such great excitement in the congregation. But when the matter became known the tumult in the congregation became so great that Christian Liebe, the second teacher, and with him four unmarried Brethren, rose up against it and placed

Häcker in a ban, although J. N. and the congregation wished only to suspend him from communion.

This godless excommunication ruined the whole congregation in the town of Krefeld. I have heard the blessed teacher, J. N., say that more than one hundred persons in Krefeld had been convinced in favor of the new baptism, but on account of this ban everything was ruined and killed. And since no Moses was there, who might have sent Aaron with the censer, the fire of the ban burned on and consumed the whole congregation, which still pains my heart whenever I think of it. But it touched poor Häcker most, who took all the blame upon himself. The spirits took possession of him so that he fell ill and died of consumption; as they were converted people they were able to accomplish something [?]. His good friend, P. B., however, was with him in his utmost need, up to his death.

After this, P. B. decided to move to Pennsylvania, and when this became known several others moved with him; but the spirit of disorder and ban also moved with them, and so wounded and corrupted them on the other side of the ocean, that they could hardly be cured in America.

George Adam Martin.[2]

Synod Records Brethren's Departure

One of the last references to the Brethren in the official records of the Reformed Church mentions the leaving of the Becker group.

Minutes of the General Synod
July 13-21, 1719.

[It] . . . is noted that the honorable preachers of the Moers District have received and forwarded the creed of the so-called *Dompelaars* who had stayed in Krefeld, and that a most respectful remonstrance concerning them has been made to the Royal Majesty of Prussia. However, the honorable brethren of the Moers Synod report to our satisfaction that these *Dompelaars*, who have been most damaging for our churches, are said to have departed by water and sailed away to Pennsylvania. Therefore, the synod recommends to the honorable preachers of the Moers District to be very much on guard lest similar enthusiasts should insinuate themselves in the future.[3]

BEGINNINGS IN AMERICA

For the beginning of the church in Pennsylvania, the *Ephrata Chronicle* is again the major source. After a three-year interval, probably owing to the concentration of all energies on situating themselves in the colony, and the ill-feeling still lingering from the Krefeld division, the church was organized under the leadership of Peter Becker. The *Chronicle's* attempt at giving Conrad Beissel credit for initiating this is probably exaggerated. The climax of the new "awakening" was the first baptism in America held on Christmas Day, 1723. This took place near Germantown in the Wissahickon Creek on the property of John Gumre, and a love feast followed in Gumre's home.

Beginnings in America Described

During this time [1720] the superintendent [Conrad Beissel] arrived at Germantown, but kept very quiet as to his projects for a solitary life, for many, who had appeared to lead pious lives in Germany, had here shelved their holy calling. What was worst, they would give no one credit for zeal or diligence. Among these were several who in the Palatinate had let themselves be driven from house and home, but here left great wealth behind them after their death. All this caused him much concern; for he everywhere saw the pious sitting at the helm and exercising magisterial offices. As he saw clearly that his trade would not be of much use to him in this country, he determined to learn the weaver's trade, and so put himself under the instruction for a year of P. B. [Peter Becker], a member of the Baptists. These good people showed him much love, and confessed their whole condition to him, namely, that on the ocean they had lost their love for one another, and now had even become scattered over the country—that the great freedom of this land was one cause of their being thus sold under the spirit of this world, through which all godly influences had been lost, and each one depended upon himself.

"See, dear friend," they further said, "that is the way it happened to us; we have become strangers one to the other, and nearly all love and faithfulness have been lost among us." In reply to this he emphatically exhorted them not to tarry any longer in so dangerous, un-Christian, and unregenerate a condition, but to reunite themselves in love to one another, and to drop all antagonisms. And then they should make an attempt sometime to see whether they could not call together a meeting; if any good is effected, a gain has been made; if not, [they should] wait a while longer. This advice was not wholly spoken to the wind, for it shows clearly that he had a hand in the awakening which soon after followed in and about Germantown; for it was through this edifying conversation that these good people were again roused from their drowsiness. All this occurred in the year 1720, in which year also the rest of the Baptists, under their minister, Alexander Mack, migrated from Schwarzenau to Westervain [Surhuister-veen] in West Friesland, from where, after having lived there for nine years, they joined their brethren in Pennsylvania in the year 1729.'

. . .

Peter Becker, mindful of the superintendent's counsel, undertook in the autumn of 1722, with two other Brethren, a journey to all their Brethren scattered throughout the land, which was their first church visitation in America. They traveled through the regions of Skippack, Falckner's Swamp, Oley, etc., and wherever they came they informed their Brethren that they were minded, with their approval, to begin to organize a meeting; also that they were willing to put aside all unkindness and hard feelings in order that the work might be the more blessed in its progress. When they came home they began to hold meetings alternately at Peter Becker's and Gumre's, until the coming of winter prevented them. Next winter, however, they resumed them, weekly, at Peter Becker's.

In August of the year 1723 a rumor was spread through the country that Christian Liebe, a famous B[aptist] teacher who had long been in the galleys, had arrived in Philadelphia. This moved some newly awakened persons on the Schuylkill to go forth to meet him. The whole matter, however, was a fiction. These persons were persuaded by the B[aptists] to go with them to their meeting, during and after which they heard so much of the Germans' awakening that they went home very much edified. Soon after, a second visit was made to Germantown, by which both parties were so much edified that the Germantown B[aptists] promised them a visit in return, which they also made four weeks afterwards with great blessing. These newly awakened ones were thereby encouraged in their love, so that at last they threw themselves at the feet of the Germantown B[aptists] and begged to be received into their church fellowship by

A Street Scene in Ladenburg

The third house from the right was the birthplace of Christopher Sauer, Sr.

holy baptism. This confronted the B[aptists] in Germantown with a heavy responsibility; for they still remembered the misunderstandings which had arisen among them and their Brethren at Krefeld. Besides, they were indeed a branch of a church fellowship, but yet not a congregation that dared to presume to administer the sacraments. The chief problem was that they were divided among themselves, and had only lately commenced to gather again.

After they had seriously pondered over all these things in the spirit, they finally agreed to consent to the request. Accordingly, after the candidates for baptism had chosen Peter Becker to be their baptizer, they were baptized in the Wissahickon stream near Germantown, on December 25, in the year 1723. And as these were the first fruits of all baptized from among the High-Germans in America, their names shall here be recorded and given to posterity, namely: Martin Urner and his companion [*Hausschwester*], Henry Landes and his companion, Frederick Lang, and Jan Mayle. The evening following they held the first love feast ever celebrated in America, at John Gumre's, which created a great stir among the people of the neighborhood; Peter Becker, as mentioned before, administered the same.

Through such a divine providence the Baptists in Pennsylvania became a church fellowship and continued their meetings through that summer with great blessing and edification, until they were hindered by the following winter. The next spring, 1724, however, when they resumed their meetings, there was given to them such a blessing that the whole region roundabout was moved thereby. Their young people were particularly affected by this movement, who, then, to the great gratification of their elders began to walk in the fear of the Lord and to love the Brethren. And as the report of this awakening spread abroad, there was such an increase of attendance at their meetings that the room could hold only a fraction of them. ([Footnote] It was remarked that the greatest force of this extraordinary awakening did not last longer than seven months, for it commenced in May and began to decline again in the following November, when the awakening in Conestoga took its beginning.)

Again the following summer there was a great movement among them, and love feasts were held, through which many were impelled to join them, and so their church fellowship experienced a rapid growth. Under these circumstances they deemed it well to make a detailed report of this new awakening to their Brethren in Germany [Friesland]. Therefore they prepared together a communication addressed to them, in which they informed them that they had become reunited in Pennsylvania, and that hereupon a great awakening had resulted in the land, which was still daily increasing—that of the awakened several had joined their church fellowship, to which they had to consent, as they dared not oppose the counsels of God.[5]

The Supposed Birthplace of Conrad Beissel at Eberbach

SCHWARZENAU—SURHUISTERVEEN—GERMANTOWN

In the meantime, the larger Schwarzenau fellowship had migrated to Surhuisterveen in Friesland. There is no one satisfactory answer for their departure. It is unlikely that it was solely because of persecution, for we have seen that Henry Albert defended his policy of toleration successfully until his death in 1723. It is true, however, that the arrival of August David as co-regent did make conditions more difficult. Further, in the year 1720 the imperial government finally took action in investigating the complaints made by Count Charles Louis in 1709-10.

It is probable that the opposition coming from the Inspirationists and other separatists played a role. The Brethren had converted by that time all in the area who were possible members. Not to be neglected is the economic problem. Wittgenstein was poor in land and poor in resources. Contemporary sources give problems of livelihood as a major reason for the move. We hear that Mack exhausted his inheritance for the common good. Undoubtedly the lure of religious freedom enjoyed in the Netherlands and Pennsylvania loomed large in the decision. The most probable conclusion is that a combination of all these factors caused the decision to leave.

LEAVING SCHWARZENAU

Grebe Sells Property

Scattered records in the Wittgenstein archive refer to Brethren who sold land prior to their departure. One of the first eight, George Grebe, the former Kassel gunsmith, sold his property near Schwarzenau. The introduction to the bill of sale follows:

Sale: George Grebe

George Grebe from the Stüntzel, and his wife, Juliana, intend to migrate to Friesland along with the other Anabaptists. They have therefore, in the presence of their son-in-law, George William Hoffmann, sold their residence with all appurtenances built on the Stüntzel to John Schreiber and Conrad Feuring, both from Puderbach, on March 18 of the current year, for two hundred fifteen *Reichstaler* (each *Reichstaler* purchased at forty-five *Albus*). These two purchasers, herewith, assume the debt of the contract, and capital which the seller, George Grebe, applied in such house and goods, of which amount one hundred *Taler* [*Hauptstuhl*] had been borrowed from the chaplaincy or deaconate at Laasphe and paid off on November 9, 1715. . . .

Wittgenstein, April 26, 1720.   Wittgenstein chancery.[6]

After years of delay, the imperial solicitor at Wetzlar began his investigation of the Brethren demanded by Count Charles Louis of Sayn-Wittgenstein ten years previously. He wrote to one of Count Henry Albert's officials, Frederick Christian Lade, asking for information about the Brethren. In the reply, the official told of the migration of the group, but disavowed that any other dissenters remained in Wittgenstein, which was something less than the truth.

Imperial Solicitor Requests Information

Honorable, especially esteemed Sir:

I cannot withhold from him [Lade] what the imperial solicitor was recently ordered by the most praiseworthy Imperial Court, namely, that he is to investigate carefully the religious enthusiasts residing in the county of Wittgenstein, who do not profess any one of the three tolerated Christian faiths established by the Peace of Westphalia. He is to take action against them according to the imperial statutes. It is rumored that this kind of persons, partly deriving from the Eva [von Buttlar] group and partly from people driven out of other areas, are residing in the manor at Schwarzenau, and that area, and are publicly tolerated. These people discard the established churches, holy baptism, and the sacraments, hold love feasts and simulate divine trials. My highly esteemed sir, as local administrator, doubtless has the best information and knowledge, whether such enthusiasts are actually and *de facto* in the village or in the area.

Therefore I have wanted to ask confidentially through official channels for his true and factual report, which may be certified under oath. I do not doubt that he will not hold back the truth, but rather will faithfully give this information to the honor of His Imperial Majesty and the high court, in which expectation and commending him to God, I remain,

Wetzlar,   your obedient servant
May 13, 1720.   Francis Erasmus von Emmerich, Imperial
                                   Solicitor.[7]

Wittgenstein Official Gives Information

Honorable Sir Imperial Solicitor:

I have seen from his [von Emmerich's] letter of the thirteenth of last month that he requests of me to learn whether various sorts of enthusiasts and persons not to be tolerated in the Roman Empire reside and stay here at Schwarzenau. I therefore report in obedient compliance to his request that many pious people resided here for a time, about whom one heard nothing evil, but rather perceived that they conducted themselves quietly and devoutly in all things. No person has ever complained about them. From this group, forty families, numbering about two hundred persons, recently left this county permanently. They were said to have been Anabaptists.

Those remaining, however, who still reside around Schwarzenau, are of Catholic, Lutheran, and Reformed faiths. That some of the persons mentioned previously as being forbidden in the Roman Empire still reside here, is unknown to me. If I can otherwise be of service to you, I will not fail therein either to prove that I am, Your Honor,

Schwarzenau,	your humble and obedient servant
June 24, 1720.	Frederick Christian Lade.[8]

Schwarzenau Census Mentions Brethren

A Schwarzenau census has some information on the dwellings left behind by the Brethren.

Schwarzenau records June 4, 1721.

All of the residents of Schwarzenau were summoned, questioned, and [their answers] were recorded in the following manner:

. . .

Mathew Lemser, Louis Matthäus, and Christian Erb inhabit Mr. Hochmann's house, called the Castle of Peace [*Friedensburg*], as an inheritance. Mathew Lemser in particular produced a certificate of exemption [*Freiheitsschein*] dated May 12, 1719.

. . .

Mr. Horbert produced a contract for the purchase of Andrew Boni's house, as well as the residence permit issued to Boni by the gracious lordship under the date of April 23, 1719. He pays a yearly tax [*Canon*] of one *florin*.

Joseph Leszle, born in Halle, lives as a tenant in the house of the tailor Sauer of Laasphe which was purchased from Alexander Mack. He pays Sauer eight *florins* a year, as the latter must pay the tax from this sum.

. . .

Bernhard Bütz showed a certificate of sale from John Henry Kalklöser, which was confirmed by the chancery on February 29, 1720. He had the gracious lordship's residence permit, dated February 28, 1720.[9]

Residence in Friesland

Just as the Marienborn Brethren found asylum with the Mennonites in Krefeld and in Germantown, the Schwarzenau Brethren sought refuge in a small village southeast of Leeuwarden in Friesland which was settled by Mennonites. The chief occupation there was cutting peat in the marshy area which was being drained for cultivation. It was here that word reached them from Pennsylvania of the awakening among the Brethren.

The only known description of the Brethren at Surhuisterveen is in the nineteenth-century history of the Dutch Mennonites, written by a leading Mennonite historian. He wrote under the assumption that the group were Swiss Mennonites.

Surhuisterveen Brethren Described

. . . At Surhuisterveen there were for some time thirty of these families who did not unite with the [Mennonite] congregation which existed there, but held their own worship services in a special house (opposite the Mennonite parsonage). They administered baptism by immersion in a clear pool at Kortewolde, a quarter of an hour distant. Otherwise they lived very modestly and quietly.

[Footnote] There were many artisans among them. There is still a clock at Surhuisterveen which was made there by one of the group, Johnathan Grebe. Tradition has it that they brought the first potatoes to Friesland. Ice-skating was unknown to them—they considered it, at first, to be a thing of the devil, that people could fly over the ice like that. These details were related to me by the Reverend F. W. Wieling. . . .

History of the Mennonites in Friesland [*1839*].

Stephen Blaupot ten Cate.[10]

Surhuisterveen Brethren Married

Four marriage proclamations preserved in the state archive of Friesland conclusively prove the presence of the Brethren at Surhuisterveen. Although records of all other marriages were entered into the church books of the Mennonite or Reformed congregations, the entries for the Brethren were placed in the back of a local government record book. These are the only known archival references to the Brethren in the Netherlands.

Marriage proclamations between:

John Juriens, groom, and Anna Catherine Kipping, bride, both of Surhuisterveen, request their marriage proclamations; they were today,

April 28, 1721, proclaimed for the first time,

May 5, 1721, for the 2nd time proclaimed,

May 19, 1721, the 3rd proclamation.

Today, May 19, 1721, the above-listed marriage was proclaimed without any objection, and the above persons were united in marriage in the presence of the Assessor Meyne Aelses as commissioner.

Witnessed by myself as secretary,

P. Huysinga.

Marriage proclamation between:

William Knepper, groom, and Veronica Bloom, bride, both of Surhuisterveen, request their marriage proclamations; they were:

Jan. 25, 1723, the 1st proclamation,

Feb. 8, 1723, the 2nd proclamation,

Feb. 22, 1723, the 3rd proclamation.

Marriage proclamations:

John Henry Kalcklöser, groom, and Anna Flys Layen, bride, both of Surhuisterveen, request their marriage proclamation; they were proclaimed for the first time today,

Jan. 31, 1724,

Two Views of Surhuisterveen

Feb. 14, 1724, the 2nd proclamation,
Feb. 28, 1724, the 3rd proclamation.

Marriage proclamations of:
    Jacob Bossert, groom, and Susan Keymen, bride, both of Surhuis-
terveen, request their marriage proclamations; they were proclaimed
for the first time today,
        Oct. 2, 1724,
        Oct. 16, 1724, the 2nd proclamation,
        Oct. 30, 1724, the 3rd proclamation.[11]

Grebe and Mack Dispute

In another section of his statement in the *Ephrata Chronicle,* George
Adam Martin related a dispute between Grebe and Mack which is said
to have taken place in Holland. As this happened soon after the release of
William Knepper from Jülich, the date must be late 1720 or early 1721.

. . . these are the very reasons, for which I took offense at the
foundation and origin, because the founders deviated from their aim
and basis, which in my opinion is the love of God toward all men,
they formed a sect, like the Inspirationists, out of the great awakening
which had taken hold of them in Germany, and aroused strife and
hatred by their disputes. This George Grebe told them to their faces
through an inspiration, and especially to A. M. [Alexander Mack], at
a public meeting in Holland, saying: "You and all of yours are dead,
and have died to the life of God." All this was listened to by W. K.
[William Knepper], who had just been liberated from the prison in
Jülich, where he had been imprisoned for the sake of the truth; he
told me all this.

At the very commencement they adopted needless restrictions, in
that they did not allow anyone who was not baptized to partake with
them of the holy sacrament. Had they not been so sectarian in this
matter, and been more given to impartial love, they would have found
entrance to more souls in their great awakening and noticeably promoted the glory of God. But, instead, sectarianism, quarrelsomeness
and disharmony spread through their whole awakening in Germany
as far as to Switzerland. Therefore, also, the incomparable teacher,
J. N. [John Naas], separated from them, and stood alone, until he

went to America and arrived in Philadelphia. At that place A. M. went to meet him and entreated him for God's sake to forget and forgive what had happened in Europe; to which he agreed.

George Adam Martin.[12]

Arrival in Pennsylvania

It was not until 1729 that Mack led the Wittgenstein group on the long and dangerous ocean voyage from the Netherlands to the New World. In 1727 Mack had sold his share of the inheritance from his father-in-law, John Valentine Kling (who died in Schriesheim in 1714), while in Surhuisterveen. Neither of the two Anna Margaret Macks given on the passenger list of the *Allen* refers to Mack's wife, who died in September 1720, according to the entry in Alexander Mack's Bible, now preserved at Bridgewater College, Bridgewater, Virginia.

It is probable that some of those listed were not members of the Brethren group, but merely passengers on the same ship. The names have been edited in an attempt to reconstruct more accurate spellings, since the lists were written by English clerks who had great difficulty spelling German names. Although there is a less complete list with actual signatures, some of the group were illiterate and their names were also written by clerks on this list as well.

Arrival of the Allen Recorded

Minutes of the provincial council.

At the Courthouse of Philadelphia, September 15th, 1729. . . . A List was presented of the names of Fifty nine Palatines, who with their Families, making in all about One hundred and twenty six Persons, were imported in the Ship *Allen,* James Craigie, Master, from Rotterdam, but last from Cowes, as by Clearance thence dated 7th of July last.[13]

Allen Passengers Listed

A list of passengers imported in the ship *Allen* from Rotterdam, James Craigie, Master, September 11, 1729.

Alexander Mack	John Ulrich Oellen
John Mack	Reinhard Hammer
Valentine Mack	Samuel Galler

Alexander Mack, Jr.
John Henry Kalcklöser
Jacob Kalcklöser
Immanuel Kalcklöser
Andrew Boni
William Knepper
Esbert Bender
Peter Lesle
John Gunde
Jacob Bossert
Jacob Weiss
Christian Schneider
Jacob Sneider
John Flickinger
Valentine Becker
Jacob Lesle
Christopher Marte
Paul Lipkip
Christopher Kalcklöser
Christian Kropf
Andrew Kropf
Jacob Kropf (sick)
Christian Kropf, Jr.
John Slaughter [Schlachter?]
John Pettighofer
John Kipping
John George Koch
John Michael Amweg
John George Kiessel
John Jacob Kiessel (sick)

Conrad Oellen
John Caspar Kolb
John Martin Kress
John Jacob Hopback
John Mickendorfer
Christian Kitsenlander
Leonard Amweg
Mathew Schneider
Joseph Bruner
John Bruner (sick)
Mathew Ulland
George Hoffart
John Perger
John Wightman
Philip Michael Fiersler
Valentine Perhart [Bernhard?]
    Hisle
John George Klauser
Henry Holstein, Germ't.
Valentine Rafer
George Fetter
John Jacob Knecht
Alexander Dihell
Henry Peter Middeldorf
Mathew Bradford (English
Nicholas Bayly   (
David Lesle
Jacob Bossert
Daniel Kropf (sick)

These following are under the age of fifteen.

John Bossert
Christopher Gottlieb Marte
John Henry Bruner

John Ulland
Christian Hoffart

These following are female passengers.

Christine Margaret Kiessel
Anna Barbara Kiessel

Anna Margaret Mack
Catherine Bender

Eva Tabaek [?] Oellen
Susan Hammer
Dorothy Galler
Margaret Oellen
Elizabeth Oellen
Marie Oellen
Anna Phillis [Felicitas?] Kolb
Anna Catherine Kress
Magdalene Hopback
Veronica Mickendorfer
Anna Barbara Kitsenlander
Magdalene Amweg
Magdalene Schneider
Catherine Elizabeth Bruner
Anna Marie Latrine
Catherine Ulland
Anna Margaret Hoffart
Anna Margaret Hoffart, Jr.
Anna Ursula Perger
Marie Phillis [Felicitas?]
  Wightman
Marie Catherine Fiersler
Susan Catherine Hisle
Anna Marie Klauser
Marie Magdalene Kamp
Anna Marie Barbara Rafer
Agnes Kalcklöser
Joanna Margaret Boni
Veronica Knepper

Anna Catherine Lesle
Marie Elizabeth Lesle
Susan Bossert
Marie Elizabeth Bossert
Susan Schneider
Christine Becker
Elizabeth Lesle
Marie Agnes Marte
Christine Lipkip
Marie Kalcklöser
Anna Margaret Mack
Phillipine Mack
Rosine Kropf
Catherine Slaughter
  [Schlachter?]
Anna Elizabeth Pettighofer
Maeta [Martha?] Lina
  Pettighofer
Gertrud Pettighofer
Anna Kipping
Sybil Kipping
Anna Catherine Koch
Anna Marie Ackhorden
Magdalene Ackhorden
Christine Lesle
Eva Bossert
Joanna Kipping
Catherine Oellen

James Craigie [Captain][14]

Chronicle Refers to Mack's Arrival

Mack's arrival in Pennsylvania is mentioned in the *Ephrata Chronicle.* Following that brief notice, the record goes on to criticize him for attempting to bring about reconciliation between the Brethren and the followers of Beissel.

In the year 1729, Alexander Mack, the founder of the Baptists,

with the rest of the congregation mentioned, left Friesland and came
to Pennsylvania. This venerable man would have well deserved to be
received with arms of love by all the pious in unity, after all that he
had had to suffer in Germany, especially from his own people. . . .[15]

Two anonymous articles on contemporary church history, which appeared in the *Geistliche Fama,* compared the Brethren to the Mennonites,
and referred to the Ephrata schism.

Brethren and Mennonites Compared (1)

Historical testimonies about the true and the false in spiritual labors.

At the time of, yes, even before, the Reformation and the split
of the Protestant church from the Papacy, there arose the Anabaptists.
They had indeed received a spark of grace in their souls for a single-
minded, childlike discipleship [*Nachfolgungs-Wesen*] of the life of
Jesus. They earnestly wanted to be guided in everything by His
teachings and life, both inwardly and outwardly, but their great aim
was to do away with infant baptism and other outward things of this
kind, and to introduce other ordinances in their place, and, indeed,
to have peace of soul therein. The good souls remained for the most
part in their peasant simplicity and natural honesty. Few attained
a deep and fervent life of grace. Still fewer achieved that state which
the masses attained under the popish husks of obedience.

About twenty to thirty years ago many farmers from the Palatinate, who were simple but honest seekers after God, were awakened.
Their great earnestness impelled them to many communal and unusual
exercises of devotion. Church life was too dead for them, and the
excessive liberty of other awakened separatists was too cold. But this
earnestness, void of all images, was soon promoted to abolish infant
baptism, first teaching the members to make them disciples, and then
admitting them to baptism and communion after their particular
manner. Simple minds gladly seized upon such simple symbols that
were easy to comprehend. Such water of rebirth to the new life can
be received without a special death of the old.

However, there soon developed opposition from within and without, so that they migrated to America. There they quarreled with
and annoyed one another as well as others, about this legalism and
that of the Seventh Day. Many join them; others leave. They barri-
cade themselves against other chosen ones, in order to preserve their

conception. The simple childlike spirit becomes sectarianism. They
have the idea that they are the undefiled congregation of the Lord;
others must turn to them.

[Anonymous][16]

Brethren and Mennonites Compared (2)

About old and new Anabaptists.

The congregations of the old Anabaptists had undergone an improvement and enlargement from the New Baptists, which, however,
was quite soon separated, hidden, and lost. The latter considered
infant baptism to be completely absent in, even against, the commandment and ordinance of Christ and the early church. Nevertheless,
baptism along with communion in the service of the New Covenant
must be changed, improved, and retained. This must be made use of
according to the custom of the early Christians and the words of
Christ, from whom they were first made disciples. The leaders
thereof were sincere and awakened laymen from the Palatinate and
the Reformed Church.

They promoted this necessity for adult baptism very zealously
among the awakened souls against much resistance, and persuaded
many to submit to this renewal of baptism. When they were tired of
promoting their cause in the Upper Rhine area, or rather, when they
could not find sufficient livelihood, and, moreover, met with all kinds
of resistance from the awakened, they turned to the area of the Lower
Rhine, even to Friesland and still further to America. Many split
off, however, and returned again to peace and solitude from that type
of activity, as they found in this "tabernacle service" as little life as
in the old church laws and ceremonies. Those who went to Pennsylvania—the few who were left—divided again into two parties. Some
considered their former brethren and baptizers apathetic, and agitated
violently with them for a new awakening. The latter fell into new
legalism in observing the Seventh Day or the Sabbath and considering
Sunday the same as any other day. They did not allow anyone in the
congregation to have more business, goods, property, etc. than was
necessary for his bare livelihood, etc. An oral and written dispute
began about this among the New Baptists, which totally destroyed
their sectarian image.

Oh, indeed, there are temptations which heavily attack the first-born of the Spirit and winnow them with heavenly malice. Yes, they hinder the transcendental life of the new creation with outer "picture-work," and new church-peculiarities. Therefore the old Baptists and the New Baptists have outward simplicity surpassing all other sects, and a likeness with the apostolic church discipline. However, in the secret wisdom and in the life of the new rebirth, the basis is not receptive and enlightened. To the contrary, in the mysticism of the foundation covered over with the dark sheet of papacy, there reveals itself the sanctuary and the Most Holy in the full glory of the divine light and right. In the antechamber, nothing shows itself but burning, washing, strangling, sweeping, and the other tabernacle services, which give little profit to those who bother with them.

Otherwise one must profess concerning the old and new Baptists, that they have a great superiority over the common mass of the large sects in outward, orderly, honorable lives of virtue. They enjoy a physical blessing, peace, and preservation from all that is idle, in their simple agricultural pursuits. The old Baptists do not seek to enlarge themselves outside of their family, but rather remain in their old simplicity, the simple lay-ministry, the house-meetings, the unlearned salvation-system, the simple administration of the sacraments, and the lowly farming and artisan life, etc.

The New Baptists, however, want to make themselves large and broad among the awakened souls with powerful teaching and con-verting to the new baptismal peculiarity and necessity. Most is, however, extinguished so that many of their most experienced teachers and leaders are ashamed of their former activities, and turn to and remain in a completely quiet and modest seeking in God.

[Anonymous][17]

OTHER MIGRATIONS

Although the two groups of 1719 and 1729 comprised the main body of the Brethren, there were others who came to Pennsylvania later. One of the first eight, Luke Vetter, arrived with his family on September 21, 1731. Abraham Dubois of Eppstein came with his family on the *John and William* on October 17, 1732. The Krefeld leader, John Naas, sailed with a group of Brethren on the *Pennsylvania Merchant,* arriving in Philadelphia on September 29, 1733. He wrote a lengthy letter to his son Jacob William, which is in the form of a diary of his ocean crossing. This can be taken as typical of the conditions which the Brethren experienced and which they gladly endured in order to migrate from the land of their origin to a land which promised them freedom of religion. The letter also gives some glimpses of life in the New World. His encouragement of his son to migrate with his family was apparently successful, for the latter arrived on the *Billender Oliver* on April 26, 1735.[18]

John Naas to His Son

Dearly beloved son, Jacob William Naas:

I greet you and your dear wife, Margaret, and her dear children very affectionately; also Brethren Grahe, Jacob Schmitz, Liebe, Lobach, Stetius, Müller, Hubert Rahr, Linge, Zwingenberg, Clemens, and also Mrs. Benders and Marie Mumert. We greet them all in affectionate love and friendship, and all their dear ones, without exception; also those who in love inquire about us. The eternal and all-sufficient God give you all mercy, light, and faith, so that you may not only choose the good in this time given us by God's mercy, but rather through the true and active faith and in true salvation and childlike obedience, you might obtain it in Christ Jesus; may the great God through Jesus Christ work this in us and all who love Him.

Amen. Yes, amen.

Because I have been requested by some to describe our trip, I have not been able to reject doing this completely, and therefore will try to describe, as briefly as possible, what I think necessary. I sent a letter back via Rotterdam from Plymouth in England with the request to make it known. Therein is described how it went from Rotterdam to England and in Plymouth—now following that, I will describe the voyage from England or Plymouth here. I certainly hope you will have received by now my last letter of September 15 from Germantown, in which is reported our happy and pleasant arrival with our dear known and unknown brethren and friends; therefore, I now describe briefly what occurred on the journey from Plymouth until here in Pennsylvania as follows.

On June 24 we sailed from Rotterdam until a half-hour from there, where we stopped, because of counter winds until July 3. We then left and the ship had to be towed by many men along the Maas

River, until near Hellevoetsluis we received a good wind so that we sailed into the sea at Hellevoetsluis. There began seasickness among the passengers, namely, running and vomiting, most of whom, as soon as they had vomited, began to eat again.

The thirteenth of the same month, in early morning, we arrived at Plymouth in the harbor, which is all rocks. There we had to lie in the middle of the harbor until the ship was cleared by customs and provisioned. We then sailed in the evening of July 21 into the great ocean and lost sight of land on the left, France and Spain. On the twenty-fourth we also lost sight of it on the right, namely England.

On the 25th a small child died, who had come on board very ill, and was buried in the sea on the next day at eight o'clock. I noticed with great amazement that as the body fell into the water from the plank, a swarm of large fish shot ahead of the ship as though they were fleeing from the dead body. We had rather good wind for about ten days, so that we sailed a good distance into the great ocean.

Before daylight on July 28, around two o'clock, a French warship came by, named *Elizabeth,* whose captain examined our captain in French; after they made themselves acquainted, they wished each other a safe trip and each went on his course. After this day we had very inconstant weather, so that in three weeks we [were in motion] less than sixty hours, [covering a distance] which otherwise would have taken one day in good wind.

On August 3, I rose one hour before daybreak in order to see how it was going, as I had decided to watch the compass during the whole trip to see if a change of course took place. As I came to the ladder, all the people were still sleeping, and a bedroll was under the ladder, and the bed-blankets lay high on the ladder. During the night it had rained a little, making it slippery under the hatch, and as I stood on the last rung of the ladder and was about to step on the deck, the persons stretched themselves in their bed and involuntarily knocked the ladder from under me, so that I fell from the level of the deck with my left side striking the ladder. I was almost unconscious and lay there a long time before I could stand up. Then I had to lie on my back for fourteen days until I could get up again, and walk a bit. I was at first afraid that I would become lame but the great God in His Son be praised, who allowed me to recover without herbs or bandages, so that I hardly feel it any more.

In the early morning of the 14th same the sailors harpooned a large fish, which was as long as a normal-sized man and had a head like a sow, also a body and entrails like a sow. On August 7, another infant died during the night and in the same hour a baby boy was born; the dead child was buried in the sea on the 8th.

On the 11th and 12th we had a storm, which, although not very severe, continued for forty-eight hours, so that all of the sails had to be lashed, the rudder tied, and the portholes covered with boards. We sat in darkness while the force of the waves broke through the glass into the beds. Some of the passengers had to vomit in every storm and strong wind.

On the 13th same another baby boy was born. On the 17th we had another storm, which for the first six or eight hours was noticeably worse than the first and drove the waves very high. It lasted one and a half days and one and a half nights, diminishing in force at the end, however. Sails, rudder, and portholes were secured very quickly, and the ship was left at the mercy of the wind and waves. Afterwards it was so still that we remained almost stationary for many days, and the passengers recovered from vomiting and running. Later came a strong side-wind, so that the ship traveled speedily. On August 23, another child died in the early morning and was buried in the sea in the evening.

On the 26th same, around five o'clock in the afternoon, we sailed with a strong wind past an unmoving mast, the tip of which stuck a foot out of the water, completely still and with a piece of sail still attached. To our great fortune our ship passed about a rod's length away. The captain had just taken tea. Many people were very frightened at this sight, because the mast could not have been stuck in the ocean floor, but despite this did not move.

On the 30th same, another child of the above-mentioned man died, and was buried in the ocean in the evening; we then saw the first small fish with wings fly over the water from two to three rods.

On the morning of September 6, the chief helmsman harpooned a dolphin, which looked much different from what they are described in Germany. This day had great heat and little wind.

On the 7th same another large fish, called a shark, was caught by the sailors; the sailors took a hook which was very large and strong and thick as a finger, and baited it with one and a half pounds of bacon. When they saw the fish near the ship they threw in the hook with the bacon, which it instantly swallowed; because the fish was very broad and five feet long, with an exceptionally strong tail, out of as well as in the water, when they heaved him on the ship they drove all of the passengers away, so that it could not injure anyone. It struck the deck with the tail with such force that if it had hit someone's legs, they would certainly have been crushed, but when the ship's carpenter hacked off its tail with barely ten strokes, the strength was gone. Its mouth was so large it could have swallowed a two-year-old child. The captain was pleased to pass out the meat for the passengers' good.

On the 11th same, another infant died, which the parents did not realize until it was nearly stiff; it was buried in the sea on the 12th.

On the 13th same, a young woman, who had always been sickly, died in labor, and was buried in the sea on the 14th, with three children, two previously, and the baby after her, so that the husband had no one else.

On the 16th, around four o'clock in the morning, a fifty-year-old woman died, who had not been well during the whole voyage and had always regretted her leaving home. She was buried in the sea on the same day. Since the trip was prolonged because of the frequently changing winds, and since most of the people had already eaten most of the provisions that they had brought along—as their mind was set on a voyage of six weeks from land to land, they had gorged and swilled from early morning until evening—so that at the last it was hard for them to live on the ship's provisions only. Then most lost their courage and were convinced they would never set foot on land again.

On the 17th same, a small land bird similar to the yellow water wagtail of Germany alighted several times on the ship, so that the people could see it well. This caused such great joy among the people that they all clapped their hands.

On the 18th a ship from Rhode Island came to us, with sheep and other things aboard for the West Indies, which our captain had hailed through the megaphone. After they had discussed with each other, both ships dropped sails, since little progress was being made anyway, and our captain had a boat lowered into the water and went with four sailors to the ship. And after they had drunk welcome with each other, he returned and brought half a sack of apples, a goose, a duck and two hens, and distributed the fine apples among the people at once. This caused great joy that they received such wonderful American fruit, which was very tasty, at sea, and he threw the apples which were left among the people to be caught; all fell over one another for the nice apples.

On the 19th same a very unusual fish came on board; it was like a large round table and had a mouth like two small baskets. The same evening a great number of large fish approached the ship from the north in schools, and when they reached the ship they shot into the depths in front of, behind, and under the ship, so that one could not see them on the other side of the ship.

On the 20th same another boy died and was buried in the sea on the same evening. And again this evening came untold numbers of large fish to the ship from the north, which, as one looked, went high above the water like the previous ones so that one did not see them from the other side. Afterwards there came such a powerful, strong rain that some people caught half pails of water with sailcloth alone, and from the captain's cabin. Then came a powerful stormwind from the northwest, so that the sea or ocean rose so high that when one looked at it it was as if one traveled in high mountains, where all mountains were covered with snow. One mountain or wave after the other struck the ship, so that the captain, chief steersman, and cook were hit by one wave leaving them without a dry stitch of clothing on their bodies. The water came into the ship with such force that many people's bedrolls which lay by portholes were completely wet. In great haste all holes were quickly closed, the rudder bound, and the ship set sideways against the wind with close rigged sails so that it did not roll so much to both sides. The storm continued throughout the night with great force. All could see without fear that it was not the strength of the ship that endured such blows, but rather the almighty hand of the Lord who preserved it in order to make known His might to the people—to Him be above all and before all the honor. Amen.

Not a person remained on the deck of the ship, except a sailor tied to the rudder who held watch. All the others—captain, steersman, and sailors—crept in their wet clothes into their beds. The ship lay for a time at the mercy of the wind, always on its side so that it shipped water, but the water always ran off again. Around midnight the waves struck so hard on the aft portholes that two porthole boards broke loose, and as the people lay partly in sleep and slumber the water poured in through the portholes, a stream as large as the hole, and immediately into the beds which caused a great panic among those who lay near the porthole. The water took a board with rope completely away again. We leaped up, because the friend who lay near the porthole had not tied the board tightly enough, and this misfortune could have been great; we took a wool sack close at hand and stuffed the porthole shut again and the other porthole with the remaining board. The ship's carpenter made a new shutter the next morning.

The storm began to let up a little bit, also the fear of the people decreased, and around two o'clock in the afternoon the sky cleared, the wind died down, the portholes were opened, and there was quiet beautiful weather. The captain had rice cooked in a kettle quickly, so that the people received a little something warm on this day, and the night until [text incomplete].

The 22nd same at noon the ship lay quite still as a house, and the people dried their things again. During the afternoon we got a good wind which held on during the night also, so strong and yet so steady that one did not realize on the ship that it was moving, yet we still progressed two and a half [?] in one hour. At midnight the first sounding was taken, over one hundred fifty fathoms deep without finding bottom.

On the 23rd same around nine o'clock another sounding was made and at fifty-five fathoms bottom was found; at eleven o'clock, thirty-five fathoms; shortly thereafter twenty fathoms deep (and still we saw no land), but were rapidly nearing the [Delaware] River. The people were very happy because of such a good wind and because we had found bottom. The captain did not think it possible to reach the river by daylight because no land could be seen, and had the sails all lowered despite the good wind around four o'clock, and the rudder bound because there were many sandbanks before and in the river.

Early the next morning all the sails were hoisted again, and directed toward the river, although the wind was not good at all, and there was a thick fog. They made soundings again and found fifteen fathoms, and an hour later seven fathoms. Around twelve o'clock we saw land with great joy; around four o'clock we approached the river closely, since when one first sees it one is six hours away. The captain and I saw three boats sailing in, and the captain cried they must be pilots or steersmen; one could hardly see them in the waves. He had all sails hoisted and was very happy that the pilots came to meet him. The first that came he did not accept, but when the second came, he knew him and took him at once aboard the ship and planned to sail into the river the same night. But when we had land on both sides, around eight o'clock, at the mouth of the river, there suddenly came a stormwind from the southwest worse than any before. All had to help lower the sails and anchor for the first time. We remained firm in one place and the water had not very much power because it was not over seven fathoms deep. Therefore we stayed at anchor the whole night and the storm died away soon after.

The 25th same the above-mentioned newly born baby died, and was buried in the river. We sailed the night of that day into the narrows of the river, which is truly very pleasant to look upon, as wide as the Rhine River, where it is broadest, and on both sides the most beautiful woods or bushes. Here and there stood houses on the river bank, and their fishing nets were hung up on the shores. We passed by New Castle on the following 27th same with a small wind and thick fog. The mentioned city is still forty English miles from Philadelphia.

Because we had very little wind then, we had to travel more than once with the flood tide, or with the water, so that we traveled on the 28th and arrived very happily on the afternoon of the 29th in Philadelphia.

Brethren and sisters came to meet us in small boats with delicious bread, apples, peaches, and other refreshments of the body, for which we praised the great God publicly on the ship, with much singing and resounding prayers. There were many tears that He had preserved us as a Father and carried us on eagles' wings, and that we had met each other in love again before eternity. This, dear children, brethren, and friends, is very briefly the description of our trip over the great ocean.

If I were to report everything that happened among the passengers, on the ship, there would be much more to write. It makes my heart sorrowful to recall that often aboard ship I said to them that I did not think it was worse in hell with all the unclean spirits than aboard ship with cursing and swearing, blasphemy, nagging, and fighting, swilling and gorging and quarreling day and night in storm and strain, so that the captain often said that he had taken many groups across the ocean, but the equal he had never seen.

He thought that they were possessed with devils and therefore he was a real example of hell [to them]. However, they treated us all in a friendly and obliging manner and had great respect for us. The captain often threatened them that he would have some of them tied to the mast by sailors and beaten from head to toe. However, they remained wicked people.

I would like to report some observations and comments concerning the great danger and difficulties of the trip to Pennsylvania.

The danger of this trip is [that] if God is against one and wishes to exact His revenge and judgment on the ocean, no one could evade Him at sea or on land. Secondly, it would be dangerous to travel in an old ship across the ocean, or with a captain who was tyrannical and did not understand sailing. If the Lord is with one (which I assumed) and one has a good ship and good sailors, the danger is not half so great as one imagines. The Lord bears the earth and the sea, and one in and upon the other, and therefore the ship on the sea, and those who travel in the heights and the depths. The eternal Jehovah has saved them, so that they should know Him and praise His name, who performs great miracles for the children of men.

The hardship of this trip lies in many factors and things. I personally did not have much hardship—very little actually—but I observed and experienced much from others: first, when people do not really need to make the trip.

Second, when people undertake the trip without enough deliberation for worldly reasons.

Third, when people set out to leave, especially married couples, and are not completely agreed to start such a long journey.

These three things are the main causes behind the hardships of this long trip, for I can and must say in truth that of the six or seven ships full of passengers, I found but few people who did not regret having made the trip. Most of them said that great need had driven them to it, even though many had been rich and they had lost much. Because of the severe pressures of the authorities, they either had to leave or become poverty stricken, and could not keep from becoming beggars and debtors. In spite of this, many regretted the trip so much that they became ill, and did not know what they were doing for anger. Neighbors accused one another; man, wife, and children picked quarrels instead of helping one another, thus not only leaving the burden for them to carry but even increasing it. People like that cause a good deal of trouble living so close together on a ship for thirteen or fourteen or fifteen weeks where they cannot do as they please.

Then there are numerous others who would consume all the supplies which they had brought along while the food on board is still good, or even throw it into the sea. In time, when the ship's food supplies have been preserved in salt for quite a long while, and part of the water begins to stink, rice, barley, peas, and the like can hardly be cooked any longer in it. Those people will have by that time stuffed themselves with all their supplies and swilled all that they had (pardon me for saying it but it is true). They are then forced to put up with the poor victuals, which is particularly hard for this type of person. As the people are so crowded together, some begin to steal whatever they can, namely foodstuffs, and liquids. Then there are the many lice among the people, so that many people have to spend the whole day in delousing and one who does not do this is practically devoured. This was a great difficulty for all, and also for my people. Now that we have arrived safely and well on land, and all of ours have met with great love and friendliness, all the previous is suddenly forgotten (so to speak) because of the great joy that we have in one another. This hardship had lasted about nineteen weeks, then it was over, for which the Highest be praised. Amen. Yes, amen.

We have not regretted that we are here and wish from our hearts that you were with us here, with your children. But that is not the case. I dare not urge you, since the trip is so difficult for persons who cannot take everything patiently as it comes, but rather are often restless when all is well. If I could, after God's good will, do everything for you children, I promise you that I would start by deciding to take upon myself another trip, for your sake, not because of the ease of earning a living here. Oh, no, this country demands an industrious people, no matter what trade they have, and then they make their way very well. There are, however, many people here who are in great difficulty, because it seems that some people would be in trouble even if they were in Paradise. Some have themselves to blame because they arrive in the country, see the beautiful plantations, the handsome livestock, and surplus of every goods, and despite the fact that they have just arrived, want to have everything right away; they not only refuse good advice, but go in debt for large pieces of land, borrow animals and such, and have a miserable time before they make good. Well, what should I say, in this world some have it better than others. Those who will be content with food and shelter can prosper with God's blessing and with a will to work.

Our people are all getting along well, one better than the next, but no one has scarcity. I was amazed at what I heard concerning those indentured emigrants, about the young and strong people and artisans, how rapidly they are gone as masons, carpenters, and all other trades, and even old people with grown children who can do only farm work. There the child takes over the indenture for both his and his father's or mother's passage for four years, and is able in that time to earn all the necessary clothing and finally a handsome outfit from head to foot, a horse or a cow with a calf; small children take on one and a half year's indenture. When they are twenty-one years old they have to be taught reading and writing, and leave well-dressed and with a horse or a cow.

One finds few houses in the city or country where the people are rather prosperous where there are not one or two children. The matter is always discussed at the city hall with great seriousness. Often parents and children are ten, eleven, twelve, thirteen, fourteen, fifteen, sixteen, seventeen, eighteen, nineteen, or twenty hours from each other. Often those indenturing themselves are better off than those who paid their passage, as they get their expenses paid by others and learn the peculiarities of the country.

I want to bring this to a close and wish patience for those who will read it.

God be with you all. Amen.

John Naas.

P.S. Well, dear children, what more should I write. It might turn out that you would come here, and then there would be no more letter writing. If you do not come and if I live, there will be more to write another time; therefore I will bring this to a close and recommend you and your dear children in the unending love of God. May He guide and direct you that you do not tread in the pathway of the sinners and do not sit in the seat of the scorner. That would not be good for you.

The Brothers Sekler, whom you know, are in eternity except Henry; his [their?] death was described in a letter in Christ to Liebe (I hope he will let you read it). The others extend their warmest greetings: Brother Becker, Brother Gantz, Gumre, Ritter, Paul, Sr., with Brother Mack, the older and younger Ziegeler, and their families greet all. Many other brethren and sisters, who do not know you, and whom you do not know, greet warmly all those in Krefeld who fear God.

In true and uniting love, your father

John Naas.

P.S. Mother and Elizabeth send their best greetings, and will also do this in their own hand. Do not forget to greet all who ask about us in love, if they have not already been named.[19]

New Testament Inscription

An interesting inscription on the flyleaves of a New Testament now in the Mennonite congregational archive in Krefeld reveals that the parents of a Herman van Laschet had sailed for Pennsylvania. The connection with the Brethren is found in a further inscription stating that his grandfather had carried this New Testament with him while imprisoned in the Berg area along with Lobach, Liebe, and others.

My grandfather had this Testament with him in the prison in the Ober-Berg area when he was persecuted because of his Christian religion by the Lutherans, along with the elder Lobach, Stetius, Liebe, Müller, Bremen, and many more.

Krefeld, the 26th of May, 1736. My dear father and dear mother with four dear brothers and one dear sister traveled to Pennsylvania and left from Oergen [?] on the 26th day of May. And I, Herman van Laschet, entered the state of matrimony with Anne Reiners the 27th of May, 1736. I wish that the Lord will bless and sustain us.[20]

REMNANTS IN EUROPE

SWITZERLAND

Information on Brethren remaining in Europe is scanty. There was considerable separatist activity in the Basel area called "Anabaptist" by the authorities. In the absence of clear-cut connection with known Brethren it is difficult to know whether to consider them as part of the Brethren movement (which was said to have expanded as far as Switzerland). A note on Andrew Boni's sister is tantalizing but indefinite. The famous anecdote about Mack and Hochmann which is said to have taken place in Switzerland is found in the Hochmann biography.

Andrew Boni's Sister Houses Dissenters

Report to the Mayor and City Council of Basel.

Report of some deputies to the mayor and council of the city of Basel of January 18, 1718, in connection with the separatist Gmehli.

. . . The wife of Rebmann in Lower Basel is the sister of the well-known Pietist Andrew Boni from Frenkendorf. Pastor Merian, who examined her privately, testifies about her that she and her husband led devout, honest, and irreproachable lives. . . . Many seek refuge with her on account of her brother, with whom they are either related or acquainted. . . .[21]

Mack Criticizes Hochmann von Hochenau

Spiritual Crumbs Concerning the Loving Disciple and Champion of Jesus Christ, Ernest Christopher Hochmann von Hochenau.

. . . Hochmann once attended there [Switzerland] a meeting of the Baptists to demonstrate outwardly his goodwill and impartiality for the sake of love. Their leader and teacher at that time, Alexander Mack, who was indeed a sincere man but a strict sectarian along with it, led in speaking the Word. It seems to me that Hochmann also spoke briefly for the edification of all. However, this Alexander Mack contradicted him, and condemned him openly before all of the people. He called him a hypocrite, a false prophet, etc., and other things.

Hochmann, however, replied to all this only with mild silence. After the close of the address or meeting, Hochmann stood up, went to Alexander Mack, embraced him, and kissed him. He then spoke to him with a smile in a most heartfelt and brotherly way, "Dear Brother Mack, when you are in heaven, and see me arrive there also, then you will rejoice and say, 'Oh, look! There comes also our dear Brother Hochmann!'" I cannot remember what else he said at that time. However, it can be easily seen what a deep impression, shame, and humility this masterpiece of divine grace and the spirit of Jesus must have caused at least with some. They must also have been dampened somewhat in their sectarian zeal, and it must have convinced them of his integrity.

Now Hochmann has certainly safely arrived in the heavenly kingdom. Not only God's Word gives a basis for this, but also the true servant of Jesus Christ, Stephen Koch, sent us some thirty years ago from Pennsylvania the happy news about it. He had seen in a vision or ecstasy Hochmann blissfully flourishing in that glorious Kingdom of Zion, and had spoken with him. This can be read with pleasure in the twentieth number of the *Geistliche Fama*. As far as his opponent, Alexander Mack, is concerned, he must have come to realize his error, if not in this life, then surely in the greater knowledge in heaven. They are, we hope, now united, to glorify the eternal God of love together.

William Weck.[22]

Anabaptism in Basel Reported

The leading anti-Pietist church periodical in Germany, *Innocent News* [*Unschuldige Nachrichten*], included an article in a 1723 issue which may refer to the Brethren.

"Report of the Fanatics and Separatists in Switzerland."

Pietism and similar enthusiastic movements are getting out of control in Switzerland. There are various persons in the canton of Basel who refuse to stand guard, participate in military drill, or in case of crisis take up arms for the fatherland. Baptism, they say, must be deferred until the person reaches full understanding. And, indeed, in most of their articles of faith, they concur with the Anabaptists. They have published their beliefs in a small tract which they distribute everywhere. They refrain from taking communion, because of their own feelings of unworthiness, but do not advise others against it.

They attend church not at all or seldom, but rather come together in private homes, and that mostly by night, to sing psalms, and read and expound upon the Holy Scriptures. They claim that they understand the Holy Scriptures better than all other Protestants. One of them sold his Bible, as he considered himself to be perfect, and therefore needed it no longer. It has been observed that the spirit of their teaching occurs more often with women than with men.

There are also in the city of Basel some families, who, it is true, do not completely profess their beliefs in this teaching, but do hold their special meetings and are in correspondence with likeminded elsewhere. They spread their seeds of teaching in the country, although if such teachers are found to be active among the peasants they are immediately driven out. As to their future success, only time will tell, as the authorities as well as the clergy seek to put an end to this disturbance, which continues to spread.

It has been discussed whether they should be driven out of the territory without confiscation of their property, or with the required abandoning of their goods and children. It is feared that when they have exhausted their savings in foreign countries, they will return again and the city of Basel might be required to provide their support.

There had been published a detailed report of their Anabaptist opinion which all tends toward the abolition of the official clergy. Nevertheless, in October the honorable theologians of Basel submitted their written opinion on the teaching of these separatists to the magistrates, in response to the order which they had received, with the following contents: this teaching is in error, and has no basis in God's Word. One must, however, seek to bring these people on the correct path again with a mild attitude and through the power of the divine Word in pure love, which requires patience. They for their part will not be lax, in the certain hope that these people will finally allow themselves to be brought to the path of truth. This opinion has pleased the magistrates very well.[23]

THE NETHERLANDS

The picture in the Netherlands is also confusing. There is one hint in a comment on Andrew Frey and his return to Europe with Count Zinzendorf in 1743. M. G. Brumbaugh listed several names of Dutch citizens called "Brethren" by Alexander Mack, Jr., who were therefore considered by Dr. Brumbaugh to be members of the church fellowship. They are known, however, to have belonged to the Dutch immersionist group, the Collegiants.[24]

Count Zinzendorf Recruits Andrew Frey

Detailed Report about the Moravians in this American Land . . .

. . . Count Louis himself left Philadelphia on January 1, 1743, at nine o'clock in the evening. Among those who were taken along and went with him from this area was Andrew Frey. He had formerly been a separatist and later a Mennonite and a Sabbatarian, but took offense at these and became a leader among the other Baptists [Brethren]. He then became involved with the Moravian movement, and was made a leader. Count Zinzendorf had long recommended and urged that Frey travel with him, because of the other Baptists in Holland, as he himself admitted. As Frey was too weak physically, he did not want to agree to this at first, but finally he was convinced and strengthened in it through the drawing of lots.

[Anonymous][25]

GERMANY

There is more information on the group remaining in Krefeld. The nucleus of this remnant were the Solingen Brethren (except William Knepper, who migrated with Mack, and John Frederick Henckels, who moved to Holland). There are records of Brethren becoming citizens of Krefeld where they tended to join the Mennonites. Their vital statistics, kept at that time in church books, were entered in the Mennonite records.

Krefeld Brethren Become Citizens

List of Krefeld citizens.

December 8, 1721; Jacob William Naas has purchased the right of citizenship and has been accepted as a citizen. According to official regulation he is to pay the city fifteen *florins*.

December 30, 1730; Christian Liebe, born in Eppstein in the Palatinate, along with his two sons, Christian, Jr., and Arnold, have purchased the right of citizenship and have been accepted and received as citizens. He will pay the fee [*Stadtsjura*] of thirty *stivers* within a month.

October 10, 1740; Gottfried Luther Stetius has purchased the right of citizenship which includes his son, John William Stetius.[26]

Last Years of Lobach Described

In the John Lobach biography is a description of the last years of Lobach and his companion, Gottfried Luther Stetius. Lobach especially was highly respected as an outstanding Christian.

. . . John Lobach and Stetius, however, moved into a small house together, where they led very secluded, peaceful, and Christlike lives in contented fellowship for several years. They both served each other and preferred each other in love. Their conduct was very quiet and edifying and they were shining lights and examples for the whole city. At first, they were alone, did their own cooking, and practiced daily silent prayer besides their usual work. Their furnishing, clothing, eating, and drinking were modest, but everything was in good order.

Later they took an elderly, very devout and quiet spinster into their home, who served them and was their housekeeper. This was so that they could devote themselves better to their outward and inward occupations. After some time, friend Stetius took as his wife the above-mentioned spinster, who was a very loyal but weak orphan, upon the consent of his dear friends. She passed away in the Lord several years later, without children, in a desired peace of mind. It is assumed that they had lived together through the years in continence. John Lobach was treated as their son and brother, and helped to keep house and care for everything.

On the fourth of May, 1750, the said John Lobach passed away in the Lord. The last years of his hidden life with Christ in God (after Colossians 3:3) as well as the brief but very edifying circumstances of his illness and death, have been recently portrayed in free verse by two close friends. This is, however, no longer present, but has been mislaid or lost through loaning. He was beloved by all manners of people in the whole city, but especially by those who had a sincere fear of God. His memory is a blessed one.

Soli Deo Gloria!

[To God alone the glory!][27]

Gerhard Tersteegen to Gottfried Luther Stetius

The Reformed poet, Gerhard Tersteegen, sent the following letter of consolation to Gottfried Luther Stetius after the death of John Lobach. The reference by Tersteegen to Stetius' wife and family is explained by the latter's second marriage in 1734.

To the Honorable Gottfried Luther Stetius in Krefeld.

Dearly Beloved Brother Stetius:

So it has pleased our Lord to call our beloved brother John [Lobach] to join Him. He had had to remain thirty years in your home and in our fellowship, until Jesus came. Jesus loved him more, and had a higher claim on him, than all of us had. He has been taken from the side of all of us, but especially from yours, in order to lie down at Jesus' side and on His breast, with content, pleasure, and proud rest, and feed on godly and pure love—thus to remain for ever and ever the disciple whom Jesus loves. Selah!

You have lost much in him, in more than one way, and all of us have lost a dearly beloved brother and fellow pilgrim. I say "lost" in a healthy sense, as we do indeed miss that which we once had. What we have through children of God is not entirely known; it is felt, though, when we no longer have it. The smallest member of the body must remain dear to us. Nevertheless, it has pleased the Lord to take a beloved disciple from our midst. Let us not mourn as do the others who have no hope, but say with Job in spirit: "The Lord gave, and the Lord has taken away; blessed be the name of the Lord" [Job 1:21].

This is already the second John who has been freed this jubilee year. They have been transplanted, as it were, from the Krefeld garden as flowers into Paradise. May the Lord grant that their absence might not be noticed in that garden, and instead of two, another twenty or more might grow up as flowers planted in Christ, to the beauty and happiness of Krefeld, to the pleasure of all initiated, and to the glory of the Great Gardener.

You, dear brother, know where you can make good your loss. May Jesus replace everything! May He become that which the departed friend was to you. May his passing away be for you, for me, and for many, a call to follow soon—to seek in the future still more completely, more ardently, and more steadily that which is above where Christ is and where our dear brothers and friends are! For the goodness we saw in them, for all of the grace given them by God, for the talents given them, for the proven support in health, illness, and death—for all this shall there be offered a "Hallelujah" to the Lord, both here and in eternity! Amen.

As I am being interrupted by visitors, I must stop. And how are you, dear brother? I heard with much brotherly sympathy that you may have suffered an attack of illness yourself. I hope, if it be God's will, that it had little effect, and that God's fatherly mercy may spare you for yet a while, to the comfort and aid of your dear wife and all your children. I am concerned about you, and, if the illness continues, please let me know. I send you warm greetings, dear brother, and warm greetings to your dear wife and all of your children. I pray to Jesus that He may embrace, bless, and guard them from evil, so that the dear Brother Lobach may again embrace with glorious joy this little flock, for whom he helped to care. I send warm greetings to all fellow pilgrims whom I know, especially those who are ill; I do not have time to name all of them. All the brethren here send their warm greetings also. I commend myself to your intercession and remain through grace,

Mühlheim/Ruhr,   your devoted feeble brother
May 12, 1750.   Gerhard Tersteegen.[28]

European Movement Completed

It is difficult to set a definite date for the completion of the Brethren movement in Europe. The group in Krefeld seems to have existed the longest. Many of them merged with the Pietist circle around Tersteegen. Others joined the Mennonites.

Two Quaker writers in Pennsylvania refer to Brethren in Europe in the 1760's and 1770's. Anthony Benezet wrote to Samuel Smith in 1765 about the latter's plan of writing a history of Pennsylvania. One of the motives for the writing of the book was to defend the pacifism of the Society of Friends. Benezet advised Smith to include descriptions of other religious bodies in Pennsylvania which also held this principle. These included the Mennonites, Schwenkfelders, Moravians, and Brethren. Benezet referred to "the Dymplers and Pietists, a People coming mostly from Germany, etc., who have many Meetings for worship both in Germany and here . . . ."[29]

In Smith's book (written between 1771 and 1773, but not published until 1913) the section on the Brethren, along with other valuable information, describes the migrations of 1719, 1729, and 1733. Smith then states: "In their native country they had not full liberty of conscience, nor in Holland, besides there, many could not maintain themselves but were helped by others, which made them all come over by degrees, except some few, who are still at Creyfeld in Friesland [*sic*]."[30]

As far as is now known, these are the last references to Brethren activity in Europe in the eighteenth century. The European phase of Brethren origins was completed.[31]

VI. Publication

They were only made more joyful through persecution, poverty, misery, and imprisonment, with which they were oppressed. Therefore, some learnéd men accosted them, and sought to confuse them with sharp arguments and crafty questions. The reader can inform himself sufficiently about this from the forty basic questions [by Eberhard Louis Gruber], along with their answers which are appended to this tract. About this time, then, the church of the Lord at Schwarzenau thought it good to publish this booklet for the instruction of singleminded souls. Every impartial reader can determine for himself, if he reads this without prejudice along with this preface, what motivated them to have this booklet printed.

However, those who then were so joyfully active in the work of the Lord, and had witnessed in great simplicity and sincerity of the truth, have all passed away peacefully. The desire has therefore arisen in the churches who bear this same testimony here in America, and who have likewise surrendered themselves to the Lord to live according to the truth, to have this simple testimony published again. This is especially for the dear young people so that they might have a simple and certain foundation in the truth in which they are instructed. However, this was especially done for the honor of God, who has so miraculously protected His truth to this very day.

—Alexander Mack, Jr.[1]

THE WRITINGS OF ALEXANDER MACK

The Reformers of the sixteenth century had quickly seized upon the new process of printing, made possible by the technical break-through of the invention of movable type, to spread their ideas. Floods of tracts and pamphlets written for the common man streamed from the crude presses. Later religious leaders followed this example in making their views known, and were often successful despite governmental censorship and regulation. Pietists, both those remaining in the church and those eventually breaking away, were prolific writers. The literature of the movement, and that of their opponents, is large.

Five years after the formation of the Brethren fraternity, the first publication presenting their principles appeared. It has commonly been called *Ground-Searching Questions,* a literal translation of part of the German title, but *Basic Questions* would be a better modern equivalent.[2] It consists of forty questions submitted by Eberhard Louis Gruber, at that time still a separatist, who later became one of the main leaders of the Inspirationists.[3] The questions were answered by an *"Artless Member"* [*Aufrichtiges Mitglied*], which reveals through the emphasized initial letters (a common practice of that day for concealing identity to all but the initiated) that the author was Alexander Mack.

We are told that these questions were submitted to the Brethren to be answered with "corporate, clear, and candid explanations" of their new form of baptism and new church fellowship. However, many of the questions are dependent upon the foregoing answers, which would make it unlikely that an actual list of questions was presented in writing. Perhaps the publication is the written outgrowth of a discussion or debate, or, less likely, it is merely a literary device.

There is also a problem about the form of publication. No copy of the first edition is known. The first American edition in 1774 by Christopher Sauer II of Germantown states that the treatise was first circulated in manuscript.[4] At the close of the American edition, Schwarzenau is given as the place of original publication, in the month of July, 1713.

However, a catalog issued in 1729 by the Berleburg book publisher and printer, John Jacob Haug, famous for his Berleburg Bible, lists *Fragen, Grundforschende, von der Wasser Taufe,* 1713, in quarto, selling for two crowns.[5] This is undoubtedly identical with Mack's writing, which would mean that there was also a printed edition in Germany. This is not necessarily in conflict with the statement on Sauer's second edition, because the tract may have first been circulated in manuscript, a common practice then, and later printed. It is probable that the title page of the second (Sauer) edition was copied from the first (German) edition, which could well have included the statement that the tract was first circulated in manuscript form.

In 1715, the Brethren published their major theological work, Alexander Mack's *Brief and Simple Exposition of the Outward but Yet Sacred Rights and Ordinances of the House of God* . . . , usually referred to incorrectly as *Rites and Ordinances*.[6] A unique copy of the original edition is in the Wittgenstein collection of Marburg University. Through the efforts of Professor Ernst Benz, Dr. Franklin H. Littell, and others, much of the theological section of the Sayn-Wittgenstein-Hohenstein library at Laasphe was preserved when that magnificent collection was auctioned off several years after the close of World War II. One of the volumes saved in this way from dispersal and irretrievable loss was Mack's publication. It was most probably printed in Berleburg.

Mack's treatise was republished in America in 1774 by Christopher Sauer II, together with the *Basic Questions*.[7] A new preface written by Mack's son, Alexander Mack, Jr., for the second edition is the best concise statement on Brethren origins, and has been quoted extensively throughout this volume. Some editorial changes were made in the second edition, mostly minor ones. More important changes have been noted in the translation here following.

One of the sons of Christopher Sauer II, Samuel Sauer, printed a third edition of both writings in Baltimore, Maryland, in 1799. He bound them together with a *Christian Hand-Book,* by Jeremias Felbinger, a seventeenth-century religious writer and translator.[8] The Samuel Sauer edition was duplicated in 1828, including the Felbinger work, by John Bär of Lancaster, Pennsylvania.[9]

In 1810 Mack's writings were translated into English for the first time by a "friend to religion"—Henry Slingluff, deacon of the Germantown church—and printed in Philadelphia by John Binns. Slingluff had begun the publication the previous year but had been interrupted. A written entry in the 1809 fragment of thirty-six pages preserved in the Cassel Library at Juniata College reads: "This book was a printing last year, till about the fifth part thereof and a friend of mine stopt the press."[10] For some unknown reasons, the last two questions of the forty questions by Gruber were omitted, and the translator added some sentences to the Alexander Mack, Jr., preface of 1774.

The next major edition came in 1860, when Henry Kurtz, the pioneer Brethren publicist, reprinted both works, with new English translations facing the German texts, in the same year as his *The Brethren's Encyclopedia,* with which they are often found bound.[11] Kurtz made the translation as "literal as possible," and it was then revised by his "English colaborer," James Quinter. The 1860 edition reinstated question thirty-nine of the *Basic Questions,* but the last question, in which Mack praised the Mennonites, was again omitted. A passage in the last portion of the tract which speaks of forty questions was evidently changed to read "thirty-nine" to correspond to the number of questions. However, that part of the preface which speaks of forty questions was left unchanged.

The Kurtz-Quinter translation was republished in 1888 by the Brethren's Publishing Company, at which time the title was changed to read *Rites and Ordinances,* rather than the correct *Rights.*[12] The meaning of the original German is "law" or "statute," and was so translated within the body of the text. The most recent publication of Mack's writings was in 1939 by the Brethren Church at Ashland, Ohio, which follows the 1860 translation, except for minor editorial changes.[13]

The following is a new translation of Mack's two short treatises. The 1799 Samuel Sauer edition of *Basic Questions,* and the 1715 original edition of *Rights and Ordinances* were used as the texts. As with the foregoing documents, the aim has been to make as close a translation as possible, but one which is still readable. The style of the originals is that of an unlearnéd but vigorous man who is very well grounded in Scripture (as was Mack). Although the meaning is occasionally obscure, the main theme of the writing—the necessity for complete obedience to Christ's teaching and example—becomes very clear through repetition.

It should be kept in mind that these were not intended as systematic and complete expressions of faith. The Brethren specifically avoided creeds and confessions, partly because they felt that they had not obtained light on all of the questions and partly because they were reacting against the extreme creedalism of the established churches which neglected the gospel in their stress on the "symbolic books." They are presentations of the early Brethren position on the *controversial* practices and beliefs. In the beginning of the discussion between father and son in *Rights and Ordinances,* Mack has the son say: ". . . I am asking you, dear father, that you might better instruct me in accordance with the witness of the Holy Scriptures and the early Christians in all these things which are yet so controversial and which cause us such criticism."[14] It is usually true that religious minorities tend to discuss their unique features, rather than those which they share with others.

The Brethren shared the post-Reformation evangelical beliefs about Christianity, and were definitely influenced by their Calvinist background. It, therefore, does violence to historical accuracy to judge them alone on these two frankly propagandistic tracts, even though they are the only statements readily available. Both must be read keeping in mind the harsh and dead orthodoxy against which the Brethren reacted by becoming Pietists, and the extreme separatist views of the radical Pietists in the Wittgenstein area and elsewhere, which they discarded when they organized as a church fellowship.

As far as is now known, Alexander Mack published but one other tract. No copy of this is known to exist. Printed in America, it was written to counteract the Sabbatarian views of Conrad Beissel, which were a contributing factor in the unhappy Brethren-Ephrata split in Pennsylvania around 1730. There are also some fragments from Mack's pen in blank leaves in his personal Bible, now at Bridgewater, Virginia.

Answers to Gruber's Basic Questions
Eberhard Louis Gruber's
BASIC QUESTIONS
which were especially submitted to be answered by the
New Baptists of the Wittgenstein Area
along with the accompanying
Brief and Simple Answers to the Same,
previously published in manuscript by an
*A*RTLESS *M*EMBER
of the church at Wittgenstein
and now publicly printed at the request of many.

[GRUBER]
In God Beloved Friends and Fellow Pilgrims:

There have been several persons who have desired a somewhat more definite explanation and report about your new baptism and church fellowship, especially since that which has been said or even written about it from time to time has still left them in great uncertainty. In order to learn about your opinion more thoroughly and accurately and thereby dispel any further doubt in regard to it, these candid and herewith-presented questions are submitted to you. We expect your clear and frank answers upon these soon.

[MACK]
Dear Friends:

You have requested from us in love our motives. The Apostle Peter teaches believers (1 Peter 3:15) that they must always be ready to give an answer to anyone who calls them to account for the hope that is in them. For these reasons, we have not been able to evade this, but rather have very briefly answered these submitted questions in a simple fashion with frankness in love and in the certainty of faith. We wish to leave them to your examination before God.

QUESTION 1: Do you maintain that for over one thousand years there has been no true and genuine baptism, and, consequently, no true church on earth?

ANSWER: We maintain and believe that at all times God has had

His church which observed the true baptism and ordinances. This was, however, always hidden from the unbelievers and often consisted of but few members. Despite this, the gates of hell could never prevail against the church of the Lord Jesus. It can also be proved from the histories that God has caused His ordinances to be revealed as a witness to the unbelievers at all times.

QUESTION 2: Could the church of God have existed at any time and in any manner even with but few members, without the original and outward ordinance of baptism, as the Israelite church (according to Joshua 5:5-7) existed for considerable time in the wilderness without practicing circumcision?

ANSWER: The church of Christ is ordained in no other way by the true Master-Builder, Jesus Christ, than that it should observe His baptism and ordinances. Christ indeed ordained everything perfectly in His congregation or church through His apostles and teachers, and sufficiently confirmed it by signs and miracles. For this reason, the fact is incontestable that a congregation or church of Christ could never have existed without the baptism and ordinances as commanded by the true Founder.

We do not deny that there could have been souls who were attracted in secret to the church of Christ. Whether, however, they followed and publicly professed Christ, or whether they preferred the honor of the world to the honor of God, we will not determine. As far as the Israelite church is concerned, it can be clearly seen that while in the wilderness the children had to bear the reproach of Egypt and suffer for the transgressions of their fathers! However, as soon as they were about to enter the promised land, and before they took the first city, Jericho, they first all had to be circumcised. God said to Joshua (5[:9]): "This day I have rolled away the reproach of Egypt from you." Only after this did they dare to celebrate the Passover and not before.

This is then a sign for us that as long as we walk in the wilderness and in great disorder and uncertainty—even though we have gone out of Egypt and have been rescued from gross sins by the mighty hand of God—we can still neither enter the house of God nor break the bread in the communion of Jesus and His members. God demands also of us that we should be baptized; He will indeed demand it of everyone, although perhaps in secret, if men will only listen to the inner voice and obey it with denial of self.

QUESTION 3: Did, then, the church of God here on earth completely cease to exist during the time that the early ordinance of baptism was no longer observed?

ANSWER: If the early ordinance of baptism had ceased to exist, then, of course, the church of Christ would also have ceased to exist. Even if there had been souls here and there who lamented the great apostasy, they could not have been called a church. However, we believe, and it can also be shown from the ancient histories, that the early form of baptism as ordained by the ordinance of Christ has never ceased to exist. Consequently, the church has likewise never ceased to exist, even if there were but few members.

QUESTION 4: How would you reconcile this with the promise of Jesus (Matthew 16:18) that the gates of hell shall not prevail against the church, and (28:20) that He will be with them always to the close of the age, and similar declarations?

ANSWER: This has already been answered because we believe that the gates of hell have *not* prevailed against the church of Christ; it has endured and will endure until the close of the age.

QUESTION 5: What, then, do you think about the salvation of those undeniable witnesses of truth who appeared from century to century, even during that time? Were they not members of Christ and His fellowship or true church which is united by the living spirit, just because they had not been baptized in accordance with the original ordinance?

ANSWER: Christ says (Matthew 7[:16]): "You will know them by their fruits." We believe that writing fine books and even prophesying are not the fruits of a good Christian, by which alone he is recognized. We cannot, therefore, consider a person to be a Christian for that alone. Yet, we will not judge anyone. Since we did not know those men in their lifetime, we leave them to their God. Neither all their writing nor even their prophesying can make us suspicious of the teaching of Jesus. We cannot consider them to be the church of Christ just because of their prophesying, if they did not walk in the teaching of Jesus, in baptism and the other ordinances.

QUESTION 6: Are you not of the opinion that the baptismal ceremony which has so long been neglected must be re-established in these latter times, and if so, why do you think so? Has not rather the all-wise God permitted this ceremony (which is not exactly part of the essence of Christianity) to be done away with, like the circumcision of the Old Covenant, for the very reason that it is as yet imperfect and does not yet make anything perfect, so that He could introduce a new economy and housekeeping of the pure spirit for His people, as all prophetic promises have foretold?

ANSWER: We are of the opinion and believe as the apostle writes (Hebrews 7:12): "For when there is a change in the priesthood, there is necessarily a change in the law as well." As long as the Levitical priesthood existed, just that long no one dared to annul the law, or circumcision, without incurring God's grave punishment and displeasure. However, when Christ came He introduced a law of life as the eternal High Priest and Son of God. He annulled the first law because it was too weak and could not make anyone perfect. He secured eternal redemption, revealed the paths to the Holy of Holies, and gave only laws of life. He confirmed His will or testament with His blood, so that we believe and profess that if an angel came from heaven and attempted to reveal another or better gospel, the angel would be accursed, according to the witness of Paul (Galatians 1:18).

Therefore, we believe that the teaching of Jesus the crucified must be kept until He himself shall come again and take vengeance with flaming fire upon those who were not obedient to His gospel, according to Paul's witness (2 Thessalonians 1:8). For this reason, then, the teachings of Jesus are rightly to be observed by believers in these days. However, there are no commandments for unbelievers.

QUESTION 7: Are you not compelled to recognize and admit that in that particular case [baptism] a direct divine calling is necessary and required for the re-establishment, just as well as for its first institution, which calling, according to the testimony of the Scriptures and the general confessions, has always been present at such great reformations of the church?

ANSWER: We do indeed believe that a direct calling and impelling by the Spirit of God is necessary for the practicing of the teachings of Christ. That, however, this calling must be confirmed and manifested before men by signs or miracles, we will not presume to dictate to

God. If the calling is of God, it is sufficient, whether men believe it or not. This must be left up to the individual.

QUESTION 8: Can any one of you stand up who is willing to state, upon his conscience and responsibility in the hour of his death and on the Day of Judgment, that he had received such a direct calling from God to re-establish the ordinance of baptism which was so long neglected, and with it to form an entirely new church of Christ here on earth such as has not existed since the time of the apostles and the early Christians?

ANSWER: When the Pharisees sent from Jerusalem and asked John whether he was the Christ or a prophet because he was baptizing, he answered: "I baptize you with water (for repentance), but among you stands one whom you do not know; he will baptize you with the Holy Spirit and with fire" [John 1:26; Matthew 3:11]. We likewise say in simplicity that we baptize in water only upon faith in Christ, who lets His voice be heard in the hearts of men in these days. Oh, if we would only follow Him and would know Him rightly, He would be the only one, and remain so forever, who shall establish, sanctify, and cleanse a church in this time with the "washing of water with the word" (Ephesians 5:26). No man would dare to appropriate this for himself, or declare before men that he was sent by God to establish a church, but he would gladly leave the honor to God. Even though God may use some as special instruments for this, they only need to be tested whether they are sent by God, as John says (3:34): "For he whom God has sent utters the words of God."

QUESTION 9: Of what does this direct calling consist? How can you justify and present this to the hearts and consciences of those who are still among the sects, as well as to those who have already withdrawn from them, for their outward or inward conviction?

ANSWER: The direct calling consists in the fact that the person is made inwardly exceedingly certain of it by the Spirit of God, and is not concerned whether men believe it or not. Jesus himself says (John 6:43, 44): "Do not murmur among yourselves. No one can come to me unless the Father who sent me draws him." It is equally true that no one can come to the teaching of Christ unless he lets himself be drawn by the Father. Whoever follows the guiding of the Father will easily recognize who the called and elect faithful are.

QUESTION 10: May it not properly be expected after the truth that if this work were indeed from God and you had received this direct divine calling to it, well-meaning souls would have gathered by the thousands? Would not the same thing have happened as that which took place at the first Pentecost of the New Testament under the direction of the Spirit at that time, and through the power of Jesus Christ in and on the apostles of the Lord?

ANSWER: Christ says (Matthew 24) to His followers that they should take heed especially in these days that no man lead them astray. He does not say that men will flock to His gospel by the thousands in such miserable times as these are, unfortunately, when love has grown cold in many hearts. Indeed, even the well-meaning souls do not come very willingly to the discipleship of Jesus, where all must be denied if Christ is to be followed rightly. On the contrary, Christ speaks of this time that the great abomination of desolation will be revealed. It only says that we must take refuge in the hills—that is, in the teachings of Jesus the crucified, which is exalted by all believers and is the city of God and the mountain of Zion, as stated in Hebrews 12:22, 23. Here, all true believers have always taken refuge. Many cannot even take their wives or children along, just as it happened to Lot, even though he was led by angels through a divine calling to escape destruction. Despite this, his friends found it ridiculous; yes, he even had to leave his wife on the way. For this reason, Christ urges His followers very briefly to bear this in mind, saying (Luke 17:32): "Remember Lot's wife."

QUESTION 11: Is water baptism so absolutely necessary that positively no one can be saved without it, no matter how holy and irreproachable his belief and life are otherwise?

ANSWER: We believe and profess that in the Old and New Testaments blessing and salvation are promised only to the faithful. We can see the way in which the faithful have been minded and disposed at all times in the believing Abraham, the father of all the faithful. He was obedient to God in everything, and therefore obtained the promise because of his living faith which effected works of obedience. Hence, we believe that if a man lives in a holy and perfect way, and his life is effected by true faith in Christ, it will indeed be easier for him to have faith to be obedient to water baptism than it was for Abraham to sacrifice his son.

When, however, this person still argues with his God, saying, "Of what use is this water for me?" this "holy life" is nothing but self-righteousness. Man seeks to establish it as did the Jews, about whom Paul speaks (Romans 10:9, 10). No salvation is promised to such selfish holiness. Christ is the fulfillment of the Law. Whoever believes in Him is justified. Faith in Christ produces obedience and submission to all of His words and commandments.

QUESTION 12: Does not the principal passage of Mark 16:16 prove the very contrary, where Jesus prudently says: ". . . he who does not believe (not he who is not baptized) will be condemned"?

ANSWER: We do indeed believe and profess that eternal life is not promised because of baptism, but only through faith in Christ (John 3:15, 18). Why should a believer not wish to do the will of Him in whom he believes? If it is the will of Christ that a believer should be baptized, then it is also the will of the believer. If he thus wills and believes as Christ wills, he is saved, even if it were impossible for him to receive baptism. Abraham was willing to sacrifice his son Isaac, but it did not happen; the son was not sacrificed. Yet obedience was fulfilled, and the blessing was received. Therefore, a believer who desires to be baptized, but cannot obtain it because of necessity—like the criminal on the cross—is still saved.

If, however, a man does not desire to be baptized, he is rightly to be judged as unbelieving and disobedient, not because of the baptism, but because of his unbelief and disobedience. Christ has rightly said, "He who believes . . ." [Mark 16:16]. If He had made salvation dependent on the water, men would be much more willing to be baptized, and retain their own will in other things. The Antichrist does this in assigning salvation to the water only, although the person lives otherwise as he pleases.

QUESTION 13: If water baptism is so absolutely necessary, why did Christ not mention it in His Sermon on the Mount when speaking of the Beatitudes (Matthew 5)? Why did He not make the least mention of it in His description of the judgment (Matthew 25), where He deals especially with all those who should be saved or condemned?

ANSWER: It is surprising how little men recognize the pure mind of God! Christ indeed speaks (Matthew 5) about many kinds of blessings. We might well ask from where such blessings may be obtained. Christ says: "Blessed are the meek . . ." [Matthew 5:5]. Now notice well how Christ calls (Matthew 11:28, 29), "Come to me . . . and learn from me." Therefore, we profess that Christ alone is the Savior. Whoever wishes to be blessed, as He preaches in Matthew 5, must necessarily accept Him in true faith, and must submit himself to Him in obedience, as clay in the hands of its potter. It is He who must make everything new and save all, and of Him all of the prophets have spoken. God himself refers to His Son.

Since then, Christ, as Savior and as the Good Physician, considers baptism necessary for believers, obedience to this commandment of baptism is also necessary for salvation. Even though Christ counts as blessed (Matthew 25) those who fed and clothed Him—and mentioned nothing of the new creature or rebirth about which He spoke (John 3), that without rebirth no one could enter the Kingdom of God, and at the latter place in turn did not say anything about visiting Him in prison or feeding His members—who would think that He counts as blessed in Matthew 25 those who were unreborn men or unbelievers, merely because of their outward works? Oh, no! Who would assume that they despised baptism? I believe that not a single person was among them who despised water baptism. There may have been some who were not baptized out of necessity, but not out of contempt for it.

QUESTION 14: How can you prove that John the Baptist was himself baptized, for he said to Christ (Matthew 3:14): "I need to be baptized by you, and do you come to me?" Or was he perhaps saved by a special exception?

ANSWER: Many questions could be asked in the same way: Where were Peter and John baptized, or where was this or that saint of the Old Covenant circumcised? More questions might be raised than would tend to edification toward God in faith. Paul records (1 Timothy 1[:4]) that there were even men who concerned themselves with endless genealogies. Nevertheless, we will also answer this in patience. John was indeed willing to be baptized by Christ, and desired this. We ascribe salvation to this faith, according to Scripture, and not to baptism. Even though it does not state explicitly in the Scriptures that he was baptized, at any rate it does say that he did not despise baptism. In addition, John will not be found among those who say, "Oh, of what use is water baptism for me?" Rather, he showed his obedience to Christ, as Abraham showed his obedience to God in the offering of his son. The son was not sacrificed, yet the obedience was fulfilled.

QUESTION 15: Were, then, all those who lived and died after the time of the early Christians who did not receive baptism in the original form completely lost and damned even though they faithfully observed the rules of Christ and true Christianity in all other respects—some even spending their blood and lives for it—only because they were content with their baptism received in infancy out of ignorance or lack of a higher motivation?

ANSWER: If they had had the same experience as Abraham when he offered his son, namely, that they had the true faith in Jesus, which is the foundation of all the rules of true Christianity, they were certainly saved. They were certainly saved even if they had not obtained outward baptism, perhaps in times of persecution or because of other circumstances. However, if they thought that their infant baptism was valid, then they were of course ignorant of the fundamentals of the Christian religion. They will probably have lived up to the fundamentals of Christianity to a small degree or not at all. They will scarcely have achieved the new creation which alone is acceptable before God. Still, we will not judge those who lived many years ago, but leave them to their God. However, similar ignorance of men today who perhaps oppose baptism because of lack of knowledge will not help them at all on the Day of Revelation.

QUESTION 16: Does not the commandment of baptism apply also to children, as did the commandment of circumcision in the Old Covenant? Consequently are not children in danger of forfeiting their salvation as long as they are not baptized? Also, will they not be damned if they die without baptism?

ANSWER: Just as circumcision did not concern children before the eighth day—to have circumcised before that time would have even been a violation of circumcision—the baptism commanded of believers does not concern children before they are able to profess their faith. The eighth day of circumcision is a prefiguration of this.

QUESTION 17: Were children damned in the Old Covenant who died without having received circumcision? If so, how are the comforting words of David (2 Samuel 12:23) to be understood which he spoke about his child conceived with Bathsheba that died on the seventh day?

ANSWER: The children who died before the eighth day had violated the commandment of circumcision as little as the female infants who were not circumcised at all, which did not hinder their salvation in any way. Enoch led a godly life, attained many hundred years, and was not circumcised; yet he was obedient to God, for that was not demanded of him. This is the way of God's commandments: where there is no law, there is no violation; where there is no violation, there is no punishment.

QUESTION 18: At what age then are the children to be baptized? Is it not proper to use all diligence to help them to be baptized as early as at all possible, even in their infancy?

ANSWER: Children are to be presented to the Lord Jesus in prayer, but baptism should be delayed until they are able to prove and profess their faith. This may be considered the "eighth day" or the first day of the new creation of a person. If they were to be baptized in their state of ignorance, it would be as if the Jews had practiced circumcision before the eighth day. This would have been a violation of circumcision rather than an obedient act.

QUESTION 19: Are not the children as capable of being baptized as of having faith (according to Luke 1:41-44; Matthew 18:3; Luke 18:16, 17; 1 Corinthians 7:14, etc.) even though they do not know how to express this with many words as do the adults? Is this not in accordance with the Word (Mark 16:16) that it is not so much a matter of an easily deceptive oral profession of faith as the truth of faith itself?

ANSWER: There is only one example of this in Scripture. John was moved in his mother's womb through the Holy Spirit because he was a child of the promise and was to be a forerunner of the Lord. Yet, it is obvious that he could not have been circumcised in his mother's womb but only after he was born. Despite this, they waited with circumcision until the eighth day. Therefore, even the moving of Saint John did not cause a change in the plan of God concerning circumcision. Rather, he was circumcised like all other children on the eighth day.

It is exactly the same with baptism. Even if the children of believing parents were to move in their mothers' wombs, they would have to wait with baptism until they were born. Again, once they were born, they would have to wait until they were moved by the Holy Spirit to desire baptism with specific words. Only then might they be baptized, because outward water baptism requires an outward expression of desire, as may be seen from Christ himself (Matthew 3:13). This desire must be effected by the true faith in the Lord Jesus. Otherwise, it is not permissible to baptize a child. Salvation is not dependent upon the water, but only upon the faith, which must be proved by love and obedience.

QUESTION 20: Does it not run counter to the evangelical character of the New Covenant to make an outward ceremony indispensably necessary for salvation? Is this not rather identical with the doctrine of the old Law-zealots against whom Paul wrote so emphatically in his letters to the Galatians and the Colossians?

ANSWER: We do not make of outward baptism anything else than what is commanded by Scripture. Since it says that believers should be baptized, we consider it disobedience to oppose that which God has commanded. Whoever opposes God in one thing—even if it is as insignificant as outward baptism—such a person will be properly punished for this disobedience. However, I do not think that a single commandment of the Lord Jesus dare be considered insignificant, if we consider the power and might of the Sovereign without reluctance. Concerning that about which Paul wrote to the Galatians and Colossians, it has only to do with the laws of the servant Moses, because they were too weak (see Hebrews 7:18). The Galatians wanted to follow these laws in order to be spared the cross of Christ and to set aside the teachings of Jesus. Paul reminded them of the baptism when he wrote: "For as many of you as were baptized into Christ have put on Christ" (Galatians 3:27). Consequently, Paul is not at all against baptism, but rather for it.

QUESTION 21: If baptism is made an absolutely necessary commandment for salvation, will this not introduce a new papacy, and bring about salvation by works?

ANSWER: It has been testified sufficiently above that we do not seek to earn salvation with these simple works, but by faith in Christ alone. If it is to be a saving faith, it must produce works of obedience. Where that faith is not present which produces obedience (not according to the pope's doctrine and command but rather by the command of Jesus the crucified), then no salvation is promised for a single work done without faith.

QUESTION 22: Can the outward ban be an essential part of the church of Christ, when Christ himself did not practice or enforce it even upon Judas, who was wicked through and through?

ANSWER: The ban is an essential and necessary part of the church of Christ, as long as it remains in combat here in this wicked world among wolves and evil spirits. There can be no church of Christ without the ban. Otherwise, the devil and his leaven of wickedness would soon contaminate the good. The true believers have never rejected this, insofar as they have remained in the faith. They have considered it an evidence of divine grace and the great love and solicitude of God. They have used it as a firm wall around the church of the Lord.

Concerning Judas, we maintain that Christ did sufficiently exercise the ban upon him. He turned him over to Satan so that he hanged himself. The fact that he was not placed in the ban by Jesus before his outward act is not against the ban, but rather in its favor. This has always been the plan of God, as can be seen in Adam. He most probably had had contact with the Tempter before, but he was not driven from Paradise until he had actually eaten of the forbidden fruit. Similarly, Judas had earlier considered treachery, but the long-suffering Jesus had borne with him, tolerated him, and urged him to repentance, until evil finally gained the upper hand and committed the evil deed. After that, he came sufficiently under the ban of Christ. The ban was practiced properly upon Judas.

QUESTION 23: Is not the binding and loosing of the apostles a prerogative granted only to them, which dare not be usurped by anyone else?

ANSWER: That the loosing and binding is a special prerogative of the apostles is true. It is, however, of the following manner. Moses had a special prerogative in that the Law was revealed to the house of Israel through him, but despite this it was not a prerogative which meant that the Law was to die with the death of Moses; rather, the descendants submitted themselves in obedience, insofar as they were faithful to God, to that which was revealed by Moses in the house of

God. Christ, the true Householder, has likewise founded a church and household and has given to His apostles, as the elect witnesses, the prerogative that they should introduce the ordinances of the house of God and confirm them by signs and miracles. This was so that none of their descendants should presume to introduce other ordinances, perhaps out of impertinence or arrogance, but that they should willingly submit themselves to the ordinances by which the apostles were appointed the stewards over God's mysteries. Since, then, the ban was commanded by Christ and His apostles, their prerogative is rightly left to them. But the believers must subject themselves to it in faith, and exercise it without the respecting of persons.

QUESTION 24: Did Christ institute a universal law for the church of the New Testament with the words of Matthew 18:17, or did He not rather speak of it with special regard to the character of the Jews? Did He not, in addition, give His followers a completely different lesson in the following twenty-first and twenty-second verses?

ANSWER: We have shown above that Christ has given a universal law for His church with the words of Matthew 18:17. They are by no means annulled by the following twenty-first and twenty-second verses, but are rather confirmed by them. This is still more clearly expressed in Luke 17:4, where Christ says: ". . . if he (your brother) sins against you seven times in the day, and turns to you seven times, and says, 'I repent,' you must forgive him." Without the admission of the sin, there is no forgiveness of sin, not even by God. Just so must believers be minded that if the sinner admits his sin, he must be forgiven. If he does not acknowledge it, then the ban is rightly to be exercised, as Christ says (Matthew 28[:20]): ". . . teaching them to observe all that I have commanded you; and lo, I am with you always, to the close of the age."

QUESTION 25: Did the apostles ever forbid administering the necessary spiritual or physical services of love to a banned person?

ANSWER: The apostles have never forbidden the administering of the necessary spiritual or physical services to a banned sinner. Rather, the banned person should be called to repentance; if he does not listen or accept it, then one is at liberty. It is the same with physical things—if there is an abundance of goods and the banned person is in need, he should be shared with as necessary.

QUESTION 26: Have you, the New Baptists, ever had the same divine effect and result with some of those whom you have banned as did the apostles?

ANSWER: We firmly believe that the ban has an inner effect and result here and now with all those on whom we have exercised it according to the Word of God. On the Day of Revelation it will indeed become outwardly manifest if they have not repented during this time of grace. However, it has not yet happened that men were immediately struck dead as was Ananias. This was recorded only once even of the apostles. Many were put into the ban by the apostles, but no other died outwardly like this. Nevertheless, the power of the ban had its full effect upon them.

QUESTION 27: Is the true spiritual rebirth inseparable from water baptism?

ANSWER: The spiritual rebirth is nothing else than true and genuine obedience toward God and all of His commandments. A reborn person will readily say with Christ (Matthew 3:15): ". . . it is fitting for us to fulfil all righteousness." We can, therefore, answer that the desire for obedience toward water baptism is inseparable from the true rebirth. If because of necessity, but not out of contempt or disobedience, water baptism does not take place, it will not be of harm for the rebirth.

QUESTION 28: Are all of those whom you baptize immediately reborn of God in truth?

ANSWER: That would indeed be a good baptism, if all those whom we baptize in water were truly reborn. It cannot be proved that all of those baptized by Christ and the apostles turned out well. If, however, true faith is present, and the Word is grasped or accepted in the water bath by faith, then a considerable rebirth or cleansing occurs in the "washing of water with the word" (Ephesians 5:26).

QUESTION 29: Could not a person be truly reborn even before he is baptized, since water baptism—as you yourselves will not deny—does not insure the true, spiritual rebirth?

ANSWER: Adam was created in Paradise in the image of God. When he was disobedient to his God, he lost his divine stature and had to accept the curse and death because of his disobedience. Therefore, a person may, of course, have attained a goodly proportion of rebirth before water baptism. But unless he becomes ever more obedient and humble, he may very easily lose again that which he had previously attained. The food of the new creation, then, for its sustenance and growth, is true obedience to the Lord Jesus. If they do not eat this food—which is indeed the food of the new creation (John 4:34)—but eat the food of the serpent—which is disobedience in manifold wisdom and cleverness against the Word—then the same thing will happen to them as happened to Adam in Paradise. Since, then, water baptism is commanded by Christ, each reborn person must humble himself in obedience and fulfill this righteousness.

QUESTION 30: Is not the true brotherhood of Christians founded much rather upon rebirth than upon water baptism?

ANSWER: The true brotherhood of Christians has always been founded upon true faith and obedience to Jesus Christ and His gospel. Therefore, true brethren in Christ have never been able to refuse outward water baptism, because they observed it in their first-born Brother, who also commanded it of them. He, Christ himself, considers only those His brethren who do the will of God (Matthew 12:50).

QUESTION 31: Are not those who have proved their rebirth by their lives before God and man to be considered rightfully as brethren, even though they have not been baptized? (See Matthew 12:49, 50.)

ANSWER: We indeed consider brethren all those who prove their rebirth by their lives before God and man. However, they will not oppose water baptism, but will let themselves be baptized upon their faith and inner motivation. Christ himself considered only those His brethren who were His disciples, and who had been baptized. (See Matthew 12:49, 50 correctly.)

QUESTION 32: Can you testify before the countenance of Jesus Christ, the omniscient Searcher of hearts and Judge of the living and the dead, that you yourselves have always been one heart and one soul?

ANSWER: God does not require of us that we should be at this time in the perfection of one heart and one soul. We cannot say that we are completely one in spirit, but we must be one in purpose. That is, we must help one another until we all attain to the same faith and to that unity of fullness in faith of which Ephesians speaks (4:11-13). No one can say that the church at Jerusalem was one heart and one soul in the state of perfection. In the beginning they were united in their discipleship of Christ with denial of everything worldly. That they were not one in understanding may be seen in Acts 15:5, etc.

Those who came from Jerusalem taught differently about circumcision than did the apostles. They had great trouble in working toward unity. It is therefore surprising that this perfect unity is demanded of us in these dreadful days, in which darkness and gloom cover all peoples. Indeed, those who boast of the inward baptism of the spirit are so disunited that they show only ignorance and discord even in the plain and clear commandments of water baptism, as well as in other fundamental points of faith.

QUESTION 33: Do you not regard your church as superior to those of all other Baptist-minded [*Taufgesinnte*] of these or previous times, and if so, in which way and why?

ANSWER: It is true that we consider our church fellowship superior to these now-deteriorated Baptists [Mennonites], with whom we are acquainted, and whom we know. The reason is that they have deteriorated in doctrine and life, and have strayed far from the doctrine and life of the old Baptists [Anabaptists]. Many of them notice this and realize it themselves. We cannot answer concerning the previous Baptists, because we did not know them in life. We are completely agreed with them as far as their doctrine is concerned, which does not teach anything in contradiction to the gospel.

QUESTION 34: What are your reasons for considering your newly established church, the practices of baptism, ban, etc., equal to those of the apostles, inasmuch as you can prove neither your divine calling, talents, nor results in your lives?

ANSWER: We consider ourselves far inferior to and still unworthy in the matter of power of working miracles, as compared to the apostles. Concerning the doctrine and the intention, we must pray to God that He might make us resemble the intention of the apostles, yes, even His Son Jesus.

QUESTION 35: Can and dare your teachers and elders bring the testimonies of their consciences before God that the Holy Spirit established them as shepherds in their churches to look after their flock as churches of God? Do they possess and can they demonstrate the spiritual gifts required and necessary for this, as given in Second Corinthians 6, etc.?

Answer: Of course, they must be able to bring it before God; otherwise they would not be true shepherds. They should not be worried or grieved if men do not believe this, but rather rejoice, if their names are cast out as evil by the people (Luke 6:22).

Question 36: Must they not admit before God in their souls that many among them were much more loving, meek, humble, and so forth before their baptism than afterwards?

Answer: Our answer to this is "No," unless it would be for those who were cut off as withered branches, or unless this meant the simulated love which is feigned for the sake of bread or honor, and which does not punish sins and errors. This kind of love says: "Leave me alone in my own will, opinion, and actions, and I will leave you alone in yours; we will love each other and be brethren." If this is meant, then we confess that it is true. Unfortunately, we stayed long enough in this pernicious hypocritical love, while we were still among the Pietists. Now we have learned, and must continue to learn, that kind of love which hates and punishes wickedness and evil.

Question 37: Is it not true that you began your new baptism with much uncertainty and wavering and have continued in this way up to now? Has this not also been shown in other things, as, for example, you once rejected the married state, and then soon permitted it again—once did away with work, then introduced it again?

Answer: We have begun the baptism of the Lord Jesus in accordance with His command in great assurance of faith. The dear God has sustained and confirmed us in this to this day by His grace amidst great opposition. We indeed can say with great certainty that those who believe should be baptized. But it is true that we had to continue discussions on marriage, work, yes, and still other matters, after the baptism. Before our baptism, when we were still among the Pietists, we were not taught otherwise by those who were deemed great saints. Therefore, we had much contention until we abandoned the errors which we had absorbed.

Question 38: On which point, then, can the undoubted divinity of your new church be recognized before all others in the whole world?

ANSWER: We indeed have neither a new church nor any new laws. We only want to remain in simplicity and true faith in the original church which Jesus founded through His blood. We wish to obey the commandment which was in the beginning. We do not demand that undoubted divinity be recognized in our church fellowship. Rather, we would wish that undoubted divinity might indeed be recognized in Christ himself, and then in the church at Jerusalem. If this and its divinity in teaching, words, and commandments were to be acknowledged, then it could be determined whether a church has this divine teaching in it or not. If this is realized, then we think that it would be sufficient to recognize a church before all other churches in the whole world, if she is subject, as a true wife to her husband Christ, to His commands, yes, if it still strives to be even more submissive. Whoever has not known Christ in the divinity of His commandments will hardly recognize His church even if the twelve apostles were serving as its bishops and teachers.

QUESTION 39: Are you yourselves assured, and have you already received the eternal assurance in the divine test of fire, that God himself recognizes you and would have you recognized? How do you propose to prove this and make it credible?

ANSWER: We must certainly have assurance before God, as Paul describes it (Romans 5[:1, 2]): "Therefore, since we are justified by faith, we have peace through our Lord Jesus Christ. Through him we have obtained access to this grace in which we stand, and we rejoice in our hope of sharing the glory of God." This assurance, however, is no longer promised, as it was also promised to the apostles, by the Lord Jesus (John 15:7): as long as they abide in Him, and His word abides with them, they are His rightful disciples. Whatever they asked for would be granted them. Thus it remains: he that is faithful in the teachings of Jesus, even to the end, will be saved.

QUESTION 40: Do you expect a better outcome for your church than that of the former Anabaptists? From where should this come? What is the assurance of your souls before and from God, who is impartial and who utterly humiliates and destroys all that is high and exalted, even all sects that pride and seek only themselves?

ANSWER: If we remain in the teaching of the New Testament, we expect this outcome, namely, that the fulfillment of our faith will be eternal life. In return for insignificant shame and suffering, we will obtain immeasurably momentous glory. We cannot testify for our descendants—as their faith is, so shall be their outcome. Nevertheless, we can say this, that the outcome of the former Baptists has turned out far better than that of all other religions. The Baptist seed is still far better than the seed of L[uther], C[alvin], and also that of the C[atholics]. These have had a completely wild, yes, bestial outcome, which is self-evident. The Jews and the Turks are scandalized by the horrible wickedness of these three religions. Not even with gallows and torture can they keep them, who are of one faith, from murdering one another in their homes, which happens often enough. What is still more horrible, they go publicly to war, and slaughter one another by the thousands. All this is the fruit of infant baptism.

No Baptist will be found in war, and few in prison or on the gallows because of their crimes. The majority of them are inclined to peacefulness. It is still possible to sleep unconcernedly among them and not need to fear robbery or even murder if one has much money. It would indeed be desirable that the whole world were full of these "deteriorated" Baptists. Their outcome has turned out far better than that of many from among the Pietists who have again taken an evil turn. Hardly had they left the great Babel several years before than they voluntarily returned to it. When the beginning is like this, the outcome will be very miserable and wretched. May God keep all Baptists in His grace so that they may not turn toward evil once more and then their outcome will be as mentioned above, namely, the eternal life of joy.

[GRUBER]

These are the most urgent questions about your new baptism and church, that were deemed necessary to present at this time to you, dear friends, for your own sake as well as that of others. You may now consider them, and prepare your corporate, clear, and candid explanations with your accompanying reasons. You should do this in such a manner as you can dare to account for such an important matter before the countenance of Jesus Christ, all His holy angels, and the elect on the inevitable day of most strict examination of this, your new work, without contradicting His noble Spirit in your consciences or those of others.

[MACK]

Beloved Friends:

Upon your request, we have published in love these answers to every one of the forty points of the searching questions which you have submitted to us upon our good consciences before God. They are answered according to our faith and good conscience before the God who sent His Son out of love to the world that we should hear, believe, and have eternal life through our faith in Him. If, then, your salvation and blessedness are dear to you, hasten and bow your necks under the scepter of this great King. Believe that His teaching is true and His baptism is saving and blessed for poor sinners. Do not say, "Of what use is this water for me?" and do not try to comfort yourselves with your infant baptism, which was introduced into the world in contradiction to God's Word.

Otherwise, may this simple testimony (which is published by the Baptists at Schwarzenau upon urgent appeal) be a witness along with your own consciences, at the great Day of Judgment of the Lord Jesus, who will come with flaming fire to take vengeance on those who were disobedient to His gospel. Now, to the strangled Lamb, who alone has might and power in heaven and on earth, be praise, honor, and glory, from eternity to eternity. Amen.

"Behold, he is coming with the clouds, and every eye will see him, every one who pierced him" [Revelation 1:7]. Amen.

Published at Schwarzenau, in the month of July, in the year of our Lord 1713.

Rights and Ordinances

A Brief
and Simple
Exposition
of the Outward but Yet Sacred
RIGHTS AND ORDINANCES
of the
House of God
as the True Householder
Commanded and Bequeathed

in Writing in His Testament;
Presented
in a Conversation
Between Father and Son
in
Question and Answer
by
ALEXANDER MACK
One also Called to the
Great Supper.
1715

- -

Psalm 119:126
"It is time for the Lord to act, for thy law has been broken."
Verse 130
"The unfolding of thy words gives light; it imparts understanding
to the simple."

[PREFACE]
Dear Reader!

God is a deity who is almighty and omnipotent; He is and always
has been very wrathful to all those who are disobedient to Him. He
very severely punished the disobedience of the first man in Paradise.
Later He severely punished even His own people for their disobedience
under the Law: whoever trespassed against the Law of Moses was
put to death without mercy, on the evidence of two or three persons.
Yes, God sent word to His people through Moses, His servant (Deuteronomy 4[:1, 2]): "And now, O Israel, give heed to the statutes and
the ordinances which I teach you, and do them; that you may live,
and go in and take possession of the land which the Lord, the God of
your fathers, gives you. You shall not add to the word which I
command you, nor take from it; that you may keep the commandments of the Lord your God which I command you."

It can be seen here how strictly God commanded that what He
had spoken to His people through His servant Moses must be kept.
Thus, it may be readily believed that God most certainly wants
everything to be kept which He has made known and revealed to

Kurtze
Und einfältige
Vorstellung/
Der äußern / aber doch heiligen
Rechten und Ordnungen
Deß
Hauses GOTTES/
Wie es der wahre Hauß-Vatter
JEsus Christus befohlen / und in sei-
nen Testament schrifftlich hinterlassen.
Vorgestellt
In einem Gespräch /
Unter Vater und Sohn
Durch
Frag und Antwort.
Von
Alexander Mack.
Einenem Mit-Beruffenen / zu dem gros-
sen Abendmahl.

✳✧✱✲✸✷✳✶✷✳✱✧✸✷✳✶✷✳✱✧✳

Anno 1715.

Title Page of the First Edition of "Rights and Ordinances"
Courtesy of Religionskundliche Sammlung der Universität Marburg.

the whole world in these latter times through His beloved Son. That is, all who call themselves Christians should live as children of one household. The good Householder [*Haus-Vater*] has given them rules and laws which they are to keep and respect well and prudently. Along with it, He has promised them life eternal, if they will obey Him in all things—insignificant as well as important ones. However, none of the teachings and ordinances of our Lord Jesus may be considered insignificant, for they were indeed commanded and ordained by an all-powerful Monarch and King. Because of the greatness of the Sovereign, even water baptism—which was commanded by Jesus to be performed in His name—must also be considered important, as well as all of His other commandments.

Just as the Ruler of the New Covenant is great, so are His statutes and laws truly great as are the promises which He added to them. These are life eternal, and all of the other gifts of grace of the Holy Spirit which believers possess. Likewise, the punishment of those who deny the gospel of Jesus Christ will be unfailingly harsh and most terrible. Paul says in the second letter to the Thessalonians in the first chapter [verse 8] that the Son of God will come with "flaming fire, inflicting vengeance upon those who do not know God and upon those who do not obey the gospel of our Lord Jesus." Yes, it is testified in the Revelation of John in the twenty-second chapter, verses eighteen and nineteen: ". . . if any one takes away from the words of the book of this prophecy (wherewith the teaching of Jesus is especially referred to), God will take away his share in the book of life. . . . If any one adds to them, God will add to him the plagues described in this book."

Therefore, we felt moved out of love to call to the attention of the kind reader the true and lawful use of the things which Christ commanded the members of His household to do, and also, to some extent, the great abuses which have prevailed among all of the Christian parties. We want to leave it up to the judgment of each one to examine this. It will be presented in the form of a dialog between a father and his son, who are journeying as travel companions.

A Conversation Between Father and Son in Question and Answer.

Son: Dear father, as we are all by ourselves in this wilderness, I shall tell you what happened to me in a certain company when I was not with you. I was criticized because of our baptism, and was called an Anabaptist, for we rebaptize those who were already baptized as infants. I was also severely criticized by those who, although they were baptized as adults but only by aspersion, are despite this baptized by us if they desire to join our church fellowship. I was criticized as well about the Lord's Supper and the ban, that we were legalistic about feet-washing, and also because of our using unleavened bread at communion. I was so attacked by all kinds of rational arguments that I could not give an adequate defense of our principles. Therefore, I am asking you, dear father, that you might better instruct me in accordance with the witness of the Holy Scriptures and the early Christians in all these things which are yet so controversial and which cause us such criticism. In this way, my faith will be confirmed and I shall be able to give to other people an accounting truly based on the Scriptures. In return for this, I shall show my gratitude to you for the rest of my life.

FATHER: Dear son, I shall give you ample instruction concerning this in as simple and satisfactory a manner as I can. Therefore, be sure to listen carefully, and ask me about those things which you were unable to answer, so that we can have a single-minded conversation.

[ON WATER BAPTISM]

SON: Beloved father, I am happy that you are willing to instruct me. I shall now diligently ask you and listen [to your replies]. Tell me then, where in Holy Scripture is outward water baptism founded?

FATHER: The eternal and almighty God is the actual founder of water baptism. As early as Noah's time, He began to reveal a prefiguration [*Vorbild*] of the water baptism of the New Covenant. Since men very quickly became wicked, the Lord God sent a flood, and these godless men were drowned in the water. The Apostle Peter said of this (1 Peter 3:20, 21): "Baptism, which corresponds to this, now saves you, not as a removal of dirt from the body but as an appeal to God for a clear conscience, through the resurrection of Jesus Christ." Yes, note further, when the Lord God wanted to make a prefiguration through His servant Moses as a testimony which should be revealed through the Son (Hebrews 3), Moses had to be lifted from the water by the daughter of Pharaoh. For that reason she also stated that "she named him Moses, for she said, 'Because I drew him out of the water'" (Exodus 2[:10]).

When God with a mighty hand led the seed of Abraham out of Egypt by this same Moses, and they were delivered from the Egyptians, this escape took place through the sea, which is a strong prefiguration of the baptism of the New Covenant. Paul calls it a baptism: ". . . all were baptized into Moses in the cloud and in the sea" (1 Corinthians 10:2). Again, as the Lord God had a tabernacle erected by Moses, which was a prefiguration of the household or church of the Lord Jesus, Moses had to make a large laver or vessel before the tabernacle where the priest Aaron and his sons were to wash themselves first before they could go into the tabernacle (Exodus 30:18-20; 40:12). This was also a strong prefiguration for the water baptism which was commanded by Jesus: no one can enter or be in the Lord's church without first being baptized in water upon confession of faith in Jesus.

Yes, you can see further how the Lord God commanded in the Law that when a leper was cleansed from his illness he had to wash his body in water (Leviticus 14:8, 9). Likewise, when the women wished to purify themselves, they had to bathe or wash in water. Again, various kinds of water baptisms were commanded by the Law, which all pointed to the water baptism of the New Testament.

Now, I will also tell you about the nature of water baptism in the New Covenant. Note well. When God the Father wished to reveal His dear Son in the world, there had to be a forerunner, namely John [the Baptist], who came into the land of Judea by divine command. He preached that men must repent, and also baptized them in water for repentance, that they should believe in Him who was to come after him—that is, in Jesus, the Son of God. He baptized at Aenon near Salim, because there was much water there.

SON: Oh, was there not great excitement among the people because John did such an extraordinary act as baptizing people in water?

FATHER: At that time, water baptism was not a strange act among the Jews, as it had already been common previously under the Law for outward cleansing. Therefore, there was no great surprise concerning the baptism as such, but in regard to his preaching the baptism was a new thing to them. He called upon men to repent and spoke of the Son of God that He would come, and called upon people to believe in Him.

SON: Did the theologians and the people in high places also submit to being baptized?

FATHER: Oh, no! The act was contemptible in their sight. They "rejected the purpose of God for themselves, not having been baptized by him," which can be read in Luke 7:30. However, Jesus, the Son of God, obeyed His Father in this, because He knew that John's baptism was from heaven. Therefore, He went quite a distance from Galilee to John at the Jordan and was baptized (Matthew 3:13).

SON: That was indeed a great miracle, and a [sign of] great humility by the Lord Jesus, that He permitted himself to be baptized in water by His servant, John.

FATHER: Yes, indeed! It was a great miracle and a great self-humiliation of the Son of God. He has left this to us and all of His followers as a mighty example in which we should follow Him.

SON: Was Jesus baptized merely so that we should follow Him on that point?

FATHER: The Son of God knew well the plan and will of His Father. For this reason He said to John, "For thus it is fitting for us to fulfill all righteousness" [Matthew 3:15]. The Son of God wished to found and ordain a water bath for His entire church, that it should be an efficacious seal and outward symbol of all those who would believe in Him. Thus, the Son of God, in the first place, fulfilled the will of His Father (because the baptism by John was commanded by God), and at the same time made a beginning of water baptism. This was no longer to be a baptism for repentance, but rather a baptism for those who had already repented and who believed in Jesus Christ, the Son of God. They were to be baptized upon their faith and confession, in the name of the Father, the Son, and the Holy Spirit.

When the Lord Jesus was baptized and came out of the water, a voice was heard from heaven which said: "This is my beloved Son, with whom I am well pleased" [Matthew 3:17]. The Holy Spirit came as a dove above the Lord Jesus. Therefore, this inception of the water baptism of the New Testament certainly had a mighty founder and author, namely, God the Father, God the Son, and God the Holy Spirit. The Lord Jesus also commanded that baptism should be performed in these three most exalted names.

SON: After Jesus was baptized, did He then immediately begin to teach and practice water baptism?

FATHER: Yes, the Lord Jesus immediately began to make disciples and to baptize them. You can read this in John 3:26; 4:1. The disciples of John came to him and said: "Rabbi, he who was with you beyond the Jordan, to whom you bore witness, here he is, baptizing, and all are going to him." John answered: "He must increase, but I must decrease. He who comes from above is above all. . . . He bears witness to what he has seen and heard, yet no one receives his testimony; he who receives his testimony sets his seal to this, that God is true." Yes, John also testifies in his first letter (5:6) that the Son of God came with water and blood and with the Holy Spirit, and that these were the three witnesses on earth.

Son: Does one also find that Christ commanded water baptism after His resurrection?

Father: Yes, I will explain this to you. In the first place, when the Lord Jesus wished to send the disciples out into all the world to preach His gospel, He gave them a specific commandment that they were to teach and baptize in His name all those who believed in Him (Matthew 28:19, 20), "teaching them to observe all that I have commanded you. . . ." You can see this further from Acts 2:37, 38; when the people asked what they should do, Peter answered: "Repent, and be baptized every one of you in the name of Jesus Christ for the forgiveness of your sins; and you shall receive the gift of the Holy Spirit."

Son: Can one read elsewhere of others who baptized?

Father: Yes, in Acts 8:5-12 it states that Philip preached at Samaria about Christ, and those who believed were baptized, both men and women.

Son: Oh, father, it says here: "They were baptized, both men and women." Were there no children baptized then?

Father: Oh, no! There is not a single example of that in the New Testament. Rather, the apostles baptized only those who publicly confessed their faith in Jesus through true repentance. Jesus, their Master, commanded them only that those were to be baptized who could be taught before and after baptism.

Son: Did not Christ command that children be baptized, and did not the apostles do that?

Father: Christ commanded only to baptize believers, and certainly not the children.

Son: Oh, but does it not say in Matthew 19[:14] that Christ

speaks: "Let the children come to me, and do not hinder them; for to such belongs the kingdom of heaven"?

FATHER: Notice well that it adds, "And he laid his hands on them, and blessed them [and went away]." It says nothing about baptism.

SON: I have also heard it said that the apostles baptized entire households, among whom there must have been children.

FATHER: Only reason says that children must have been among them. The Holy Scriptures do not say a single word about it.

SON: Water baptism is indeed an important commandment as you have shown me from the Old and the New Testament. However, if a child dies before it is baptized, does it not suffer the loss of its salvation by dying without baptism? Many say that baptism was introduced instead of circumcision; when a male infant was not circumcised on the eighth day, it had to be killed.

FATHER: I am glad you asked that. Note well the plan and intent of God at all times. Whenever God commanded something, He wanted it to be kept just as He commanded it. The circumcision of the Old Testament was demanded only of male infants on the eighth day. If then, a child had died before that time, he would not have violated God's commandment. Doubtless many died before the eighth day, and they were certainly not rejected, as little as the female infants, who were not circumcised at all, and despite this were under the promise.

Therefore, if a child dies without water baptism, that will not be disadvantageous for it, because this has not been commanded of the child. It has not yet experienced the "eighth day"—that is, the day on which it could have repented and believed in the Lord Jesus, and could have been baptized upon this, its faith. This was the point of the eighth day with circumcision. That is the reason why baptism is commanded only of adults and believers, and not at all of children. The children are in a state of grace because of the merit of Jesus Christ, and they will be saved out of grace. On such important matters of faith there must be specific commandments.

SON: Does one not find in histories that the early Christians baptized their children?

FATHER: We find in Gottfried Arnold's *Portrayal of the First Christians* that infant baptism began to be practiced only at the end of the second century after Christ's birth. At first, they did it only upon request for those who desired it. Later, baptism was only at Easter. Finally, a certain pope issued an order that no child should die without being baptized. Thus, it has prevailed through long-continued custom until everyone now thinks that infant baptism was commanded by Christ.

SON: You have already told me much about water baptism and its importance. Now, I would like to ask whether there is something special about water, because God commanded so many cleansings in water in the Old Testament, and again in the New Testament He ordained and founded water baptism for His believers.

FATHER: Observe well. Water is an element created by God. All things are created through water; yes, the entire earth subsists of water and is based upon it. Man himself is born in water in his mother's womb. Indeed, the Spirit of God first moved upon the waters, and therefore there is in water a divine mercy. Christ also sanctified water by His baptism. For this reason He has spoken (John 3[:5]): "Unless one is born of water and the Spirit, he cannot enter the Kingdom of God."

Nevertheless, believers do not look to the power of water in baptism, but rather they look to the power of the Word which has commanded it. Christ ordained a water bath for His church and wished to cleanse them by the water bath in the Word, as Paul says (Ephesians 5:26). The faithful, therefore, believe that obedience to the commandment of water baptism cleanses them and frees them from future punishment. This is true only if the person does not let himself sink again into filth by sinning and violating the Word after this washing. God looks only upon obedience, and believers are bound to obey the Word. Then they will achieve eternal life by obedience.

SON: If a person denied himself everything—gave his goods to the poor, prayed and fasted much, but did not wish to be baptized because it was an outward act—could not such a person please God?

FATHER: Note well. If a person did these things out of true faith and love of God, they would be good and saving things. Such a person would certainly not refuse to submit himself willingly to this commandment of water baptism. "For this is the love of God that we keep his commandments. And his commandments are not burdensome" (1 John 5:3). Moreover, Paul says (1 Corinthians 13:3): "If I give away all that I have, and if I deliver my body to be burned, but have not love, I gain nothing." He then describes the way of love as believing everything that God has commanded. Yes, Christ says (John 14:23, 24): "If a man loves me, he will keep my word. . . . He who does not love me does not keep my words. . . ."

Therefore, a man may indeed do much by his own sanctity, and despite this, still not hold to the love of Jesus as the Head. There were people like this in Paul's time. He writes in his letter to the Colossians (2:18) about those who go about in "worship of angels." Paul says that they have "a sensuous mind" (verse 19), because they did not rely on the Head.

SON: Cannot then a man love God despite this, even if he does not want to obey in just one point, but performs all of the rest?

FATHER: Are you not yet able to realize what James says (2:10): "For whoever keeps the whole law but fails in one point has become guilty of all of it" [?] Think about it yourself. If you had been obedient in everything to me for ten or even more years, and I requested you to pick up a piece of straw, and you did not want to do it and did not do it, I would have to consider you a disobedient child. Even if you said a thousand times, "Father, I will do everything; I will work hard; I will go wherever you send me, but it does not seem necessary to me to pick up the piece of straw because it neither helps you nor me," I would say to you, "You are a disobedient wretch."

SON: Father, you say this about yourself, but is God who is love similarly minded toward His children? If so, how can this be proved?

FATHER: I will prove it to you very clearly from the Holy Scriptures that God is so minded. Just consider what the first man in Paradise did. God said to him that he should eat from all of the trees except one, from which he was not to eat. Behold, as soon as he ate of the forbidden tree, he lost all of his happiness and was expelled from Paradise for his disobedience. Yes, consider further what God did and commanded in the Law (Numbers 15:30, 31): "But the person who does anything with a high hand . . . because he has despised the word of the Lord, and has broken his commandments, that person shall be utterly cut off."

Again, when the sons of Aaron brought unholy fire before the Lord, they suffered death (Leviticus 10:12). King Saul was rejected because of his disobedience to the Lord (1 Samuel 15:22, 23). Similarly, Achan and his entire family had to die because he disobeyed the commandment of God in that he took some of the prohibited spoils, which was forbidden by God, at the taking of the city of Jericho (Joshua 7:20). Yes, it would be possible to cite many more similar testimonies from Holy Scripture, but these are sufficient. You can see from them that God demands absolute obedience from all of His creatures.

SON: I well perceive that man should not only heed that which is commanded, but also the Master himself, and especially His greatness. Therefore, all of the commandments of the great God shall be esteemed great.

FATHER: *Yes, that has always been the true faith and the true love of all saints and believers. They have done what God has commanded them to do, and have bowed all of their reason and will before the will of their God. It can be heard or noticed of no believer that he has ever rebelled against a single commandment of God.*

SON: If then so much, indeed, everything depends upon the keeping of God's commandments, why is it that God has always commanded men to do but simple things, as can be seen in the Old and New Testaments?

FATHER: Notice well, God is himself a simple and good Being, and does not need the service of men. He has many thousand times a thousand angels and spirits who serve Him. The commandments which God has always given men are for their sake, so that men shall become truly lowly and simple through them. Man rose to great heights through the fall of Adam and wants to be great, mighty, and holy in his own sight. In order to redeem man from his perilous condition, God ordered through His Son that [certain] simple things be done. If man does them in true faith and in obedience holds his reason captive, he will gradually become single-minded and childlike. It is just in this single-mindedness that the soul again finds rest, peace, and security. Therefore, Christ says: "Truly, I say unto you, unless you turn and become like children, you will never enter the kingdom of heaven" [Matthew 18:3].

SON: I now well understand that all commandments point only to true obedience. The same is true of water baptism, which Christ commanded His apostles to perform, and which they then did. Was this commandment given to all believers that they should be baptized, and is this commandment to remain until the end of the world?

FATHER: This is very clearly expressed in Matthew 28:19, 20, where our Savior says: "Go therefore and make disciples of all nations, baptizing them (etc.) . . . teaching them to observe all that I have commanded you; and lo, I am with you always, to the close of the age."

SON: After the death of the apostles, were other men allowed to baptize who had not been sent to do this as were the apostles?

FATHER: Mark well the household plan and ordinances of God already under the Law: When God had a house built by Moses in which the priests were to serve, the tribe of Levi was chosen for this by God. From this tribe, God himself elected Aaron and his sons as the ones who were to carry out the offices of priests. Whenever the temple and everything else was destroyed and ruined, and they again wished to observe their worship services, no other than someone from the tribe of Levi could conduct it. However, the godless King Jeroboam appointed people as priests who were not from the tribe of Levi. They could also perform idol worship (1 Kings 12:31). But when they chose priests from the tribe of Levi, they appointed those who were well versed in the Law of Moses. They dared not have blemishes or infirmities of the body (Leviticus 21).

Therefore, note this well that it was the Son of God himself who established in His church first of all apostles, and later teachers and others like them. The apostles soon chose others in the service of the household of God to baptize, to administer the ban and the like, so that the divine ordinances might be well maintained. However, at all times they chose only those who were descended from the royal priesthood, that is, those who had the Spirit of Jesus. They were permitted to baptize, and to do other things by this same Spirit. Now, the apostles had already in their time noticed men who were indeed Christians in appearance, but did not have the Spirit of Christ. Paul speaks of them to the elders in Ephesus (Acts 20:29, 30): "And from among your own selves will arise men speaking perverse things, to draw away the disciples after them."

This has always been a characteristic of the false spirits: whenever a person seeks honor for himself, he is not of the manner of Christ, who had not placed himself in the priesthood, but rather was placed by His Father. It can be seen in Acts 20:18-28, that the first teachers and elders of the churches were appointed by the Holy Spirit. The apostle Paul had the elders and teachers of the church of Ephesus called to him, and he gave them this admonition, among others, "Take heed to yourselves and to all of the flock, in which the Holy Spirit has made you guardians, to feed the church of the Lord which he obtained with his own blood."

When, however, men appointed themselves to the service of the church by their own spirit and their own honor, the great abuse and every evil originated and spread. There are many thousand preachers in the world, but only a handful have the royal priesthood of the holy nation (1 Peter 2:9). Only a handful have the Spirit of Christ. Only a handful were appointed bishops by the Holy Spirit. It is for that reason that they preach only for their own honor and profit.

On the other hand, after the death of the apostles the faithful church which remained pure and undefiled always chose men from among them who had the Spirit of Jesus and denied themselves. Just as Christ chose His apostles outwardly, so has the church of the Lord (as the body of Christ) in turn chosen those whom they recognized as capable. These have then also baptized. The commandment of the Lord Jesus in its purity has never been lacking nor ceased, as He says (Matthew 28:20): ". . . teaching them to observe all that I have commanded you." Rather, this command will remain until Christ comes again to judge His own servants and also His enemies on His teaching.

Cyprian and other devout men of the early church required of a person who wished to baptize, a true and sound belief in Christ, and proper appointment thereto by his church. The Council at Ilibris likewise wrote and demanded of one who wished and was to baptize that he must be correctly baptized himself, and not have fallen again from grace by sinning after his baptism. Gregory also reports: "Consider each worthy and capable enough to administer the office of baptism if he can be counted among the godly."

Son: I understand now very well about baptism, that it is a command from Christ to His believers until the end of the world. Now, I would like to know for certain about the mode of baptism. Should one baptize in water, or can baptism also be performed in a room with a handful of water and still fulfill the act of obedience of the commandment?

Father: Note well; I will explain this to you from the Holy Scriptures. In the first place, Christ, the true forerunner of His entire church, was baptized by John in the Jordan (Matthew 2[3]:13, 16). John baptized at a place near Salim, because there was much water there (John 3:23). You should be able to see sufficiently from these two testimonies that if the commandment of baptism could have been fulfilled on dry land, John would not have gone where there was so much water. It is indeed much more convenient to baptize in a room than in the water, because the water is often cold and tends to weaken the constitution.

For good measure, I will tell you of yet other testimonies. The Greek word for the command *to baptize* actually means to immerse. It is so translated by most translators.* However, since the practice of aspersion [sprinkling] has developed, and the theologians have shied away from the water because of their frailty, they maintained that the Greek word can also be taken to mean to asperse, to pour, or to make wet. Nevertheless, they have to admit that it means to immerse. Further, when Philip baptized the eunuch, it states: ". . . and they both went down into the water, Philip and the eunuch, and he baptized him" (Acts 8:38, 39). Much can be found in the histories about the early Christians baptizing in rivers and streams and wells.

In addition, it can be seen in the *Martyrs Mirror* [*Bloedig Tooneel* . . .] of the Mennonites (page 265), that in 980 A.D. many persons were baptized in the River Euphrates. It further states (page 207) that Paulinianus [Paulinus] baptized at noon in the River Trentha [Trent] near the city of Truvolsinga in the year 1620 [620]. It is written there that this baptism was called by the ancients an immersion or dipping [*Unterdomplung*]. It further states (page 220) that the English were baptized in the Rivers Schwalbe and Rhine, and that it could not be done in any other way or manner. Yes, people must be quite blind and prejudiced, because this is written so clearly even in the Holy Scriptures. In Romans 6:5 it is called a burial of sins. Paul further calls it a water bath (Ephesians 5:26). Christ says (John 3:5) that one must be "born of water and of the spirit."

The early Christians spoke thus of baptism: "The carnal children of Adam (they said) enter the water, and after they have become spiritual children of God must rise from the water." Justinian gave this account of it to the emperor himself: "Those who are converted

---

* Later editions add: ". . . by Jeremias Felbinger."

and believe that what we teach is true, and who also promise that they wish to live in this way through the grace of God, are taught how they are to pray, fast, and seek forgiveness for their sins from God. After this, we lead them to a place where there is water, and they are reborn, just as we were reborn; they are cleansed in the water in the name of God the Father and the Lord of all things, and of our Lord Jesus Christ, and of the Holy Spirit." The above-mentioned Justinian said to Caesar: "We have received this manner from the apostles."

Bede (book 2, chapter 14) also testifies that from time to time at the beginning of the first congregations the English people were immersed in rivers. Wallfried Strabo writes in his book, *On Ecclesiastical Matters [De rebus eccles.]* (chapter 26), that it should be made known that the believers originally were baptized in flowing waters or wells. Our Lord Jesus himself was baptized by John in the Jordan so that He would sanctify this bath for us, as can be read: "John also was baptizing at Aenon near Salim, because there was much water there" (John 3:23).

Yes, Nicodemus testifies in his description of the crucifixion of the Lord Jesus that after the Lord Jesus' resurrection many saints rose [from the dead] and appeared in Jerusalem and testified that Jesus had risen. Among those risen were the two sons of the old Simeon who had taken the Lord Jesus in his arms in the temple and praised God. They, namely Karinus and Lentzius, testified that the Lord Jesus had also awakened them, and that the archangel Michael had commanded them to go along the Jordan to a lovely place where many others were who had also risen. They were baptized in the river of Jordan, and received exceedingly bright robes as white as snow.

Further, the above-mentioned Nicodemus testified that the Emperor Tiberius, during whose reign the Lord suffered, sent a great prince named Wolusin to Jerusalem to bring the Lord Jesus to him to heal him, because he had heard that He could do that. When, however, the prince arrived in Jerusalem and learned of the deeds and teachings of the Lord Jesus and that Pilate had crucified Him, he had Pilate put in chains, and then he returned to the emperor. He told him everything and also said that Jesus wanted all who believed in Him also to believe in being immersed three times in water and baptized. Upon this, the emperor said: "Woe is me, that I was not worthy of seeing Jesus myself." He had Pilate placed in prison, where he committed suicide out of desperation.*

SON: It seems to me that you have shown me sufficient testimonies to prove that Christ, John, the apostles, and very many of the early Christians were baptized in water.

FATHER: That would, of course, be adequate, but I wish to refer you to even more testimonies from the histories of the early Christians. Hononus Aug. [Honorius Augustodunensis] writes in his book, *The Soul's Jewel* [*Gemma animae*] (book 3, page 106): "It should be known that the holy apostles and their disciples used to baptize in flowing waters and wells." Tertullian reports in his book, *On the Chaplet* [*De corona militis*]: "Those who are to be baptized profess some time previously in the church before the teachers that they renounce the devil, his pomp and angels; after this, they are immersed three times and baptized. This custom was maintained until 801, and the time when Ludovicus [Leo V] was made emperor in 815."†

SON: Do tell me also whether the apostles immersed the entire person or just a hand or the head, or how was it done? I have heard many say that it can be clearly seen from Scripture that one should go into the water, but how the baptism is to take place is not certain.

FATHER: You reveal with this question that you lack inner light. Those who say that it is not known how baptism should be performed reveal that they have a miserable teacher. Is it possible that Jesus is the kind of a teacher who requires His own to do something in His name, such as an act as important as baptism, and would not let it be known in what manner it is to be done? [If that were so] they

---

* The preceding two paragraphs are omitted in later editions.

† This obviously incorrect quotation may have been taken from a sixteenth-century statement against infant baptism. The following passage, found in the writing of an Anabaptist martyr, Thomas Imbroich (1533-1558), was reprinted in the eighteenth century by the Mennonites: ". . . thus says Tertullian (in his book *On the Chaplet*): 'Those who are to be baptized profess there, and also some time previously in the church before the bishop that they renounce the devil, his pomp and angels; after this they are immersed three times and baptized.' Renan notes at this passage that the old custom was that the adults were baptized and washed with the bath of rebirth, [and that] this custom was maintained until the time of Charles the Great, Ludovici the emperor, in the year 801; Ludovicus became emperor in the year 815 after Christ's birth." ['Widerspruch von einem, der sich nennet *Petrus* (und sein Gegentheil *Thomas*). Welcher die Kinder-Tauffe ohne Grund und Zeugnisz heiliger Schrifft wil erhalten und bewähren,' in *Confessio Pulchra* . . . , part of *Güldene Aepffel in Silbern Schalen* . . . (Ephrata, Pennsylvania: the Community, 1745), page 74; first printed in Europe in 1702.]

would have to ask the teacher how they should do it, and better refrain from it than perform it in uncertainty. Just consider that those men want to be the stewards over the mysteries of the House of God, and do not even know how one should baptize in water. Where, or from which teacher, did they learn that they could sprinkle the head with a handful of water or make it wet, in a dry place in a room or meeting place? This cannot be found in one single place in Holy Scripture and the exact opposite can be seen from Jesus and His apostles.

Since you have asked me about this, I will explain it briefly. You have heard about Christ and His apostles, and many testimonies of the early Christians, that they baptized in flowing waters and wells, and that baptism is nothing else but immersion. This is as the Word and the commandment require, for Christ said to His apostles (Matthew 28:19): "Go therefore and make disciples of all nations (mankind), baptizing them (immersing them)," and not [baptizing] the bells, such as happens under the papacy. The Lord Jesus did indeed not say to baptize the head or some other part of the body of the person, or sprinkle the person a little with water in His name. No, the Lord Jesus did not command this, but rather that the whole person should be immersed in water. As I have already told you about the significance of the baptism, it must have inner significance.

Son: Cannot the water bath or burial of sins be symbolized by a handful of water or the like?

Father: That is impossible, for that which should symbolize an outward thing cannot be different from what it is essentially.

Son: Would it really matter if the essence were inward, and its outward symbol were different from the inward substance?

Father: Note well. Suppose a great lord should say to his servant (who wished to be a painter) that he should make a portrait of him so that others could see and recognize the lord who do not see him physically. And suppose that the servant, when he did this, did not pay strict attention to his lord, but rather his mind was occupied with other things—he did not really love his lord, but nevertheless wanted to fulfill the command—and he painted his lord with great carelessness. Further suppose that he painted him without one eye, or one foot or one hand, and the portrait was therefore completely distorted, so that there was absolutely no resemblance with the subject. What should the lord then say to a servant like that? He would dismiss him from his service as a worthless servant.

There are unfortunately many such worthless painters in the world, especially where water baptism and all of the other commandments of Christ are concerned. The hearts of most of them are filled with the love of the world and of self. As the love of Jesus the crucified and the love of denying themselves is not in them, they have also forgotten the image of Jesus in His teaching and His mighty example. They have, therefore, completely distorted the teaching of Jesus. Each one paints as he wishes according to his own will, or as it is customary here and there. They do not look singly and alone to their Lord and Master. Some sprinkle small children a bit on the head. Others, who approach it somewhat closer, sprinkle adults with a handful of water on the head; some take three handfuls, others but one handful of water. All say, "I baptize you." This is supposed to be a water bath or a burial of sins.

SON: I perceive clearly that the teaching of Jesus is very much distorted, and that no accurate image of it can now be seen or felt.

FATHER: Yes, a great darkness now covers all of the people and the entire world. However, it will be soon illuminated again, as is prophesied (Zechariah 14:7; Revelation 18:1).

[ON THE LORD'S SUPPER]

SON: I thank you, dear father, that you have told me all this. I am very much astonished about the great abuses concerning baptism in these times. There must have indeed been great darkness covering the nations. I must, however, ask you now something else, concerning the Lord's Supper. How was it instituted by Christ? How should it be held? Is this also in a state of decay as is baptism?

FATHER: You can well assume that if people err so much in one thing, they will err in all others too. You will see this clearly from the ordinance of Christ and the present custom. In the first place, it is called a supper which the Son of God established as a memorial for His beloved disciples. He commanded that they should thereby proclaim His death on the cross, break the bread of communion, drink the cup of communion, and covenant with one another in love as members of Christ to be ever more faithful to their Lord and Master. Further, that they should remain steadfast with Him in true obedience of faith even to the cross, so that they may partake of the Great Supper with Him at the end of the world.

SON: Are only the true followers of the Lord Jesus, who keep His commandments and help to bear His cross, permitted and intended to partake of the Lord's Supper, or should and may others partake of it?

FATHER: The true Householder, Jesus Christ, commanded this only of the members of His household who have entered the Kingdom through true repentance and faith and baptism, and who willingly keep all of the rules of the Householder in obedience of faith. The Lord God commanded under the Law that whoever wished to keep the Passover of the Lord must first be circumcised (Exodus 12:48). Therefore, whoever wants to keep the Lord's Supper worthily must first be separated from the body of Satan, the world, yes, from all unrighteousness, and from all false sects and religions. He must cling to Jesus the Head as a true member in faith and in love. He must be ready to give his body, and even life, unto death, if it is demanded of him, for the sake of Jesus and His teachings according to the will of God in the evangelical manner. Whoever still lives knowingly in sin and disobedience toward God, and will not follow Christ in the denial of self and all things of the world according to the counsel of Jesus in Luke 14:26, 27, is still unworthy. "For any one who eats and drinks without discerning the body eats and drinks judgment upon himself" (1 Corinthians 11:29).

SON: Oh, father, how does it then happen that it is called a Lord's Supper and despite this it is usually held in the mornings or at noon, and not in the evening?

FATHER: Just as I told you above about baptism, that it has fallen into great decay and disorder, so it is with the Lord's Supper. Some hold it in the morning, others, at noon, but none have it as a supper. When an evening or a noon meal is to be held, there must be something to eat! But here the people go to their so-called "supper" and return from it hungry and thirsty. Some do not even receive a bit of bread and others not a drop of wine. Again, others do receive a bit of bread and a little wine, but at the same time are filled with great extravagance of clothes, sensual debauchery, selfish pride, and the like. This can be seen in the great parties in all religions, when they claim to keep the Lord's Supper.

SON: Must it then be held in the evening and must there be a real meal with it, or is it not also good to hold it without the other meal in the morning or at noon?

FATHER: Observe well, that the true believers and lovers of the Lord Jesus have always looked steadfastly and single-mindedly to their Lord and Master in all things. They follow Him gladly in all of His commands, just as He has told them to do, and as He has shown them by His own example. They thus learn in their simplicity to understand well the intention of their Master, even in the simplest matters. In the first place, it says in the Scriptures, a "supper" (1 Corinthians 11:20). The believers observed it that way, having learned it from Paul this way, as is stated in the same chapter (verse 1). Paul, in turn, had himself received from the Lord Jesus that which he gave to the Corinthians (verse 23). They thus held an evening meal or a supper.

Now, blind reason can (if it but wanted!) indeed recognize and make the differentiation that an evening meal could not mean a noon meal. As early as Paul's time the people came together and held the supper. But Paul says (1 Corinthians 11:20) that they did not [really] hold the Lord's Supper. When, however, the believers gathered in united love and fellowship and had a supper, observing thereby the commandments of the Lord Jesus that they wash one another's feet after the example and order of the Master (John 13:14, 15), yes, when they broke the bread of communion, drank the chalice (the cup) of communion, proclaimed the death and suffering of Jesus, praised and glorified His great love for them, and exhorted one another to bear the cross and endure suffering, to follow after their Lord and Master, to remain true to all of His commandments, to resist earnestly all sins, to love one another truly, and to live together in peace and unity—that alone could be called the Lord's Supper.

They can then rejoice and comfort themselves in the suffering of the Lord Jesus. By such a supper they portray that they are members and house companions of the Lord Jesus. They will one day observe the Great Supper with the Lord Jesus at the close of the world and enjoy eternal happiness.

Paul says about this above-mentioned supper that "any one who eats and drinks without discerning the body eats and drinks judgment upon himself" [1 Corinthians 11:29]. When, however, people eat a morning or noon meal, who have not truly repented, who do not believe in the commandments of the Lord Jesus, who are not baptized upon true repentance and true faith, who still love the world, the lust of the eye, the lust of the flesh, and the pride of life, who live in envy, hate, gluttony, drunkenness, and the like—that is not the Lord's Supper. Rather, it is a custom which has been introduced by reason and by the worldly spirit through the wrongly praised artfulness of the theologians in their many rational conclusions; through long habit it has become fixed in the simple people. Everyone now thinks that he goes to the Lord's Supper, but in reality it is not what he thinks it is.

SON: Can obvious sinners be permitted at the Lord's Supper?

FATHER: Obvious sinners cannot be permitted at the Lord's Supper, even if but one work of the flesh is evident in them (about which Paul writes in Galatians 5), if repentance or improvement does not take place after admonishment. Moreover, not only do they not belong at the Lord's Supper; they do not even belong in the Kingdom of God, and do not belong in the church of the Lord. Just as they are excluded from the Kingdom of God because of their sins, so must they also be excluded from the church of the Lord.

[ON SEPARATION]

SON: Oh, father, I thought that each person must give an account for himself alone. What damage does it do if my fellow member has something evil in him, when I myself am devout? If despite this, I told him in love that he should abstain from his sin, and he did not want to, I could still treat him with love and remain in fellowship with him. He would have to give an account for himself.

FATHER: Listen and observe well! This idea has a very good appearance of love, but it is only a feigned love and is absolutely unlike the manner of God's love. Divine love cannot be minded other than God [is]. Yes, it cannot love other than that which God, who is eternal love, has commanded and ordained. It cannot believe other than that which God has commanded to believe. The true divine love cannot and may not prescribe to the Spirit of God in meaning, wisdom, and counsel. The true love of God looks only to God, its eternal source. The person in whom the love of God really exists looks to and learns from God about His character and nature.

Now then, a true child of God (because of the exclusion mentioned above) has learned from his heavenly Father at all times a division and separation—namely, that between the pure and the impure, between light and darkness, between His people and the Gentiles. This can well be seen in the creation; when God created heaven and earth there was light and darkness, earth and water all intermingled; then God separated the light from the darkness, and called the light day and the darkness night. Further, when God planted a Paradise, and created out of love all kinds of delightful things, He also created out of love man in His own image. He made him so worthy that he was allowed to live in Paradise and even eat of the fruits of Paradise which God had offered to him. As soon, however, as man became disobedient to his God, he became unclean, and as an impure being could not any longer remain in Paradise. He had to leave, until he was cleansed by Christ (the second Adam); then he could re-enter Paradise. Adam had to wait many hundred years, until Christ, the promised seed of woman, led him back into Paradise. Along with Adam, many other saints rose after the resurrection of the Lord Jesus, and He led them all with Him into His Kingdom. This can be seen in Matthew 27:52. Here may be seen how sin and disobedience separate us from God and His Kingdom.

Again, God revealed to Abraham, the father of all of the faithful, about a separation and division in respect to circumcision. This was that his seed should be a people separate from the heathen. He thus led them with a mighty hand from Egypt, and pledged to give them a promised land. The Lord God gave His people a special Law upon the Mountain Sinai in the desert, whereby they should be completely separated—not only from the unclean heathen, but also from the unclean animals, fish, and birds. God said to them (Leviticus 20:24-26): "I am the Lord your God, who have separated you from the peoples. You shall therefore make a distinction between the clean beast and the unclean, and between the unclean bird and the clean; you shall not make yourselves abominable by beast or by bird or by anything with which the ground teems, which I have set apart for you to hold unclean. You shall be holy to me; for I the Lord am holy, and have separated you from the peoples, that you should be mine."

You thus see how God has herein revealed His plan and will in the separation of the clean from the unclean, the Lord's people from the heathen (who were indeed also God's creatures, but were not granted any part or fellowship with the people of God).

Son: Yes, dear father, I have understood clearly from you about the separation among the people of God in the Old Testament with the Levitical priesthood, which taught such outward ceremonies. However, Jesus Christ fulfilled the Law as an eternal High Priest and did not promise an outward Canaan but proclaimed an eternal Kingdom which is spiritual. Therefore all of His laws are spiritual. How, then, does one understand the separation in the New Testament, or is separation necessary? I would like to be thoroughly instructed about this.

Father: Note well, and pay close attention to the Word of the Lord Jesus and His apostles. You will thus recognize an inevitably necessary separation in the New Covenant between believers and unbelievers. The Lord Jesus says (Matthew 13:24) that the present world is like a field in which good and bad seeds are planted. The Lord Jesus sows the good seed through His gospel; these represent the children of His Kingdom who are brought forth by the Word of Truth (James 1:18). The weeds, however, are the bad seeds, the seed of the devil, planted by him through his false, cunning, and lying word so agreeable to human wisdom. Now the harvest from these seeds is the end of the world. At that time the Lord of the Harvest will gather the good seeds into His barn, but He will burn the bad seed with everlasting fire.

Now, notice well, as is mentioned above, that the separation in the Old Testament was commanded through Moses, which was all spoken by the servant Moses as a testimony toward the Son and His household (Hebrews 3:5, 6). There no uncircumcised, no lepers, no one who had made himself unclean by touching a corpse, was permitted to enter the temple. In like manner Jesus, the Son of God, instituted and ordained a temple, a church, and a household by His death on the cross and by His Holy Spirit. In the Holy Scriptures this temple or church is called the body of the Lord Jesus (Romans 12:5; 1 Corinthians 12:27; Ephesians 1:22, 23; 4:12; 5:30; Colossians 1:18). All members of Jesus are planted and baptized into this holy temple or church. Paul says (1 Corinthians 12:13): "For by one Spirit we were all baptized into one body."

This body, temple, or church (which is all one) is cleansed by Jesus as the Head by the "washing of water with the word" (Ephesians 5:26). This body or church is separated from the world, from sin, from all error, yes, from the entire old house of Adam—that is, according to the inner part in faith. This church is named in the Holy Scriptures a "chosen race, a royal priesthood, a holy nation" etc. (1 Peter 2:9), because this body, according to Romans 6:2-4, is dead to sin and is buried by baptism into death and is risen again to a newness of life in Christ Jesus; it remains and lives in it as a fruitful vine. However, this body or the church of Christ still walks outwardly in a state of humiliation in this wicked world. It thus happens through divine permission that Satan is allowed to tempt each member with sins, with various errors, and all kinds of wicked and harmful deeds day and night, in order to test his faith and love. Therefore, the Lord Jesus and the apostles call upon the faithful to watch and pray, struggle and strive.

Nonetheless, it can easily happen that one of these members, who once died to sin and put on the Lord Jesus in the newness of life, sins again, perhaps against one of his fellow members or even against the ways and statutes of the Lord, if he does not remain constant in prayer and watching. In this case, the Lord Jesus teaches, as the true Head of His body (Matthew 18:15): "If your brother sins against you, go and tell him his fault, between him and you alone. If he listens to you, you have gained your brother. But if he does not listen, take one or two others along with you, that every word may be confirmed by the evidence of two or three witnesses. If he refuses to listen to them, tell it to the church; and if he refuses to listen even to the church, let him be to you as a Gentile and a tax collector."

Behold, you can see who is the founder of the separation and the ban in the New Testament, namely, the Lord Jesus, the true House-holder. This is then a separation of those sinners whose sins can be forgiven without their being disowned, when the sinner is willing to hear. If he will not hear, he is not excluded because of the sin, but rather because of his hardness of heart and arrogant pride. He rejects the counsel of the Spirit of God, and grieves and despises the church even though he is obligated to die for his fellow members rather than grieving them and despising their good counsel.

The Law has already spoken of such wicked men (Numbers 19:13): "Whoever touches a dead person . . . (which is a slight matter in itself) and does not cleanse himself, defiles the tabernacle of the Lord, and that person shall be cut off from Israel," etc. That which is the water of aspersion in the Old Testament by which the unclean were cleansed is the brotherly discipline in the New Covenant. If then, a member sins, and does dead works of sin and despises the brotherly discipline, the deceitfulness of sin has already hardened that heart. Paul warns (Hebrews 3:13) the believers to take care that "none of you may be hardened by the deceitfulness of sin. For we share in Christ, if only we hold our first confidence firm to the end." That is, we have become partakers in the new life from Christ Jesus. Let us also remain steadfast therein until the end, and by no means abandon again the true life in Christ and the living God by the old life of sin.

SON: If then a man can be excluded from the body and church of the Lord and even from the eternal Kingdom of God because of a minor sin (which could be easily forgiven if he listened), what will then happen if a member knowingly commits a premeditated sin, a lie or the like, or even fights against the statutes and law of the Lord?

FATHER: Note well the mind of the Spirit of God in all things. He is the best counselor (knowing everything beforehand), and has therefore arranged everything wisely in His household. God already commanded under the Law (Numbers 15:27-30) that if a person or an entire congregation sins unknowingly against a commandment of the Lord, they are to bring a sacrifice to the Lord and the sin shall be forgiven. When, however, a person sins against the commandment and ordinances of the Lord out of wickedness, there is no sacrifice for this, but such a person shall be cut off, and his iniquity shall be upon him because he has despised the word of the Lord and has broken His commandment. Yes, if an entire congregation or city should sin like that, and serve other gods—that is, do those things which the Lord God has forbidden—that entire city should be destroyed (Deuteronomy 13:12).

Now see how this must be observed in the church of the Lord according to the spirit of the New Testament, so that the gates of hell, which are sin, may not prevail against it. Now, each member of the body of Jesus knows full well that he was buried into death through baptism (Romans 6[:4]) and that he should walk in newness of life. At the time of his baptism he was also charged that he must renounce completely all sins and the devil, along with his own will, and that he must obediently follow after the Lord Jesus, being steadfast in all suffering, until death. Now, the works of the flesh are indeed plain according to the witness of Galatians 5:19. They are: adultery, immorality, licentiousness, impurity, idolatry, sorcery, enmity, strife, envy, anger, contention, dissension, partisan spirit, hatred, murder, drunkenness, gluttony, and the like. If a single one of these evils becomes manifest in a member, to all such the Kingdom of God is completely denied by the Holy Spirit.

If then, a work like this is evident in a member of the body of the Lord, so that the church can clearly recognize it, then it is only just that such a member be expelled from the church according to 1 Corinthians 5:13, until he is cleansed of it by true penitence and repentance. This is so that the entire body or church is not contaminated by it. How wicked and corrupt must then a member like this be, if he wishes to justify himself in doing the works of the flesh.

[ON DISSENSION]

Son: I well see herein the plan of God. But this work of "dissension"—I cannot rightly recognize what that is. I would like to know it.

Father: This is the kind of spirit which those persons who are not sufficiently enlightened encounter on the paths of the Lord, just as Eve met the serpent in Paradise. It said: "You will not die. For God knows that when you eat of it [the forbidden fruit] your eyes will be opened, and you will be like God, knowing good and evil" [Genesis 3:4, 5]. This then also took place in part; namely, as soon as they had eaten, the eyes of both were opened, and they saw that they were naked. Therefore, Paul says to the Corinthians, "I am afraid that as the serpent deceived Eve by his cunning, your thoughts will be led astray from a sincere and pure devotion to Christ" (2 Corinthians 11:3).

As long, then, as a faithful member of Christ remains in this conflict, and he "destroys arguments and every proud obstacle to the knowledge of God and takes every thought captive to obey Christ" (2 Corinthians 10:5)—so long will the carnal spirit of dissension be unable to capture his soul. Rather, the member walks in simplicity, in obedience of faith, in peace, and in unity with his fellow members. He willingly leaves in peace and in simplicity to his fellow members that which he does not understand. He humbly submits himself to his fellow members, after the counsel of Peter (1 Peter 5:5).

As soon, however, as this spirit—that is, the spirit of dissension—

becomes master of those who do not know it, the person is slowly but surely separated inwardly from peace and love toward his fellow members. He takes offense, now against this, then against that, and gradually loses the true power of faith. The meetings of his fellow members, where he should rightly be edified, will also become burdensome for him. If this is noticed, and he is asked about it in love, then he can more readily listen to frivolous and trifling conversation than to the loving admonitions of his fellow members, who notice and recognize this. If the person refuses to listen to the loving exhortations of his fellow members, but rather listens to the false and deceitful spirit which disguises itself as an angel of light, he will be made to think himself so clever and wise that he sees with keen eyes all of the faults of his fellow members, is repelled and offended by them, and afterwards begins to censure them as well as the entire congregation.

This person eventually opposes the whole congregation. This kind of spirit of dissension always works through such a member to bring about the separation of all other members to abolish all order and to be his own master. He usually wins a following. This is called by the Spirit of God dissension and party-spirit; it is plainly a work of the flesh. It does not belong in the Kingdom of God, nor in the church of the Lord, but rather in the old house and kingdom of Adam, which is complete division and therefore will not endure. It must fall because division has always been the origin of all evil. No earthly household can endure in blessing where there is dissension, much less a divine household.

Therefore, true believers must avoid all such spirits within themselves and also all such persons must be avoided outwardly who create scandal and division in this and other ways, as Paul admonishes (Romans 16:17). Those are works of the flesh and a carnal spirit, and that is a carnal person, even though he disguises himself outwardly in angelic humility. Paul also calls and refers to such people in this way (Colossians 2:18). Yes, he even calls it "heresy," which should be avoided (Titus 3:10).

[ON THE BAN]

Son: I have clearly understood about the spirit of dissension, and about those who should be avoided. But, dear father, I ask you to tell me what kind of person it must be who conducts and administers this ordinance of the ban. We all have many faults and fall short of the glory of God. James says, "If any one makes no mistakes in what he says he is a perfect man" [3:2]. Since, then, we all lack faith, who is it that should avoid others because of their shortcomings or sins?

FATHER: It is very good that you ask me about everything so that you do not remain ignorant on any point, for ignorance causes great damage to the soul. Take notice, then, and pay attention. In the first place, no other people are promised salvation except the faithful, who believe in the Son of God. They shall have eternal life. Those who do not believe shall remain under the wrath of God. Now note this manner and quality of faith, as Jesus the Son of God has described it (Mark 16:17). The Lord Jesus says there to His disciples: "And these signs will accompany those who believe: in my name (that is, in His teaching, word, and commandments) they will cast out demons; they will speak in new tongues; they will pick up serpents, and if they drink any deadly thing, it will not hurt them; they will lay their hands on the sick; and they will recover."

These believers are promised eternal life, and these believers are commanded by Christ to eject the sinful, offensive, self-seeking spirits, to exclude them from their fellowship. Whatever these believers bind on earth, that will be certainly also bound in heaven; what they loose on earth, that will also be loosed in heaven. These believers put into effect the royal statutes and ordinances of His house and walk amid much temptation with great joyfulness of faith, according to the rule of their Lord and Master, even when they are rejected by men for this as evildoers. Even though these faithful members of Jesus may unwittingly also make mistakes and commit sins, they do not do it intentionally, but rather are truly sorry for it in their hearts. They are the kind who suffer because of their weakness. When they are corrected by their fellow members, they listen very willingly, and allow themselves to be told where they have fallen short. They are those of whom John speaks: "My little children . . . if any one does sin, we have an advocate with the Father, Jesus Christ, the righteous" (1 John 2:1). They stand in an unrelenting battle and war within themselves and by continually doing so mortify the sinful members of earth. Yes, they would rather be outside of the church of the Lord than that they should sin and not desist when they are disciplined.

These believers can then with good conscience also help to exclude and avoid even their beloved fellow members when the latter sin and will not listen to loving admonition. This is possible because they have in themselves already rejected and banned such a mind and spirit. These believers can also say with assurance of faith that which John says (1 John 4:6): "We are of God. Whoever knows God listens to us, and he who is not of God does not listen to us. By this we know the spirit of truth and the spirit of error." These believers then can with a good conscience exclude from their midst a member who no longer will permit himself to be disciplined and edified in love. When a member sins and no longer listens, then this is a mortal sin and is one which cannot be prayed about, as John records (1 John 5:16).

Thus, you see the great difference in sinning. Two men can commit the same sin: one may be lost and the other may attain mercy. You can see this in the two criminals who were crucified with Jesus. The one went with Jesus to Paradise because he confessed his sin and believed in the Lord Jesus. It can likewise be the same in a church that two members commit the same sin. One listens and is sorry for his sin, and will be forgiven. The other will not listen to the discipline of love and sits in arrogance and selfishness, and will be lost. Therefore there is a great difference in sins. David says: "Blessed is the man to whom the Lord imputes no iniquity, and in whose spirit there is no deceit" (Psalm 32:2). These are the upright souls who are regretful when they, perhaps, were overhasty and made mistakes. They listen, however, very willingly to the admonition of love from their fellow members. James says about them: ". . . we all make many mistakes" (James 3:2).

Nevertheless, they are in Christ Jesus, and there is "therefore now no condemnation for those who are in Christ Jesus" (Romans 8:1). They "walk not according to the flesh, but according to the Spirit" (verse 4). They cannot sin to condemnation, for they are born of God, and God's seed keeps them (1 John 3:9). These are the blessed seeds of woman who are in daily combat against sin, which is the seed of the devil. There is continual enmity between believers and the seed of the serpent. They must also feel its bruises on their heels, although its head—that is, its dominion—has been crushed and removed. Therefore, the faithful are called the church militant as long as they live in a state of humiliation. They "have conquered him by the blood of the Lamb" (Revelation 12:11).

Son: I now understand somewhat about the difference between sinners, as well as about avoidance and its causes. However, I have heard many say after they had been banned that they felt perfectly well. They did not feel any ban. I have also heard from others that the ban had neither power nor effect, because those who are placed under it do not feel it, but say that they are in good spirits.

Father: Note also here the mind of God, and you will easily see how such poor souls who know neither themselves nor God are deceived by the slyness of the serpent. When they first repent of their sins, and believe in the teachings of Jesus, they enter by faith into the church and the divine ordinances. They themselves help to conduct the ban for a time, and believe that whatever the church of the Lord binds on earth, that will also be bound in heaven. However, such poor souls do not want to "contend for the faith" according to the counsel of the Apostle Jude (verse 3), but rather abandon the faith again. They incline in their hearts toward seductive spirits, whom they look upon as good angels, as Paul clearly writes about (1 Timothy 4:1). They listen to those spirits who promise them nothing but good things, and complete freedom, as also the Apostle Peter wrote about (2 Peter 2:18, 19).

If, then, these poor souls abandon the faith, their consciences are branded as with a hot iron. But, because they have left the faith they do not feel the ban until the day of revelation. Yes, they can speak proudly to the church of the Lord: "You can ban me as you will; I shall still come into grace with God." The others, however, who are banned because of their sins, and have not abandoned the faith, indeed feel the ban. They repent, and are restored again through faith.

Now consider well the great blindness of these people who find fault with a church because some of its members who have abandoned it say, as mentioned above, that they feel no ban, but rather can still contend against the church of the Lord. Now note that God himself conducts a ban like this with the majority of mankind. All unreborn men lie under the wrath of God. His eternal damnation awaits them if they do not truly repent and are reborn to Jesus through belief and live according to the will of God. Now, look at these men. They are merry and cheerful, and have within them a hope of salvation, which has been planted there by the false gospel. They are the kind of people about whom Jesus speaks (Matthew 24:38, 39) as they were in the day before the flood: "... they were eating, and drinking ... ," etc. They were happy until the flood came and swept them all away. They let Noah preach and build his ark; they even mocked him and did not believe.

It will be exactly like this with mankind when the coming of the Son of man shall be revealed. They will not believe that their condition is so bad, and, therefore, they will not feel the divine ban within themselves, although it already rests upon them. Unbelief has hardened their hearts and made them stubborn, like Lot's wife, who turned into a solid pillar of salt. Likewise, the poor souls who once departed from the sinful Sodom and who looked back on their way became pillars of salt who no longer believe the gospel. The Apostle Peter says: "For it would have been better for them never to have known the way of righteousness than after knowing it to turn back from the holy commandment delivered to them" (2 Peter 2:21). Therefore, the Lord Jesus calls to His followers with a strong voice, "Remember Lot's wife" (Luke 17:32).

Consider further the angels who sinned. God "cast them into hell and committed them to pits of nether gloom to be kept until the judgment" (2 Peter 2:4). See how these angels conducted themselves. They again fought against the good angels, which can be seen in the letter of Jude (verse 9) and in Revelation (12:7). Notice, the strife with Satan and with the Lord Jesus himself (Matthew 4). In such a case, these poor and blind men could also say to God that His ban had no effect. If the angels banned by God could still fight against the good angels, do not be surprised that the banned people, who have abandoned the faith and follow such banned spirits, can still contend against the faithful and cause them much trouble. This is, however, only for the increasing of their damnation, and to test the faith of the believers and increase their salvation.

Therefore, do not be concerned about what other men say, for in most cases their testimony is false and goes against the mind of God. Even though the testimony of such men is accepted, the divine testimony is still much greater (John 5). God has testified about His Son; whoever believes in the Son of God has the divine witness in him, which is more certain than all of man's testimonies, no matter how it appears. Here you have heard sufficiently the reason and the cause of those who are banned and their manner of contending against the church of God.

SON: If then a church conducts a ban and separation for itself, would the civil authorities permit this?

FATHER: Mark well, that this good ordinance is not opposed to the authorities, but, on the contrary, is conducive to the station of civil government. The faithful are taught by Paul (Romans 13:1-7) that they should be subject to the human regulations made by the authorities for the sake of the Lord, who instituted them. They should give the government taxes, imposts, honor, and respect, for all authorities are ordained of God to punish the evil, and to help to protect the good, provided that they desire to carry out their offices in accordance with the will of God. The authorities should rightly rejoice if they had only those subjects who walk in the fear of God by not permitting any evident sinners within their communion, and who willingly, in the fear of God, give the authorities what is owed them and who give the Lord, their God, that which belongs to Him. The Lord has foretold such a time [in which] the kings will be the wet-nurses of the church of the Lord (Isaiah 60:16).

[ON OATH-TAKING]

SON: Will the government also be satisfied if one does not swear the oath, according to the teaching of Christ?

FATHER: If the true believers affirm with "Yes" what is "Yes" and deny with "No" what is "No" in accordance with the teaching of Christ, that is much better than many oaths which are mostly sworn and not kept. Therefore, the government can feel much more secure and more sure of the truth with those subjects who tell them truthfully "Yes" and "No" in the fear of God and remain in the truth than with those who swear the oath and are still not to be trusted or believed.

[ON EXAMINATION]

SON: Dear father, I thank you that you have instructed me upon all of these points. I perceive well that to have a sure foundation in sacred things, it is necessary to look to God. He has revealed himself in His Word at all times and remains steadfast in faithfulness, and thus the heart is made firm through grace. I want to ask you something else which I also heard said, and about which I would like to be certain. Why are people not tested prior to their baptism and acceptance into the church, rather than first being baptized and then being put into the ban? They claimed that this shows that the spirit of examination is not present which is certainly necessary for this work.

FATHER: Dear son, listen and remember again herein how people still do not recognize and understand the divine mind and way. Because of this they judge and reject a thing which they do not understand according to human opinions. I will also clearly explain this so that you can understand or grasp it well. In the first place, the faithful dare not be of a different mind in the household of God than God has revealed himself to be in His household. They dare not wish to be more wise than God. Even if they should all be looked down upon by men as fools, they must despite this still abide with divine wisdom. Therefore Paul speaks: "If any one among you thinks that he is wise in this age, let him become a fool that he may become wise. For the wisdom of the world is folly with God" (1 Corinthians 3: 18, 19).

Now, since the believers must look only to God in all things, it is but just that they look to God in the testing of men. Now, one cannot see and learn from God any other way than this: when He wished to test a man or a people He first laid His laws and commandments upon this man or the entire people. Only then were they really tested under His laws and commandments. This has been the manner of divine wisdom at all times and still is (Ecclesiasticus 4:19; 6:22). That this is true can be seen, in the first place, in that Adam did not have to be tried outside of Paradise, but rather within it. He was under the will of God to see whether or not he would eat the fruit which God had forbidden him to eat. Secondly, Noah had to be tested in his faith in the construction of the ark, and in his entering into it.

Again, Abraham, the father of all the faithful, was severely tested in that God ordered him to go out from his own country and from his friends. The most difficult test occurred for him after he had already received the covenant of circumcision, when he was to sacrifice his son Isaac (Genesis 12:1; 22:1). Again, it can be seen that God severely tested the entire seed of Abraham in Egypt, and also after they had been led with a mighty hand from Egypt. Then God began to tempt them and test them in the wilderness. Although they had already received God's pledge of the promised land, they were first tested in the wilderness, so that it would be revealed what was in their hearts—

whether they would keep God's commandments or not. This can be seen in Deuteronomy 8:2.

In this wilderness of temptation, most of them were struck down because of their disbelief (unfaithfulness). God had no pleasure in them. Although they were already baptized in the cloud and in the sea under Moses, and all of them had eaten the same food—even angel food, as the Book of Wisdom calls it (Wisdom of Solomon 16:20). Yes, they had "all eaten the same supernatural food, and all drank the same supernatural drink. For they drank from the supernatural Rock which followed them, and the Rock was Christ" (1 Corinthians 10:3, 4). They did not stand the test, when God demanded obedience for his evidenced love and favors and toward His commands, ordinances, and laws.

Now, see and observe the intent of God in the New Covenant. In the first place, we read that there was no examination before the baptism of the Son of God. However, when he was baptized by John in the Jordan, and the voice was heard from heaven [saying], "This is my beloved Son, with whom I am well pleased" (Matthew 3:16, 17), then temptation began. It was then that the devil tempted Him, that the scribes and the Pharisees tempted Him, that He had to learn obedience (Hebrews 5:8). He was obedient unto death, even death on a cross (Philippians 2:8).

In the same manner and in no other way as the Father led and tempted the Lord Jesus, the Son of God, does Jesus lead His followers. "The kingdom of heaven is like a net which was thrown into the sea and gathered fish of every kind . . . but [the men] threw away the bad" (Matthew 13:47, 48). The Lord Jesus called a great many who became His disciples by faith and baptism (John 4:1). However, they were then tested and made elect by the cross in His faith. The Lord Jesus never examined men except for His teaching and gospel, but rather all those who came to Him and believed in Him were accepted as disciples. He said to them: "If you continue in my word, you are truly my disciples, and you will know the truth, and the truth will make you free" (John 8:31, 32).

Again, the dear Jesus said to His disciples: "He who abides in me, and I in him, he it is that bears much fruit, for apart from me you can do nothing. If a man does not abide in me, he is cast forth as a branch and withers" (John 15:4-6). The church of the Lord Jesus must have this mind and no other. If a man repents and publicly renounces the devil, the world, and all sins, and desires to enter the teachings of the Lord Jesus, and supposing that it could be suspected that perhaps this man would not remain steadfast but nothing evil were known about him at that moment, then this man could not, upon his public profession, be excluded from the church. The man will first be tested by the discipleship of Christ; then it will be revealed whether he rejects the teaching of Jesus, which is the true stone of examination.

This is attested by [the Book of] Wisdom (Ecclesiasticus 6:22 [21]). Divine wisdom invites all men to come to it, yes, even the fools (Proverbs 9:1-4). It excludes no man who accepts the invitation, forsakes the path of folly, and takes the path of wisdom. Man is tested afterwards in the household of God, when he must put his feet into the fetters and his neck into the yoke (Ecclesiasticus 6:25 [24]). If he then does not remain loyal, then the guilt is upon him alone.

This is the divine intention that man, after he has entered into a relationship with his God, is only then tested in the commandments of God. Otherwise, God himself could be blamed for instances in the Old Testament, that He had not been able to test the men who accepted His promises but did not remain steadfast. Yes, even Jesus Christ could be accused that He accepted men who did not remain true to Him. Why did He not make as His disciples only those who remained true to Him? It states: "After this, many of his disciples drew back, and no longer went about with him" (John 6:66). All of the apostles could be accused in the same way. It can be seen from their letters that they made many disciples by their preaching of the gospel, and at all times many turned away again in all kinds of manners and ways.

Now, notice well this simple comparison; if two persons love each other and decide to marry, when can they really test each other? Before marriage they are still free of the burdens of the household, the woman is still free from obedience to the man, and he is still free from the cares and weaknesses of the woman—all they know is love. As soon, however, as they enter into a public marriage relationship, and begin a household, then begins the real test. Then the wife dare not flirt with any other man, for she must be obedient to her husband. Then the husband becomes aware of the weakness of the wife, and the like. The first passionate love is dissipated and a divine love is required if they are to live together in peace. Then a love is necessary which must be steadfast until death. They must share joy and sorrow, the sweet and the bitter, and cleave to each other until death. That is the state of marriage among the faithful, which symbolizes the Lord Jesus and His church (Ephesians 5:32).

When worldly people desire to marry and have not decided upon any one, they commonly are first inclined to the one and then to the other, and are completely fickle. They find fault with the married people and think that they will live much better when they are married. When, however, they are actually married, then they must first learn how to run a household, and many become adulterers. They do not have enough love and patience to endure in the testing period.

Notice well what happens similarly in the spiritual realm. How many souls have been awakened and have forsaken the great harlot—have gone out of the great outward Babel—and have fallen in illicit love in various ways with the teachings of Jesus? One takes here a verse of the [New] Testament, and another takes there a verse, and with these they make love illicitly. They also pretend great love for one another, call one another "brethren" and "sisters" and are also able to live in this love. They are, however, not joined or baptized into one body through one Spirit (1 Corinthians 12:13). Therefore, they have freedom among themselves for each to indulge where and how he will. One inclines to this opinion, the other to that. The one holds to this spirit, the other to that. All this time they remain together in this illicit love. Yes, it is said among them, "Love covers all, and condemns none."

It is true that this uninhibited illicit love covers all, for it is not a marriage with Christ and His church to walk according to His rules, in which there is no room for illicit love, but rather a love which hates all that is evil, wicked and sinful, if it is not to be false (Romans 13:9). These lovers may be judged and criticized by those who have entered into the marriage with Christ and have committed themselves, who edify one another, work, and admonish. It may happen that among them one inclines to a different spirit and illicitly loves it, so that they judge this person an adulterer and exclude him from the church if he will not listen. Then this person goes at once to the company of illicit lovers, where he can illicitly love all of the false spirits outside the house and church of the Lord. That is then called a great liberty of the spirit, and it is indeed so, but it is also outside of the house of God, outside of His church, and outside of His Kingdom.

In the Kingdom of God there is no disorder and no false freedom, but it is all order and unity. All of the angels and spirits in heaven must will what God wills or they cannot remain in His Kingdom. As soon as the angels desired something different from [what] God [willed], they were ejected and bound with the chains of darkness to be kept until the judgment (2 Peter 2:4). This is the nature of the true love of God, and therefore all believers must be minded as their Lord and Master has taught them. He has also portrayed it in this understanding, namely, if one of the members of your body "causes you to sin, cut it off and throw it from you" (Matthew 8[18:8]). Jesus has given this commandment especially to His church, which is His body, to cut off all sinful and offensive members, lest the entire body be spoiled. This love was commanded by God already under the Law: ". . . [if] your friend who is as your own soul, entices you secretly, saying, 'Let us go and serve other gods,' which neither you nor your fathers have known . . . you shall not yield to him or listen to him, nor shall your eye pity him" (Deuteronomy 13:6). The illicit lovers know nothing of this kind of love, as long as they do not enter the state of marriage with Christ in His teachings and ordinances.

Nevertheless, they pride themselves greatly on their unpartisan love which they have and pretend. They are also considered by uninitiated souls to be men who walk in a great divine love and in good faith. It will be revealed that this was only a false, illicit love, which was indeed well disguised by eloquent and clever speeches, by which many innocent hearts have been deceived. Therefore, say the Scriptures: "Let love be genuine" (Romans 12[:9]). The essence of the commandment is ". . . love that issues from a pure heart and a good conscience and sincere faith. Certain persons by swerving from this have wandered away into vain discussion . . ." (1 Timothy 1:5). Here you see that an adulterated faith and also an adulterated love can exist.

[ON LOVE AND FAITH]

Son: Yes, but how can we test the true love and the true faith, or the false love and the adulterated faith?

Father: The true faith which is genuine and which is promised eternal life must be a Scriptural faith, just as the Lord Jesus says:

"He who believes in me, as the Scripture has said, 'Out of his heart shall flow rivers of living water'" (John 7:38). Where there is a Scriptural faith, it will also produce the true love according to the Scriptures. "This is the love of God, that we keep his commandments" (1 John 5:3). The Lord Jesus says of the true love: "He who has my commandments and keeps them, he it is who loves me; and he who loves me will be loved by my Father, and I will love and manifest myself to him" (John 14:21). By this Scriptural love His disciples will be known (John 13:34, 35). Just as the Lord Jesus was born in accordance with the Scriptures and crucified and resurrected in accordance with the Scriptures (1 Corinthians 15:3, 4), so He taught all of His own a Scriptural faith and promised them eternal life in accordance with the Scriptures. But an adulterated faith and an adulterated love cannot be founded on Scripture, but rather only on human opinion.

The one believes that which he was taught by the theologians, the other as he was convinced by this or that book, the third, according to his own mind's opinion and self-will. But the Scripture says specifically: "There is [but] . . . one Lord, one faith, one baptism" (Ephesians 4:5). If there were ten men who were still standing in an adulterated faith, and if they were to be examined in accordance with Scripture, it would be learned that each of the ten had his peculiar faith, and not one of them would be completely in accord with the Scriptures. There is only one single unadulterated faith, and all those who have true faith according to Scripture are also unified according to Scripture as far as the rules of faith are concerned.

[ON THE SCRIPTURES]

Son: I have, however, heard it said that all sects appeal to Scripture, and therefore one cannot prove one's faith with Scripture.

Father: Whoever says that because all sects appeal to Scripture a true believer dare not do so must really be a miserable and ignorant person. Rather, it greatly strengthens the faith of a believer to know that all sects recognize the Holy Scriptures as divine and appeal to them, even though they do not believe. To appeal to Scripture and to believe in Scripture are two vastly different things. This can well be seen from the words of the Lord Jesus, who said to the Jews: "If you believed Moses you would believe me, for he wrote of me" (John 5:46). Now, the Jews had all referred to Moses, but they had not believed in his writings. Likewise, all of the sects are based not only on the Scriptures, but also on the Lord Jesus himself. However, the way they believe in the Lord Jesus is the way they believe in the Scriptures. Now, if a true believer were so blind as to think or say: "Oh, all sects appeal to the same crucified Savior, therefore I may and can not appeal to Him," that would certainly please the devil. But no! The true believers have learned more and better wisdom from their Lord and Master.

When the devil appealed to Scripture during the temptation of the Lord Jesus, Jesus answered in faith from the Scriptures and referred to them (Matthew 4:6, 7). Let the devil and all false spirits appeal to Scripture; they do not really believe it. You will learn that the very people who try to confuse a believer by saying that all sects appeal to Scripture will nevertheless appeal to it themselves. Therefore, a faithful child of God looks only to his heavenly Father, and believes and follows Him in His revealed Word, because he is certain of and believes that God and His spoken Word are completely one. Otherwise a believer would have to abstain from many things, if he did not wish to do in faith that which the godless and unbelievers do in disbelief.

He would not dare to pray, sing, work, eat, sleep, and the rest, because these are all sin for the wicked and abominations before God. "To the pure all things are pure, but to the corrupt and unbelieving nothing is pure" (Titus 1:15). Therefore, learn well the true Scriptural distinction in all things, so that you do not become confused, as have, unfortunately, many souls in this day. They see that also the godless perform acts of worship such as prayer, singing, holding of meetings, baptizing, holding of the Lord's Supper, and the like. The unenlightened mind says: "If the godless do these things, they are not very important. They can be completely rejected." Such people become so confused in different ways that finally they do not know what they think or believe. They have to make a faith for themselves which is not taught by Scripture. They think that they have achieved more than the apostles. Moreover, they no longer take counsel from the writings of the apostles.

During my life I have known and heard many such people. I have also experienced that the outcome of their path has brought with it complete disaster, for they very quickly fell and perished so that they were destroyed. Finally, they did no longer believe in anything, but again fell victim to the world and the wide path. May God protect in grace all simple believers in Christ that they do not desire to climb so high, but "associate with the lowly" (Romans 12:16). Paul admonishes Timothy with these words: ". . . from childhood you have been acquainted with the sacred writings which are able to instruct you for salvation through faith in Christ Jesus. All scripture is inspired by God and profitable for teaching, for reproof, for correction, and for training in righteousness, that the man of God may be complete, equipped for every good work" (2 Timothy 3:15-17).

Son: Can and may we believe the witness of the Holy Scripture in all things, and is a believer obligated to believe and follow the Scripture? Does not the Spirit of God lead him on other paths, of which the outward letter of the Scripture knows nothing?

Father: No one may say to a believer that he should and must believe and obey the Scriptures, because no one can be a believer without the Holy Spirit, who must create the belief. Now, the Scriptures are only an outward testimony of those things which were once taught and commanded by the Holy Spirit. The prophecies and warnings were also spoken through it. If, then, through true penitence and repentance, a person receives the Holy Spirit from God, the Father of all spirits, then it is the same spirit of faith which was present and worked in Peter, Paul, and John hundreds of years ago. True, the Holy Spirit was in the apostles in greater measure for the expansion of the gospel, yet it is the same Holy Spirit in all believers.

Whatever then Paul, Peter, and John wrote, ordained, and commanded at that time was all agreed to by all of the faithful of that time, insofar as they were still sound in the faith. Since there is one Spirit and only one, then this holy and unique Spirit cannot will other than that which He willed for salvation many hundred years ago. That which the Holy Spirit ordained for the faithful was written outwardly. All believers are united in it, for the Holy Spirit teaches them inwardly just as the Scriptures teach them outwardly. However, when men come to the Scriptures with their wisdom and carnal minds, they do not have the spirit of faith within themselves. Therefore, they cannot believe the testimony of the Scriptures outwardly, nor follow in obedience of faith. Indeed, it is not written for them, and therefore they are free from the commands which are contained therein.

This is just as if a king had commands written to his subjects, making great promises along with them if they followed his orders, and great threats if they did not keep them. Other people who are not subjects of that king are indeed able to read the commands and speak at great length about them. However, if they are not the king's subjects, nor wish to become subjects, they do not respect the threats and do not believe the promises. They do not submit themselves to his commandments, statutes and laws.

Exactly the same is true with the Holy Scriptures in the New Testament. Whoever reads it can see what Jesus, the King of all kings, has promised to all men who truly repent, believe in Him, and are willing to follow Him obediently in all of His commandments. He can also see and read in the Holy Scriptures with what the Lord Jesus threatens all unrepentant sinners who are not willing to repent and believe in His gospel, and who will not allow Jesus to reign over them by His Spirit through the commandments which He had left behind in written form. A man can indeed read the Scriptures outwardly and talk and write about them, but, if the spirit of faith is not in him, he will not be concerned with the commandments therein, nor be frightened very much by the threats which they contain. This is because the inner ears are not yet opened.

Therefore, the Lord Jesus said to the people who personally heard him preach: "He who has ears to hear, let him hear" (Matthew 11:15; 13:43). In the Holy Revelation of Saint John, the Spirit of God calls to each of the seven churches: "He who has an ear, let him hear what the Spirit says to the churches" (Revelation 2:7). Therefore, when a believing person whose inner ears are opened reads the Holy Scriptures outwardly, he will hear as the Lord Jesus intends His teaching to be understood. He hears that which the apostles want to express in their writings. He will also be impelled, through his inner hearing, to true obedience which makes him obey even in outward matters. Outwardly, he reads the Scriptures in faith and hears the inner word of life which gives him strength and power to follow Jesus. Where, however, faith is lacking, a person can indeed hear and read outwardly, and say: "It is a dead letter which I cannot follow. I am not inwardly convinced of what it states outwardly." He does not know, however, that he lacks faith, and the true divine love (John 14).

[ON THE OUTWARD AND INWARD WORD]

Son: I have, nevertheless, heard many say that the Christians stand in the New Covenant, and that the Law of God is written in their hearts. Consequently, they do not need to accommodate themselves to the outward Scriptures and follow them.

Father: I am glad that you have also asked me about this. Observe closely the true intention of God. You will easily realize that this talk contains some truth, but that it is also intermingled with lies. When, in times past, the Lord God revealed His Law to His people through Moses, God wrote the Law on two stone tablets. He gave them to Moses, who had to put them into the ark of the Covenant (Deuteronomy 10:1-5; Hebrews 9:4). They had to make a copy of them and write them on the doorposts of their houses (Deuteronomy 6:6-9). There it states: "And these words which I command you this day shall be upon your heart; and you shall teach them diligently to your children. . . . [And] you shall bind them as a sign upon your hand. . . . And you shall write them on the doorposts of your house . . . ."

The outward copy was to be nothing else than, much less contrary to, that which God himself had written upon the stone tablets, and which lay hidden in the Holy of Holies in the ark of the Covenant. Therefore, the outward and the inward Law retained the same meaning. The Holy of Holies in the ark of the Covenant, in which the tablets of the Law lay, now corresponds in the New Covenant to the heart of each true believer. In it undoubtedly lie the tablets of the law of his God. They are written in each believer's heart, not by the hands of men, but rather by the Holy Spirit. This law which is inwardly written by the Spirit of God is completely identical with that which is outwardly written in the New Testament. All of the latter had flowed from the inward, and is an express image of the inward living Word of God.

However, when a person says, out of haughtiness alone, that the laws of his God are written in his heart, while he opposes the orders, statutes, and laws which the Son of God and His apostles have ordained (of which the Scriptures testify outwardly) you may be quite sure that he is still of the world. The law which he claims to have in his heart was written by the spirit of errors and lies. Moreover, this is a clear indication of the law of God and the law of the deceiving spirit: all those on whose hearts the law of God is written are united in the one faith, the one baptism, and the one spirit in accordance with Jesus Christ. This is the perfect will of the true Law-giver that they who are His should be one even as the Father and the Son are one (John 17:12 [21]).

But the law which the spirit of error writes in hearts by its false gospel is of such a nature that it is, in the first place, completely uncertain about divine testimonies (Psalm 5:10). Secondly, it separates men from God's commandments and ordinances, and divides men into manifold creeds and confessions. I have observed this of many who said that they were free men, that they did not need to subject themselves to the letter of the New Testament—meaning the written word—for the law of God was written in their hearts. But I have further seen and recognized that no two of them were agreed concerning the basic principles of the Christian life according to the Scriptures, but rather they had as many laws as there were persons maintaining such haughty opinions.

It has often occurred to me that this must be a foreign spirit which plants these various laws in the hearts of men. The Lord God complained about this already in the book of the prophet Jeremiah: the people of Israel, led astray by false prophets, abandoned the one Law of God and the one altar of the Lord. In their false freedom, they made other gods and altars as they thought best (Jeremiah 11:13). The same thing happens today with people of this time who boast of great freedom and do not follow divine counsel and commandments in accordance with Holy Scripture. Here is truly a case of "as many men—as many spirits and as many laws." Despite its great spiritual pretensions, Babel, confusion, and disunity remain. Even so, these builders will not refrain from their intentions, disregarding the fact that the Lord has confused their languages. Yes, they see that many learnéd and wise men have already built in this manner apart from the ordinances of the Lord Jesus, and have utterly failed, yes, some even made fools. Still, more builders begin once again to continue this chaotic construction. It becomes more and more confused and terrible. If they do not soon refrain from this, there will finally be "men of corrupt mind and counterfeit faith; but they will not get very far, for their folly will be plain to all, as was that of these two men [Jannes and Jambres]" (2 Timothy 3[:8, 9]).

Now then, you have learned about the true and the false laws which are both written in the hearts of men. The false law is written in the hearts of the unbelievers by the spirit of errors. The true law of life is written in the children of the New Covenant, the true believers, by the Holy Spirit of truth. It is in every way identical with that which Christ commanded outwardly, and that which the apostles have written.

[ON BLOOD AND STRANGLED ANIMALS]

SON: I have now understood this sufficiently. It is very useful and necessary for me that I have been so well instructed in many things, because in this day keen eyes are needed to differentiate between and recognize the true and the false. Now I must ask you something else. I have read in Acts 15:29 that the apostles at Jerusalem forbade the believers among the Gentiles to eat blood and strangled [animals]. Must this still be observed?

FATHER: Note well that since blood in the Old Testament was for atonement, God said, as soon as He had permitted Noah and his sons to eat meat: ". . . you shall not eat flesh with its life, that is, its blood" (Genesis 9:4). God had this told to His people by Moses: "Moreover you shall eat no blood whatever, whether of fowl or of animal, in any of your dwellings. Whoever eats any blood, that person shall be cut off from his people" (Leviticus 7:26). God expressed this still more clearly when He said: "If any man of the house of Israel or of the strangers that sojourn among them eats any blood, I will set my face against that person who eats blood, and will cut him off from among his people. For the life of the flesh is in the blood; and I have given it for you upon the altar to make atonement for your souls; for it is the blood that makes atonement by reason of the life" (Leviticus 17:10-12).

There you see why God, in the Old Testament, forbade His people to eat blood. At the time of the apostles, those who had become believers from among the Jews had already learned from the Law not to eat blood. The believers from among the Gentiles, however, knew nothing about it. Therefore, it pleased the Holy Spirit to command through the apostles as a necessary part that they refrain from eating blood, just as well as from unchastity (Acts 15:29). Since for the Christians the blood of the Son of God is their atonement, it is but right that they should eat no blood. It is also forbidden to do this in the New as well as in the Old Testament. The early Christians said to the Gentiles: "We are not so cruel as the beasts that when we eat the meat of animals we should also eat their blood and hunger for it." They placed the ban on those who ate blood, which can be seen in the *Portrayal of the First Christians* by Gottfried Arnold.

SON: I have heard stated, however, that the Lord Jesus said: ". . . there is nothing outside a man which by going into him can defile him" (Mark 7:15). Further, that the apostle said: "Eat whatever is sold in the meat market . . ." (1 Corinthians 10:25).

FATHER: The men who say this do not yet understand the unity of the Spirit. Rather, because they are disunited, they think that the Scriptures and the Spirit of God are likewise disunited—that in one place something is forbidden, yet in another place it is allowed. If Christ had meant forbidden things, one could drink to excess in good conscience, which is a great sin. And, if Paul permitted that everything might be purchased without discrimination which is offered to be sold at the meat market and eaten, there are of course many things for sale which cannot be eaten at all. Just as little as Paul referred to other things than natural food that can be eaten, he did not refer to the buying and eating of blood. It remains, then, a settled point that the eating of blood and of strangled things is forbidden to all true Christians just as much as is unchastity by the Holy Spirit through the apostles.

[ON MARRIAGE]

SON: Tell me then, what is the place of marriage in the New Covenant? May believers marry, or how should marriage be practiced?

FATHER: The Lord God himself instituted marriage in Paradise, and the Lord Jesus himself said to the Pharisees: "Have you not read that he who made them from the beginning made them male and female, and said . . . the two shall become one?" [Matthew 19:4, 5]. Now, the state of marriage of two persons who are one in the fear of God and in faith in God is ordained and blessed by God himself. This can be seen in Abraham, Isaac, Jacob, and the other saints of the Old Testament. That the state of marriage is to be carried on in unity is already expressed under the Law. In the first place, the people of Israel were forbidden by God to marry outside of the descendants of Abraham (Deuteronomy 7:3). When the Lord God wanted to have His Law heard by the people of Israel, He had Moses tell them: "Be ready by the third day; do not go near a woman" (Exodus 19:15). Furthermore, God ordered under the Law that if a woman bore a female child, "she shall continue in the blood of her purifying for sixty-six days" (Leviticus 12:5); during this time there was to be complete continence. When a woman had her sickness, then continence was strictly commanded.

From all these commandments of God can be clearly seen that the state of marriage must be conducted in purity and in continence, and not in the plague of lust as do the heathen who do not know God. It may well be seen that God wanted the state of marriage in the Old Testament to be conducted in purity and continence. Now, under the New Testament, the state of marriage should and must be conducted not in a less holy, but rightly in a much holier manner. Paul said about unmarried persons that it would be good for them if they remained as he, Paul, was. If the unmarried state is conducted in purity of the Spirit and of the flesh in true faith in Jesus, and is kept in true humility, it is better and higher. It is also closer to the image of Christ to remain unmarried.

Nevertheless, if an unmarried person marries, he commits no sin, provided it occurs in the Lord Jesus, and is performed in the true belief in Jesus Christ—that is, that they are one in true faith in Jesus Christ according to the teachings of Jesus and according to His commandments. This is what is meant by "The two shall become one," just as Christ and His church are one (Ephesians 5). There is no other way for a person to be one flesh of Christ and His members except when he accepts in faith the Word which was Jesus and that which He taught and follows Him in obedience. Then he is "bone of my bones and flesh of my flesh." This cannot be understood as the believers' corruptible flesh, for the flesh of Christ indeed cannot be corrupted. Therefore, the true state of marriage which God has instituted must consist of this unity, that they should be one not only after the outward and corruptible flesh, but that they must much rather be one in their hearts after the will of their God and of one faith in Christ Jesus. In no other manner is the state of marriage established or blessed by the Holy Spirit, than as here described.

When, however, people marry each other because of the lust of the eyes, lust of the flesh, and for the sake of wealth, and they do not take into consideration the unity of the faith in Christ—this marriage is cursed, and must rightly be rejected by true believers. Nor is it legitimate in the house or church of the Lord, and it has always been punished by God. This may be seen in the instance when the "sons of God (fell away from God, became sensually minded, and they) saw the daughters of men were fair, and they took to wife such of them as they chose" [Genesis 6:2]. Then the flood had to come and kill them all. The Scripture calls those the children of God who were from the family of Seth, a son of Adam, and created in His likeness (Genesis 5:3). The children of man were, however, of the house of Cain, who was cursed by the Lord because of the murder of his brother. These two families were not to be intermingled, but they would not obey God, and so they all perished. But from the family of Seth, one seed was preserved, namely, Noah and his sons.

However, the devil soon succeeded in bringing Ham, that is the son of Noah, under the curse, so that his father Noah cursed him (Genesis 9:25). From the house of Ham, God chose no one, but from the family of Shem, Noah's son, is descended Abraham, the father of all of the faithful. Now, Abraham already understood the mind of God, for when his son Isaac wished to be married, Abraham told his oldest servant not to take a wife for his son from the daughters of the Canaanites, among whom he dwelt, but to go to his country and to his kindred, and take a wife for his son Isaac [Genesis 24:3, 4]. Isaac was of the same mind, because he ordered his son, Jacob, as he blessed him saying: "You shall not marry one of the Canaanite women. Arise, go to . . . the house of . . . your mother's father; and . . . take . . . [a] wife from there . . ." [Genesis 28:1, 2].

But Esau, also a son of Isaac, was an uncouth man and hated God, for he did not respect the mind of God in marrying, but rather followed his own lust and pleasure. He took two women from the Hittites, who were not of his family, and they caused Isaac and Rebekah much grief.

This may be seen in the example of the wise King Solomon when love and lust for foreign women overwhelmed him, and he married contrary to the Law. Thus he fell into the disgrace of God, and finally his entire kingdom was disrupted. Again, it can be seen that when the Jews there were converted, and rebuilt the temple during Nehemiah's time, they had to divorce their foreign wives whom they had married, among whom there were also some with child. This may be read in Ezra, chapter ten.

SON: If people outside of the true faith marry, and one partner is converted and becomes a believer, may he stay with the unbeliever?

FATHER: Indeed, it must have happened often among the early Christians that one partner became a believer and the other did not. Paul teaches that if the unbeliever desires to remain with the believer, the believer should not divorce him. If, however, the unbeliever wishes to be divorced, he may do it, and the believing partner is not bound in such a case (1 Corinthians 7:12-15). It is good to note what Paul says in the previous verses about the state of marriage among believers, namely, that the Lord says that "the wife should not separate from her husband (but if she does, let her remain single . . .) . . . . To the rest I say, not the Lord, that if any brother has a wife who is an unbeliever, and she consents to live with him, he should not divorce her" [1 Corinthians 7:10-12].

By this we understand that the unbelieving partner must not be a wolf or a brute, as are some men who are like dogs, lions, or wild beasts. They quarrel, blaspheme, and continually try to destroy and ruin with violence all that is good. If the unbeliever were to break out into all kinds of outrage and adultery, so that the believing partner were only a cloak for his scandals, the believer should definitely not be bound to remain with such a vicious person.

[ON ADULTERY]

SON: If then, among married people, one partner were to allow himself to be seduced by the devil to commit adultery, but still wished to remain with the spouse, may this be permitted?

FATHER: In the first place, it is commanded under the Law that adulterers be killed, for there should be none among the people of the Lord. If, however, a man set his wife at liberty by a letter of divorce, she was no adulteress even if she took another husband. However, if the second husband died, the first was not allowed to take her again, because she had become unclean. This was "an abomination before the Lord" (Deuteronomy 24:3, 4).

Now it can easily be seen that if a woman became unclean even if her husband released her by the permissible method, how much more was she unclean if she fell into adultery. How much less then dare a believer, whose body is to be holy, have any further relationship with an adulterous harlots-body? This is certainly a great abomination in the sight of God and can absolutely not be permitted in the church of the Lord. The entire church would be defiled by this. In case such a woman or man truly repented, he or she could continue to live with the innocent partner. However, it would be unclean to have relationships with each other again, according to the pure mind of God.*

[ON AVOIDANCE]

SON: If, among believers, one partner sins, be it husband or wife, so that he or she has to be placed in the ban by the church, must then the other partner also avoid the first, and especially in marital relationships?

FATHER: Note here again the plan of God! In the Old Testament, God commanded: "If your brother, the son of your mother, or your son, or your daughter, or the wife of your bosom, or your friend who is as your own soul, entices you secretly, saying, 'Let us go and serve other gods,' which neither you nor your fathers have known, . . . you shall not yield to him or listen to him, nor shall your eye pity him, nor shall you spare him, nor shall you conceal him; but you shall kill him; your hand shall be first against him to put him to death, and afterwards the hand of all the people" (Deuteronomy 13:6-9). You see here that no kinship could help anyone who had to be killed in accordance with the Law. This prefigured the ban of the church in the New Covenant. The Lord Jesus says that if your brother sins against you (and here is also to be understood husband, wife, child, and parent, if they are united with one another in the covenant of God), and if he refuses to listen to you and the church ". . . let him be to you as a Gentile and a tax collector" (Matthew 18:17).

This is indeed avoidance in spiritual as well as physical relationships. Those persons who are closest to the one banned must justly be the first to avoid him as already mentioned above, if they do not want to be defiled. This is powerfully prefigured in Deuteronomy 17:7; when a person had sinned so that he had to die "the hand of the witnesses shall be first against him to put him to death, and afterward the hand of all the people." When Israel committed sin with

---

* In some English versions, Matthew 18:8, 9 is here inserted.

the golden calf, according to the Word of the Lord the Levites had to slay in the camp, first, each man's brother, friend, and neighbor, and then the blessing was conferred upon them by Moses.

Therefore, it is the most necessary thing in Christianity to deny the very best for the sake of the Lord. The teachings of Jesus have the same emphasis of self-denial. There are still some unenlightened souls who are willing to help carry out the ban against someone where it requires no self-denial, but if it happens that they themselves, or their dearest friends, or husband, wife, or children should be denied, then, unfortunately, often natural love is much stronger than divine love, and this proves their ruin. There is no eluding this word of the Lord Jesus: "Whoever loves something more than me, he is not worthy of me."

[ON OUTWARD WORSHIP]

Son: You have now told me about various things, but I hear from many that it is not necessary to pay attention to these things, because believers are transformed into heavenly beings, and no longer need to trouble themselves with such things.

Father: Yes, I have myself seen enough of such men who speak, teach, and write like that. However, they are badly mistaken; they lack humble hearts which gladly submit to divine counsel and ordinances and learn to be faithful in humble tasks. When this is done they will be placed over high and great things. There is a time of humiliation and a time of exaltation. The Lord Jesus first appeared very humbly and lowly in this world in humble and willing submission to the will of His Father. The second time, however, He will appear in great power and glory as an exalted Christ.

All souls who desire to be with Him in His exaltedness must certainly first accept Him as a humbled Christ. They must confess Him before men in all of His commandments, and not be ashamed of them. In this way they will become humble in the humble commandments, and then finally they shall be exalted in due season. It will be impossible otherwise.

For this reason, the church of the Lord has always been lowly and despised in this world. It has always been considered as filth [by the unbelieving world]. For this reason those men err badly in their thinking who claim that it is not necessary for believers to be baptized with elementary water; likewise, they do not consider it necessary to drink the common wine of the communion to proclaim the death of Jesus, but rather say that they drink spiritual wine and are baptized with spiritual water, and other similar pretensions contrary to the clear testimony of the Holy Scriptures. Therefore, it is very good to look only to the express word of the Lord Jesus and to His own perfect example. If people would just follow after Him in the obedience of faith, taking reason captive in obedience to the Lord Jesus, they would not be led astray by the high-sounding talk of men.

[ON HUMAN TESTIMONY]

SON: I have also heard many who appeal to the saints, such as Tauler, Thomas a Kempis, and others, who have written such beautiful and gifted books but have not recorded anything about observing the outward teachings of Christ.

FATHER: Those persons who appeal to the testimonies of men reveal that they do not possess the divine testimony of Jesus. Therefore Saint John says: "If we receive the testimony of men, the testimony of God is greater; for this is the testimony of God that he has borne witness to his Son. He who believes in the Son of God has the testimony in himself. He who does not believe God, has made him a liar, because he has not believed in the testimony that God has borne to his Son" (1 John 5:9, 10). This testimony is necessary for salvation, and all of the saints have had it. It is unfortunately very dangerous to appeal to this testimony of men who have remained within the great Babel. In general, all those who appeal to such men are despite this not in agreement with them. Who, indeed, could be agreed with those who were still in monasteries and under the papal dogma? Perhaps they did not profess what they had actually come to recognize as the truth because of fear of men.

This appealing to holy men is just as blind as the entire world's appealing to Christ and His apostles when it is not one with the latters' lives and teaching. Therefore, those poor souls are indeed to be pitied who wish to build their faith upon such a poor foundation, which always fails when temptation comes. The Son of God taught this: "Every one then who hears these words of mine and does them will be . . . a wise man" (Matthew 7:24). Again, the Savior speaks: "Truly, truly, I say to you, he who hears my word and believes him who sent me, has eternal life; he does not come into judgment . . ."

(John 5:24). Again, ". . . whoever lives and believes in me shall never die" [John 11:26].

These are positive testimonies for him who believes. How wretched is it to appeal to testimonies of men and to look to men who are considered holy and wise, so that one is led to think or say: "Truly, if they taught in this way and believed according to the Scriptures, we shall believe it also!" The Apostle Paul speaks against it: "But even if we, or an angel from heaven, should preach to you a gospel contrary to that which we preached to you, let him be accursed" (Galatians 1:8). Behold, this is the only gospel which Moses and all the prophets emphasized that it might be heard, and which was revealed to us by Christ and His apostles. This gospel cannot be altered or violated by the holiness of angels, much less by that of men, or even the might or power of the entire world. They can neither add anything to it nor take anything away, without incurring the great displeasure of God. It stands firm like the mountain of God. It is a stone such as Christ speaks of: "And he who falls on this stone will be broken to pieces; but when it falls on anyone, it will crush him" (Matthew 21:44).

[ON THE REWARD FOR BELIEVERS]

Son: You have told me much about the teaching of Jesus Christ, and that it is necessary to walk according to it under the cross and in trials. What may a man expect if he denies himself and follows Christ, and endures the cross and suffering to the very end?

Father: Blessings and glories of such great dignity will be obtained through Christ that no human tongue can express it, nor can be described what God has prepared for those who love Him. Nevertheless, I will tell you as much as has been expressed in the Holy Scriptures by the Spirit of God. The Son of God himself testifies that whoever believes in Him may have eternal life (John 3:15). That is in itself a great pronouncement of eternal glory. This is not the kind of a life that kings and monarchs have in this world, which is scarcely a handsbreadth, and is full of infirmity, illness, fear, unrest, danger of death, and the like and at last is of no avail. Rather, it is a life of joy which is no longer subject to death and remains everlasting. For eternity there is no illness, pain, fear, want, discomfort, war, or disputes; neither weeping nor mourning will be heard.

In the same measure that life will be everlasting, so will joy be everlasting. God spoke this through the prophets: "Everlasting joy [shall be] upon their heads; they shall obtain joy and gladness, and sorrow and sighing shall flee away" (Isaiah 35:10). There will be "the river of the water of life, bright as crystal, flowing from the throne of God and of the Lamb . . .; on either side of the river, the tree of life," bearing the most delicious fruit (Revelation 22:1). In this life of joy, the Holy City of God will reveal itself (Revelation 21). The city and its streets will be of pure gold and precious stones, and the faithful will sing the joyous *Hallelujah* in the streets of the city (Tobit 13:22 [18]). They will wear crowns on their heads, and have palm branches of victory in their hands (Revelation 7). They will sing and make music, and rejoice with great joy. The Lamb will lead them to the spring of the water of life, and they will enjoy the fruits of immortality.

Yes, the joy will always be heightened when they behold the Lord Jesus in His great glory and majesty with His many thousand times a thousand saints and angels who surround His throne and sing *Hallelujah* with holy fervor and joy so that heaven and earth will resound with it. The creatures who have been made free will be led because of this to utter praise, honor, glory, and power from eternity to eternity before the strangled Lamb (Revelation 5:15 [13]). More than all this, the greatest delight will be to behold the Lord Jesus in His transfigured humanity. Indeed, they will wonder why so few people loved and followed after Jesus, who alone is all-powerful and glorious.

Yes, the believers will wonder why they were not more willing, while in this world, to sacrifice body and soul and all that they had out of love for this heavenly King and His holy teaching. They will realize that the Lord Jesus had left this glory to come to the valley of misery out of love for them—even died out of love for them so that they could obtain this great blessing. This will then move them to give more honor, praise, and gratitude in all eternity.

> Then what a life of jubilee,
> Will there in that period be,
> To the thousands whose happy home,
> Is before, and near to God's throne.
> With rays of glory surrounded,
> With the seraphic host joined

In the heavenly song, thrice holy
Are the Three unit'd in testimony.*

[ON PUNISHMENT OF UNBELIEVERS]

Son: If, then, the true and believing soul shall enjoy such great and, indeed, inexpressible blessedness, what will happen to the unbelievers who were not obedient to the commandments of the Lord Jesus, and did not love Him and His Kingdom but rather the world and its glories, and who died in sin?

Father: Just as the glories of the believers will be inexpressible, the torment of the condemned and unbelievers will be equally inexpressible. The Scriptures say: "Behold, he is coming with the clouds, and every eye will see him, every one who pierced him; and all tribes of the earth will wail on account of him" (Revelation 1:7). They will cry to the mountains and hills in sheer fear and terror: "Fall on us and hide us from the face of him who is seated on the throne, and from the wrath of the Lamb" (Revelation 6:16). That will no longer help them, for they will have to listen as Christ says: "Depart from me, you cursed, into the eternal fire prepared for the devil and his angels . . ." (Matthew 25 [:41]). "If any one worships the beast and its image . . . he shall be tormented with fire and brimstone in the presence of the holy angels and in the presence of the Lamb. And the smoke of their torment goes up for ever and ever; and they have no rest, day or night . . ." (Revelation 14:[9] 10, 11).

If anyone's name is not found in the Book of Life, he will be thrown into the lake of fire, where the worm does not die and the fire will not be quenched (Revelation 20:15; Mark 9:48; Isaiah 66:24). They will be an abomination to all flesh. In all of their torment, the pain will be increased the more when they realize how they frivolously forfeited through folly the great blessedness and glories which they now see in the children of God, when they still lived in the time of grace. They did not respect them then, but heedlessly spent the time in every sin. Then the righteous will stand with great gladness opposite those who had so persecuted them and rejected their work (their teaching and faith in Jesus Christ). Then the damned will see this and stand in dreadful awe of such blessedness, and will say to one another with penitence, and sigh with anguish of the spirit: "This is

---

* From the Kurtz translation.

the man we fools once laughed at . . . . We thought his life was madness . . . . How did he come to be reckoned among the sons of God, and why is his lot among the saints? Then we must have wandered from the true way . . . . What good did our arrogance do us? And what have wealth and ostentation done for us?" (Wisdom of Solomon 5:1 [4-8]).

They will ponder all of these things—how they spent their lives in sin, how they did not love God as the highest good, and lost through this folly all this great blessedness. Then they will experience torment, grief, and misery which no tongue can express, for they are banished from the presence of God and all the saints.

[ON UNIVERSAL RESTORATION]

Son: These things are most horrible to hear. Do tell me, are these torments and tortures to last for eternity, without end?

Father: According to the testimony of the Holy Scriptures, "the smoke of their torment goes up for ever and ever" (Revelation 14:11). However, that it should last for eternity is not supported by Holy Scripture. It is not necessary to talk much about it or speculate about it. The joyous blessedness is definitely forfeited by their folly. Even if at some time the torment should end after long eternities, they will never attain that which the believers have achieved in the time of grace through Jesus Christ if they obey Him. Many who have heard about universal restoration commit the great folly not to deny themselves completely but rather hope for the restoration. This hope will most certainly come to naught when they enter the torment, and can see no end to it. Their pitiful comfort will vanish like smoke.

Therefore, it is much better to practice this simple truth that one should try to become worthy in the time of grace to escape the wrath of God and the torments of hell, rather than deliberate how or when it would be possible to escape from it again. It is as if a thief were to console himself like this: "Oh, even if I am seized because of the theft, my punishment will have its end." Would not that be a miserable consolation! Therefore, that is a much better and more blessed gospel which teaches how to escape the wrath of God than the gospel which teaches that eternal punishment has an end. Even though this is true, it should not be preached as a gospel to the godless. Unfortunately, in this day, everything is completely distorted by the great power of imagination of those people who teach and write books about restoration.

[ON SPIRITUAL FOOD]

There are very few faithful stewards who were established by the Lord Jesus over His house who "give them their portion of food at the proper time" (Luke 12:42). "Give children milk, youths more nourishing food, and to the mature the most solid food. But there are so many unfaithful stewards who were not set over the servants of the house by the Lord himself, but run according to their own pleasures by human wisdom. They wish to be clever people, but they distort the plan and intent of the Lord. They give solid food to those to whom they should give milk. Of this, the Apostle Paul said at Corinth: "I fed you with milk, not solid food, for you were not ready for it . . .; you are still of the flesh" (1 Corinthians 3:1, 2).

The same is true in the spiritual as in the natural life. If milk were to be withheld from a young infant, and it were given instead a delicious roast, one would certainly find out that the child would soon die, even though the meat itself was very good and delicious. The same happens, unfortunately, also in these troubled times, when many souls have been awakened by grace to repentance, and are still young children in the faith. They should rightly be given the first principles of the Christian life—the proper milk-food, as Peter points out (1 Peter 2[:2]), that they should grow up as do the newborn babies. However, this pure milk is withdrawn from them by making them suspicious of it, and by presenting them with more solid food.

The consequences of this cannot be enough lamented, because they result in nothing but harm, death and ruin, distraction and division. When such a teacher and steward has presented solid food for a long time, he departs again, and the poor people do not know what it really was. It is true, they were long led by a beautiful sound, but it was an indistinct tone. Therefore, no one has been able to prepare himself properly for the strife against the devil and his following. Paul compares such people to a "noisy gong or a clanging cymbal" (1 Corinthians 13:1), because they do not have the teaching and love, through which the ordinances and commandments of God can be kept (John 14; 1 John 5:3).

[CONCLUSION: FATHERLY ADVICE]

Son: Dear father, I thank you again for your good instructions,

Because this journey is just about over, I would like to ask yet this question: I have well understood from you, and also believe, that the way to life is very narrow and straight, and the deception of the world is great, there being so many false spirits, false teachers, and false prophets. How should I conduct myself in these times so that I might obtain eternal salvation, and avoid being misled?

FATHER: I will give you good and sure counsel out of fatherly love. Bear this in mind all your life; never let it escape your heart, but remember it wherever you go and are—when you lie down and when you rise. Let this be your greatest concern that all of your sighs and desires be directed toward loving your God (who has created you) and toward loving Jesus Christ (who has redeemed you with His precious blood) with all your heart, all your soul, and all your mind above all things of the world, be it beauty or wealth, yes, whatever may come within your sight or your hearing.

Fear God in this love with a childlike heart, contemplate all of His commandments day and night, keep them with a pure heart, let them be your counselors, and pray unceasingly for the Holy Spirit, who will guide you in truth in all of the commandments of God. Let continually ring in your ears that which David says: "How can a young man keep his way pure? By guarding it according to thy word" (Psalm 119:9). Again, "The promises of the Lord are promises that are pure, silver refined in a furnace on the ground, purified seven times" (Psalm 12:7[6]). Further, "The law of the Lord is perfect, reviving the soul; the testimony of the Lord is sure, making wise the simple; the precepts of the Lord are right, rejoicing the heart; the commandment of the Lord is pure, enlightening the eyes . . . . More to be desired are they than gold, even much fine gold; sweeter also than honey and drippings of the honeycomb" (Psalm 19:8, 11 [7, 8, 10]).

Moreover, let continually resound in your mind the words of the Lord Jesus: "If a man loves me, he will keep my word . . . . He who does not love me does not keep my words" (John 14:23, 24). Again, "My sheep hear my voice, and I know them, and they follow me; and I give them eternal life" (John 10:27 [and 28]). Besides this always remember in your heart what the Lord Jesus says about His commandments when He speaks: "For I have not spoken on my own authority; the Father who sent me has himself given me commandment what to say and what to speak" (John 12:49, 50). Always keep the dear counsel of the Lord Jesus, which He gives to His own, when He says: "Beware of false prophets, who come to you in sheep's clothing but inwardly are ravenous wolves" (Matthew 7:15). Further: "Take heed, that no one lead you astray. For many will come in my name, saying, 'I am the Christ,' and they will lead many astray" (Matthew 24:4, 5).

Always bear your soul in your hands as your most precious treasure, and walk in holy fear at all times. Speak with David with a pure heart to God: "With regard to the works of men, by the word of thy lips I have avoided the ways of the violent" (Psalm 17:4). You may encounter such men and be in the company of those who seem to you much more holy than John, more zealous than Elijah, more miracle-working than Moses, and appearing more humble and spiritually minded than Christ himself or His apostles. If they do not walk in the teachings of Jesus the crucified Savior, as written in the New Testament, and they wish to lead you away from these simple commandments of the Lord Jesus, remember this and believe it in your heart—they are false apostles and deceitful workers. Close your eyes to their gospel, be wise as a serpent which stops its ears to the charmer, and call and cry to Jesus as a sheep to its shepherd.

SON: I must ask you yet something else. It seems to me somewhat harsh that I should consider those men false prophets who prove themselves with such sanctity and gift of working miracles, even if they do not walk in the ways of the Lord and are opposed to what is written outwardly in the [New] Testament.

FATHER: I should have thought that you would have well understood the divine plan after this long conversation. I will repeat it in accordance with the testimony of the Holy Scriptures, of both Old and New Testaments. When God revealed His Law to the people of Israel through Moses, it was a definite rule that whoever broke the Law of Moses must die (Numbers 15:35; Hebrews 10:28). But the person who did anything with a high hand reviled the Lord, and that person was cut off from among the people and his iniquity was upon him. So strict was the word of the Lord given through Moses!

Now, all those who added to or took away from the Law were false prophets. The true prophets all adhered to and observed the Law, as the servant Moses had spoken it. The false ones walked according to their hearts' desires but did say to the people, "Thus spoke the

Lord." But these were only lies. Now, notice well what kind of teaching, statutes, and laws were introduced by the Son of God himself, and were confirmed by "signs and wonders and various miracles and by gifts of the Holy Spirit distributed according to His own will" (Hebrews 2:4) by the Son of God, through whom the Father has spoken to us "in these last days" (Hebrews 1:1, 2)—by whom the Father "made the whole world"; who is that living "Word become flesh" (John 1[:14]); to whom the Father has given "all authority in heaven and on earth" (Matthew 28:18); which law is "far above all rule and authority and power and dominion . . . not only in this age but also in that which is to come" (Ephesians 1:21). It is the Son of God who "has gone into heaven and is at the right hand of God, with angels, authorities, and powers subject to him" (1 Peter 3:22).

Now, consider how much better the teaching of the Son of God must be kept, how much more strictly and unfalteringly, by all those who believe in His teachings, commandments, good counsel, and laws. From this you can easily determine how wicked, how arrogant, how blind, and how dark a soul must be to despise a single command of the Lord Jesus. How much more wicked must those teachers and prophets be who despise in their wisdom the wisdom of Jesus and wish to make a different path from that which Jesus ordained. They seek to mislead those souls who wish to follow Jesus in His commands in a simple way—some try it through eloquent speeches, disguised in sheep's clothing; others threaten with imprisonment and seek to prevent these souls from the good counsel of Jesus by threats and all kinds of persecution.

What do you think? Are they not the deceivers, false prophets, yes, thieves and murderers, who have always tried to climb over the wall, and will not enter by the door—which is Jesus himself (John 10 [:1, 2]). There is nothing more abominable and more sinful in the sight of God than when a mortal man does not believe His God in all His commands and prohibitions. You will not find another salvation in the Old and New Testaments outside of this, except only that the will of God has been the salvation of the souls, and will always remain so.

This is the way to God if a soul does that which is agreeable to the will of God. If he does not do it and opposes himself to his God with his will because of deprecating Him, thinking and speaking that certain things are not necessary for him although God has commanded them—then this soul is an enemy of God. Saint John says: "Any one who goes ahead and does not abide in the doctrine of Christ does not have God" (2 John, verse 9). Whoever remains in the teaching of Christ has both Father and Son. Therefore, I will advise you this, in conclusion, that you should look alone to Jesus your Redeemer and Savior (Hebrews 12:2). If you have learned from Him the teaching as it is outwardly commanded in the Testament, so that you will remain steadfast in it, and resolve yourself to sacrifice your life, your property, family, yes, all that you have in the whole world—rather than waver from His teaching—you must become used to taking His cross upon yourself daily with denial of your will. Otherwise, you cannot be a disciple of the Lord Jesus, much less an heir of His Kingdom (Luke 14:27).

Now, may the Lord Jesus bless your soul, and strengthen your faith, and let this simple instruction grow within you and bear fruit which will remain for life eternal. We will together praise and glorify our God forever. Amen.

The Sin-Expunging Jesus

(Der Sünden austilgende Jesus)*

A pard'ning Lord I am,
In love I will be found.
The Son of God and man,
To heal the sinful wound.
All is now gained,
My death has bought,
And pardon wrought
That you be spared.

Your sin I cast away,
It shall return no more;
Your debt I had to pay,
And suffered for it sore.

---

* The poem, probably written by Alexander Mack, is missing from the copy of the 1715 edition, although there is evidence that it was the last page of the original publication. The translation is that used by Henry Kurtz in 1860, with minor revisions.

My blood I gave,
My life I spent,
Through death I went
For you to save.

This have I done for you;
Be faithful then, and true;
Do not depart from me,
I shall be faithful too.
Then watch and pray,
And love me too,
Who first loved you
And am your stay.

THE FIRST BRETHREN HYMNAL

Also included in the Wittgenstein collection in Marburg is a tiny volume which is of great importance for Brethren history—the first Brethren hymnal. There is an additional copy from the collection on permanent loan to the library of the Reformed Synod of Wittgenstein. The hymnal is entitled *Spiritual Hymnal for All Loving Souls of Truth, Especially for the Church of the Lord* . . . [*Geistreiches Gesang-Buch/ Vor alle Liebhabende Seelen der Warheit/ sonderlich Vor die Gemeine Des Herrn* . . .] printed in Berleburg in 1720 by Christopher Konert.[15]

These are the reasons for attributing this virtually unknown hymnal to the Wittgenstein Brethren. The preface states that the hymnal was composed of songs from various hymnals used in the meetings of the Baptist-minded [*Taufgesinnte*], who had decided to compile their own hymnbook. It contains one hundred new hymns, most of them composed by "brethren" who had at that time been imprisoned for almost three years for the sake of their faith. This corresponds exactly with the Solingen Brethren, who, as we know, composed many hymns while imprisoned in Düsseldorf. (See page 250.) The hymnal stresses distinctive Brethren practices such as baptism by immersion and feet-washing, and Brethren concerns such as discipleship. Finally, it contains a hymn known to have been written by Alexander Mack in Germany, which was later used in America. This is given in English translation following.

The hymnal is evidently patterned after the like-named Halle hymnal, edited by John Anastasius Freylinghausen, which was widely used in

Geistreiches

Gesang-Buch/

Vor alle Liebhabende

Seelen der Warheit/

sonderlich

Vor die Gemeine

Des

HERRN

In sich fassend

Die Auserlesenste und nöthigste

Lieder/

Aus andern Gesang-Bü-
chern ausgezogen/

Nebst 100. neue Lieder / so zum ersten
mahl aufgesetzt worden / zum Trost und
Erquickung allen wahren Nachfolgern des
HErrn JEsu/ und in gegenwärtiger Form
ans Licht gegeben/

Zum

Lobe GOTTES.

BERLENBURG/
Gedruckt bey Christoph Konert/Anno 1720.

Title Page of the First Brethren Hymnal (1720)

Pietist circles.[16] A great majority of the non-Brethren selections of the 1720 hymnal appear in the earlier Halle hymnal, the first part of which was published in 1704. Other hymns appear in *Davidisches Psalter-Spiel der Kinder Zions,* first published in 1718 by the Inspirationists in Switzerland, and often republished. This 1718 Inspirationist hymnal became the standard hymnbook of all German sectarians in colonial America, and went through edition after edition on the Sauer press.[17]

This raises an important question. If this 1720 hymnal is the first Brethren hymnal, why did they not bring it with them to America? There is no known record of its being used by the Brethren in America. Instead, they used the hymnal of the rival Inspirationists! The answer is not known. A possible explanation is that the hymnal may have been ordered by the Schwarzenau Brethren who then left Wittgenstein in the late spring of 1720 before the hymnal was completed later the same year. At any rate, the hymnal provides an important document for understanding early Brethren belief and piety.

A translation of the preface of the hymnal follows, as well as rhymed English translations of four of its original Brethren hymns, including the Mack hymn. Unfortunately, the names of the authors of the other three hymns are not known.

PREFACE

May God grant much blessing and mercy.

Dear Friends and Brethren:

Several years ago, dissatisfaction was felt, in the meetings of the Baptist-minded, about the many different hymnals. For this reason, we have been led to select the most edifying hymns from all of them and compile them in one volume. One hundred new hymns were added, most of which were written by brethren who have been imprisoned now for almost three years for the sake of their witness to Jesus, in which imprisonment God's goodness has not been lacking. Rather, it has refreshed and strengthened the inward man, so that they have written these spiritual hymns for the comforting and strengthening of all those who are resolved to follow Jesus, the crucified Savior, in His saving words and commandments, and because of this must take upon themselves cross, shame, and various temptations.

Yes, I say it again, these hymns will be able to serve them to the awakening and joy of their hearts to look even more steadfastly to Jesus, the Author and Completer of the faith, to bear always more willingly the shame of Jesus with the people of God, and to rejoice in the imminent great happiness when we will hear the hymns of praise resound from all corners of the earth to the honor of the righteous (Isaiah 24:16). Yes, eventually, all creatures in heaven, on earth, and under the earth—yes, on the sea and all that is in it—will bring praise and gratitude to God and the Lamb. To this end may the almighty God also bless this little book for all who have turned their faces toward the heavenly Jerusalem (which is the mother of all true believers). May he grant all blessing and grace here in this world-wilderness to serve God in spite of this in spirit and in truth, and also to sing hymns to the Lord in spirit, to whom alone belongs honor from all creatures. To Him, the only true and living God and to Jesus, His most beloved Son, the crucified Savior, and also to the Holy Spirit, be praise, honor, glory, gratitude, fame, might, . . . from eternity to eternity. Amen. Hallelujah.[18]

Count Well the Cost
[by Alexander Mack, Sr.]

1

Christ Jesus says, "Count well the cost
When you lay the foundation."
Are you resolved, though all seem lost,
To risk your reputation,
Your self, your wealth, for Christ the Lord
As you now give your solemn word?

2

Into Christ's death you're buried now
Through baptism's joyous union.
No claim of self dare you allow
If you desire communion
With Christ's true church, His willing bride,
Which, through His Word, He has supplied.

3

When from the heart all sin you loathe,
Then you will be succeeding

Yourself with righteousness to clothe.
The struggle still proceeding,
Your righteousness can hold at bay
This world's false god, athwart your way.

4

Within the church's warm embrace
The child of God is molded,
God's Spirit lighting up his face
And by His grace enfolded.
His childlike steps trace out Christ's plan
And he becomes a godly man.

5

In Christian growth he is matured,
Of fruitful vines a token.
That this good growth may be assured,
Ofttimes to him is broken
The bread of fellowship replete
When Christ's redeemed together meet.

6

Within the church's sheltering fold
God is His truth revealing;
Through Christ, His Son, all men are told
To heed His warm appealing,
For all the truth through Him made known
Is sealed with blood that is His own.

7

His testimony is as true
As when the church received it
Long years ago, while it was new,
And with glad hearts believed it.
Through signs that dare not be denied,
The new has pushed the old aside.

8

By means of wonder and of sign
God brought the old to being.
As later years brought its decline
There was no need of seeing.
When Joshua had heard it read,
His faith required no sign, he said.

9

He who has faith in God's sure Word
Will not demand a token.
When Christ rebuked the evil horde,
Their unbelief plain spoken,
He showed a sign, at their request,
But they remained quite unimpressed.

10

Consider well what Abraham said
When the rich man suggested,
From that realm of the tortured dead,
That Lazarus be requested
To warn his brothers of hell's pain
While in this world they yet remain.

11

That boon by Abraham was denied.
From all that is deceiving
The heart must be made right inside
Ere there can be believing;
The Law and the prophetic Word
Project faith's light upon our Lord.

12

Against false teaching guard your heart.
Some practice at deceiving
And make it seem, by sinful art,
As if to Christ they're cleaving.

If from Christ's Word one does not teach,
His words are but deceptive speech.

13

Up, sons of men! The time is right
To ward off ills impending,
For Christ himself joins in the fight,
His righteous realm defending.
To do this, have the mind of Christ;
His Word at all times has sufficed.

—Translated by Ora W. Garber[19]

The Christian Pilgrim

1 (1)

Wouldst thou pursue the pilgrim's way
And find the rest that calms thee,
If thou wouldst see bright Canaan's day
The narrow way must thine be.

2 (3)

Thou must a hero ever be,
To prayers and vigils given,
And must to heaven make thy plea,
From sin completely riven.

3 (4)

The cost must heed with greatest care,
In pain and anguish building,
Lest thou be caught right unaware
In what was only gilding.

4 (6)

Thou art a pilgrim true and tried,
If self from pelf thou sever,

And see that mind and will have died
And are subdued forever.

5 (8)

The narrow way is fraught with pain
And shame thy soul assailing;
Wouldst thou have joy, from ease refrain,
Or grief will be prevailing.

6 (9)

He is a righteous pilgrim true
Whose soul on God is founded,
With love and patience kept in view,
And hate of self unbounded.

7 (15)

The lavish robe holds no appeal
Which men so highly cherish;
The sumptuous fare is not his meal;
On this his soul would perish.

8 (16)

A pilgrim thus denies himself
And counts the world as useless;
All worldly goods are held as pelf;
How can a pilgrim do less!

9 (14)

An earthly house he'll not adorn;
He knows it's not eternal.
A pilgrim looks for heaven's morn
And turns from things infernal.

10 (28)

When troubles thwart the pilgrim's path,
Love causes them to vanish;

The joy a sainted pilgrim hath
Helps all his trials to banish.

11 (33)

O pilgrim saint, bow down thy soul,
The narrow way ascending;
Thou wilt with joy perform thy role,
The crown on thee descending.

—Translated by Ralph W. Schlosser[20]

Love Feast Hymn

1 (1)

O ransomed saints, consider
The wondrous works of God;
May nought on earth bewilder
Our souls so prone to nod.
Behold our Savior slain;
His face bespeaks His anguish;
His soul for us did languish
That we the crown might gain.

2 (2)

In spirit let us ponder
Jehovah's acts of old;
How hearts were made to wonder
As He preserved His fold!
See how Jehovah brought
His people out with power,
And made the waves devour
The hosts that Israel fought.

3 (7)

As Egypt was confounded
Through God's triumphant might,
So sinners will be hounded
Who grope in Satan's might.

To save from death and hell
And us from pain deliver,
Our Christ became the giver
Of blood that sounds death's knell.

4 (8)

On Calvary's tree redemption
Was purchased with Christ's blood;
His mercy brought exemption
From sin's polluting flood.
O Jesus, with Thy might
Hast Thou destroyed death's power,
Hast toppled Satan's tower,
His pomp hast put to flight.

5 (10)

This night we come intending
Our minds to purify,
Our lips Thy praise attending,
Our hearts to sanctify.
Now meet we with accord
Our hearts to blend in singing,
Thy goodness ever praising
Here at Thy table, Lord.

6 (11)

O Jesus, we exalt Thee;
Thy blessed death we praise;
Thy rising e'er extolled be,
As hearts to Thee we raise.
In faith we break this bread,
In loving contemplation,
In deepest adoration,
And by Thy Spirit led.

7 (12)

Our minds we bring adoring
Thy matchless glorious name;

This night we come imploring
Our hearts be set aflame,
That we may grow in love
For Thee, our Lord, more dearly,
Obey Thy Word sincerely,
Directed from above.

8 (13)

Lord, grant us Thy protection
And keep us from all sin;
Lord, bring us to perfection,
Eternal joys to win.
Teach us to watch and pray;
From Satan's wiles protect us;
From earth's dark woes direct us
To heaven's blissful day.

9 (18)

This night Thy bread we've broken;
The cup we too have shared;
Thus Thou to us hast spoken,
For whom Thy soul has cared.
In faith to break this bread
Christ's children it will strengthen;
The cords of love will lengthen,
As in His paths we tread.

—Translated by Ralph W. Schlosser[21]

A Hymn of Feet-Washing

1

How pleasant is it and how good
That those who live as brothers should,
   In faith and love uniting,
Like servants wash each other's feet
When at the feast of love they meet,
   In fellowship delighting.

2

'Tis precious and of honored worth.
Our Lord himself, while here on earth,
   His deep love demonstrating,
In true humility of heart
Stooped down to play the servant's part,
   This practice consecrating.

3

To His disciples He decreed,
"Your sovereign Lord am I indeed,
   As you have well asserted.
This model, given in love, is right."
Thus spoke He on that selfsame night
   Iscariot deserted.

4

In your remembrances hold true
All that your Master did for you
   That you may do it later
In loving service day by day,
Nor choose to pull yourselves away
   As Judas did, the traitor.

5

Then let us give the clearest thought
In this our time, as servants ought,
   Unto this new ablution
So that we too in it may share
In humble love as we prepare
   For certain persecution.

6

Likewise then in true unity
Love one another fervently,
   In humble consecration.

Oh, that no Judas may be there
In this most sacred rite to share
　　And thus incur damnation.

7

He who engages in this rite
Must note how Christ did it that night
　　In deep humiliation,
And also see that being whole
Requires the cleansing of the soul
　　Through Christ's outpoured salvation.

8

Who spurns the washing of his feet
Thus spurns a fellowship replete,
　　No vital touch sustaining.
His life in Jesus cannot start;
His selfish soul must stand apart,
　　A withered vine remaining.

9

Within Thy vineyard, Lord, we pray,
Make us green, fruitful vines today,
　　To each his part assigning.
Fill us with love and peace this hour;
Endow us with Thy Spirit's power,
　　Our hearts to Thee inclining.

10

In order that we may proclaim
Thy suffering love, Thy death, Thy Name,
　　And cause the world to hear it
And also thereby break the bread,
May we in fellowship be led
　　By Thy most gracious Spirit.

11

And now, Lord Jesus, finally
May Thy good Spirit outpoured be,
    Thy grace and might displaying;
And thus shall we in this hour start
To live like Thee, with the whole heart
    Thy holy love obeying.

—Translated by Ora W. Garber[22]

This simple testimony of truth is therefore laid again at the feet of His grace, and commended to the mighty protection of the good God, who alone is wise. May the kind reader be granted a God-pleasing, truth-loving spiritual state in which occurs the most divine, useful and blessed spirit of examination, and which strives to direct the flock of Christ in all truth. Blessed is the person who does not resist Him, who will remember everything which Jesus, the eternal truth, himself spoke and taught.

Now to the same innocent Lamb of God who has taken away the sins of the world, be honor, praise, and adoration in the fellowship of the first-born in heaven and on earth, in the communion of the Father, and of the Holy Spirit. Amen.

—Alexander Mack, Jr.[23]

Notes

INTRODUCTION

1. Georg W. F. Hegel, cited in Egon Friedell, *A Cultural History of the Modern Age*, translated by Charles F. Atkinson (New York: Alfred Knopf, 1931), II, 14.
2. Emil Ermatinger, *Deutsche Kultur im Zeitalter der Aufklärung* (Potsdam: Akademische Verlagsgesellschaft Athenaion, 1935), p. 127.
3. *Ibid.*, pp. 125, 126.
4. Friedell, *op. cit.*, p. 117.
5. Ermatinger, *op. cit.*, p. 65.
6. For an excellent discussion of the military history, see John B. Wolf, *The Emergence of the Great Powers (1685-1715)*, one of the volumes in the Rise of Modern Europe series edited by William L. Langer (New York: Harpers, 1951), pp. 15-96.
7. Ermatinger, *op. cit.*, p. 30.
8. Friedell, *op. cit.*, p. 50.
9. Veit Valentin, *The German People: Their History and Civilization from the Holy Roman Empire to the Third Reich*, translated by Olga Marx (New York: Alfred Knopf, 1946), p. 217.
10. Ermatinger, *op. cit.*, p. 25.
11. Wolf, *op. cit.*, p. 286.
12. J. Jüngst-Stettin, *Pietisten* (Tübingen: J. C. B. Mohr, 1906), p. 4.
13. Karl von Hase, cited in Friedell, *op. cit.*, p. 16.
14. Jüngst-Stettin, *op. cit.*, p. 5.
15. Heinrich Jung-Stilling, *Theobald, oder die Schwärmer: Eine wahre Geschichte* (Stuttgart: J. Scheible, 1837), p. 24.
16. Heinz Renkewitz, *Hochmann von Hochenau (1670-1721): Quellenstudien zur Geschichte des Pietismus. Berichte des theologischen Seminars der Brüdergemeine in Herrnhut, No. XII, 1934* (Breslau: Maruschke und Berendt, 1935), p. 224.
17. Ermatinger, *op. cit.*, p. 67ff.
18. For the life of Untereyk, see Max Goebel, *Geschichte des christlichen Lebens in der rheinisch-westphälischen evangelischen Kirche* (Coblenz. Karl Bädeker, 1849-1860), II, 300-312; Albrecht Ritschl, *Geschichte des Pietismus in der reformirten Kirche* (Bonn/Rhine: Adolph Marcus, 1880), I, 371-377; James I. Good, *History of the Reformed Church of Germany, 1620-1890* (Reading, Pa.: Daniel Miller, 1894), pp. 323-332.

For Lampe, see Goebel, *op. cit.,* II, 398-435; Ritschl, *op. cit.,* I, 427-454; Good, *op. cit.,* 374-394.

19. The standard biography of Spener is still Paul Grünberg, *Philipp Jakob Spener* (Göttingen: 1893-1906), three volumes; see also Kurt Aland, *Spener-Studien,* No. 28 in the series, Arbeiten zur Kirchengeschichte (Berlin: Walter de Gruyter, 1943); Goebel, *op. cit.,* II, 537-591; and Ritschl, *Geschichte des Pietismus in der lutherischen Kirche des 17. und 18. Jahrhunderts* (Bonn/Rhine: Adolph Marcus, 1884-1886), II, 97-225 (continuing volumes of the first cited).

20. For the life of Francke, see the writing of Gustav Kramer, *August Hermann Francke. Ein Lebensbild* (Halle: 1880-1882); also Ritschl, *op. cit.,* II, 249-294; and Erich Beyreuther, *August Hermann Francke (1663-1727): Zeuge des lebendigen Gottes* (Marburg/Lahn: Francke Buchhandlung, 1956).

21. Erich Seeberg has written the standard life—*Gottfried Arnold. Die Wissenschaft und Mystik seiner Zeit* (Meerane: E. R. Herzog, 1923); see also Goebel, *op. cit.,* II, 698-735, and Ritschl, *op. cit.,* II, 294-322.

22. Goebel, *op. cit.,* II, 819.

23. The standard biography is Renkewitz, *op. cit.;* see also Goebel, *op. cit.,* II, 809-855; Ritschl, *op. cit.,* II, 339-340; Martin G. Brumbaugh, *A History of the German Baptist Brethren in Europe and America,* second edition (Elgin, Illinois: Brethren Publishing House, 1907), pp. 16-28.

I: SEPARATION

1. Alexander Mack, Jr., "Vorrede," . . . *Rechten u. Ordnungen des Hauses Gottes . . .* (Baltimore: Samuel Saur, 1799), p. [7]. Mack's description was taken partly from papers which had belonged to his father and to Peter Becker, and partly from what he had heard from his parents and other early Brethren.

2. Almost all of the documents given here in translation concerning Pietist activity in the Palatinate are found in the folder, "Acta über den Pietismus in der Pfalz 1703-1709," Pfalz Generalia 77: 4330, Badisches Generallandesarchiv, Karlsruhe. Documents will be identified by their page numbers, with the archive cited as BGLA Karlsruhe. The documents are drafts, unless otherwise identified. For a written account using these materials, see Renkewitz, *op. cit.,* pp. 218-236.

3. BGLA Karlsruhe, pp. 3-7.

4. BGLA Karlsruhe, p. 11.

5. For a sketch of Mack's life, see Hermann Brunn, "Alexander Mack,

the Founder, 1679-1735," in Lawrence W. Shultz, *Schwarzenau, Yesterday and Today* (Winona Lake, Indiana: Light and Life Press, 1954), pp. 37-43.

6. BGLA Karlsruhe, p. 15, copy.

7. BGLA Karlsruhe, pp. 21, 22, original.

8. BGLA Karlsruhe, pp. 24, 25.

9. Städtisches Archiv, Mannheim, Ratsprotokollbuch 1706-1707, pp. 126-130, 132.

10. BGLA Karlsruhe, pp. 26, 27.

11. BGLA Karlsruhe, pp. 31, 32, original.

12. BGLA Karlsruhe, p. 36.

13. Gemeindeamt, Schriesheim, Wehrbuch 1676-1707, pp. 285, 286, 298; Grundbuch 1707-1714, pp. 30, 66. For information on Mack and his mill, see Hermann Brunn, *Schriesheimer Mühlen in Vergangenheit und Gegenwart: Ein Beitrag zur Ortsgeschichte* (Mannheim: Wilhelm Burger, 1947), pp. 108-123.

14. Goebel, *op. cit.,* II, 819.

15. BGLA Karlsruhe, pp. 56-58, original.

16. BGLA Karlsruhe, p. 59, copy.

17. BGLA Karlsruhe, p. 60.

18. BGLA Karlsruhe, pp. 61, 62, copy.

19. BGLA Karlsruhe, p. 63, original.

20. BGLA Karlsruhe, p. 66.

21. BGLA Karlsruhe, p. 67, original.

22. BGLA Karlsruhe, p. 67 verso, original.

23. BGLA Karlsruhe, p. 68, original.

24. BGLA Karlsruhe, pp. 69-80, minutes.

25. BGLA Karlsruhe, pp. 81-91, minutes.

26. BGLA Karlsruhe, p. 95.

27. BGLA Karlsruhe, p. 96.

28. BGLA Karlsruhe, p. 97.

29. BGLA Karlsruhe, p. 97 verso.

30. Städtisches Archiv, Heidelberg, Ratsprotokolle 1709, pp. 157, 158.

31. On the Eckerlin family, see the *Chronicon Ephratense,* by Lamech [pseud.] and Agrippa [John Peter Müller], translated by J. Max Hark (Lancaster, Pa.: S. H. Zahm, 1889), pp. 224-234; Brumbaugh, *op. cit.,* pp. 465-469; Julius F. Sachse, *The German Sectarians of Pennsylvania 1708-1742, 1742-1800* (Philadelphia, Pa.: P. C. Stockhausen, 1899-1900), II, 331-355.

32. Archiv de la Ville, Strassburg, No. 99/33/a, Enquête contre les

pasteurs piétistes à Barr et à Goxwiller, etc., minutes. The archive will hereafter be cited as AV Strassburg.

33. For information on the Petersens, see Goebel, *op. cit.*, III, 74-77; Ritschl, *op. cit.*, II, 225-249. On Gross, see Goebel, *op. cit.*, III, 104ff.; Ritschl, *op. cit.*, II, 364, III, 307, 367.

34. Printed in [Zentgraf], *Desz Evangelischen Kirchen-Convents in Straszburg Abgenöthigter Bericht* . . . (Strassburg: D. Lerse, 1706), pp. 66, 67. This book is a polemic written against a publication defending the Pietists who were suppressed by the Strassburg authorities. It is valuable for its publication of a great number of documents, primarily intercepted Pietist correspondence.

35. AV Strassburg, No. 78, Acta Pietistica III/6, Examen Rödereri, minutes.

36. AV Strassburg, No. 78, Acta Pietistica III/7, Examen Dr. M. Ruopp, minutes.

37. AV Strassburg, No. 99/33/b, Executionsbericht, copy.

38. AV Strassburg, AA 2573, No. 6/23, Ordre d'expulsion des piétistes transmis par M. de Chamilladt an preteur royal, (French) original.

39. Staatsarchiv Basel-Land, Liestal, Kirchenakten E 9 Frenkendorf, Das Touff Buch und Infürung der Eeluten zü Munzach . . . 1542 Jor, [no pagination].

40. Städtisches Archiv, Heidelberg, Ratsprotokolle 1702, p. 140 verso.

41. Städtisches Archiv, Heidelberg, Ratsprotokolle 1703, p. 7 verso.

42. For a thorough description of the activity of the Bonis and others in the Basel area, see Eduard Thurneysen, "Die Basler Separatisten im ersten Viertel des achtzehnten Jahrhunderts," [*Basler*] *Jahrbuch,* edited by A. Burckhardt and others, 1895: pp. 30-78; 1896: pp. 54-106.

43. Staatsarchiv, Basel-Stadt, Criminalia I B/b, Wiedertäufer Literatur B, original. This folder is not paginated. Documents from it will be cited hereafter Wiedertäufer; the archive, StA Basel-Stadt.

44. StA Basel-Stadt, Wiedertäufer, original.

45. StA Basel-Stadt, Kleiner Raths-Protokolle No. 78, p. 208.

46. StA Basel-Stadt, Wiedertäufer, minutes.

47. StA Basel-Stadt, Kleiner Raths-Protokolle No. 78, pp. 232 verso to 235 verso.

48. StA Basel-Stadt, Wiedertäufer, original.

49. StA Basel-Stadt, Kleiner Raths-Protokolle No. 78, p. 249.

50. StA Basel-Stadt, Wiedertäufer, original.

51. StA Basel-Stadt, Wiedertäufer, original.

52. StA Basel-Stadt, Wiedertäufer, minutes.

53. StA Basel-Stadt, Kleiner Raths-Protokolle No. 78, pp. 279 verso to 280.

II: FORMATION

1. Alexander Mack, Jr., *op. cit.,* p. [7].

2. For literature on Wittgenstein see Friedrich Goebel, *Historische Fragmente aus dem Leben der regierenden Grafen und Fürsten zu Sayn-Wittgenstein-Hohenstein* (Siegen: Vorländer's Buchdruckerei, 1858); Max Goebel, *op. cit.,* II, 736-855; Karl Hartnack, "Schwarzenau," *Wittgenstein: Blätter des Wittgensteiner Heimatvereins,* edited by Wilhelm Hartnack and Fritz Vitt, XLIV (1956), Vol. 20, No. 1/2, 83-93; L. Hinsberg, *Streifzüge durch Berleburgs Vergangenheit* (Berleburg: 1915); Renkewitz, *op. cit.,* pp. 263-273; and Günther Wrede, *Territorialgeschichte der Grafschaft Wittgenstein,* with atlas (Marburg: N. G. Elwert, 1927). A recent book in English is Lawrence W. Shultz, *Schwarzenau: Yesterday and Today* (Winona Lake, Indiana: Light and Life Press, 1954).

3. Johann Christian Edelmann, *Selbstbiographie,* edited by C. R. Wilhelm Klose (Berlin: Karl Wieganat, 1849), p. 228.

4. Wilhelm Weck, compiler, Geistliche Liebes-Brocken, von dem liebvollen Jünger und Streiter Jesu Christi Ernst Christoph Hochmann von Hogenau [*sic*], 1771, first part, twenty-fourth letter, pp. 149-157. This is a handwritten, bound volume containing a biography of Hochmann and a collection of his letters. It is now in the possession of Herr Fritz Behmenburg, Duisburg-Meidrich. The letter was published by Pastor Friedrich Augé in his article, "Acht Briefe Ernst Christoph Hochmanns von Hochenau," *Monatshefte für rheinische Kirchengeschichte,* edited by W. Rothscheid, XIX (1925), No. 7/10, 133-154. The above translation combines both versions, which vary slightly. The volume will hereafter be cited as Weck, *Liebes-Brocken.*

5. Thüringisches Landeshauptarchiv, Weimar, Landesarchiv Greiz, C 198, Vb 2/2, pp. 5-8, copy. The archive will hereafter be cited as TLHA Weimar; the folder, Greiz.

6. Alexander Mack, Jr., *op. cit.,* pp. [7-10].

7. *Chronicon Ephratense,* pp. 1, 2; as in other citations from the *Chronicon,* this is Dr. Hark's translation, with some modifications.

8. TLHA Weimar, Greiz, pp. 1-3, copy.

9. TLHA Weimar, Greiz, p. 4, copy.

10. For information on Gichtel, see Goebel, *op. cit.,* II, 233ff., III, 80ff.; Ritschl, *op. cit.,* II, 229ff.

11. Johann Georg Gichtel, *Sämmtliche Werke, oder: Theosophia Practica* . . . , third improved edition (Berlin: Arnold Weber, 1768), V, 3592, 3593.

12. *Ibid.,* I, 572, 573.

13. *Ibid.,* V, 3437.

14. *Ibid.,* VI, 1720, 1721.

15. For the Callenberg sisters, see Goebel, *op. cit.,* II, 754ff., 787ff.; III, 202-228; and Ritschl, *op. cit.,* I, 418, 425. The main source is the handwritten autobiography of the later husband of Lady Clara, Das Leben des Herrn Charles Hector Marquis St. George de Marsay, which also contains a biography of her. One bound copy is in the possession of Dr. J. F. Gerhard Goeters, Bonn/Rhine; another copy is in the Archiv der Evangelischen Kirche im Rheinland. This will be cited as Marsay, Leben.

16. Marsay, Leben, p. 92.

17. Marsay, Leben, p. 106.

18. Marsay, Leben, p. 122.

19. Marsay, Leben, p. 124.

20. See Renkewitz, *op. cit.,* pp. 270-273; and Hartnack, *op. cit.,* pp. 86, 87.

21. Printed in *Abgenöthigte Abwendung irriger Concepte über die in der Reichs-Grafschafft Wittgenstein . . . vornehmlich zu Schwarzenau lebender . . . frommer und guter Christen . . .* (n.p.: 1711), pp. 20, 21. This is the defense published by the four Wittgenstein countesses against Count Charles Louis's attack.

22. Fürstlich Sayn-Wittgenstein-Hohensteinisches Archiv, Laasphe/Lahn, K 291, pp. 1-4, original. This archive will hereafter be cited as FWA Laasphe. A copy of this letter is found in the Fürstlich zu Solms-Braunfelsisches Archiv, Braunfels, Kirchensachen 61/1, pp. 1-6; this archive and folder will be cited hereafter as FSBA Braunfels. A second copy is in the Staatsarchiv, Münster, Mscr. VII/6607, pp. 54-57 verso. This archive and folder will hereafter be cited as StA Münster.

23. FSBA Braunfels, pp. 10-14, copy. A second copy is in the StA Münster, pp. 63-68.

24. FSBA Braunfels, p. 15, copy.

25. FWA Laasphe, K 291, p. 10, copy. Another copy is in the FSBA Braunfels, pp. 16, 17; a third copy is in the StA Münster, pp. 83 verso-84.

26. FSBA Braunfels, pp. 18-26, copy. A second copy is located in the StA Münster, pp. 176-179.

27. FWA Laasphe, K 290, p. 6, original. A copy is in the FWA Laasphe, K 290, p. 2.

28. FWA Laasphe, K 290, pp. 7-9, copy.

29. FWA Laasphe, K 291, p. 116, original.

30. FWA Laasphe, C/2, copy; no pagination.

31. The standard treatment of the Inspirationists in Germany is by Max Goebel, "Geschichte der wahren Inspirationsgemeinden von 1688-1850," in *Zeitschrift für historische Theologie,* edited by J. Niedner, 1854: 267-322, 377-438; 1855: 94-160, 327-425; and 1857: 131-151. He also devoted a section of his book (*op. cit.,* III, 126-165) to them. See also Renkewitz, *op. cit.,* pp. 280, 281, 289-294.

32. *J. J. J. XVI. Sammlung. Das ist: der XVI. Auszug aus denen Jahr-Büchern der wahren Inspirations Gemeinschaften . . . ausgesprochen im Jahr 1727* (n.p.: 1772), p. 242. This rare volume is in the Universitäts-Bibliothek, Bonn/Rhine; the library will hereafter be cited as UBibl Bonn.

33. *Historische Umstände zur Prüfung des Geistes der Inspirierten* (n.p.: 1715), p. 13. This book is in the Zentralbibliothek, Zürich.

34. Johann Adam Gruber, *J. J. J. Kurtze Anmerckungen und einfältiges Bedencken über Herr. Doctor Kaysers Zweyte Beylage zu seinen geistl. Weg-weiser . . .* (n.p.: 1748), pp. 56, 57; in the UBibl Bonn. Gruber wrote this from America, where he had lived in Germantown since 1726.

35. Ursula Meyer, Conlectanea Mystica, a handwritten volume, once in the UBibl Bonn, but destroyed in the last war. This citation is taken from Renkewitz, *op. cit.,* p. 293, footnote 110.

III: EXPANSION

1. Alexander Mack, Jr., *op. cit.,* p. [10].

2. FYBA Büdingen, *Privilegia und Freyheiten/ Der Hoch-gebohrne Graf und Herr Ernst Casimir/ Graf zu Ysenburg und Büdingen/etc. . . .* (Offenbach/Main: Bonaventura de Launoy, 1712). This edict was republished in Christian F. Meyer, *Geschichte der Stadt und Pfarrei Büdingen* (Büdingen: Ernst Eberling, 1868), p. 145ff.

3. On conditions in Ysenburg-Büdingen, see Renkewitz, *op. cit.,* pp. 274-282; and Meyer, *op. cit.*

4. Fürstlich Ysenburg- und Büdingisches Archiv, Büdingen, Protokolle und Diaria 17, Extra Judicial Protokoll. The archive will hereafter be cited as FYBA Büdingen.

5. FYBA Büdingen, Kulturwesen 27/211, draft [no pagination]; Kulturwesen is hereafter abbreviated as K.

6. FYBA Büdingen, K 27/211, original.

7. FYBA Büdingen, K 27/211, copy.

8. FYBA Büdingen, K 27/212/3, original. This letter is the only known letter in existence signed by Alexander Mack; it is given in translation

and photostatic reproduction in Floyd E. Mallott, *Studies in Brethren History* (Elgin, Illinois: Brethren Publishing House, 1954), pp. 296-301, as well as in this volume. The section K 27/212/3 is entirely devoted to the Brethren; it is titled: Widertaufferey 1711, 1712, 1714; in specie die Neue Wiedertauffer betr[effend].

9. FYBA Büdingen, K 27/212/3, original.
10. FYBA Büdingen, K 27/212/3, draft.
11. FYBA Büdingen, K 27/212/3, draft.
12. FYBA Büdingen, K 27/212/3, original.
13. FYBA Büdingen, K 27/211, draft.
14. FYBA Büdingen, K 27/212/3, original.
15. FYBA Büdingen, K 27/212/3, draft.
16. FYBA Büdingen, K 27/212/3, draft.
17. FYBA Büdingen, K 27/212/3, original.
18. FYBA Büdingen, K 27/212/3, draft.
19. FYBA Büdingen, K 27/212/3, copy.
20. FYBA Büdingen, K 27/212/3, original.
21. FYBA Büdingen, K 27/212/3, draft.
22. FYBA Büdingen, K 27/212/3, original.
23. FYBA Büdingen, K 27/212/3, draft.
24. FYBA Büdingen, K 27/212/3, copy.
25. For information on Neumann, see Goebel, *op. cit.,* III, 132; Eduard E. Koch, *Geschichte des Kirchenlieds und Kirchengesangs der christlichen, insbesondere der deutschen evangelischen Kirche,* third edition (Stuttgart: Christian Belser, 1866-1877), V, 336ff.; VIII, 649; Renkewitz, *op. cit.,* p. 276ff.; and Theodore Wotschke, "Gottfried Neumann . . .," *Monatshefte für rheinische Kirchengeschichte,* XXVI (1932), 48-57, where three letters from Neumann to August Hermann Francke are published.
26. Archiv der Franckeschen Stiftungen, Universitäts- und Landesbibliothek, Halle/Saale, HSS A 113, p. 4. Published in Wotschke, *op. cit.,* pp. 54, 55.
27. Gottfried Neumann, ". . . Historische Erzehlung . . .," *Unterschiedliche Erfahrungs-volle Zeugnisze . . . von der . . . Inspirations-Sache . . .* (Himbach: 1715), pp. 50, 51; in the Zentralbibliothek, Zürich.
28. *Ibid.,* pp. 53, 54.
29. FYBA Büdingen, K 27/212/3, original.
30. FYBA Büdingen, K 27/212/1, original.
31. FYBA Büdingen, K 27/212/3, original.
32. FYBA Büdingen, K 27/212/3, draft.

33. FYBA Büdingen, K 27/212/1, original.

34. FYBA Büdingen, K 27/212/1, draft.

35. FYBA Büdingen, K 27/211, draft. There is another draft in K 27/212/3.

36. FYBA Büdingen Protokolle und Diaria 18.

37. On Krefeld, see Gottfried Buschbell, *Geschichte der Stadt Krefeld*, edited by Karl Heinzelmann (Krefeld: 1953), two volumes; Goebel, *op. cit.*, II, 294ff.; III, 71ff.; Friedrich Nieper, *Die ersten deutschen Auswanderer von Krefeld nach Pennsylvanien: Ein Bild aus der religiösen Ideengeschichte des 17. und 18. Jahrhunderts* (Neukirchen (Moers): Erziehungsverein, 1940), extremely important for the history of the Brethren in this area; Renkewitz, *op. cit.*, pp. 282-285. On the Berg area, see Goebel, *op. cit.*, II, 49ff.; III, 2ff.; W. H. Alfred Hengstenberg, *Geschichte der reformierten oder gröszern evangelischen Gemeinde zu Solingen und ihre Besitzungen* . . . (Solingen: 1847), pp. 107, 108; Renkewitz, *op. cit.*, p. 194ff.

38. [John Lobach], Ein Neues Merckmahl der Göttlichen Liebes-Wunder dieser Zeit . . . von J. L., pp. 1-73 [translation greatly shortened]. This handwritten volume is in the possession of Dr. J. F. Gerhard Goeters, Bonn/Rhine. It was copied and compiled by Wilhelm Weck. This volume, with the additional writings appended to it, will be cited hereafter as Lobach, Merckmahl.

39. Lobach, Merckmahl, pp. 74-78.

40. Archiv der Evangelischen Kirche im Rheinland, Düsseldorf, A I Ic 11, Einige erbauliche Briefe von Johann Lobach in Creyfeld, Nachtrag pp. 53-57, copy. This folder will hereafter be cited as Lobach, Briefe, and the archive, AEvKR Düsseldorf.

41. Evangelisches Pfarramt, Solingen-Wald, Protokollbuch der Reformierten Gemeinde 1701-1734, pp. 235, 235 verso.

42. Evangelisches Pfarramt, Solingen-Wald, Protokollbuch der Reformierten Gemeinde 1701-1734, pp. 238, 238 verso.

43. Lobach, Merckmahl, pp. 78-81.

44. AEvKR Düsseldorf, A I/ Ia 3, Acta Syn. Gen. 1687-1731, XXXII, paragraph 44. This was published in Nieper, *op. cit.*, p. 215.

45. For Brethren-Mennonite relationships in this area, see the sources listed in footnote 37 and the following: Dirk Cattepoel, "Das religiöse Leben in der Krefelder Mennonitengemeinde des 17. und 18. Jahrhunderts," *Beiträge zur Geschichte rheinischer Mennoniten*, Schriftenreihe des Mennonitischen Geschichtsvereins, No. 2 (Weierhof (Pfalz): 1939), pp. 5-28; and the articles—Christian Neff, "Dompelaars"; Karl Rembert, "Krefeld"; and O. Schowalter, "Goyen, Gossen,"

all found in the *Mennonitisches Lexikon,* edited by Christian Hege and Christian Neff (Frankfurt/Main and Weierhof (Pfalz): 1913ff.).

46. [Jan Crous], "Eine Mennonitische Taufpredigt aus dem Jahre 1716," *Die Heimat* [Krefeld], IV (1924), 197, 198. A microfilm of the Dutch original is in the Mennonitische Forschungstelle, Göttingen.

47. Weck, Liebes-Brocken, pp. 92-103.

48. Evangelisches Pfarramt, Duisburg, Consistorialakten 1689-1721.

49. AEvKR Düsseldorf, A I/IIIa 3, Acta Syn. Cliv. 1709-1785, CIV, paragraph 74; published in Nieper, *op. cit.,* p. 216.

50. Staatsarchiv, Schloss Brühl, Mennonitisches Gemeindebuch. A copy is in the Standesamt, Krefeld.

51. Städtisches Archiv, Krefeld, copy. This archive will hereafter be cited as StdA Krefeld.

52. AEvKR Düsseldorf, A I/Ia 3, Acta Syn. Gen., Conv. Ext. 1687-1731, paragraph 14; published in Nieper, *op. cit.,* p. 217.

53. Bürger Bibliothek, Bern, Mss. Hist. Helv. III/272b, copy. For information on Tscheer, see Paul Wernle, *Der schweizerische Protestantismus im XVIII. Jahrhundert* (Tübingen: J. C. B. Mohr, 1923-1925), I, 125, 129, 178. Expelled from Bern as a follower of the Pietist Samuel König, Tscheer became the editor of Jacob Boehme's writings.

54. Staatsarchiv, Düsseldorf, Reg. Moers Generalia, I/7, p. 59 verso, original; the poem was published in the article by Neff, *op. cit.,* I, 459.

IV: SUPPRESSION

1. Alexander Mack, Jr., *op. cit.,* pp. [10, 11].

2. For a detailed description of the Liebe imprisonment, see Ernst Müller, *Geschichte der Bernischen Täufer* (Frauenfeld: J. Huber, 1895), pp. 226-232; and an article by Christian Neff, "Christian Liebe," in the *Mennonitisches Lexikon,* II, 649. A contemporary description is that of Nicolas S. de Treytorrens, *Lettre Missiue: Ecritte au Chef de la Chambre de Religion dans la Ville de Berne en Suisse, par une Personne du Pays* (n.p.: 1717), especially the forty-seven-page third section. This rare book is found in the Bürger Bibliothek, Bern.

3. Staatsarchiv des Kantons Bern, Raths-Manual No. 61, pp. 61, 62. This archive will hereafter be cited as StAK Bern.

4. StAK Bern, Geheim-Manual, No. 1b, pp. 272-275.

5. StAK Bern, Raths-Manual, No. 63, pp. 147, 148. On Wattenwyl, see Wernle, *op. cit.,* I, 194ff.

6. Algemeen Rijksarchief, the Hague, Requesten 7557, (Dutch) original. This archive will hereafter be cited as ARA, the Hague.

7. Verenigde Doopsgezinde Gemeente Archief, Amsterdam, AA 1780, (Dutch) copy. This archive will hereafter be cited as VDGA Amsterdam.
8. ARA the Hague, Missives, original.
9. VDGA Amsterdam, AA 1376, (Dutch) copy.
10. StAK Bern, Raths-Manual, No. 66, p. 229.
11. StAK Bern, Raths-Manual, No. 66, p. 280.
12. VDGA Amsterdam, AA 1378, copy.
13. VDGA Amsterdam, AA 1377, original; most probably written by Liebe. The letter was published in Dutch translation in the article by S. Cramer, "Brief van een Doopsgezinden galeislaaf," *Doopsgezinde Bijdragen*, edited by S. Cramer, XLVIII (1908), 116-130.
14. VDGA Amsterdam, AA 1381, (Dutch) copy.
15. VDGA Amsterdam, AA 1379, copy.
16. StAK Bern, Raths-Manual, No. 66, pp. 406, 407.
17. VDGA Amsterdam, AA 1382, (French) copy.
18. VDGA Amsterdam, AA 1384, original.
19. VDGA Amsterdam, AA 1385, original.
20. Goebel, *op. cit.*, III, 239-263; [Wilhelm Grahe], "Egt Verhaal van de Gevangeneeming, Gevangenis en Wederloslating van zeven Persoonen, namelijk Wm. Knepper, Jacob Grahe, Joh. Lobach, G. L. Stetius, Joh. Henckels, Wm. Grahe, en Joh. Carl," *Doopsgezinde Bijdragen*, edited by D. Harting and P. Cool, I (1861), 51ff.; and [Wilhelm Grahe], "Aufrichtige Nachricht von denen um der Wahrheit, um Christi willen in Verhaft gezogenen Sieben Persohnen," *Die Heimat* [Krefeld], 1877, 188ff. (incomplete).
21. Wilhelm Grahe, Aufrichtige Nachricht von denen um der Wahrheit, und Christi willen in Verhaft genohmenen Sieben Persohnen . . . Gesamlet und beschrieben von Wilhelm Grah in Creveld, 1763 (sixty-pages), now in the possession of Dr. J. F. Gerhard Goeters, Bonn/Rhine; it is bound with Lobach, Merckmahl. A second copy is in the StdA Krefeld, Abt. B, IX/2/33.
22. AEvKR Düsseldorf, Lobach Briefe, pp. 1-14, copy.
23. AEvKR Düsseldorf, Lobach Briefe, pp. 35, 36, copy.
24. AEvKR Düsseldorf, Lobach Briefe, pp. 48, 49, copy.
25. AEvKR Düsseldorf, Lobach Briefe, Nachtrag, pp. 1-4, copy.
26. ARA the Hague, Requesten 7576, (Dutch) original.
27. ARA the Hague, Missives 6222, (Dutch) original.
28. ARA the Hague, Missives 6222, (Dutch) original.
29. Bayrisches Geheimes Staatsarchiv, Kasten Blau 83/29, Acta der Baron Ullner Gesandtschaftverrichtung im Haag 1720-1723, original.

V: EMIGRATION

1. *Chronicon Ephratense,* p. 3 [revised].
2. *Ibid.,* pp. 248, 249 [revised].
3. AEvKR Düsseldorf, B, A I/ Ia 3, Acta Syn. Gen. 1687-1731, XXXIII, paragraph 21; published in Nieper, *op. cit.,* p. 219.
4. *Chronicon Ephratense,* pp. 15, 16 [revised].
5. *Ibid.,* pp. 22-24 [revised].
6. FWA Laasphe, W 64/II, copy.
7. FWA Laasphe, K 291, p. 38, original.
8. FWA Laasphe, K 291, p. 39, copy.
9. FWA Laasphe, N 72, Actum Schwarzenau, June 1721.
10. Steven Blaupot ten Cate, *Geschiedenis der Doopsgezinden in Friesland* (Leeuwarden: W. Eckhoff, 1839), p. 200.
11. Rijksarchief Friesland, Leeuwarden, Proclamation B. Achtkarspelen 1721—Huwelÿken.
12. *Chronicon Ephratense,* pp. 246, 247 [revised].
13. "Minutes of the Provincial Council," *Colonial Records,* III, 368; cited in Ralph B. Strassburger and John W. Hinke (editor), *Pennsylvania German Pioneers,* Pennsylvania German Society Proceedings and Addresses, Vols. XLII-XLIV (Norristown, Pa.: Pennsylvania German Society, 1934), I, 29.
14. *Ibid.,* List 10A, pp. 27, 28 [revised].
15. *Chronicon Ephratense,* p. 48 [revised].
16. *Geistliche Fama, mittheilend einige neuere Nachrichten von Göttlichen Erweckungen/Wegen/Führungen/und Gerichten,* edited by J. S. Carl and others (Berleburg: 1730-1744), II, Stück 19, 22, 23.
17. *Ibid.,* I, Stück 10, 86-89.
18. For the arrivals, see Strassburger and Hinke, *op. cit.,* I, 47, 102, 122, 154.
19. [Johannes Naas], "Krefelder Auswanderer auf der Fahrt nach Amerika vor 200 Jahren. Beziehungen und Erwägungen," edited by Karl Rembert, *Die Heimat* [Krefeld], XII (1933), No. 2, 101-109. Also published in "Reisetagebuch des Joh. Naas aus Crefeld vom 17. Oktober, 1733," *Krefelder Zeitung,* No. 25, January 29, 1881; "Reisetagebuch des Johannes Naas aus Crefeld, von Rotterdam bis Germantown in Pennsylvanien," *Der Deutsche Pionier,* XII (1880-1881), 340-350; given in English translation in Brumbaugh, *op. cit.,* pp. 108-124.
20. *Das Neue Testament* (Herborn: Joh. Andrea, 1715); in the Mennonitisches Gemeinde Archiv, Krefeld.
21. StA Basel-Stadt, Kirchen-Archiv A 16, Bericht . . . in Zusammenhang mit dem Separatisten Gmehli, paragraph 3.

22. Weck, *Liebes-Brocken,* pp. 80-82.
23. "Nachricht von denen Fanatiquern und Separatisten in der Schweitz," in *Unschuldige Nachrichten von alten u. neuen theologischen Sachen und der fortgesetzten Sammlung,* edited by Valentin Löscher (Leipzig: 1723), XXXIX, 844-846.
24. For the Dutch names, see Brumbaugh, *op. cit.,* pp. 54-70.
25. "Ausführliche Nachricht, welchergestalt die Herrnhutische Sache in diesen Americanischen Landen . . . Eingang und Aufnahm gesucht und gefunden . . . ," *Johann Philip Fresenius bewährte Nachrichten von Herrnhutischen Sachen* (Frankfurt/Main and Leipzig: Heinrich Brönner, 1748), III, iii, No. 1, 227.
26. StdA Krefeld, VII/3, Bürgerbuch, pp. 54, 67, 85.
27. Lobach, *Merckmahl,* pp. 81, 82.
28. Barmen-Gemarke Gemeinde Archiv, A II d 62, *Zur Erinnerung an den 100-jährigen Todestag G. Tersteegens 3. April, 1869.*
29. Historical Society of Pennsylvania, Philadelphia, A.L.S.
30. Samuel Smith, *History of the Province of Pennsylvania,* edited by William M. Mervine (Philadelphia: J. B. Lippincott Company for the Colonial Society of Pennsylvania, 1913), pp. 189, 190. See also Roger Sappington's article, "Eighteenth-Century Non-Brethren Sources of Brethren History, IV," in *Brethren Life and Thought,* II (1957), iv, pp. 65-75.
31. Two existing groups in Europe claim the Schwarzenau eight as their ancestors. One is the group of *Brüder* meeting in Schwarzenau who cherish folk traditions about the early Wittgenstein Brethren. They are theologically aligned with the nineteenth-century English movement led by John Nelson Darby. The Danish church, *Christi Menighed* or the Assembly of Christ, trace their origin from the first eight through two Danish brethren, Simon and Sören Bolle, who went to Denmark in 1737. On the Christi Menighed, see the note, "Brethren in Denmark and the Scandinavian Countries," in the *Brethren Missionary Herald* (Winona Lake, Indiana), October 6, 1956, XVIII, No. 40, 608; a letter from Pastor E. J. P. Hansen, Copenhagen, to D. F. Durnbaugh, November 16, 1956.

VI: PUBLICATION

1. Alexander Mack, Jr., *op. cit.,* p. [11].
2. [Alexander Mack], *Eberhard Ludwig Grubers Grundforschende Fragen, welche denen Neuen Täufern im Witgensteinischen, insonderheit zu beantworten, vorgelegt waren, nebst beygefügten kurzen und*

einfältigen Antworten auf dieselben, vormals schriftlich heraus gegeben von einem Aufrichtigen Mitglied der Gemeine zu Witgenstein, und nun auf vieles verlangen zum öffentlichen Druck befördert, third edition (Baltimore: Samuel Saur, 1799).

3. See page 149.

4. *Ibid.,* second edition (Germantown, Pa.: Christoph Saur, 1774).

5. *Catalogus, oder Verzeichnüsz derjenigen Bücher welche in der Berlenburgischen Buchhandlung bey Johann Jacob Haug in beygesetztem Preisz anjetzo zu haben seynd* (Berleburg: 1729).

6. *Kurtze Und einfältige Vorstellung/Der äuszern/aber doch heiligen Rechten und Ordnungen Desz Hauses Gottes/Wie es der wahre Hausz-Vatter* [sic] *Jesus Christus befohlen/und in seinen Testament schrifftlich hinterlassen. Vorgestellt In einem Gespräch/Unter Vater und Sohn durch Frag und Antwort. Von Alexander Mack. Einenem* [sic] *Mit-Beruffenen/Zu dem groszen Abendmahl* (Berleburg?: 1715).

7. *Ibid.,* second edition (Germantown: Christoph Saur, 1774).

8. *Christliches Hand-Büchlein . . . , Von Jeremias Felbinger./ Rechten und Ordnungen des Hauses Gottes, in Frag und Antwort./ Grundforschende Fragen . . . , Von Alexander Mack,* third edition (Baltimore: Samuel Saur, 1799).

9. *Ibid.* (Lancaster, Pa.: printed for the publisher by Johann Bär, 1822).

10. *A Short and Plain View of the Outward, Yet Sacred Rights and Ordinances of the House of God, As commanded to be Observed by the True Steward, Jesus Christ, and deposited in His last Will and Testament, arranged in a Conversation between Father and Son. By Alexander Mack: Translated into English by a Friend to Religion* (Philadelphia: John Binns, 1810); also includes *Eberhard Ludwig Gruber's Enquiries . . . .*

11. *A Short and Plain View of the Outward, Yet Sacred Rights and Ordinances of the House of God—As commanded by the True Steward, Jesus Christ, and left on record in His last Will and Testament, arranged in Conversation between a Father and Son in Questions and Answers./ Also Ground Searching Questions answered by the author Alexander Mack./ A New English Translation with Memoir of the Author* (Columbiana, Ohio: Henry Kurtz, 1860).

12. *A Plain View of the Rites and Ordinances of the House of God: Arranged in the form of a Conversation between a Father and Son, to which are added Ground-Searching Questions answered by the Author./ By Alexander Mack* (Mount Morris, Ill.: The Brethren's Publishing Company, 1888).

13. *Ibid.* (Ashland, Ohio: The Century Printing Co., 1939).

14. Mack, . . . *Rechten und Ordnungen* . . . (1715), p. 7.

15. *Geistreiches Gesang-Buch/Vor alle Liebhabende Seelen der Warheit/ sonderlich Vor die Gemeine Des Herrn In sich fassend Die Auserlesenste und nöthigste Lieder/Aus andern Gesang-Büchern ausgezogen/ Nebst 100. neue Lieder/so zum erstenmahl aufgesetzt worden/zum Trost und Erquickung allen wahren Nachfolgern des Herrn Jesu/und in gegenwärtiger Form ans Licht gegeben/Zum Lobe Gottes* (Berleburg: Christoph Konert, 1720).

16. *Johann Anastasii Freylinghausen* . . . *Geistreiches Gesang-Buch, den Kern alter und neuer Lieder in sich haltend* . . . (Halle: the Orphanage, 1704ff.). See Koch, *op. cit.,* IV, 300ff., 322ff., V, 586ff.

17. *Davidisches Psalter-Spiel der Kinder Zions, Von Alten und Neuen auserlesenen Geistes-Gesängen; Allen wahren Heils-Begierigen Säuglingen der Weisheit, Insonderheit aber Denen Gemeinen des Herrn, Zum Dienst und Gebrauch mit Fleisz zusammengetragen und In gegenwärtig beliebiger Ordnung und Form, Nebst einem doppelt dazu nützlichen Register, ans Licht gegeben von Einem MitGeNossen Zions in Philadelphia* (Schaffhausen: 1718). For the origin of this hymnal, see Goebel, "Geschichte der wahren Inspirationsgemeinden von 1688-1850," *op. cit.,* 1854, p. 277, and Wernle, *op. cit.,* I, 449. For a recent discussion of its use in colonial America, see Nevin W. Fisher, *The History of Brethren Hymnbooks* (Bridgewater, Va.: The Beacon Publishers, 1950), pp. 3-15.

18. *Geistreiches Gesang-Buch* . . . , pp. [v, vi].

19. *Ibid.,* No. 4, pp. 7-9.

20. *Ibid.,* No. 284, pp. 440-445.

21. *Ibid.,* No. 88, pp. 151-154.

22. *Ibid.,* No. 24, pp. 43, 44.

23. Alexander Mack, Jr., *op. cit.,* pp. [11, 12].

Index

O